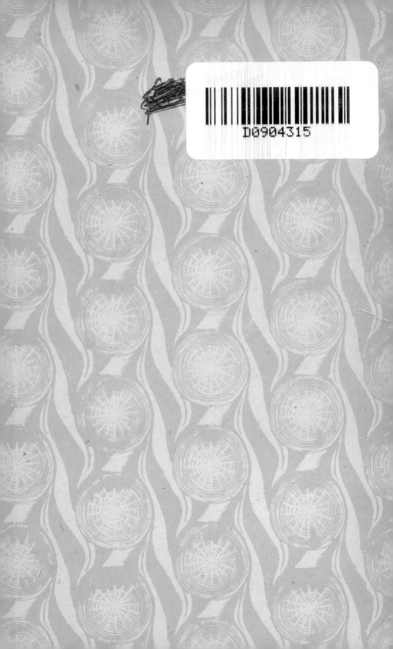

Everyman, I will go with thee, and be thy guide,
In thy most need to go by thy side.

EVERYMAN'S LIBRARY

Founded 1906 by J. M. Dent (d. 1926)
Edited by Ernest Rhys (d. 1946)

No. 982

THEOLOGY

ST. AUGUSTINE: THE CITY OF GOD
JOHN HEALEY'S TRANSLATION, WITH A
SELECTION FROM VIVES' COMMENTARIES
EDITED BY R. V. G. TASKER, M.A., B.D.
INTRODUCTION BY SIR ERNEST BARKER
IN TWO VOLS.   VOL. I

AUGUSTINE, born in 354 in Tagaste in Numidia. Went to the university of Carthage and embraced Manichaeism. While living in Milan the oratory of Ambrose led to his conversion to the Christian Church in 386. Died at Hippo in 430.

THE CITY OF GOD
(DE CIVITATE DEI)

SAINT AUGUSTINE

LONDON: J. M. DENT & SONS LTD.
NEW YORK: E. P. DUTTON & CO. INC.

U 303/10 m

EDITOR'S PREFACE

THESE two volumes contain a thoroughly revised edition of John Healey's famous translation of St. Augustine's *De Civitate Dei*, followed by a selection of notes from the Commentaries of Ioannes Lodovicus Vives, which were attached to the original edition of Healey's work. This translation was first published in 1610, and was followed by a revised edition in 1620. A reprint of the earlier edition with modernized spelling was published in 1890 by Griffith Farran & Co.

This reprint, which contains a large number of misprints and mistakes, has hitherto been the only accessible edition of Healey's work, containing the complete text, which has been available for students; though in 1903 an abridged edition of this reprint was published in the Temple Classics, which was re-issued later with an illuminating introduction by Sir Ernest Barker.

The aim, which I have had continually in mind while making this revision, has been to retain as far as possible the vigour and eloquence of Healey's version, which, though a free translation, is usually accurate, but at the same time to enable St. Augustine's meaning to become clearer to the modern reader in such places where it is in danger of being obscured or rendered unintelligible either by the archaic vocabulary, the chaotic punctuation, or the prolixities of Elizabethan prose, or where the translator has indulged in a degree of freedom that can scarcely be justified.

I have embodied most of the corrections made in the 1620 edition, have changed all words which have passed out of general use, or which are now used in a different sense, and have reconstructed sentences which were needlessly obscure. In a few places I have found Healey's version so completely obscure that I have had no other alternative than that of making my own translation. This I have done from the text edited by the late Bishop Welldon, and published by the S.P.C.K. This text I have had open in front of me throughout. I can only hope that these re-written passages will not appear too glaringly obvious to the reader. In order to render the book more useful to students, I have inserted the very full classical and biblical references from Welldon's edition by kind permission of the publishers.

Lovers of the archaic in our language will regret the disappearance of many Elizabethan words; but I became more and more convinced as the work progressed that in preparing *The City of God* (a work that makes considerable demands on the reader's powers of concentration) for Everyman's Library, the claims of clarity and lucidity must as far as possible be paramount. While therefore I have been anxious for the reader to enjoy the magnificence of Healey's prose, I have been still more anxious that he should be able with the minimum of difficulty to grasp the meaning of what St. Augustine has to say in this his greatest and most important work, especially at the present time, when there is much confusion of thought concerning the nature of the 'two cities' to the detriment of true Christianity and the general disillusionment of humanity.

Considerations of space made it possible to give only a selection from Vives' long and for the most part rather dull and tedious commentaries. It seems incredible that Henry the Eighth, who knew not which to congratulate the more, St. Augustine or Vives, could really have had either the time or the inclination to read through these notes in full. I have not attempted in making the necessary selection to follow any definite principles. I have merely chosen such passages as appeared in my judgment to be of the most general interest. Rarely do Vives' comments throw much light on St. Augustine, but they tell us something about Vives himself and the views and opinions of his contemporaries. I have reprinted these comments for the most part as they were originally written, except for the modernizing of the spelling; for the language is one of their more attractive features.

I should like to express my thanks to Sir Ernest Barker for the encouragement and help he has given me in what has been a somewhat exacting piece of work. Part of the incentive which has kept me at it has been the knowledge that it would enable his introduction to form the preface to the complete text of Healey's translation, instead of to a maimed version of it as heretofore.

R. V. G. TASKER.

ABRIDGE, 1944.

SAINT AUGUSTINE, b. 354; d. 430

St. Augustine's works include (autobiographical) *Confessions*, **circ.** 397, *Retractations*, 427-8, to which may be added *Letters*; (philosophical) *Contra Academicos*, 386; *De Vita Beata*, 386; *Soliloquia*, 387; *De Musica*, 387-9; *De Magistro*, 389; *De Anima et ejus Origine*, 419; and others, including his works on Grammar, Geometry, Rhetoric, etc.; (critical and polemical) *De Doctrina Christiana*, 397; *De Civitate Dei*, 413-26; *Enchiridion*, or *De Fide*, 421; *De Vera Religione*, 390, etc. (among these the Anti-Pelagian contain what is known as the Augustinian System of Theology); (exegetical, etc.) *De Genesi ad literam*, 401-15; *Enarrationes in Psalmos*, Homilies, and *De Consensu Evangelistarum*. Three hundred and ninety-six Sermons and various treatises on moral virtues are still to be added. Works, edited by Pilkington and others, *Select Library of Nicene and Post-Nicene Fathers*, vols. i-viii, 1887-92.

INTRODUCTION

By Sir Ernest Barker

MANY scholars, with a far more abundant equipment, have written introductions to *The City of God*. Why should a new introduction be added? The answer is simple. I have long been anxious for the publication, in an accessible form and at a moderate price, of a translation of *The City of God* for the use and the benefit of students of history and political ideas. The publishers of this edition have generously consented to republish a translation which has been for some years out of print. They have asked me to write an introduction. I am sadly aware of my own limitations; but I feel that I owe them a debt of honour. . . . That is the origin of this introduction.[1] I will only add that what I have written is directed mainly to some of the political aspects of St. Augustine's teaching, and, more particularly, to the argument of the nineteenth book.

I

St. Augustine was born (A.D. 354), and spent his life, in the eastern part of what is now the French province of Algeria; and for the last thirty-five years of his life he was bishop of what is now the French port of Bona. In his lifetime, and to the very year of his death (A.D. 430), when the Vandal Gaiseric began a Teutonic conquest, the land was part of the Roman province of Africa. St. Augustine was thus an 'African'; and he shows in *The City of God* some traces of that nationalism which, in Africa as well as elsewhere, but perhaps more than elsewhere, emerged from the decline and fall of Rome. The Roman province of Africa, many centuries ago, had been governed by ancient Carthage; the language of ancient Carthage, Punic, still lingered in the province, and formed a vernacular basis of African nationalism. St. Augustine drew illustrations from the old speech: he urged on the Christian clergy of the province the need for acquainting themselves with it; and when he speaks, in *The City of God*, of the Punic Wars, he betrays a sympathy with the *victa causa* of Carthage.

The archaeological research of our own day proves more and more abundantly the culture of Roman Africa. Born among this culture, St. Augustine began to imbibe it at an early age. By the year A.D. 370, at the age of sixteen, he was engaged in study at

---

[1] The introduction was originally written for an edition of the year 1931. It is printed here as it was originally written, except for some small verbal alterations and some omissions at the end.

Carthage. He mastered the Latin classics—particularly Cicero, Virgil, and the encyclopaedic Varro, whose *Antiquitatum Libri* (in forty-one books, now lost) is quoted again and again in *The City of God*. He also read (in translations) the *Categories* of Aristotle and many of the dialogues of Plato. He was particularly influenced by Plato; and one of the chapters of *The City of God* is headed: 'Of the means by which Plato was able to gain such intelligence that he came near to the knowledge of Christ.' He became a teacher of classical culture: he professed 'rhetoric' at Carthage as early as 377, and was professing the same subject at Milan in 384. . . . And then, by the ways which he has himself described in his *Confessions*, he was led to the Christian cause. Henceforth there are, in a sense, two men in St. Augustine—the antique man of the old classical culture, and the Christian man of the new Gospel. It is the great fascination of *The City of God* (and particularly perhaps of the nineteenth book) that we see the two men at grips with one another. This is what makes the work one of the great turning-points in the history of human destiny: it stands on the confines of two worlds, the classical and the Christian, and it points the way into the Christian. For there is never a doubt, in all the argument, from the first words of the first chapter of the first book, of the victory of that 'most glorious city of God' proclaimed, as with the voice of a trumpet, in the very beginning and prelude.

St. Augustine was baptized in 387 at the age of thirty-three. After an absence of five years in Italy, he returned to Africa in 388. Three years later, in 391, he was directly ordained a presbyter, omitting all minor orders; and he was set by his bishop (the Bishop of Hippo, which, as we have said, is the modern Bona) to expound the Gospel and to preach in his presence. He was thus directed, early in his career, to the task of Christian exegesis; and having a ready pen as well as an eloquent voice—burning, in every way, with a great gift and a fine passion of communication—he set to work on his lifelong task of justification and interpretation of the Christian faith. He was consecrated bishop in 395. His episcopal duties were far from light. For one thing, he had a heavy burden of judicial duties: the episcopal court, in the custom of the age, was a court of general resort, even for civil cases.[1] For another thing, he was organizing around him (as he had already begun to do when he was first made presbyter) a community of clergy, or canons, living a common life under a rule; and he was thus occupied in the foundation of what, in the language of a later day, would have been called a religious order—a task which a St. Benedict or a St. Francis found engrossing enough in itself. But whatever the burden of his judicial work, and whatever his obligation to the

---

[1] When St. Augustine (e.g. in Book xix. vi) speaks of the difficulties of the judge and 'the error of human judgments when the truth is hidden,' he is speaking from a full experience.

clerical community gathered round him, he never ceased to write till the very year of his death. He began in 397 a work *De Doctrina Christiana*: it was not finished until 426. He began in 413 *The City of God*; and that too was not finished until 426. (We have to remember, in reading it, that it appeared, part by part, over a period of thirteen years; and then we can understand its length, its repetitions, its diffuseness, its lack of a single controlling scheme of arrangement. The bishop was giving to his flock and to the world —part by part, and section by section—the thoughts that had poured into a fermenting brain, the experiences which had filled a rich life, in the intervals between the publication of one section and the appearance of the next; and his flock, and the world of his readers, had come to expect their recurrent food in its season.) But the treatise on *Christian Doctrine* and that on *The City of God* are only two among a multitude of others. There are the *Confessions*, for instance, which were finished in A.D. 400; there are commentaries on Genesis, the Psalms, and the Gospel of St. John; there are homilies, *De Bono Conjugali* and *De Nuptiis*; there are treatises on Free Will and Predestination, the Trinity and the Grace of Christ; there are, at the end of his life, the *Retractationum Libri*. It was an indefatigable pen which finally ceased its work in the last days of August 430 in that city of Hippo in which he had spent more than half of the seventy-six years of his life. The city was being besieged by the Vandals as he died; and within five years of his death they had settled on a large tract of the Roman province, with their capital at Hippo. For his own city, at any rate, St. Augustine had been the 'last of the Romans.'

He was a man of vital personality, with an abounding gift of self-expression. One of his phrases, as Mr. Bevan has remarked in an essay on the 'Prophet of Personality,' [1] is the solemn and profound phrase, 'abyssus humanae conscientiae,' 'the abysmal depths of personality.' He knew the depths of the soul, and he could express its secrets, in a way which was new among the writers of the ancient world. He had at his command a remarkable style and a Latinity which was at once nervous, subtle, and sinuous. 'We should perhaps never have dared to forecast,' Mr. Bevan writes of his Latin, 'how this speech of massive construction, made for rock-graven epigram or magisterial formula, could be used to convey the outpourings of mystical devotion, to catch the elusive quality of shadowy moods, to enter into the subtleties of psychological analysis.' The glory of his Latinity, and of the vision which it expressed, was destined to work permanently on the imagination of all the Middle Ages. When Abelard sings his great hymn:

> O quanta qualia sunt illa sabbata,
> Quae semper celebrat superna curia,

[1] Essay VII in *Hellenism and Christianity*.

he is borrowing the very words of St. Augustine, and particularly of that last chapter of the last book of *The City of God* which is entitled, 'Of the eternal felicity of the city of God and its perpetual sabbath.' And when Dante climbs into paradise, he is following St. Augustine's footsteps.

It is tempting to quote some of the great sayings of St. Augustine.[1] 'Thou hast made us for Thyself, and our heart is restless until it find rest in Thee.' 'This is the sum of religion, to imitate whom thou dost worship.' 'A man shall say unto me, *Intelligam ut credam*; and I will reply to him, *Immo crede ut intelligas*.' 'There is one commonwealth of all Christian men.' 'That heavenly city which has truth for its king, love for its law, and eternity for its measure.' 'Whosoever reads these words, let him go with me, when he is equally certain; let him seek with me, when he is equally in doubt; let him return to me, when he knows his own error; let him call me back, when he knows mine.' All these sayings show the man. Many of them became the great commonplaces of future ages. To remember them is to remember the essence of the writer's thought. Who can forget the deep meaning of his cry to God: *Da quod jubes—et jube quod vis*?

II

The occasion of the writing of *The City of God* was the sack of Rome by Alaric and his Goths in 410. The sack was not in itself the most terrible of visitations. Gaiseric and his Vandals sacked it again in 455, plundering at leisure for a fortnight. The Normans under Guiscard sacked it once more in 1084, and their ravages exceeded the ravages of Goths and Vandals. But the sack of A.D. 410 impressed the imagination of the age profoundly. Rome herself, intact from a foreign invader for nearly a thousand years—Rome, the founder, the mistress, and the capital of the Empire, had fallen. She had fallen in the hour of the victory of Christianity; she had fallen (murmured those who clung to the ancient ways) in consequence of that victory. News of the fall of Rome had come flying over the seas to Carthage; and fugitives from Rome had come flying in the wake of the news. Here was a great question for Christian apologetics. Were the barbaric invasions and the decline of the empire, which had just culminated in the resounding crash of the 'eternal city,' the result of abandoning the old civic gods and the old civic faith? If they were not, what was their meaning, and what 'philosophy of history' could Christians produce to explain and justify the march of events? These were the questions to which Augustine turned, and which formed the original inspiration of *The City of God*.

[1] They are collected in Bishop Welldon's edition of the *De Civitate Dei*, vol. ii, pp. 656–8.

But a work which, as we have already had occasion to notice, took thirteen years in composition, and eventually ran to twenty-two books, was bound to transcend its original design. St. Augustine indeed deals with history in *The City of God*; but he left a good deal of the historical theme to Orosius, a Spanish monk who had come to Hippo in 414 (the year after *The City of God* had been begun), and was entrusted with the writing of an *Historia adversus Paganos* by way of an appendix or corollary—not of a very high order—to his master's work.[1] St. Augustine himself took a higher flight. He had been drawn into a connection with Volusianus, the proconsul of Africa, a philosophical pagan engaged in the study of Christian evidences. The connection gave a new theme and fresh motive to the development of his treatise on *The City of God*. He was no longer only concerned to provide a philosophy of history in answer to pagan murmurings; he was also concerned to provide a justification of the whole *philosophia Christi* in answer to the human philosophy of the ancient world. It was this double purpose which determined the trend and the argument of *The City of God* as the work developed down to 426.

St. Augustine himself has given his own account of the scope of his work in a passage of the *Retractationum Libri*. The twenty-two books, he explains, fall into two parts—which, as we shall see, correspond to the two purposes of which we have spoken. The first part, embracing the first ten books, falls itself in turn into two divisions. The first division (Books I–V) is directed against the belief that human prosperity depends upon the maintenance of a civic worship of the many gods of the pagan pantheon; and in particular it is intended to disprove the opinion that the prohibition of such worship, which had been recently enacted by Gratian and Theodosius (*circiter* A.D. 380), was responsible for the late calamities—the barbarian invasions, the decline of the Empire, and the sack of Rome. The second division (Books VI–X) is directed against a more moderate trend of pagan belief and opinion: it is intended to refute the thinkers who, admitting that calamities were the inseparable and perpetual companions of humanity—admitting, therefore, that the late calamities needed no special explanation of ancient gods irate at the special oppression of their worship—nevertheless believed that for the course of the life to come (if not for the course of this life) the worship of the ancient gods had its own advantages. The argument of both the divisions of the first part is thus critical and destructive: it is an *argumentum adversus paganos*. But criticism was not enough: St. Augustine desired to

---

[1] 'Orosius' cue was this: the world, far from being more miserable than before the advent of Christianity, was really more prosperous and happy. Etna was less active of old, the locusts consumed less, the barbarian invasions were no more than merciful warnings.'—Dr. H. F. Stewart, in the *Cambridge Ancient History*, i, pp. 576–7.

be constructive as well as destructive; he desired not only to put to flight pagan murmurings about the sack of Rome, but also to draw over to the Christian side the thoughtful pagan (such as Volusianus) who was pondering the truth of Christian evidences. 'As I did not wish,' he says, 'to be accused of having merely controverted the doctrines of others, without stating my own, this [that is to say, the statement of his own doctrines] is the theme of the second part of this work, which is contained in twelve books.' This second part is divided by St. Augustine into three divisions. The first (Books XI–XIV) 'contains the *origin* of the two cities, the city of God and the city of this world'; the second (Books XV–XVIII) 'contains their *process or progress*'; the third (Books XIX–XXII) deals with 'their appointed *ends*'—in other words, with the goal towards which they move and the consummation in which the logic of their process necessarily culminates.

III

St. Augustine, taking over the idea from the philosophers of antiquity, distinguishes four grades (or, we may say, concentric rings) of human society. The first is the *domus* or household. Above that, and wider than that, is the *civitas*—which had originally meant the City, and the State founded upon and co-extensive with the City, but had been extended (as Rome, for example, grew, and from a city became a great State) to mean the State in general. Above the *civitas*, and wider than it, comes the *orbis terrae*—the whole Earth and the whole human society which inhabits the Earth. Finally, and widest of all societies, there is the Universe, *mundus*, which embraces the heavens and their constellations as well as the earth, and includes God and His angels and the souls of the departed, as well as the human society now sojourning upon the earth. In the light of this classification we may make some preliminary observations on St. Augustine's conception of the City of God.

Strictly, the city of God transcends the grade (or the concentric ring) of the *civitas*. It belongs to the great society of the Universe; it is co-extensive with the *mundus*. But for centuries past, by a natural metaphor, the conception of *civitas* (or πόλις) had been applied to Universal Society; and such society had been regarded, and described, as a city. Men naturally sought to import the warmth and the intimacy of the close and familiar civic community into the Universe, as soon as they began to regard it as a unity or society; they felt that they had made themselves at home in the Universe when they had called it a 'city,' in which the divine and the human dwelt together in a common 'citizenship.' The Stoics, about 300 B.C., had already begun to go this way; and indeed the Cynics had already trodden the way before them. They had spoken of the _κοσμόπολις,_ the City which is as wide as the whole _κόσμος_ (the Greek word for Universe which was translated by the Latin _mundus_); and in the process of time, as we find in the _Meditations_ of Marcus Aurelius (IV. xxiii), the very term 'City of God' began to be applied to the Cosmos. Turning to it, the emperor cries: 'All fits together for me which is well-fitted for thee, O thou Universe; from thee are all things, in thee are all things, to thee come all things; the poet saith: "Dear City of Athens," but wilt thou not say: "Dear City of God"?' (ὦ πόλι φίλη Διός.) St. Augustine had thus the great phrase ready to his hand; but he had even more than the phrase. He had a picture, inherited from the past, of the lineaments of the City of God.

The picture was a double picture, and it had been painted by two men, both of whom came from the same corner of the eastern Mediterranean.[1] One of them was Posidonius of Apamea, an eclectic philosopher who blended Stoicism with Platonism, and gave to the world of the first century B.C. (the world into which Christianity was born) its prevalent body of philosophic ideas. Mr. Bevan has described, in his book on _Stoics and Sceptics_, the picture which Posidonius drew of the Universe. The outer spheres of the Universe (the spheres of the fixed stars and the planets and the sun) were composed of pure ether; and this pure ether was the place of God, and indeed it _was_ God. As you came inward, towards the earth, purity diminished with the admixture of baser substance; and from the sphere of the moon to the central earth there was an increasing degree of impurity. What happened within this Universe was simple. At death the soul of man (now a _daimon_) tried to fly away to the pure ether and to be with God. It got as far as its life on earth warranted; and so the inner Universe, between the earth and the outer spheres, was peopled with _daimones_. 'You will see,' Mr. Bevan writes, 'that when the Stoic books talked about the world as one great city, of which gods and men were citizens, it was really a much more compact and knowable whole which was presented to their imagination than is suggested by the Universe to ours. Even to Posidonius, indeed, the spaces of the heavens were vast, as compared with the globe of earth; yet he could see the fiery orbs which marked the outer boundary of the Universe, _flammantia moenia mundi_, and there was nothing beyond it. . . . The whole of reality was contained for him

---

[1] It is one of the curiosities of history that three great thinkers came from the neighbourhood of the Gulf of Cilicia, and all went to Athens to learn or to teach. The first was Zeno, from Citium in Cyprus, who came to Athens about 300 B.C. and founded Stoicism. The second was Posidonius of Apamea, who was in Athens about 100 B.C. The third was St. Paul of Tarsus, who was preaching in Athens about A.D. 50. An Englishman can hardly refrain from adding the the name of Theodore of Tarsus, who became Archbishop of Canterbury in A.D. 668, and organized the English Church. He too had studied in Athens, and was called 'the philosopher.'

within the envelope of fiery ether, one world, knit together by a natural sympathy between all the parts.'

The other man who painted a picture of the city of God was St. Paul. A number of inspirations combined to produce his picture. In the first place he was a Jew, and he knew the City of Jerusalem; he knew too the old Hebrew dreams of the Holy City of Zion, to which all the nations should resort, and which should gather the world into its glory. Again he was versed (like St. Augustine himself in his day) in the teachings of the Greek philosophers; and a knowledge of Stoic philosophy peeps again and again through his Epistles. Above all he was an apostle, and he knew the teaching of our Lord: he had received the gospel of the 'Kingdom of Heaven,' into which all men might enter by regeneration, if they believed in God and His Son and their belief were counted to them for 'righteousness.' Under these various inspirations, but especially and particularly under the last, St. Paul spoke of a commonwealth (a πολίτευμα, or organized civic body) as 'existing in the heavens,' [1] and yet as including Christian believers here on earth who had attained (or, more exactly, had been given by the grace of God) the gift of 'righteousness.' It is to that divine commonwealth, or city of God, that all Christians really belong; and St. Paul thus speaks of them as fellow-citizens (συμπολῖται) of the Saints.[2] But meanwhile Christians are sojourning on earth in another polity; and in that other, or earthly, polity they may be called 'strangers and pilgrims' [3]—or, as a Greek would have said, 'resident aliens' (ξένοι μέτοικοι), who, belonging as citizens to another city, are temporarily resident as strangers in a foreign body of citizens. It is here, and in this picture (sketched with a few bold strokes) of the commonwealth in the heavens and the pilgrimage on earth, that we find, as it were, the original drawing from which St. Augustine painted the great canvas of *The City of God*.

We must pause, at this point, to notice some fundamental differences between the picture of St. Paul and the picture of Posidonius and the Stoics. For the latter there is really but a single city, reaching from earth to heaven—a city in which the baser sort (the *stulti*, as the Stoics called them) will indeed occupy a far lowlier position, never attaining near to the outer ether, but which, none the less, includes the divine and the *daimones* and all humanity in its wide embrace. St. Paul implies two sorts of cities —the divine commonwealth in the heavens, and the human commonwealths on earth. (Just in the same way St. Augustine distinguishes the *civitas Dei* and the *terrena civitas*.) And the

---

[1] Phil. iii. 20.   [2] Eph. ii. 19.

[3] The words are those, not of St. Paul, but of St. Peter (1 Pet. ii. 11). I would add that I owe these references to Bishop Welldon's edition of the *De Civitate Dei*.

reason for this distinction of the two sorts of cities is, in one word, 'righteousness.' For the divine city is the city only of the righteous; and no unclean thing may enter into it. Here, in this one word righteousness, which in Latin is *justitia*, we touch one of the great key-words of human thought—a key-word to the thought of St. Augustine, a key-word to the thought of the Middle Ages. It is a word which we must study; and we shall find that its study takes us back to Plato.

Language plays great tricks with the human mind. Words of a mixed and wavering content are the greatest of all tricksters. Among these words is the Latin word *justitia*. When the thought of the Greeks—the thought of Plato and of St. Paul—came to the Latin West, there came with it the word δικαιοσύνη, which (so far as it has an equivalent in our language) may be translated 'righteousness.' The translation which it received in the Latin language was *justitia*; and that translation had large (and sometimes disastrous) consequences in the field of theology and of moral philosophy. It legalized a term which in the original Greek was something more than legal; and a legal tone (a tone of wrongs, penalties, sanctions, and 'justification') thus came to affect the thought of Latin Christendom. This had not been the tone of Greek writers. Plato, for example, had written a dialogue called *The Republic, or Concerning Righteousness* (πολιτεία ἢ περὶ δικαιοσύνης); but the right (τὸ δίκαιον) had meant for him the ideal good of a society in the whole range of its collective life (and not merely in the field of legal relations), and righteousness had meant the ideal goodness of a whole society and all its members. The idea of righteousness in Plato was a moral idea (which at its highest seemed to pass into a religious idea) rather than an idea of law; and what is true of Plato is also true, and even more true, of St. Paul and his use of the idea of righteousness. It is also true, as we must now proceed to show, of St. Augustine.

St. Augustine, as we have already had occasion to mention, was particularly influenced by Plato. He had read his dialogues in a Latin translation; he had read the Neoplatonists' interpretations of their master; and he cites Plato again and again in the course of *The City of God*. We are here concerned only with the influence of the Platonic conception of righteousness, and only with that as it bears on the social and political theory of St. Augustine; but the influence of Plato upon St. Augustine goes farther than this. St. Augustine carried the *general* thought of Plato into his own *general* thought; and through him, as we shall later have reason to notice, Plato influenced the subsequent course of Western theology throughout the Middle Ages and down to the Reformation, which was indeed itself, in some of its aspects, a return to Plato and St. Augustine. 'The appeal away from the illusion of things seen to the reality that belongs to God alone, the slight store set by him on institutions of time and place, in a word, the philosophic idealism that underlies and colours all Augustine's utterances on doctrinal and even practical questions and forms the real basis of his thought, is Platonic.' [1]

In *The Republic* Plato had constructed an ideal city, based upon right and instinct with righteousness, which might almost be described as a city of God, and is actually described by Plato as 'laid up somewhere in heaven.' This ideal city was to be a model; and looking upon it, and trying to copy it, men might blot out some features from their cities, and paint in others, until 'they had made the ways of men, as far as possible, agreeable to the ways of God.' [2] Over against the ideal city Plato had set, in the later books of *The Republic*, a description of the actual and earthly cities of men, tracing the progressive corruption of the ideal in their successive forms. The ground of the distinction and contrast was simple. In the ideal city there was righteousness. Each of its citizens took his particular station; each of them performed— performed only, but performed to the best of his power—the appointed functions of that station; and since righteousness consisted in 'performing the function of station' (τὸ αὑτοῦ πράττειν), a city on such a foundation was righteous. In the actual and earthly cities, on the other hand, unrighteousness reigned; men departed more and more from their station, and encroached more and more on the stations of others; there was no order; there was no system of stations; there was no system of right relations duly based on a system of stations.

We may almost say that St. Augustine takes the Platonic distinction, and Christianizes it. Righteousness is lifted to a higher plane: it ceases to be a system of right relations between men, based on the idea of social stations, and it becomes a system of right relations between man and God (but also, and consequently, between man and man), based on the idea, first of man's faith in God's will for a system of right relations, and secondly, of God's grace as rewarding such faith by creating (or rather restoring), through the 'election' of the faithful, the system of right relations interrupted by sin but renewed by faith and election. *Ordo* is a great word in St. Augustine; and *ordo* is closely allied to what I have called a 'system of right relations,' [3] as that in turn is closely allied to, and indeed identical with, the idea of righteousness. We can now understand St. Augustine's transfiguration of the old Platonic conception; we can understand his distinction of the city of God and the terrene city; we can understand his saying (IV. iv): 'Remove righteousness, and what are kingdoms but great bands of

[1] Dr. Stewart in the *Cambridge Modern History*, vol. i, p. 579.
[2] *The Republic*, vi, 501.
[3] Ordo est parium dispariumque rerum sua cuique loca tribuens dispositio XIX. xii).

brigands?' The city of God is the city of the righteous, a city pervaded by a system of right relations (*ordo creaturarum*) which unites God and His angels and the saints in heaven with the righteous on earth. It is a city of the Universe (*mundus*); and yet it does not embrace the whole Universe, for it excludes the fallen angels, the souls of the unrighteous, and the unrighteous who are living on earth. It is an invisible society: it cannot be identified with any visible society; it cannot, in strictness, be identified with the Church, because the Church on earth contains baptized members who belong to *its* society, and yet are not righteous, and cannot therefore belong to the society of the city of God. Look at the city of God in its earthly membership (remembering that this is only one part of the whole), and you will see that, so far as religious society on earth is concerned, the city contains most, but not all, of the members of the Church: you will see again that, so far as secular societies are concerned, the city 'summoneth its citizens from all tribes, and collecteth its pilgrim fellowship among all languages, taking no heed of what is diverse in manners or laws or institutions' (XIX. xviii). Compare it then with its opposite, and you will readily see the nature of the earthly city. That again, in strictness, is no formal, visible, enumerable society. It is simply all the unrighteous, wherever they be in the Universe—the fallen angels, the souls of the unrighteous, the unrighteous who are living on earth. You cannot identify it with any actual organized society: you cannot, for instance, identify it with the Roman Empire. It is something more—it includes fallen angels as well as men; it is something less—it does *not* include the righteous, who are to be found in any actual State.

We can now see, as it were face to face, the lineaments of the city of God. 'Two loves have created two cities: love of self, to the contempt of God, the earthly city; love of God, to the contempt of self, the heavenly' (XIV. xxviii). Of the heavenly city St. Augustine writes further in one of his letters (cxxxvii), saying: 'The only basis and bond of a true city is that of faith and strong concord, when the object of love is the universal good—which is, in its highest and truest character, God Himself—and men love one another, with full sincerity, in Him, and the ground of their love for one another is the love of Him from whose eyes they cannot conceal the Spirit of their love.' . . . And these two cities, and these two loves, shall live together, side by side, and even inter-mixed, until the last winnowing and the final separation shall come upon the earth in the day of judgment.

Two things remain to be said—one concerning the State and its institutions in their relation to this distinction of the heavenly and the earthly cities; the other concerning the Church and its relation to the same distinction.

We might think, at first sight, that the State corresponded to, or was somehow identical with, the earthly city or some form of that city. But, as we have just seen, it would be as great a mistake (or an even greater mistake) to identify the earthly city with the Roman Empire, or with any form of actual State, as to identify the heavenly city with the Catholic Church. The earthly city, like the heavenly city, is an ideal conception; or rather, and to speak more exactly, it may be called the ideal negation, or antithesis, of the ideal. It is a city of unrighteousness. The actual State, as it really exists, is something different. It is not absolutely unrighteous. On the contrary, it has a sort of *justitia* of its own; and not only so, but the citizens of the heavenly city avail themselves of the aid of this *justitia* in the course of their pilgrimage, so that the State is thus, in its way, a coadjutor of the city of God.

In order to understand this view of the State we must make a distinction between absolute and relative righteousness. Absolute righteousness is a system of right relations to God—relations which are at once religious, moral, and, if you will, legal: relations which are, in a word, *total*. This system, or *ordo*, has not to reckon with, or to be adjusted to, any defects; it has not to reckon with, or to adjust itself to, the defect of sin, for sin has been swallowed up in faith and grace. Relative righteousness is a system of right relations mainly in the legal sphere, and it is a system of right relations reckoning with, and adjusted to, the sinfulness of human nature. It is the best possible, *granted the defect of sin*; but again, and just because that defect has to be assumed, it is only a second best. This is the basis of St. Augustine's conception of the State and all the institutions of the State—government, property, slavery. All of these institutions are forms of *dominium*—the *dominium* of government over subjects, the *dominium* of owners over property, the *dominium* of masters over slaves. All *dominium* is a form of *ordo*, and to that extent good; but the order is an order conditioned by, and relative to, the sinfulness which it has to correct, and it is therefore only relatively good. The argument may be illustrated from the example of property. Ideally, for the righteous, all things are in common, and we read of the early Christians that 'they had all things common.' But sinfulness continues and abounds; and a form of sinfulness is greed. Partly to provide a punishment for greed, and partly to provide a remedy, private property becomes a necessity and an institution of the organized State. It is not *quod postulat ordo creaturarum*; but at any rate it is *quod exigit meritum peccatorum* (XIX. xv). We may say, therefore, that property is an institution, not indeed of absolute, but at any rate of relative righteousness. We may even say that it is willed by God, ordaining a relative righteousness where sin makes absolute righteousness unobtainable. What is true of the institution of property is true of the whole State. 'God willed the State,' in the view of St. Augustine (as afterwards in that of Burke); but He willed it *propter remedium peccatorum*.

The State, therefore, if it falls far below the heavenly city, may be said to rise above the earthly city of the unrighteous. It stands somewhere between the two—though it must be admitted that the language of *The City of God* often seems to suggest that the State and the earthly city touch and blend. From this point of view we can understand how St. Augustine can speak of the heavenly city as using the aid of the State. The State has its *ordo*, though it is not the order of creation: the State has its *pax*, though it is not the true and eternal peace. 'Therefore the heavenly city rescinds and destroys none of those things by which earthly peace is attained or maintained: rather it preserves and pursues that which, different though it be in different nations, is yet directed to the one and selfsame end of earthly peace—provided it hinder not religion, whereby we are taught that the one highest and true God must be worshipped. Therefore, again, the heavenly city uses earthly peace in this its pilgrimage: it preserves and seeks the agreement of human wills in matters pertaining to the mortal nature of men, so far as, with due regard to piety and religion, it can; and it relates that earthly peace to the heavenly peace, which truly is such peace that it should be accounted and named the only peace of the rational creature, being as it is a most ordered and most concordant companionship in the enjoyment of God, and, again, in the enjoyment of one another in God' (XIX. xvii).

Here, it might seem, we touch St. Augustine's theory of the relation of Church and State. In a sense that is true, though we have to remember that, so far as our argument has hitherto gone, the Church and the heavenly city are not the same, and it is of the heavenly city that St. Augustine is speaking in the passage which has just been quoted. This much, at any rate, we may believe about the State, that it is not an unblessed or Satanic institution. It has its own 'order': it has its own relative 'righteousness.' It is not a *magnum latrocinium*; for you *cannot* remove righteousness from it, and St. Augustine only said that kingdoms were great bands of brigands *if you remove righteousness*. Nor again was it founded by Satan (even though Gregory VII, at a far later date, might say in a hot moment that kings took their beginnings from those who were instigated by the prince of this world to desire dominion over their fellows); on the contrary, it is willed or intended by God. It can stand up, on its own basis, with its own justification, to aid the heavenly city. The State has thus assumed a clear character; but we are still left with the question of the position of the Church, of its relation to the distinction of the heavenly and the earthly cities, and, again, of its relation to the State.

We may begin by noticing that, at the time at which St. Augustine was writing, a distinction had already established itself between the Church in the East and the Church in the West. The Eastern Church had become something of the nature of a State Church, with a reverential awe for its Emperor and a veneration for the memory of Constantine as 'equal to the apostles.' The Church of the West was far more independent. St. Ambrose had but lately rebuked and controlled the great Emperor Theodosius; the pope at Rome, all the more as the Emperor had recently withdrawn to Ravenna, stood ready to assume the purple. Did *The City of God* prepare the way for the pretensions and the power of the medieval papacy? A great ecclesiastical scholar has written the words: 'St. Augustine's theory of the *Civitas Dei* was, in the germ, that of the medieval papacy, without the name of Rome. In Rome itself it was easy to supply the insertion, and to conceive of a dominion, still wielded from the ancient seat of government, as world-wide and almost as authoritative as that of the Empire.' [1] In what sense, if any, may it be said that *The City of God* was the germ of the medieval papacy?

What St. Augustine might be interpreted into meaning, or used to suggest, is a different thing from St. Augustine's own teaching. We may admit, and admit readily, that the whole picture of the *gloriosissima civitas Dei* might easily be transferred to the medieval Church and the papacy. After all, that Church was based on the 'righteousness' of the *lex evangelica* (*justitia* was the cry of Hildebrand, and his dying words were *Dilexi justitiam*); after all, it sought to spread the reign of 'righteousness' by the action of its papal head in every State and upon every estate: why should it not be counted the heir of *The City of God*? But we are here concerned with St. Augustine himself, living and writing in nationalist Africa (and no little of a nationalist himself, as witness his references to ancient Carthage) between the years 413 and 426. What was his actual conception of the Church? [2]

We must turn to some of his other writings to get the outlines of his conception clear. He believed in a universal Church comparable to the moon; he believed in particular Churches (*particulatim per loca singula Ecclesiae*) comparable to the stars. He held that an especial authority resided in the particular Churches founded by the apostles; and among these he recognized a primary, or a still more especial, authority in the Roman Church. The Roman Church might therefore be particularly consulted for an authoritative pronouncement on disputed questions, though at the same time St. Augustine speaks of an appeal to 'a plenary Council of the Church Universal.' Roughly, we may say that he believes in a universal Church as a single unit of faith and Christian society;

[1] The late Mr. C. H. Turner, in the *Cambridge Mediaeval History*, i. 173.
[2] In seeking to answer this question, I have drawn on Appendix H of Bishop Welldon's edition.

he believes in particular churches as units of organization; he allows a special authority to some, and a still more especial authority to one, of these; but he has no single church which is at one and the same time a unit of faith, of organization, and of authority.

We may now inquire into the relation of the Church, as a unit of faith, to the city of God. We can only say that the thought of St. Augustine about this relation varies, according as his thought glows into a fervour of incandescence, or restricts itself within the bonds of his theological logic. Logically, there is a difference between the Church and the city of God. Not all who formally belong to the Church as a unit of faith—not all who have been baptized and confirmed—are righteous; and the Church may thus contain members who are not also members of the city of God. But the fervour of faith may sweep away the difference; and there are passages in which the Church is made the same as the city of God. 'The ark is a figure of the city of God on its pilgrimage in this world, *that is to say of the Church*, which is saved by the wood on which hung the mediator of God and men, the man Christ Jesus (xv. xxvi). 'Therefore even now the Church is the kingdom of Christ and the kingdom of the Heavens' (xx. ix). A number of other passages might readily be collected to the same effect. We can only say that the Church, as a unit of faith, sometimes glows with the greatness of the city of God, and sometimes falls short of that measure.

What, then, shall we say of the relation of Church and State? It is a question that hardly enters into St. Augustine's thought, in the form in which it presented itself to the Middle Ages, or presents itself to us to-day. There is no question, in *The City of God*, of any system of 'concordat' between Church and State, or of any State 'establishment' of the Church, or of the superiority of the *sacerdotium* over the *regnum*, or of the power of the keys, or of the Donation of Constantine,[1] or of anything of the sort. The Church is a pilgrim society, living by faith and looking to the hereafter. It lives on earth by the side of the State; it uses the *terrena pax* of the State; it acknowledges the divine institution and the relative righteousness of the State. But it simply moves as a pilgrim past the grandeurs and dignities of this world, *nihil eorum rescindens vel destruens, immo etiam servans et sequens*, but always looking beyond, and always with eyes fixed elsewhere. What has a pilgrim to do with a king, except to acknowledge that he is king, to render to him due obedience in matters of worldly peace, and to pass on?

Yet there is a sense in which the doctrine of *The City of God* is inimical to the State, and even subversive of its existence. St. Augustine shifts the centre of gravity. The men of the ancient world had thought in terms of the *civitas Romana* as the one and only society; they had deified the Roman Emperor as its living

[1] The idea of the Donation first emerges in the eighth century.

incarnation, and they had thereby given a religious sanction to its claims: they had pent all life—religion, politics, everything—in a single secular framework. Writing at a time when the framework seemed to be cracking and breaking, St. Augustine says, in effect: 'This is not all; nor indeed is it the half of the matter. There is another and a greater society; and it is towards that society that the whole of creation moves.' The ultimate effect of *The City of God* is the elimination of the State: it is the enthronement of the Church (or at any rate of the heavenly city which again and again is identified with the Church) as the one and only *final* society. Rome has fallen: Christ has risen. The process of history is a process making for His kingdom. When we remember that St. Augustine himself, as a consecrated officer of the Church, was already doing justice from his own episcopal tribunal in all sorts of cases, we can see that the way was prepared, alike in his thought and his life, for the enthronement of the Church upon earth.

IV

The student who seeks to acquaint himself with the thought of St. Augustine may well be dismayed by the many pages of the *De Civitate Dei*. Perhaps he may be wise to steep himself in some single book of the twenty-two. The argument of *The City of God* is not a sustained argument in distinct and successive logical steps. Writing as he did in separately published parts, and repeating and reinforcing his cardinal views, St. Augustine may be studied, as it were, in a 'sample.' The sample will not give the whole of his thought; but it may indicate its general drift and tendency. Such a sample may be found in Book XIX.

The City of God, it was said above, 'stands on the confines of two worlds, the classical and the Christian, and points the way forward into the Christian.' The nineteenth book particularly illustrates this sentinel attitude. On the one hand, St. Augustine looks back upon the theories of classical philosophy in regard to the nature of the Supreme Good, and reviews the attempts of antiquity to construct a gospel of human happiness within the confines of our mortal existence; on the other hand, he looks forward to the peace and happiness of the heavenly city of God, alike in the time of its earthly pilgrimage and in the eternity of its perpetual Sabbath.

In the early chapters (i–iii) St. Augustine, using, as he so often does, the compilation of Varro, begins by stating the best features of the theories of classical antiquity in regard to the nature of the Supreme Good. He finds these features represented in the opinions and doctrines of the Old Academy—that is to say, in the

Platonic tradition. We may summarize these opinions and doctrines in two propositions: (1) The Supreme Good, in which lies happiness, is composed of the goods both of the body and of the mind; but since virtue, the highest quality of the mind, is incomparably the greatest of all goods, the life of man is most happy (and the Supreme Good is most perfectly attained) when he enjoys virtue, with the other goods of mind and body without which virtue is impossible. (The Christian answer to this theory is stated by St. Augustine in the fourth chapter.) (2) The happy life is social, and the Supreme Good can only be attained in society. Men desire the good of their friends: they desire that good for its own sake; they wish for their friends, for their friends' own sake, the good which they wish for themselves. Society thus arises, and appears in four grades—the grades we have already mentioned—the *domus*, the *civitas*, the *orbis*, the *mundus*; and society is essential to happiness. (To this line of thought St. Augustine cannot but give, as he says, a 'far ampler approval'; and therefore, partly in agreement with it, and partly in correction of it, he devotes twelve chapters (v–xvii) to a consideration of society and its relation to the Supreme Good and the happiness of men. It is these twelve chapters which give to the nineteenth book its particular interest for students of the social and political thought of St. Augustine.)

In stating these two propositions, we have incidentally indicated the gist of the first seventeen chapters, which form more than two-thirds of the nineteenth book. But there is another and final section of the book which also bears particularly on St. Augustine's political theory. After three intervening chapters (xviii–xx), which are partly occupied with some details of the opinions of the Academy, and partly with an insistence on the idea that Christian happiness is an anticipatory happiness (*spe*, as he says, rather than *re*), he starts, in chapter xxi, to discuss Cicero's definition of *populus*. It was natural that, after discussing *societas* in general, he should turn to a discussion of *populus* and *respublica*; and thus a final and peculiarly political section is added to the book (xxi–xxvii). But there is a long theological digression early in the section (xxii–xxiii, but particularly xxiii); and the conclusion of the section, rising to higher than political themes, first treats of the relations between religion and morality, and then ends with the end of the wicked.

There are three themes which emerge from this brief analysis of the nineteenth book. The first is St. Augustine's criticism of the moral theory of the ancient philosophers. The second is his own theory of *societas*. The third is his definition of *populus* and *respublica*.

(1) His criticism of the moral theory of the ancient world begins and ends in the affirmation of the opposing tenets of the Christian faith. 'The city of God will make answer that eternal life is the Supreme Good, eternal death is the Supreme Evil; and it is therefore

for the sake of gaining the one, and shunning the other, that we must live rightly.' There can be no Supreme Good or Happiness in this life only—and it is to this life only that pagan philosophy has its regard. Sickness assaults the body: afflictions threaten the senses; insanity menaces reason itself; and even virtue, the highest reach of mere mortal faculty, is always a struggle against the lusts of the flesh—a battle, and not a felicity. One by one St. Augustine examines the four cardinal virtues of ancient theory—Temperance, Prudence, Justice, and Fortitude—and of each in turn he proves that, so long as it is a merely mortal virtue, without the comfort of faith in God and the corroboration of the hope of eternal life, it must necessarily absent itself from felicity. Consider, he urges, Fortitude; consider its culmination in Stoic theory, which was a theory of Fortitude; and what do you find at its peak but suicide, glorified as the last and greatest fling of the brave heart? And how can a theory which ends in *that* be a theory of the Supreme Good or of Happiness? This is a shrewd and vital criticism of the moral theory of the ancient world: the gaunt figure of suicide standing on its summit is the index of its inherent inconsistency. *O vitam beatam, quae ut finiatur mortis quaerit auxilium*—O strange happiness, that seeketh the alliance of Death to win its crown. From the gospel of Death St. Augustine turns to point to the gospel of Life, the Life of Eternity. Seek the righteousness which comes from faith in God, and you shall have the hope of immortality; and in that hope you shall have both *salus* and *beatitudo*—the salvation and the happiness which philosophy seeks in vain. *Talis salus, quae in futuro erit saeculo, ipsa erit etiam finalis beatitudo.* The supreme Good and Happiness are not in the Here and Now: they are in the Yonder and the Hereafter; it is in terms of eternal life alone that the 'Good' of man can be understood, and won.

(2) The philosophers have said that the moral life is *vita socialis*. Therein they spoke wisely, and we may agree with their saying; for how could the city of God, itself a society, have its beginning, or its course, or its consummation, *nisi socialis esset vita sanctorum*? But if happiness be social, society (in itself) is not happiness; and St. Augustine (looking always to Eternity) proceeds to show the troubles and the misfortunes to which society is prone. He takes each of the four ranges of society. The *domus, commune perfugium*, has none the less its losses and griefs, its disputes and its angers. The society of the *civitas* suffers from the problems of litigation and the perils of civil war. (On the problems of litigation St. Augustine, himself a judge, writes a pregnant chapter (vi). How difficult it is for the judge to find the truth, and yet how necessary is his office; how gladly would he leave his bench, and how strictly is he constrained to his duty by human society, 'which he thinks it a crime for him to desert'; how fervently can he repeat the psalmist's cry to God: *De necessitatibus meis erue me*.)

On the *civitas* follows the *orbis terrae*, the third range of human society (vii); and lo! the earth is full of misfortunes and troubles. The difference of languages has kept the human race sundered; and if the *imperiosa civitas* of Rome has imposed her own language on conquered nations through the peace of the great society she has achieved, the price of her achievement in the past has been war, as the price of its maintenance to-day is still war—war without, the war on the frontier: war within, the civil war, which the very extent of the empire inevitably breeds. And if it be said that there is such a thing as 'just war' (the Christian canonists were later to elaborate a theory of *justum bellum*), it may also be said that even the just war is a 'cruel necessity,' unavoidable, indeed, if the unjust aggressor is to meet his due, but none the less, in itself, a trouble and a misfortune.

At this point St. Augustine turns aside to speak of friendship (viii). It is a consolation and a delight; but when we give our heart to our friends, we give it over to perils. Our friends may suffer—and then we suffer; they may be corrupted—and then we suffer even more. The society of friends is precious, but it is as perilous as it is precious; and in it, as in all the three ranges of society through which the argument has run, there is no exemption from misfortune and trouble. Nor is there any exemption in the fourth and highest range of society, the *mundus*, which brings us into the society of spirits (ix). We cannot see the angels familiarly; and Satan sends false angels for our deception. It is these false angels, masquerading as gods, who have produced pagan polytheism. Even the true Christian, who has not yielded, like the pagan, to such guile, is never secure from the assaults of deception (x). . . . But the trouble from which he suffers serves only to whet the fervour of his longing for that final security in which peace—peace as complete as it is certain—is at the last to be found.

Peace now becomes the note of St. Augustine's argument (xi). Society is a good thing; but we want a society free from trouble and misfortune; we want a society which is at peace. We may say therefore that the Supreme Good, which was defined before as eternal life, is also, and at the same time, peace. It is not idly, continues St. Augustine, that Jerusalem, which is the mystical name of the Heavenly City, should also signify peace; for the Hebrew *Salem* is the Latin *pax*. And yet peace is not enough in itself to denote the Supreme Good (for peace may also exist in a lower sense); nor again is eternal life enough in itself (for we read of the eternal life of the wicked, which is the Supreme Evil); and we must therefore put both together, and define the Supreme Good as 'Peace in Eternity' or 'Eternity in Peace.'

Having thus vindicated eternal peace as the Supreme Good, St. Augustine proceeds to show that the highest peace is but the finest music of a chord which runs through all creation (xii). Peace is the diapason [1] of the Universe. Peace is the object of war: the breaker of peace desires peace—only a peace more after his own mind; conspirators and robbers need peace—if it be only peace with one another. The very animals seek peace and ensue it; and it is by the gate of their instinct for peace that they pass into the life of the herd or society, of which that instinct is the condition and (we may almost say) the origin. Man is especially moved by the laws of his nature to enter upon society and peace with all men. It is only a perversion of a genuine instinct when a man seeks, by conquering and dominating others, to make his will their peace. Properly, naturally—by the law of his nature, which is part of the universal law of all nature—man should seek to live in equality with others under the peace of God: improperly, unnaturally, violating that law, he seeks to make others live in inequality and subjection under a peace of his own imposition. But even in violating nature (that is to say, in instituting *dominium* over others to the end of securing an imposed peace), man does homage involuntarily to nature; and he does so because he seeks and ensues, in his own way, the peace which is nature's purpose and chord and law. 'No man's vice is so much against nature that it destroys even the last traces of nature.' This great phrase is like that of Shakespeare:

> There is some soul of goodness in things evil,
> Would men observingly distil it out.

The free will of man cannot entirely defeat the purpose of nature; and all nature, as the creation of God, is intrinsically good. 'Even what is perverse must be peaceably set in, or in dependence on, or in connection with, some part of the order of things.' St. Augustine's idea of universal peace is thus closely connected with an idea of a universal order or law, proceeding from God and pervading creation. *Pax* and *ordo* go together; they are like obverse and reverse of the same coin. From the connection of *pax* and *ordo* St. Augustine rises to one of the finest and most philosophical of his arguments (xii, end). Imagine a living human body suspended upside down. It is a thing contrary to the order, the natural law, the peace of that body. Imagine the body left alone, day upon day, day upon day. Order, natural law, peace, all return. The body dies, dissolves, is resolved into the earth and air: it returns to its order, its nature, its peace. 'It is assimilated into the elements of the Universe; moment by moment, particle by particle, it passes into their peace; but nothing is in any wise derogated thereby from the laws of that Highest and Ordaining Creator by whom the peace of the world is administered.' The words (with their suggestion of the sovereignty of nature's great

---

[1] Diapason, if we go back to the Greek, is ἡ διὰ πασῶν τῶν χορδῶν συμφωνία.

laws and the conservation of all nature's energy) have the ring of modern science;[1] but they have at the same time the solemn overtone of Christian faith.

We now see that many things work together, and are fused, in St. Augustine's thought. We spoke of righteousness as a system of right relations, an order; and St. Augustine himself (iv) speaks of righteousness as a *justus ordo naturae*. Peace, too, is an order—the order of an 'ordaining' God who pervades an 'ordinate' creation, and always and in everything acts by law, in heaven above and on the earth beneath. This order of peace is an order which everywhere, and in all creation, composes part to part (both among things animate and among things inanimate) according to law; it is an order, therefore, issuing in society—the society of the whole articulated Universe as well as, and in the same way as, the societies of men. *Pax*, *ordo*, *lex*, *societas*—the words are like four bells ringing a peal in all the Universe. Burke, who knew the writings of the Fathers, has a noble passage in the *Reflections on the Revolution in France*, which is a modern counterpart of St. Augustine. *Pactum*, or contract, is his key-note rather than *pax*; but he makes *pactum* pervade the Universe just as St. Augustine made *pax*. 'Each contract of each particular State is but a clause in the great primeval contract of eternal society, linking the lower with the higher natures, connecting the visible and invisible worlds, according to a fixed compact sanctioned by the invisible oath which holds all physical and all moral natures each in their appointed place.'[2]

In the following chapter (xiii) St. Augustine proceeds to enumerate the phases and manifestations of peace. There is a peace of the body, a peace of the irrational soul, a peace of the rational soul, a peace of both body and soul in their union with one another. There is a peace between man and God, which is 'ordered obedience in faith under eternal law'; there is a peace between man and man, which is 'ordered concord'; and, as species of this latter, there are the peace of the household ('ordered concord of its members in rule and obedience') and the peace of the *civitas* or State ('ordered concord of citizens in rule and obedience'). Finally, there is the peace of the city of God, 'a most ordered and concordant companionship in enjoying God, and one another in God'; and there is the universal peace of all things, which is 'the tranquillity of order.' This peace of order, in all the range of its phases and manifestations, is a system of righteousness; but it embraces even the unrighteous. They have, in one sense, gone out of the order; they are, in another sense, caught fast in the order. So far as they are miserable, and justly miserable, their misery is

---

[1] See Dr. Cunningham, *St. Austin*, Appendix A (*St. Austin and the Observation of Nature*).

[2] Burke's *Works*, ii. 368 (Bohn edition).

only the 'return' upon them of the order which they have violated; so far as they are free from disturbance, it is because they are adjusted, by a sort of harmony, to the conditions in which they are placed; and in this way they possess a sort of tranquillity of order, and therefore a sort of peace. We may gloss St. Augustine by saying that the institutions adjusted to unrighteousness (the State and its government, slavery, property) are institutions fundamentally righteous, because they represent the return — the inevitable return—of interrupted right and order and peace. Nothing can exist outside order. Nothing can be in its nature utterly bad.[1] God made creation, and made it good. If His creatures, by their will, introduce evil, the overruling order of His will returns, and instils good into that evil. The State is the return of the order of God upon the evil introduced by man's sin.

In the fourteenth chapter the argument begins to trend more definitely in a political direction, and the fifteenth and sixteenth chapters (more especially the former) contain some of the most essential elements in the political thought of St. Augustine. He goes back to one of the phases or manifestations of peace which he has mentioned in the previous chapter. The highest peace of man (considered, for the moment, simply as man) is the peace of his highest faculty. This is his rational soul; and its peace may be defined as an 'ordered harmony of knowing and doing.' Knowing precedes doing; but for any true knowledge man needs a Divine Master whom he can follow in certainty, and a Divine Helper whom he can obey in liberty. The Master and Helper has given us two commandments—that we should love God, and that we should love our neighbour as ourselves. It follows that we should serve and aid our neighbours to love God, since that is the greatest love and the highest service we can give them. If we do that, we shall be living in peace—which is 'ordered concord,' which again is 'society'—with our neighbours. The rules of this society will be, first and negatively, to injure no man, and secondly or positively, to aid all men whom we can. The first circle of such society will be the family; and in the family there will be authority and subjection. But since the rule of the society is love, and love means service, any authority will only be a mode of service, and it will be exerted in the spirit of service. 'They who exercise authority are in the service of those over whom they appear to exercise authority; and they exercise their authority, not from a desire for domination, but by virtue of a duty to give counsel and aid.'

St. Augustine here started a line of thought which was long to

[1] 'There cannot be a nature in which there is no good. Not even the nature of the devil, in so far as it is nature (and therefore the creation of God), is evil; but perversity maketh it evil. He abode not in the tranquillity of order; but he hath not therefore escaped from the power of the Ordainer.'

endure. More than a thousand years afterwards, in 1579, the author of the *Vindiciae contra Tyrannos* echoed his words when he wrote: 'Imperare ergo nihil aliud est quam consulere'; and a writer of our days has similarly said of the State: 'It commands only because it serves.' But St. Augustine has no sooner started this line of thought than he sees, and faces, a difficulty. He has been speaking of the circle of the family; and the family, in his day and generation, included slaves. Can the position of the slave be reconciled with the idea that authority is only a form of service? St. Augustine attempts an answer in the fifteenth chapter. The free society, in which *imperare est consulere*, is here argued to be both the prescription of natural order and the rule imposed at the moment of creation. God gave the first man dominion only over the animal world. 'He would not have reasonable man, made in His own image, to exercise dominion save over unreasoning beings: He set man not over man but over the beasts of the field. Therefore the righteous of the first days were rather made shepherds of flocks than kings of men, in order that God might, even after this manner, suggest what it is which is required by the order of created beings, and what it is which is demanded by the desert of sin.' For there is a great gulf between these two things; and slavery is explained, and justified, by that gulf.

Slavery is the result of sin; and it is a condition rightly imposed on the sinner. It comes to pass by the judgment of God; it is justified by His judgment. There is even a sense in which it is the result, or rather the 'return,' of natural order. 'No man, indeed, is a slave to man, or to sin, by the nature in which God first created man. But penal slavery is ordained by that law, which commands the preservation and forbids the violation of natural order.' Thus even the unrighteous, as we have already had reason to notice, are caught fast in the system of righteousness; and even what seems the unnatural institution of slavery is but the 'return' (in the form of retribution for 'the desert of sin') of the order of nature. The question one naturally asks to-day (though St. Augustine did not pause to put it) is whether an actual slave has ever really committed any unrighteousness other than, or beyond, that committed by the rest of mankind. And if the answer to that question be 'No,' it is difficult to explain why he should be placed none the less in a totally different condition from other men.

But if slavery be a result, or a 'return,' of natural order, the true master of slaves must nevertheless look to their eternal happiness (xvi). He must serve and aid them (for they too are his neighbours) to love God; and meanwhile he may hope to be released from the burden of his mastership in the hereafter. For it *is* a burden, in the same way and the same sense as St. Augustine has argued before that the office of judge is a burden: it involves, in the same way,

the duty of discipline and the office of correction. The master,
like the judge, may cry for deliverance (*De necessitatibus meis erue
me*), 'longing and praying to reach that heavenly home, in which
the duty of ruling men is no longer necessary.' (How often must
any 'administrator' echo that cry!)

We might expect, after this discussion of the household, to be
carried onwards into a fuller discussion of the *civitas* or State than
has been given before in chapter vi. But St. Augustine, omitting
to treat of the *civitas* in the same detail as he has just been treating
of the *domus*, flies away at once, in a chapter (xvii) which concludes
his long discourse on society, to a consideration of the heavenly
city. His theme is its relations—its relations both of agreement and
of disagreement—with the earthly city. It is, in a way, the theme
of the relations of Church and State. In some things, says St.
Augustine, 'the things which are necessary to this mortal life'
(roughly, we may say, the preservation of law and order), both cities
can readily share together. The heavenly city (or, more exactly, the
part of it which is now making its earthly pilgrimage) accordingly
uses the earthly peace of the earthly city; its members enter into the
agreement of wills concerning the things pertaining to mortal life;
they obey the laws regulating these things, 'that as mortality is
common to both cities, so concord may be preserved between both
in matters pertaining thereto.' But there is a sphere of things, 'the
things pertaining to immortality,' in which no concord is possible.
Polytheistic thinkers have introduced supposed gods as civic
deities into the affairs of the earthly city; and the heavenly city,
devoted to the one true God, cannot therefore have any laws of
religion in common with the earthly city. It has therefore followed
the way of dissent; it has trodden the path of persecution—'until
the days [they had already come in St. Augustine's time] when at
length it might make the spirits of its adversaries recoil before the
terror of its multitude.'

(3) The final theme of the nineteenth book is the nature of a
populus and of the *respublica* in which a *populus* is organized.
The theme, as we have already had occasion to notice, naturally
follows on the discussion of *societas*; but it is treated separately,
and the chapters concerned with the theme are in the nature of
an appendix. St. Augustine had promised, in an earlier book
(II. xxi), to prove that, on Cicero's definition of the term, there had
never existed a *respublica* at Rome. What he has now said in the
nineteenth book about the heavenly city, as the only home of true
righteousness, reminds him of his promise, and he sets about its
performance.

A *respublica* is *res populi*: what then is a *populus*? In Cicero's
definition it is 'the union of a number of men associated by the
two bonds of common acknowledgement of right (*jus*) and common
pursuit of interest' (xxi). It is the word right, or *jus*, which

offends St. Augustine.   In the Latin usage *jus* is a legal term; and it signifies simply the body of legal rules which is recognized, and can be enforced, by a human authority.   On the basis of this significance of *jus* there is little in Cicero's definition with which we need quarrel.   It might, perhaps, go farther; but it is correct enough so far as it goes.   But St. Augustine had his own pre-conceptions; and they made him resolved to quarrel with Cicero's definition.   With his mind full of the idea of righteousness (the Greek δικαιοσύνη, as it appears in Plato and in St. Paul), he twists the sense of *jus*.   He identifies *jus* with *justitia*; he identifies *justitia* with *vera justitia*; and he argues accordingly that 'where there is no true righteousness, there cannot be a union of men associated by a common acknowledgment of right.'   Here he has already departed far from Cicero's sense; but he proceeds to depart farther.   *Justitia,* he argues, is the virtue which gives to each his due.   It must include, and include particularly, the giving of His due to God.   In other words, it must include true religion; for it is only true religion which gives to God His due.   But if *justitia* thus involves true religion, and if *justitia*, as has already been assumed, is necessary to the existence of a *populus*, it follows that true religion is necessary to the existence of a *populus*.   The worship which gives to God His due is the *sine qua non* of the existence of a *populus*, and therefore of a *respublica*.   It is therefore proven that, on Cicero's definition, there never existed a *populus* at Rome; for the *populus Romanus* never gave God His due.

We may rejoin that this has only been proven on the basis of assumptions about the significance of *jus* which Cicero would never have admitted.   But if we make that rejoinder, we must also make an admission.   We must admit that century upon century was destined to hold, and to hold tenaciously, the view which St. Augustine implies—the view that a people, in order to be a true people, must not only be a legal society, but also, and in the same breath, a religious society worshipping God in union and uniformity.   This is the Elizabethan view, implied in the Act of Uniformity and expressed in the philosophy of Hooker: the commonwealth of the people of England must be a Church, as well as a State, in order to be a true commonwealth, and its members must be Churchmen as well as citizens in order to be truly members.   Indeed, so long as a form of Establishment lasts, there still remains a relic of the idea that religion is necessary to the existence of a *respublica*.

And yet St. Augustine is willing, after all, to allow that there may be a people without any confession of true religion.   He had only set out to prove, and he was content with having (as he thought) proved, that *on Cicero's definition of the term* there could not be a people without a confession of true religion.   *If* (he had argued) you say that there must be 'common acknowledgment of right,' *then* there must be common acknowledgment of God, for that is involved in common acknowledgment of right. But you need not say that there must be common acknowledgement of right. You may pitch the key lower, and simply say that a people is 'the union of a reasoning multitude associated by an agreement to pursue in common the objects which it desires' (xxiv). On this definition the end and criterion of a people is not *jus*; it is simply —whatever it is. On this definition, again, the objects desired may be higher or lower; and a people will be better or worse accordingly. On this definition, finally, the Roman people was a people, and the *respublica Romana* a *respublica*; but history shows the quality of the objects it desired, and history testifies how it broke, again and again, by civil wars, the agreement on which the salvation of any people depends. This is equally true of Athens and other States of antiquity. We may allow that they were 'peoples': we must also allow that they were 'cities of the ungodly, devoid of the truth of righteousness.' And therefore the conclusion of the matter is that, though a people may be a people without confessing the true God, no people can be a good people without that confession.

And so St. Augustine argues, in the last chapters of the book (xxv–xxvii), that true virtue cannot exist apart from true religion. Indeed, virtue which does not come from the knowledge and love of God is a vice rather than a virtue; it is a matter of peacock pride and idle vainglorying. 'Not from man, but from above man, proceedeth that which maketh a man live happily.' [1] And yet (the argument proceeds, as St. Augustine turns to the other side of the matter), even a people alienated from God, destitute as it is of virtue, has 'a certain peace of its own, not to be lightly esteemed' (xxvi). It is indeed to the interest of the Christian that it should have this peace; 'for so long as the two cities are mixed, we too use the peace of Babylon.' Here St. Augustine returns to the old problem of the relations of the heavenly and the earthly cities (*supra*, p. xix); but he adds a fresh tribute to the service and the claims of the earthly city when he cites the apostle's exhortation to the Church to 'pray for kings, and those in authority.' The peace of this world, after all, deserves its acknowledgment. Not but what the Christian, even in this world, has a peace of his own which is higher than the peace of this world—the peculiar peace of his faith (xxvii). And yet even that higher and peculiar peace has its miseries, so long as it is enjoyed, precariously enjoyed, in this mortal life. Sin besets us always: even upon the brave fighter *subrepit aliquid . . . unde, si non facili operatione, certe labili*

---

[1] 'He felt, and St. Paul confirmed the conviction, that the whole movement was from God, that faith as much as grace is His gift, and that both are determined by the inscrutable decree of His predestining counsel.'—Dr. Stewart, op. cit., i, p. 585.

locutione, aut volatili cogitatione, peccatur. (The words have a beauty and a subtlety beyond translation.) Only at the last 'will there be such felicity of living and reigning as there shall also be serenity and facility of obeying; and this shall there, in all and in each, be eternal, and its eternity shall be sure; and therefore the peace of this beatitude, or the beatitude of this peace, shall be the Supreme Good.'

V

We have seen the philosophy of sunrise seeking to dispel the philosophy of night. It only remains to say some words on the future influence of *The City of God*. It was studied by Gregory the Great: it was read and loved by Charlemagne, who believed that hs had inaugurated the *civitas Dei* upon earth. Abelard wrote hymns in the strains, and even the words, of the great prose of St. Augustine; and Dante, though he only refers to him twice in the *Divina Commedia*, uses his teaching in *De Monarchia*.[1] But the deeper influence of St. Augustine is not to be traced in particular writers. It is to be traced in the general theory of the canonists and the general theological tradition of the Middle Ages.

One element in the theory of St. Augustine which particularly influenced the canonists was his teaching with regard to property —that by the natural order all things are enjoyed by the righteous in common: that private property is the result of sin; but that none the less it is justified (on that doctrine of the 'return' or recoil of natural order of which we have spoken), because it is, after all, a remedy for sin, and because it canalizes, as it were, and reduces to order the greed of possession which came with sin. This teaching passed to Gratian and the canonists; and it gave them, as Dr. Carlyle has shown (*Mediaeval Political Theory in the West*, II. ii. 6), their technical doctrine in regard to property—that it is not a primitive or natural institution; that its origin must be sought in sinful appetite; that its title rests on the sanction of custom and civil law. It is tempting, but it is impossible in this place, to investigate the debt of Wyclif's theory of *dominium* to the teaching of St. Augustine. It can only be said that Wyclif, in this as in other points of his theory, was steeped in St. Augustine, even if he carried the premises of his teacher to conclusions at which the teacher himself might have stood aghast.

If the teaching of St. Augustine certainly influenced the canonists'

---

[1] On Dante and St. Augustine, see Moore, *Studies in Dante*, i. One might have dreamed that Virgil would have been succeeded by St. Augustine (who, by the way, loved Virgil) when the end of the *Purgatorio* was being reached. But Beatrice appears instead to guide Dante upward to the heavenly city. In the *Paradiso* Dante simply mentions St. Augustine as the founder of canons, by the side of St. Benedict the father of monks and St. Francis the founder of friars.

theory of property, it is a much more difficult thing to say how far his teaching influenced their theory of the relations of *regnum* and *sacerdotum*. Of this theme we have already spoken; and there is but little to be added here. It is sufficient to say that, between the time when St. Augustine finished *The City of God*, in 426, and the outbreak of the War of Investitures, in 1075, a whole stock of new weapons had been added to the armoury of polemics. There is the Gelasian theory of the parity or 'diarchy' of the two powers (*circiter* 500); there is the weapon of the 'Donation of Constantine,' fabricated about 760; there is the argument from the 'Translation of the Empire,' deduced from Charlemagne's coronation in 800; there are the theories drawn by later controversialists from the 'Keys' and the 'Two Swords' and the analogy of 'Sun and Moon'; there is the application of feudal theory to the relations of Church and State. It was from materials such as these that the Middle Ages proper constructed a theory of the relations between *regnum* and *sacerdotum*; and the teaching of St. Augustine could only be one ingredient in a large and varied amalgam. It is tempting to trace a connection between the saying of St. Augustine: 'Remove righteousness, and what are kingdoms but great bands of brigands?' and the outburst of Gregory VII in his letter to Hermann of Metz: 'Who can be ignorant that kings took their beginnings from those who by way of rapine, at the instigation of the prince of this world, desired to have dominion over their fellows?' But before we attempt to trace the connection, or to conclude that St. Augustine taught Gregory VII that States were organizations of brigands, we must remember two things. The first is that, as we have already seen, St. Augustine taught nothing of the sort. The second is that the outburst of Gregory VII stands in isolation, and is contradicted by his other statements. Little can be made of the influence of St. Augustine in this particular connection; and it must remain doubtful how much can be made of it in other respects. Scholars have differed upon the issue whether the teaching of St. Augustine tended, or did not tend, to depress the State and to promote the rise of a theocracy. Harnack has said: 'He roused the conviction that the empirical Catholic Church *san phrase* was the kingdom of God, and the independent State that of the Devil.' [1] (This is a saying which cannot be justified.) Gierke has said: 'The theory of *The City of God* left the worldly State practically destitute of importance, except in so far as it ranged itself, as a subordinate member, within and below the divine State which was realized in the Church.' (This is a saying, again, which the reader of St. Augustine's actual text can hardly accept.) Dubief has said (as it seems to me with more justice): 'It is impossible to find in St. Augustine's words those

---

[1] I have borrowed these quotations mainly from Bishop Welldon's edition, *i*, pp. 51–2. The reference to Troeltsch is my own.

comparisons between the spiritual power and the temporal power which are intended to establish the pre-eminence of the former above the latter, and denote the intention of subordinating the State to the clergy.' Perhaps Ernst Troeltsch, in his massive way, gives the best and soundest view of the matter: [1] 'St. Augustine admitted that view of the State and its laws which brings them both into connection with natural law, but he confined that view within narrower limits than the other Fathers: he wanted room for the possibility of irreligious Emperors (regarded as a visitation of God and a punishment of sin), and for the moral rejection of the powers that be in so far as they did not allow themselves to be guided by divine righteousness.' There were, Troeltsch argues, two elements in the thought of the age of St. Augustine. One was a belief in the *Naturrecht* of the State (in other words, a belief that it was based on what St. Augustine calls *naturalis ordo*); the other was the theocratic belief of a victorious religious society that its principles were the sovereign principles, and must therefore prevail even in the area of political organization. 'The latter, as is well known, was particularly expounded by St. Augustine in his great work. But what is less noticed is that in it he also enunciated and maintained the former. In the irreconcilable struggle of the two points of view lies the double nature of the work of this great thinker—a work which, for this very reason, transmitted also to the future a double tendency. Theocracy and *naturalis ordo* are both made to consecrate the State: what the one cannot do the other will; and the Emperor is in any case primarily determined by his quality of existing *Dei gratia* and by his theocratic connections. But the State itself remains, for all that, the incarnation of "the world."' After this account of St. Augustine's own position, Troeltsch turns to his influence on the Middle Ages. 'Chrysostom, Leo I, Gelasius I, St. Augustine might all indeed demand the theocratic subjection of the Emperor under the clergy, on the analogy of the Old Testament, and they might sketch the "Programme of the Middle Ages." But the programme was never realized at all in the East, and it was only realized in the West after five centuries had passed.' When these five centuries had passed, and the realization of the programme was attempted, St. Augustine's treasures of thought were used. But (and this is the important point), if 'the harsh sayings of St. Augustine about the State were again brought into play, they underwent a radical intensification in the process; and an exorbitant exaggeration of emphasis was laid on the sinfulness of the State, on which St. Augustine had indeed laid stress, but behind which he had always recognized the existence of a basis of natural law.'

The influence of St. Augustine on the theological tradition (as

[1] I have translated or summarized four passages in his *Soziallehren der christlichen Kirchen*, pp. 168, 170, 191, 215

distinct from the social and political doctrines) of the Middle Ages is a vast theme, upon which we cannot embark, but which it would be almost a treason not to mention. St. Augustine enters into the *Summa* of St. Thomas; he influenced Wyclif profoundly; he influenced Luther no less profoundly. 'The history of Church doctrine in the West,' Harnack has said, 'is a much disguised struggle against Augustinianism.' This is a deep saying, and we must attempt to gloss it. St. Augustine, we may say, imbued as he was with Platonic philosophy, always believed in the unchanging perfection of a God who always and everywhere acted by law. In his theory, God is always determined (or to speak more exactly He always determines Himself) by *rationes exemplares* [1] (or, as Plato would have said, 'ideas'); His relations to His creatures are always relations in the sphere of immutable order; any apparent change is a change not in God, but in the creature, and God must adjust Himself to the changing creature in order to remain unchanged in His own unchanging essence. Against this clear and pure rigour of an unswerving general order (the rigour which Wordsworth celebrates in his *Ode to Duty*), it was natural that those should revolt who wanted a mysterious and emotional world, rich in insoluble riddles, and needing a mediatory and miraculous Church to give a mystical clue. Such a revolt was that of the Nominalists of the later Middle Ages; and here we find one of those 'much disguised struggles against Augustinianism' of which Harnack speaks. *Latet dolus in generalibus,* said the Nominalists; and they accordingly laid their emphasis on the Particular in its unique and concrete 'reality.' Their emphasis on the Particular led them to lay stress on individuality and personality, alike in man and in God; and their study of human individuality helped them to make some of the first modern researches in psychology. But the trend of their thought turned them also towards obscurantism. The individual became an ultimate mystery: God Himself became an inscrutably omnipotent individual, acting indeterminately by His individual will. The Nominalists thus came to magnify the authority of the Church as the only escape from 'the burden of the mystery'; they believed in *fides implicita*; and in them may be traced the tendency of the over-subtle intellect to pass through obscurantism to the acceptance of mere authority. It was against the Nominalists that Wyclif and Luther were both in revolt; and they both went back to St. Augustine for comfort and countenance. It would be too bold to say that St. Augustine inspired the Reformation. But it would perhaps be true to say that he took the sixteenth century back to the idea of a divine general order of the Universe, and back to a conception of righteousness based upon that idea.

---

[1] I have borrowed the phrase from Wyclif.

VI

It may be worth while, in conclusion, to give some indications of the origin of the translation which is now printed in full in the Everyman series.

The great edition current in the sixteenth century was an edition printed by Froben at Basle in 1522. Erasmus wrote the introduction; but the work of editing and of adding a commentary was undertaken, at his request, by the Spanish scholar and educationalist, Luis Vives. Vives produced a fine book, which he dedicated to Henry VIII; and he was rewarded by a letter in which the king declared: 'It has raised the doubt within us whom we should chiefly congratulate, whether first you, who have brought to a close by such learned labour so choice a work; or secondly, St. Augustine, who has been for so long a time so imperfectly accessible, and who now at last is brought from darkness to light, restored to his ancient integrity; or thirdly, all posterity, for whose great profit your *Commentaries* are now at hand.'

Whether Vives or St. Augustine or posterity was most to be congratulated may be left, as it was left by Henry, an open question. But posterity has certainly benefited by Vives' work. Nearly a century afterwards, John Healey, an Elizabethan translator armed with the wonderful style of his age, took Vives' edition in hand. Healey was a friend of Thomas Thorpe, a publisher (if indeed he can so be called) who published Shakespeare's *Sonnets*; and after providing Thorpe with 'Philip Mornay, Lord of Plessis, his Tears' and 'Epictetus his Manuall and Cebes his Table,' he produced for him, in 1610, 'St. Augustine of the Citie of God, with the learned comments of Io. Lod. Vives.'[1] Healey was a translator of the stamp of Sir Thomas Hoby (translator of Castiglione's *Il Cortegiano*), Sir Thomas North (translator of Plutarch), and Florio (translator of Montaigne).

[1] There are two editions of Healey's translation—one of the year 1610, and one of the year 1620. The edition of 1620 contains an interesting 'dedicatory epistle' by W. Crashaw. This Crashaw was a notable man, the father of the poet Crashaw: he had been a Fellow of St. John's College, Cambridge: he became a Puritan divine, and wrote a number of learned works. In his dedicatory epistle of 1620 he writes: 'I set one about it' (i.e. the translation), which suggests that he started Healey in his work of translation before 1610. Healey died in that year—the year of the publication of the first edition—perhaps leaving his work, as indeed the dedicatory epistle in the edition of 1620 implies, incompletely corrected. The edition of 1620 is accordingly a revised edition, 'compared with the Latin edition,' as it is stated on the title-page, 'and in very many places corrected and amended.' Is it possible that W. Crashaw had not only suggested the translation to Healey before 1610, but had also corrected and amended it for the new edition of 1620? It may be noted that in 1618 he had been made incumbent of St. Mary, Whitechapel, and was thus living in London at the time when the second edition was printed there. This note is largely a matter of conjecture; but it may suggest to some scholar an inquiry into Crashaw's connection with the translation of the *Civitas Dei*.

But students of this translation will not find it easy reading. Elizabethan English is noble, but its sentences are couched in long and often involved periods, and the turns of phrase are often different from our own. A student will be well advised to have at hand a Latin text of St. Augustine's own words, and to turn occasionally for reference to the simpler (but prosier) translation of Dr. Dods[1]. But he must remember that much of the difficulty of St. Augustine is intrinsic. He had been nurtured in the ancient schools of learning: he had collected there a large store of faggots of information. He cannot away with them when he is writing; and though the fire of his faith burns gloriously through, it leaves an abundance of charred sticks and ashes. (The first three chapters of the nineteenth book are a good example.) The method of his mind and the turn of his style add to the difficulty. Trained in the schools, he has a subtle and antithetical—one may almost say a scholastic—mind; he refines and dichotomizes; he pursues a thought into all its ramifications and divisions. Add to this a rhetorical style—sometimes glowing into a noble beauty, but sometimes overloaded with ornaments and epithets—and the difficulty of the student reaches its culmination. But to read him is supremely worth while. It is an education, and a very liberal education.

ERNEST BARKER.

31st December 1930.

NOTE. Where I have quoted St. Augustine in English in the course of the introduction I have translated for myself.

[1] Published in 1871, in the Select Library of the Nicene and Post-Nicene Fathers of the Church. The most convenient modern edition of the Latin text is that edited by Bishop Welldon and published by the S.P.C.K. in 1924.

To the Right Honourable,

The Three Most Noble Brothers,

William Earl of Pembroke, Lord Chamberlain: Thomas Earl of Arundel:

Two of the Lords of His Majesty's most Honourable Privy Council:

and Philip Earl of Montgomery:

Knights of the most Noble Order of the Garter:

Grace and Peace in Christ.

Right Honourable Lords:

As man amongst creatures, and the Church amongst men, and the Fathers in the Church, and St. Augustine amongst the Fathers, so amongst the many precious volumes, and in the rich store-house of his works, his books on the City of God have a special pre-eminence. For St. Augustine himself. He was a glorious light in his time, and one of the worthiest Champions that ever the Church had since the Apostles. For though he was but one of the four Doctors of the Latin Church, yet fought he with four of the foulest heretics, and cut off the heads of four of the foulest monsters that ever oppressed the Church, namely the Arians, the Manichees, the Donatists, and Pelagians. Such a Hercules was this holy Father that he feared not four together.

Almost forty years of his life he misspent, partly in the errors of those times, partly in the lusts of his life; but the latter forty he consecrated to God and the Church's service, and spent them with such profit, as few have done the like since the world began; for it is written of him that, besides his daily preaching (which alone is now held impossible for any man to do), and his visiting of the sick, and reconciling of people at variance, and giving counsel and directions when he was consulted, he wrote so many worthy volumes and learned works, as a man can scarce advisedly peruse in a great part of his life. Amongst which these of the City of God have a special pre-eminence; for as in his other labours he went before other men, so in this he exceeded himself, insomuch as not only for excellency of divinity, but for variety of all learning it is called and esteemed a storehouse of knowledge.

If any object that Augustine had some errors, I answer: Who was ever free since the Apostles? Again, regarding the times he lived in, it is no wonder he had errors, but that he had no more. In a word, his errors are few, and not fundamental, therefore not

to be regarded where so many truths are so faithfully taught, and
so manfully maintained. Add hereunto that his errors are such
as gain the adversaries but a little. Take for example the point of
purgatory, touching which they brag so much of St. Augustine.
He that looks shall find that if he does hold any purgatory after
this life, it is such a one as the pope will not give a pin for: for
the pope's purgatory is a lake of torments, into which all are cast
but monks and martyrs, and out of which the pope at his pleasure,
and for paying and praying, and doing as he appoints, can deliver
when he will. This St. Augustine and the old Fathers never knew
nor taught, but such an one, if any at all, as every man must endure
till God release him. And he that teacheth no other purgatory
than this in Rome, the pope would burn him. But to do right to
this holy Father and the truth itself, it is more likely that he is
wronged, and his works corrupted and altered since he died; for
else it is impossible that so wise a man as he should be so contrary
to himself, for he saith plainly:

'There is no middle place for any; but he must needs be with
the devil that is not with Christ.'

And 'We must either be with Christ or Satan; there is no middle
place.' And in this very book: 'They that have not possession of
the Kingdom of God are liable to eternal punishment, for there is
no middle place.'

He that teacheth this, how can he teach a popish purgatory?
Wherefore undoubtedly either he might incline to the opinion of
purgatory in his younger days, and in his riper age reformed his
judgment (as many men do in many things); or else his works have
passed the popish censures, and in the Romish forge have been
forged anew, which is now proved to be the daily practice of that
generation.

If any say that he wanted the tongues, they do him wrong; for,
if he was not so exquisite in the Oriental tongues as Hierome, no
marvel, he living in the Latin Church all his life; whereas Hierome
spent a great part of his in the Eastern Churches among them that
spake the Hebrew and Syriac tongues, and knew the Chaldee and
Arabic; yet it is certain he was well seen in all the learned languages. He was an excellent Latinist for those times, and a
competent Grecian and Hebraist; and otherwise so excellent a
scholar, and of so rare a wit, as it is uncertain whether his parts
of nature or of art were more admirable in him: but I am sure
for neither of them was he so admirable as for humility and holiness of life after his conversion, commendable, honourable, and
imitable to all posterity.

His works are of such excellent matter, as some of them are not
only translated into many vulgar tongues, but, which is rare, into
Greek also. This work of the City of God was long ago translated
into French. I saw not therefore any reason why it should be

denied to our English people, so many desiring it as did daily. Wherefore I set one about it, who if he had time enough (for he is now with God) wanted not, I am sure, neither will nor skill to do it well. And now that our British world hath it, seeing many in France thanked Maldonat though a Jesuit for persuading Gentian Hervet to put it into French, I need not doubt that many in this island will thank him that was the means of putting it into English.

And in whose names rather should this book pass into England, Scotland, and Ireland, than in yours (Right Honourable), a triplicity of noble brethren, known and loved and honoured in all three Kingdoms? You are brethren many ways, two of you brethren in blood, two of you brethren by marriage, two of you brethren in one Honourable place, all of you brethren in one Honourable Order, all brethren in the service of one great King, all loved of your Sovereign, all honoured of his subjects, and, which is most of all, all brethren in the religion and service of the most high God.

Vouchsafe therefore to be all three brethren in giving this honour to holy St. Augustine, that great saint of God and servant of His Church; and I shall pray you may still and ever continue brethren in all loyalty to your Sovereign, love one to another, and in all the honour and happiness of this life: and for the life to come, that you may be brethren in grace here, and in glory hereafter.

Your Honours' devoted in Christ to do you service,

W. CRASHAWE.

EXTRACT FROM THE DEDICATION OF THE COMMENTARIES UPON
ST. AUGUSTINE'S 'DE CIVITATE DEI' BY JOANNES LODOVICUS
VIVES TO THE RENOWNED PRINCE HENRY THE EIGHTH, KING OF
ENGLAND, LORD OF IRELAND, etc.

This work, not mine, but St. Augustine's, is also suitable unto
your greatness, whether the author be respected, or the matter
of the work. The author is Augustine, good God, how holy,
how learned a man, what a light, what a pillar to the Christian
Commonwealth, on whom alone it depended for many rites, many
statutes, customs, holy and venerable ceremonies. And not
without cause. For in that man was most plentiful study, most
exact knowledge of holy writ, a sharp and clear judgment, a wit
admirably quick and piercing. He was a most diligent defender
of undefiled piety, of most sweet behaviour, composed and conformed to the charity of the Gospel, renowned and honoured for
his integrity and holiness of life; all of which a man might hardly
prosecute in a full volume, much less in an epistle. It is well that
I speak of a writer known of all, and familiar to you.

Now the work is not concerning the children of Niobe, or the
gates of Thebes, or mending clothes, or preparing pleasures, or
manuring grounds, which yet have been arguments presented even
to kings; but concerning both cities, of the world and of God,
wherein angels, devils, and all men are contained; how they
were born, how bred, how grown, whither they tend, and what
they shall do when they come to their work: which to unfold he
hath omitted no profane nor sacred learning, which he doth not
both touch and explain. . . .

And all this with a wonderful wit, exceeding sharpness, most
neat learning, a clear and polished style, such as became an author
traversed and exercised in all kind of learning and writings, and
as beseemed those great and excellent matters, and fitted those
with whom he disputed.

Him therefore shall you read, most famous and best-minded
king, at such hours as you withdraw from the mighty affairs and
turmoils of your kingdom to employ on learning and ornaments
of the mind, and withal take a taste of our commentaries; whereof
let me say, as Ovid said of his book *De Fastis*, when he presented
them to Germanicus Caesar:

> A learned Prince's judgment t' undergo,
> As sent to read to Phoebus, our leaves go.

Which if I find they dislike you not, I shall not fear the allowance of others; for who will be so impudent as not to be ashamed to dissent from so exact a judgment? Which if any dare do, your even silent authority shall yet protect me.

Farewell, worthiest king, and reckon Vives most devoted to you in any place, so he be reckoned one of yours.

From Louvain the 7th of July M.D.XXII.

HENRY KING OF ENGLAND
TO
IOANNES LODOVICUS VIVES
GREETING

Worthy Sir, and our very well-beloved friend,

As soon as St. Augustine *De Civitate Dei*, enlightened with your comments, came to our hands, being right welcome unto us, it caused us to doubt, whom we should most congratulate; either you, by whose so learned labour so choice a work is finished; St. Augustine, who long time in last brought from darkness to li integrity; or posterity, whom the finitely profit. But whereas it pleased mentaries unto our name, we cannot but retain a grateful and return you great thanks; in that especially your mind therein seemeth to manifest no vulgar love and observance towards us. Wherefore we would have you persuaded that our favour and good-will shall never fail in your affairs, whatsoever occasion shall be offered that may tend to your avail. So fare you happily well.

From our Court at Greenwich, the xxiiii of January, M.D.XXIII.

...nished; or
...mperfect and obscure, is now at
...ght, and restored to his ancient
...se your Commentaries shall in-
...d you to dedicate these Com-
...mind,

CONTENTS

VOLUME ONE

THE THIRD BOOK:

THE FOURTH BOOK:

THE SEVENTH BOOK:

THE EIGHTH BOOK:

THE ELEVENTH BOOK:

THE TWELFTH BOOK:

VOLUME TWO

THE THIRTEENTH BOOK:

THE SEVENTEENTH BOOK:

THE EIGHTEENTH BOOK:

THE TWENTIETH BOOK:

THE TWENTY-FIRST BOOK:

THE TWENTY-SECOND BOOK:

THE FIRST BOOK OF THE CITY OF GOD

CHAPTER I

*Of the adversaries of the name of Christ, spared by the barbarians in
the sacking of Rome, only for Christ's sake*

THAT most glorious society and celestial city of God's faithful,
which is partly seated in the course of these declining times, wherein 'he that liveth by faith,' [1] is a pilgrim amongst the wicked; and
partly in that solid estate of eternity, which as yet the other part
doth patiently expect, until 'righteousness be turned into judgment,' [2] being then by the proper excellence to obtain the last
victory, and be crowned in perfection of peace; have I undertaken
to defend in this work, which I intend unto you (my dearest Marcellinus) as being your due by my promise, against all those that
prefer their own gods before this city's founder. The work is
great and difficult, but God is our helper. For I know well what
strong arguments are required to make the proud know the virtue
of humility, by which (not being enhanced by human glory, but
endowed with divine grace) it surmounts all earthly loftiness, which
totters through the one transitory instability. For the King, the
builder of this city, whereof we are now to discourse, hath revealed
a maxim of the divine law to His people, thus: 'God resisteth the
proud, and giveth grace to the humble.' [3] Now this which is
indeed only God's, the swelling pride of an ambitious mind affecteth
also, and loves to hear this as parcel of His praise:

> Parcere subjectis et debellare superbos. [4]
> To spare the lowly, and strike down the proud.

Wherefore touching the temporal city (which longing after
domination, though it hold all the other nations under it, yet in
itself is overruled by the one lust after sovereignty) we may not
omit to speak whatsoever the quality of our proposed subject shall
require or permit; for out of this arise the foes against whom God's
city is to be guarded. Yet some of these reclaiming their impious
errors have become good citizens therein: but others burning with
an extreme violence of hate against it, are thankless to the Redeemer
of it for benefits of His so manifest, that at this day they would not
be able to speak a word against it, unless in the holy places thereof,

[1] Hab. ii. 4; Rom. i. 17; Gal. iii. 11.   [2] Ps. xciii. 15.
[3] Jas. iv. 6; 1 Pet. v. 5.   [4] Virg. *Aen.* vi. 853.

flying thither from the sword of the foe, they had found that life
and safety wherein now they glory. Are not these Romans become
persecutors of Christ, whom the very barbarians saved for Christ's
sake? Yes, the churches of the apostles, and the martyrs can
testify this, which in that great sack were free both to their own
and strangers. So far and no farther came the rage of the bloody
enemy: even there the murderer's fury stopped: even thither were
the distressed led by their pitiful foes (who had spared them, though
finding them out of those sanctuaries) lest they should light upon
some that should not extend the like pity. And even they that
elsewhere raged in slaughters, coming but to those places, that
forbade what law of war elsewhere allowed—all their headlong fury
curbed itself, and all their desire of conquest was conquered. And
so escaped many then, that since have detracted from Christianity:
they can impute their city's other calamities wholly unto Christ,
but that good which was bestowed on them only for Christ's honour
(namely, the sparing of their lives) that they impute not unto our
Christ, but unto their own fate: whereas if they had any judgment,
they would rather attribute these calamities and miseries at the
hands of their enemies all unto the providence of God, which is
wont to reform the corruptions of men's manners by war and
oppressions, and laudably to exercise the righteous in such afflictions; and having so tried them, either to transport them to a more
excellent estate, or to keep them longer in the world for other ends
and uses. And whereas the bloody barbarians, against all custom
of war, spared them both in other places, for the honour of Christ,
and in those large houses that were dedicated unto Him (made
large, to contain many, for the larger extent of pity); this ought
they to ascribe to these Christian times, to give God thanks for it,
and to have true recourse by this means unto God's name, thereby
to avoid the pains of eternal damnation: which name many of them
as then falsely took up, as a sure shelter against the storms of
present ruin. For even those that you may now behold most
petulantly insulting over Christ's servants, most of them had never
escaped the general massacre, had they not counterfeited themselves to be the servants of Christ. But now, through their ungrateful pride, and ungodly madness, they stand against that name
(in perverseness of heart, and to their eternal captivation in darkness) to which they fled with a dissembling tongue, for the obtaining
and enjoying but of this temporal light.

CHAPTER II

There never was war wherein the conquerors would spare them, whom they conquered, for the gods they worshipped

THERE have been thus many wars chronicled, partly before Rome was built, and partly since her founding: let them read, and find me any one city taken by a stranger foe, that would spare any that they found retired into the temples of their gods, or any barbarian captain, that ever commanded that in the sack of the town none should be touched that were fled into such or such temples. Did not Aeneas see Priam slain before the altar, and with his blood

> Sanguine foedantem quos ipse sacraverat ignes? [1]
>
> Sprinkling the flames himself had hallowed?

Did not Diomede and Ulysses, 'having slaughtered all the keepers of the high tower,

> '. . . caesis summae custodibus arcis,
> Corripuere sacram effigiem, manibusque cruentis
> Virgineas ausi divae contingere vittas'? [2]
>
> 'Snatch up the sacred statue, and with hands
> Besmeared in blood, durst touch the Virgin's veil'?

Yet that is not true which followeth:

> Ex illo fluere ac retro sublapsa referri
> Spes Danaum.
>
> From thence the Grecians' hopes decline, and fail.

For after all this, they conquered: after this they threw down Troy with sword and fire: after this they smote off Priam's head while fleeing to the altar. Neither perished Troy because it lost the Palladium: for what had the Palladium lost first, that itself should perish? perhaps the keepers? indeed it is true, they being slain, it was soon taken away: for the image kept not the men, but the men kept the image. But why then was it adored as the preserver of the country and citizens, when it could not preserve its own keepers?

CHAPTER III

Of the Romans' fondness in thinking that those gods could help them which could not help Troy in her distress

BEHOLD unto what patrons the Romans rejoiced to commit the protection of their city! Oh, too, too piteous error! Nay, they are angry at us when we speak thus of their gods; but never with their teachers and inventors, but pay them money for learning them such

[1] Virg. *Aen.* ii. 501–2.   [2] *Aen.* ii. 166–70.

fooleries: yea, and moreover have vouchsafed their authors both stipends from the common treasury and ample honours besides. Forsooth in Virgil, who was therefore taught unto their children, because that they think this great and most renowned poet, being fastened in their minds whilst they are young, will never easily be forgotten (according to that of Horace:

> Quo semel est imbuta recens servabit odorem
> Testa diu.[1]
>
> The liquors that new vessels first contains,
> Behind them leave a taste that long remains)

—even in the forenamed poet Virgil is Juno presented as the Trojans' foe, inciting Aeolus, the King of Winds, against them in these words:

> Gens inimica mihi Tyrrhenum navigat aequor
> Ilium in Italiam portans, victosque penates.[2]
>
> The nation that I hate in peace sails by,
> With Troy and Troy's fall'n gods to Italy.

Yea, would any wise man have commended the defence of Rome unto gods already proved unable to defend themselves? But suppose Juno spoke this as a woman in anger, not knowing what she said, what says (the so-often surnamed godly) Aeneas himself? Does he not say plainly:

> Panthus Othryades, arcis, Phoebique sacerdos,
> Sacra manu, victosque deos parvumque nepotem
> Ipse trahit, cursuque amens ad limina tendit?[3]
>
> Panthus, a priest of Phoebus and the Tower,
> Burdened with his fall'n gods, and in his hand
> His poor young nephew, flies unto the strand?

Does he not hold these gods (which he dares call fallen) rather commended unto him than he to them; it being said to him:

> Sacra suosque tibi commendat Troia penates?[4]
>
> To thee doth Troy commend her gods, her all?

If Virgil, then, call them fallen gods, and conquered gods, needing man's help for their escape after their overthrow and fall, how mad are men to think that there was any wit shown in committing Rome to their keeping, or that it could not be lost, if first it lost not them? To worship conquered and cast gods as guardians and defenders—what is it but to put by good deities, and adore wicked devils?[5] Were there not more wisdom shown in believing not that Rome had not come to this calamity unless it had first lost them, but that they had long since come to nothing had not Rome

[1] *Epist.* i. 2, 69, 70.   [2] *Aen.* i. 67–8.
[3] *Aen.* ii. 319–21.   [4] *Aen.* ii. 293.
[5] Healey reads *daemonia.* If *nomina* is read translate 'and rely on false securities.'—ED.

been as the especially careful keeper of them? Who sees not (that will see anything) what an idle presumption it is to build any impossibility of being conquered upon defenders that have been conquered? and to think that Rome therefore perished because it had lost the gods as guardians, when the only possible cause why it perished was because it would choose guardians soon to perish? Nor were the poets disposed to lie when they sung thus of these subverted gods; it was truth that enforced those prudent men to confess it. But of this, more fitly in another place hereafter. At this time (as I resolved at first) I will have a little bout (as well as I can) with those ungrateful persons, whose blasphemous tongues throw those calamities upon Christ, which they worthily suffer for their own perversity. But whereas Christ's name alone was of power to procure them their undeserved safety, that they do scorn to acknowledge; and being mad with sacrilegious petulancy, they practise their foul terms upon His name, which, like false wretches, they were before glad to take upon them to save their lives by; and those filthy tongues which, when they were in Christ's houses, fear kept silent, to remain there with more safety, where, even for His sake, they found mercy; those selfsame, getting forth again, shoot at His deity with all their envenomed shafts of malice, and curses of hostility.

CHAPTER IV

Of the sanctuary of Juno in Troy which freed not any (that fled into it) from the Greeks at the city's sack, whereas the churches of the apostles saved all comers from the barbarians at the sack of Rome. Cato's opinion touching the enemy's custom in the sack of cities

NOR could Troy itself that was (as I said before) the mother of the Romans' progeny, in all her hallowed temples, save any one from the Grecian force or fury, though they worshipped the same gods: nay did they not in the very sanctuary of Juno,

> Ipso Junonis asylo
> Custodes lecti Phoenix, et dirus Ulysses
> Praedam asservabant. Huc undique Troia gaza
> Incensis erepta adytis, mensaeque deorum,
> Crateresque auro solidi, captivaque vestis
> Congeritur, etc.? [1]

> To Juno's sanctuary
> Comes all the prey, and what they thither carry
> Is kept by choice men; the Phoenician
> And dire Ulysses: thither the whole state
> Of Troy's wealth swarms, the gods, their temple's plate,
> There lies the gold in heaps, and robes of worth
> Snatched from the flaming coffers, etc.?

[1] *Aen.* ii. 761–7.

Behold, the place dedicated unto so great a goddess was chosen out not to serve for a place whence they might lawfully pull prisoners out, but for a prison wherein to shut up all they took. Now compare this temple, not of any vulgar god, of the common sort, but of Jupiter's sister, and queen of all the other gods, unto the churches built as memorials of the apostles. To the first, all the spoils that were plucked from the gods and flaming temples were carried, not to be bestowed back to the vanquished, but to be shared amongst the vanquishers. To the second, both that which was the place's own and whatever was found also elsewhere to belong to such places, with all religious honour and reverence was restored. There, was freedom lost, here, saved: there, was bondage shut in, here, it was shut out: thither were men brought by their proud foes, for to undergo slavery; hither were men brought by their pitiful foes to be secured from slavery. Lastly the temple of Juno was chosen by the inconstant Greeks to practise their proud covetousness in, whereas the churches of Christ were by the naturally cruel barbarians chosen to exercise their pious humility in. Perhaps the Greeks in that their victory spared those that fled into the temples of the common gods, and did not dare to hurt or captivate such as escaped thither: but in that, Virgil plays the poet indeed, and feigns it. Indeed there he describes the general custom of most enemies in the sacking of cities, and conquests; which custom Caesar himself (as Sallust,[1] that noble, true historian, records) forgets not to avouch, in his sentence given upon the conspirators in the senate house: that (in these spoils) the virgins are ravished, the children torn from their parents' bosoms, the matrons made the objects of all the victors' lust, the temples and houses all spoiled, all things turned into burning and slaughter: and lastly all places stuffed full of weapons, carcasses, blood, and lamentation. If Cato had not named temples, we might have thought it the custom of a foe to spare such places as are the habitations of their gods: but the senators feared the ruin of their temples, not by an unknown or stranger enemy, but by Catiline, and his followers, who were senators and citizens of Rome themselves. But these were villains though, and their country's parricides.

CHAPTER V

That the Romans themselves never spared the temples of those cities which they conquered

BUT why should we spend time in discoursing of many nations, that have waged wars together, and yet never spared the conquered habitations of one another's gods: let us go to the Romans

[1] *Catil.* 51.

themselves; yes, I say, let us observe the **Romans** themselves, whose chief glory it was

> Parcere subjectis et debellare superbos.[1]
>
> To spare the lowly, and pull down the proud.

And 'being offered injury they preferred rather to pardon than persecute.' [2]   In all their spacious conquests of towns and cities, in all their progress and augmentation of their domination, show us unto what one temple they granted this privilege, that it should secure him that could fly into it from the enemy's sword.   Did they ever do so, and yet their histories not record it?   Is it likely that they that hunted thus for monuments of praise, would endure the suppression of this so goodly a commendation?   Indeed that great Roman, Marcus Marcellus, that took that goodly city of Syracuse, is said to have wept before the ruin, and shed his own tears before he shed their blood: having a care to preserve the chastity even of his foes from violation.   For before he gave leave to the invasion, he made an absolute edict, that no violence should be offered unto any free person: yet was the city in hostile manner subverted utterly, nor find we anywhere recorded, that this so chaste and gentle a general ever commanded to spare such as fled for refuge to this temple or that: which (had it been otherwise) would not have been omitted, since neither his compassion, nor his command for the captives' chastity, is left unrecorded.   So is Fabius, the conqueror of Tarentum, commended for abstaining from making booty of their images.   For his secretary asking him what they should do with the images of the gods, whereof they had as then taken a great many: he seasoned his continency with a conceit, for asking what they were, and being answered that there were many of them great ones, and some of them armed: 'Oh' (said he), 'let us leave the Tarentines their angry gods.'   Seeing therefore that the Roman historiographers neither concealed Marcellus his weeping, nor Fabius his jesting, neither the chaste pity of the one, nor the merry abstinence of the other, with what reason should they omit that, if any of them had given such privilege to some men in honour of their gods, they might save their lives by taking sanctuary in such or such a temple, where neither slavery nor slaughter should have any power or place?

[1] Virg. *Aen.* vi. 853.   [2] Sallust, *Catil.* 9.

CHAPTER VI

*That the cruel effects following the losses of war did but follow the
custom of war: and wherein they were moderated, it was through
the power of the name of Jesus Christ*

THEREFORE all the spoil, murder, burning, violence, and affliction,
that in this fresh calamity fell upon Rome, were nothing but the
ordinary effects following the custom of war. But that which was
so unaccustomed, that the savage nature of the barbarians should
put on a new shape and appear so merciful, that it would make
choice of great and spacious churches, to fill with such as it meant
to show pity on, from which none should be haled to slaughter or
slavery, in which none should be hurt, to which many by their
courteous foes should be conducted, and out of which none should
be led into bondage even by cruel enemies; this is due to the name
of Christ, this is due to the Christian profession; he that seeth not
this is blind, he that seeth it and praiseth it not is thankless, he that
hinders him that praiseth it is mad. God forbid that any man of
sense should attribute this unto the barbarians' brutishness. It was
God that struck a terror into their truculent and bloody spirits, it
was He that bridled them, it was He that so wondrously restrained
them, that had so long before foretold this by His prophet: 'I will
visit their offences with the rod, and their sin with scourges: yet
will I not utterly take My mercy from them.'[1]

CHAPTER VII

*Of the commodities and discommodities commonly communicated both
to good and ill*

YEA, but some will say: Why doth God suffer His mercy to be extended unto the graceless and thankless? Oh! why should we
judge, but because it is His work 'that maketh the sun to shine
daily both on good and bad, and the rain to fall both on the just
and unjust'?[2] For what though some by meditating upon this,
take occasion to reform their enormities with repentance? and
some others (as the apostle saith) despising the riches of God's
goodness and long-suffering, in their hardness of heart and im-
penitency 'do lay up unto themselves wrath against the day of
wrath, and the revelation of God's just judgment, who will reward
each man according to his works'?[3] Nevertheless God's patience
still inviteth the wicked unto repentance as this scourge doth

---

[1] Ps. lxxxix. 32, 33.   [2] Matt. v. 45.   [3] Rom. ii. 4-6.

instruct the good unto patience. The mercy of God embraceth the good with love, as His severity doth correct the bad with pains. For it seemed good to the almighty providence to prepare such goods, in the world to come, as the just only should enjoy and not the unjust: and such evils as the wicked only should feel, and not the godly. But as for these temporal goods of this world, He hath left them to the common use both of good and bad: that the goods of this world should not be too much desired, because even the wicked do also partake them: and that the evils of this world should not be too cowardly avoided, wherewith the good are sometimes afflicted. But there is great difference in the use both of that estate in this world, which is called prosperous, and that which is called adverse. For neither do these temporal goods extol a good man, nor do the evil deject him. But the evil man must needs be subject to the punishment of this earthly unhappiness, because he is first corrupted by this earthly happiness: yet in the distributing of these temporal blessings God showeth His provident operation. For if all sin were in the present punished, there should be nothing to do at the last judgment: and again, if no sin were here openly punished, the divine providence would not be believed. And so in prosperity, if God should not give competency of worldly and apparent blessing to some that ask them, we would say He hath nothing to do with them: and should He give them to all that ask them, we should think He were not to be served but for them, and so His service should not make us godly, but rather greedy. This being thus, whatever affliction good men and bad do suffer together in this life, it doth not prove the persons undistinct, because so they both do jointly endure like pains. For the sufferers remain distinct even while enduring the same sufferings, and virtue and vice remain distinct beneath the burden of the same affliction; for as in one fire gold shineth and chaff smoketh, and as under one flail the straw is bruised and the ear cleansed; nor are the lees and the oil confused because they are both pressed in one press; so likewise one and the same violence of affliction proveth, purifieth, and clarifieth the good, and condemneth, wasteth, and casteth out the bad. And thus in one and the same distress do the wicked offend God by detestation and blasphemy, and the good do glorify Him by praise and prayer. So great is the difference wherein we ponder not what, but how a man suffers. For one and the same motion maketh the mud smell filthily, and the unguent smell most fragrantly.

CHAPTER VIII

Of the causes of such corrections as fall both upon the good and bad together

BUT tell me now in all this desolation what one thing did the Christians endure, which due and faithful consideration might not turn unto their edification? For first they might with fear observe to what a mass iniquity was increased, at which the just God being displeased had sent these afflictions upon the world, and that though they themselves were far from the society of the wicked, yet should they not hold themselves so purely separate from all faults, that they should think themselves too good to suffer a temporal correction for divers faults that might be found in their conversations: for to omit this—that there is no man however laudable in his conversation, that in some things yields not unto the concupiscence of the flesh; and that though he decline not unto the gulf of reprobate offence and habitation of all brutish filthiness, yet slips now and then into some enormities, and those either seldom, or so much more often as they are less grave— to omit all this, how hard a thing is it to find one that makes a true use of their fellowship, for whose horrible pride, luxury, avarice, bestial iniquity, and irreligiousness, the Lord (as His prophets have threatened) doth lay His heavy hand upon the whole world! How few do we find that live with them, as good men ought to live with them! For either we keep aloof, and forbear to give them due instructions, admonitions, or reprehensions; or else we hold their reformation too great a labour: either we are afraid to offend them, or else we eschew their hate for our own greater temporal preferment, and fear their opposition either in those things which our greediness longeth to enjoy, or in those which our weakness is afraid to forgo: so that though the lives of the wicked be still disliked of the good, and that thereby the one do avoid that damnation which in the world to come is the assured inheritance of the other, yet because they wink at their damnable exorbitances, because they fear by them to lose their own vain temporalities, justly do they partake with them in the punishments temporal though they shall not do so in the eternal; justly do they in these divine corrections taste the bitterness of these transitory afflictions with them, to whom when they deserved those afflictions, they through the love of this life forbear to show themselves better. Indeed he that forbears to reprehend ill courses in some that follow them, because he will take a more fit time, or because he doubts his reprehension may rather tend to their ruin than their reformation, or because he thinks that others that are weak may by this correction be offended in their godly endeavours or diverted from the true faith: in this case forbearance arises not from occasion of greediness, but from the counsel of charity. But theirs is the fault indeed who live a life quite contrary, wholly abhorring the courses of the wicked, yet spare to tax the others' sins whereof they ought to be most severe reprehenders and correctors, because they fear to offend them, and so be hurt in their possession of those things whose use is lawful both unto good and bad, desiring temporalities in this kind far more greedily than is fit for such as are but pilgrims in this world, and such as expect the hope of a celestial inheritance. For it is not only those of the weaker sort that live in marriage, having (or seeking to have) children, and keeping houses and families, whom [1] the apostle in the Church doth instruct how to live, the wives with their husbands and the husbands with their wives; children with their parents and the parents with their children; the servants with their masters and the masters with their servants: it is not these alone that get together these worldly goods with industry, and lose them with sorrow, and because of which they dare not offend such men as in their filthy and contaminate lives do extremely displease them: but it is also those of the higher sort, such as are no way chained in marriage, such as are content with poor fare and mean attire. Many of these through too much love of their good name and safety, through their fear of the deceits and violence of the wicked, through frailty and weakness, forbear to reprove the wicked when they have offended. And although they do not fear them so far as to be drawn to actual imitation of these their vicious demeanours; yet this which they will not act with them, they will not reprehend in them (though herein they might reform some of them by this reprehension): by reason that (in case they did not reform them) their own fame and their safety might come in danger of destruction. Now herein they do at no hand consider how they are bound to see that their fame and safety be necessarily employed in the instruction of others, but they are solely influenced by their own infirmity, which loves to be stroked with a smooth tongue, and delighteth in popularity; fearing the censure of the vulgar, and the torture and destruction of body: that is, they forbear this duty, not through any duty of charity, but merely through the power of avarice and greedy affection. Wherefore I hold this a great cause, why the good livers do partake with the bad in their afflictions, when it is God's pleasure to correct the corruption of manners with the punishment of temporal calamities. For they both endure one scourge, not because they are both guilty of one disordered life, but because they both do too much desire this transitory life; not in like measure, but yet both together: which the good man should contemn, that the other by him being corrected and amended might attain the life eternal: who if they would not join with them in this endeavour of attaining beatitude, they should be borne

[1] Eph. v. 22–vi. 9; Col. iii. 18–25.

withal and loved as our enemies are to be loved in Christianity: we being uncertain whilst they live here, whether ever their heart shall be turned unto better or no; which to do, the good men have (not the like, but) far greater reason, because unto them the prophet saith: 'He is taken away for his iniquity, but his blood will I require at the watchman's hand,' [1] for unto this end were watchmen, that is, rulers over the people, placed in the churches, that they should not spare to reprehend enormities. Nor yet is any other man altogether free from this guilt, whatsoever he be, ruler or not ruler, who in that daily commerce and conversation, wherein human necessity confines him, observeth anything blameworthy and to be reprehended, and refraineth from so doing, seeking to avoid the others' displeasure, being drawn hereunto by these vanities which he does not use as he should, but desireth much more than he should. Again, there is another reason why the righteous should endure these temporal inflictions, and which was cause of holy Job's sufferance, namely that hereby the soul may be proved and fully known whether it hath so much godly virtue as to love God freely, and for Himself alone. These reasons being well considered, tell me whether anything happens unto the good, that tendeth not to their good: unless we shall hold that the apostle talked idly when he said: 'We know all things work together for the best unto them that love God.' [2]

CHAPTER IX

That the saints in their loss of things temporal lose not anything at all

THEY lost all that they had: what? their faith? their zeal? their goods of the inward man; which enrich the soul before God? These are a Christian's riches, whereof the apostle being possessed said: 'Godliness is a great gain if a man be content with what he hath: for we brought nothing into this world, nor can we carry anything out: therefore when we have food and raiment, let us content ourselves therewith, for they that will be rich fall into temptation and snares, and into many foolish and hurtful desires, which drown men in perdition and destruction, for covetousness of money is the root of all evil, which while some lusting after, have erred from the faith, and cast themselves in many sorrows.' [3] Such therefore as lost their goods in that destruction, if they held them as the aforesaid apostle (poor without, but rich within) taught them: that is, if they used the world so as if they used it not at all, then might they truly say with him that was so sore assaulted and yet never overthrown: 'Naked came I out of my mother's womb, and naked shall I return thither again. The Lord hath

[1] Ezek. xxxiii. 6.   [2] Rom. viii. 28.   [3] 1 Tim. vi. 6–10.

given it, and the Lord hath taken it away, as it hath pleased the
Lord so cometh it to pass: blessed be the name of the Lord.' [1]   He
held his Lord's will (as a good servant) for great possessions, and
by attending that, enriched his spirit: nor grieved he at all at the
loss of that in his lifetime, which death perforce would make him
leave shortly after.   But those far weaker souls who, though they
prefer not these worldly things before Christ, yet stick unto them
with a certain exorbitant affection, and must needs feel such pain
in the losing of them, as their offence deserved in loving of them:
and endure the sorrows in the same measure that they cast themselves unto them: as I said before out of the apostle.   For it was
meet for them to taste a little of the discipline of experience, seeing
they had so long neglected instruction by words: the apostle
having said: 'They that will be rich fall into temptation,' [2] etc.
Herein doth he reprehend the desire after riches only, not the use
of them: teaching likewise elsewhere: 'Charge them that are rich
in this world that they be not high minded, and that they trust not
in their uncertain wealth, but in the living God, who giveth us
plentifully all things to enjoy: that they do good and be rich in
good works, ready to distribute and communicate: laying up in
store for themselves a good foundation against the time to come,
that they may obtain the true life.' [3]   They that did thus with
their riches, by easing small burdens, reaped great gains; taking
more joy in that part which by their free distribution unto others
they had kept more safely, than they felt sorrow for that which by
their care to preserve to themselves they lost so easily.   For it was
likely that would perish here on earth which they had no mind to
remove into a more secure custody.   For they that follow their
Lord's counsel, when He saith unto them: 'Lay not up treasures
for yourselves upon the earth where the moth and rust corrupt, or
where thieves dig through and steal, but lay up treasures for yourselves in heaven, where neither rust nor moth corrupt, nor thieves
dig through and steal: for where your treasure is, there will your
heart be also': [4] these, I say, in the time of tribulation were sure
to find how well they were advised in following that master of all
truth, and that diligent and dreadless keeper of all good treasure:
for seeing there were many that rejoiced because they had hidden
their treasure in a place which the foe by chance overpassed and
found not; how much more certain and secure might their comfort
be, that by their God's instruction had retired thither with their
substance, whither they were sure the foe could not come!   And
therefore one Paulinus, being Bishop of Nola, and having refused
infinite riches for voluntary poverty (and yet was he rich in holiness),
when the barbarians sacked Nola, and held him prisoner, thus
prayed he in his heart (as he told us afterward): 'Lord, let me not
be troubled for gold nor silver, for where all my treasures are, Thou

[1] Job i. 21.   [2] 1 Tim. vi. 9.   [3] 1 Tim. vi. 17–19.   [4] Matt. vi. 19–21.

knowest': even there had he laid up all his, where He had advised
him to lay it who foretold these miseries to fall upon the world.
And so others, in that they obeyed God's instructions for the choice
and preservation of the true treasure indeed, had even their worldly
treasures preserved from the fury of the barbarians: but others paid
for their disobedience, and because their precedent wisdom could
not do it, their subsequent experience taught them how to dispose
of such temporal trash.   Some Christians by their enemies were
put unto torture, to make them discover where their goods lay: but
that good, whereby themselves were good, they could neither lose
nor discover.   But if they had rather have endured torture than
discover their mammon of iniquity, then were they far from good.
But those that suffered so much for gold, were to be instructed
what should be endured for Christ: that they might rather learn
to love Him that enricheth His martyrs with eternal felicity, than
gold and silver for which it is miserable to endure any torment,
whether it be concealed by lying, or discovered by telling the truth.
For no man that ever confessed Christ could lose Him amongst all
the torments: whereas no man could ever save his gold but by
denying it.   Wherefore even those very torments are more profitable, in that they teach a man to love an incorruptible good, than
those goods in that they procure their owners' torture through the
blind love they bear unto them.   But some that had no such goods,
and yet were thought to have them, were tortured also.   Why?
Perhaps they had a desire to them though they had them not, and
were poor against their wills, not of their own election: and then
though their possessions did not justly deserve those afflictions,
yet their affections did.   But if their minds flew a loftier pitch,
beholding both the possession and the affection of riches with an
eye of scorn, I make a doubt whether any such were ever tormented in this kind, or being so innocent, incurred any such
imputation.   But if they did, truly, they in these their tortures,
confessing their sanctified poverty, confessed Christ Himself.   And
therefore though the extorted confession of such holy poverty
could not deserve to be believed of the enemy, yet should he not
be put to this torment without a heavenly reward for his pains.

CHAPTER X

Of the end of this transitory life, whether it be long or short

THE extremity of famine they say destroyed many Christians in
these invasions.   Well, even of this also the faithful, by enduring
it patiently, have made good use.   For such as the famine made
an end of, it delivered from the evils of this life, as well as any other
bodily disease could do: such as it ended not, it taught them a

sparing diet, and ableness to fast.   Yea, but many Christians were destroyed by the foulest variety that might be, falling by so many sorts of death: but this ought not to be a burden grievous to be endured, since it is common to all that ever have been born.   This I know, that no man is dead that should not at length have died. For the life's ending makes the long life and the short all one: neither is there one better and another worse, nor one longer and another shorter, which is not in this end made equal.   And what skills it what kind of death do dispatch our life, when he that dieth cannot be forced to die again?   And seeing that every mortal man, in the daily casualties of this life is threatened continually with innumerable sorts of death, as long as he is uncertain which of them he shall taste; tell me whether it were better to suffer but one in dying once for ever, or still to live in continual fear of all those extremes of death?   I know how unworthy a choice it were to choose rather to live under the awe of so many deaths, than by once dying to be freed from all their fear for ever.   But it is one thing when the weak sensitive flesh doth fear it, and another when the purified reason of the soul overcomes it.   A bad death never follows a good life: for there is nothing that maketh death bad but that estate which followeth death.   Therefore let not their care that needs must die be employed upon the manner of their death, but upon the estate that they are eternally to inherit after death. Wherefore seeing that all Christians know that the death of the religious beggar amongst the dogs, licking his sores, was better than the death of the wicked rich man in all his silks and purples, what power hath the horror of any kind of death to affright their souls that have led a virtuous life?

CHAPTER XI

Of burial of the dead: that it is not prejudicial to the state of a Christian soul to be forbidden it

OH, but in this great slaughter the dead could not be buried: tush, our holy faith dreads not that, holding fast the promise: it is not so frail as to think that the ravenous beasts can deprive the body of any part to be wanting in the resurrection, where not a hair of the head shall be missing.   Nor would the Truth have said: 'Fear not them that kill the body but are not able to kill the soul': [1] if that which the foe could do unto our dead bodies in this world should in any way prejudice our perfection in the world to come: unless any man will be so absurd as to contend that they that can kill the body are not to be feared before death lest they should kill it, but after death, lest having killed it they should not permit it burial.   Is it false

[1] Matt. x. 28.

then which Christ saith: 'Those that kill the body, afterwards can do no more,'[1] and that they have power to do so much hurt unto the dead carcass? God forbid that should be false which is spoken by the Truth itself: therefore it is said they do something in killing, because then they afflict the bodily sense for a while: but afterwards they can afflict it no more, because there is no sense in a dead body. So then suppose that many of the Christians' bodies never came into the earth: what of that? No man hath taken any of them both from earth and heaven, have they? No: and both these doth His glorious presence replenish that knows how to restore every atom of His work in the created. The psalmist indeed complaineth thus: 'The dead bodies of Thy servants have they given to be meat unto the fowls of the air: and the flesh of Thy saints unto the beasts of the earth: their blood have they shed like waters round about Jerusalem, and there was none to bury them.'[2] But this is spoken to intimate their villainy that did it, rather than their misery that suffered it. For though unto the eyes of man these acts seem bloody and tyrannous, yet: 'Precious in the sight of the Lord is the death of His saints.'[3] And therefore all these ceremonies concerning the dead, the care of the burial, the fashions of the sepulchres, and the pomps of the funerals, are rather solaces to the living, than furtherances to the dead. For if a goodly and rich tomb be any help to the wicked man being dead, then is the poor and mean one a hindrance unto the godly man in like case. The family of that rich gorgeous glutton prepared him a sumptuous funeral unto the eyes of men: but one far more sumptuous did the ministering angels prepare for the poor ulcered beggar in the sight of God: they bore him not into any sepulchre of marble, but placed him in the bosom of Abraham. This do they scoff at, against whom we are to defend the city of God. And yet even their own philosophers have contemned the respect of burial: and oftentimes whole armies, fighting and falling for their earthly country, went stoutly to these slaughters, without ever taking thought where to be laid, in what marble tomb, or in what beast's belly. And the poets were allowed to speak their pleasures of this theme, with applause of the vulgar, as one doth thus:

> Caelo tegitur qui non habet urnam.[4]
>
> Who wants a grave, heaven serveth for his tomb.

What little reason then have these miscreants to insult over the Christians that lie unburied, unto whom a new restitution of their whole bodies is promised, to be restored them in a moment,[5] not only out of the earth alone, but even out of all the most secret folds of all the other elements, wherein any body is or can possibly be included.

[1] Luke xii. 4.   [2] Ps. lxxviii. 2, 3.   [3] Ps. cxv. 15.
[4] Lucan, *Phars.* vii. 819.   [5] 1 Cor. xv. 52.

CHAPTER XII

The reasons why we should bury the bodies of the saints

NOTWITHSTANDING, the bodies of the dead are not to be contemned and cast away, especially of the righteous and faithful, which the Holy Ghost used as organs and instruments unto all good works. For if the garment or ring of one's father be so much the more esteemed of his posterity, by how much they held him dearer in their affection; then are not our bodies to be despised, seeing that we wear them more near unto ourselves than any attire whatsoever. For these are no part of external ornament or assistance unto man, but of his express nature. And therefore the funerals of the righteous in the times of old were performed with a zealous care, their burials celebrated, and their monuments provided, and they themselves in their lifetime would lay charges upon their children concerning the burying or translating of their bodies. Tobias [1] in burying of the dead was acceptable unto God, as the angel testi-fieth. And the Lord Himself being about to arise again on the third day, commended the good work of that religious woman,[2] who poured the precious ointment upon His head and body, and did it to bury Him. And the gospel hath crowned them with eternal praise that took down His body from the cross, and gave it honest and honourable burial. But yet these authorities prove not any sense to be in the dead carcasses themselves, but signify that the providence of God extendeth even unto the very bodies of the dead (for He is pleased with such good deeds) and do build up the belief of the resurrection. Whereby also we may learn this pro-fitable lesson, how great the reward of alms-deeds done unto the living may be, since this duty and favour shown but unto the dead is not forgotten of God. There are other prophetical places of the holy patriarchs concerning the entombing or the translation of their own bodies. But this is no place to handle them in, and of this we have already spoken sufficiently: but if the necessaries of man's life, as meat and clothing, though they be wanting in great extremity, yet cannot subvert the good man's patience, nor draw him from goodness: how much less power shall those things have which are omitted in the burying of the dead, to afflict the souls that are already at quiet in the secret receptacles of the righteous? And therefore, when, as in that great overthrow of Rome, and of other cities, the bodies of the Christians wanted these rights, it was neither fault in the living, that could not perform them, nor hurt to the dead, that could not feel them.

[1] Tobit, ii. 7; xii. 12.   [2] Matt. xxvi. 6–13.

CHAPTER XIII

Of the captivity of the saints, and that therein they never lacked spiritual comfort

AYE, but many Christians (say they) were led into captivity: this indeed had been a lamentable case, if they had been led unto some place where they could not possibly have found their God. But for comforts in captivity, the scriptures have store: the three children were in bondage: so was Daniel, so were others of the prophets: but they never lacked God, their comforter. No more did He here abandon His faithful being under the command of barbarous men, who forsook not His prophet being even in the belly of a beast. This now they with whom we are to deal had rather scorn than believe, yet of that fable in their own books they are fully persuaded, namely that that same excellent harper Arion of Methymna, being cast overboard, was taken up on a dolphin's back, and so borne safe to land. Is our history of Jonas more incredible than this? yes, because it is more admirable; and it is more admirable, because more powerful.

CHAPTER XIV

Of Marcus Regulus, who was a famous example to animate all men to the enduring of voluntary captivity for their religion: which, notwithstanding, was unprofitable unto him by reason of his paganism

YET for all this our enemies have one worthy example proposed by one of their most famous men, for the willing toleration of bondage in the cause of religion. Marcus Atilius Regulus, general of the Roman forces, was prisoner at Carthage: now the Carthaginians being more desirous to exchange their prisoners than to keep them, sent Regulus with their ambassadors to Rome to treat upon this exchange, having first sworn him, that in case he effected not what they desired he should return as captive unto Carthage; so he went unto Rome, and having a day of audience granted him, he persuaded the direct contrary unto his embassage: because he held it was not profitable for the Romans to exchange their prisoners. Nor after this persuasive speech did the Romans compel him to return unto his enemies, but willingly did he go back again for saving of his oath. But his cruel foes put him to death with horrible and exquisite torments: for shutting him in a narrow barrel, stuck all full of sharp nails, and so forcing him to stand upright, being not able to lean to any side without extreme pains, they killed him even with over-watching him. This virtue in him

is worthy of everlasting praise, being made greater by so great
infelicity. Now his oath of return was taken by those gods, for
the neglect of whose forbidden worship those infidels hold these
plagues laid upon mankind. But if these gods (being worshipped
only for the attainment of temporal prosperity) either desired or
permitted these pains to be laid upon one that kept his oath so
truly, what greater plague could they in their most deserved wrath
have inflicted upon a most perjured villain than they laid upon this
religious worthy? But why do not I confirm mine argument with a
double proof? If he worshipped his gods so sincerely, that for
keeping the oath which he had taken by their deities, he would
leave his natural country to return not unto what place he liked,
but unto his greatest enemies; if he held that religiousness of his
in any way beneficial unto his temporal estate (which he ended in
such horrible pains) he was far deceived. For his example hath
taught all the world that those gods of his never further their worshippers in any prosperity of this life; since he that was so devout
and dutiful a servant of theirs, for all that they could do, was conquered and led away captive. If on the other hand the worship of
these gods return men's happiness in the life to come, why then do
they calumniate the profession of the Christians, saying that that
misery fell upon the city, because it gave over the worship of the
old gods, whereas were it never so vowed unto their worship, yet
might it taste of as much temporal misfortune as ever did Regulus:
unless any man will stand in such brainless blindness against the
pure truth, as to say that a whole city duly worshipping these gods
cannot be miserable, when one single man may, as though the gods'
power were of more ability and promptness to preserve generals,
than particulars; what? doth not every multitude consist of
singularities? If they say that Regulus even in all that bondage
and torment might nevertheless be happy in the virtue of his constant mind, then let us rather follow the quest of that virtue by
which a whole city may be made truly happy, for a city's happiness
and a particular man's do not arise from any several heads: the city
being nothing but a multitude of men united in one conformity of
religion and estate: wherefore as yet I call not Regulus' virtue
into any question. It is now sufficient that his very example is of
power to enforce them to confess that the worship exhibited unto
the gods, aims not in any way at bodily prosperity, nor at things
externally incident unto man; because Regulus chose rather to
forgo all these, than to offend his gods before whom he had passed
his oath. But what shall we say to these men, that dare glory
that they had had one citizen of that quality whereof they fear
to have a city? If they have no such fear, let them then acknowledge, that what befell Regulus, the same may befall a whole
city, though its devotion may parallel his in this worship of
its gods; and therefore let them cease to slander the times of

Christianity. But seeing that our question arose about the captive Christians, let such as hereby take especial occasion to deride and scorn that saving religion, mark but this, and be silent: that if it were no disgrace unto their gods, that one of their most zealous worshippers, by keeping his oath made unto them, should be nevertheless deprived of his country, and have no place left him to retire to, but must perforce be returned to his enemies, amongst whom he had already endured a hard and wretched captivity, and was now lastly to taste of a tedious death, in most execrable, strange, and cruel torments: then, far less cause is there to accuse the name of Christ for the captivity of His saints, for that they, expecting the heavenly habitation in true faith, knew full well, that they were but pilgrims in their native soils and habitations here upon earth, and subject to all the miseries of mortality.

CHAPTER XV

Whether the rapes that the holy virgins suffered against their wills in their captivities could pollute the virtues of their mind

OH, but they think they give the Christians a foul blow, when they aggravate the disgrace of their captivity, by urging the rapes which were wrought not only upon married and marriageable persons, but even upon some votaresses also: here are we not to speak of faith, or godliness, or of the virtue of chastity, but our discourse must run a narrow course, betwixt shame and reason. Nor care we so much to give an answer unto strangers in this, as to minister comfort unto our fellow Christians. Be this therefore granted as our first position, that that power by which man liveth well, resting enthroned, and established in the mind, commands every member of the body, and the body is sanctified by the sanctification of the will: which sanctimony of the will, if it remain firm and inviolate, what way soever the body be disposed of or abused (if the party enduring this abuse cannot avoid it without an express offence), this sufferance layeth no crime upon the soul. But because every body is subject to suffer the effects both of the fury and the lusts of him that subdueth it, that which it suffereth in this latter kind, though it be not a destroyer of one's chastity, yet is it a procurer of one's shame: because otherwise it might be thought that that was suffered with the consent of the mind, which it may be could not be suffered without some delight of the flesh: and therefore as for those, who to avoid this did voluntarily destroy themselves, what human heart can choose but pity them? yet as touching such as would not do so, fearing by avoiding others' villainy to incur their own damnation, he that imputes this as a fault unto them, is not free from the fault of folly.

CHAPTER XVI

Of such as chose a voluntary death to avoid the fear of pain and dishonour

FOR if it be not lawful for a private man to kill any man, however guilty, unless the law have granted a special allowance for it, then surely whosoever kills himself is guilty of homicide: and so much the more guilty doth that killing of himself make him, by how much the more guiltless he was in that cause for which he killed himself. For if Judas' act was worthily detestable, and yet the Truth saith, that by hanging himself, he did rather augment than expiate the guilt of his wicked treachery because his despair of God's mercy in his damnable repentance left no place in his soul for saving repentance; how much more ought he to forbear from being cause of his own death, that hath no guilt in him worthy of such a punishment as death: for Judas in hanging himself hanged but a wicked man, and died guilty, not only of Christ's death, but of his own also: adding the wickedness of being his own death to that other wickedness of his, for which he died.

CHAPTER XVII

Of the violent lust of the soldiers executed upon the bodies of the captives against their consents

BUT why should he that hath done no man evil, do himself evil, and by destroying himself, destroy an innocent man, for fear to suffer injury by the guilt of another, and procure a sin unto himself, by avoiding the sin of another? Oh, but his fear is, to be defiled by another's lust! Tush, another's lust cannot pollute thee; if it do, it is not another's but thine own. But chastity being a virtue of the mind, and accompanied with fortitude, by which it learns rather to endure all evils, than consent to any; and no man of this fortitude and chastity being able to dispose of his body as he will, but only of the consent and dissent of his mind; what man of wit will think he loseth his chastity, though his captived body be forcedly prostitute unto another's bestiality? If chastity were lost thus easily, it were no virtue of the mind; nor one of those goods, whereby a man lives in goodness; but were to be reckoned amongst the goods of the body, with strength, beauty, health, and such like: which if a man do decrease in, yet it doth not follow that he decreaseth in his uprightness of life: but if chastity be of another kind, why should we endanger our bodies to no end, who fear to lose it? for if it be a good, belonging to the mind, it is not lost though the body be violated. Moreover it is the virtue of holy continency, that when it withstands the pollution of carnal concupiscence, thereby it sanctifies even the body also: and therefore when the intention stands firm, and gives no way to vicious effects, the chastity of the body is not lost, because the will remains still in the holy use, and in the power too, as far as it can.   For the body is not holy in that it is whole, or untouched in every member, for it may be hurt and wounded by many other casualties: and the physician oftentimes for the preservation of the health doth that unto the body which the eye abhors to behold.   A midwife trying a certain maid's integrity of the virginal part (whether for malice, or by chance, it is uncertain), spoiled it.   Now I think none so foolish as to think that this virgin lost any part of her bodily sanctity, though that part endured this breach of integrity.   And therefore the intent of the mind standing firm (which firmness it is that sanctifies the body), the violence of another's lust cannot deprive so much as the body of this sanctity, because the perseverance of the mind in continency ever preserveth it.   But shall we say that any woman whose corrupt mind hath broken her promise unto God, and yielded herself willingly to the lust of her deceiver (though but in purpose), is as yet holy in her body, when she hath lost that holiness of mind which sanctified her body?   God forbid.   And here let us learn, that the sanctity of body is no more lost, if the sanctity of mind remain (though the body be ravished), than it is kept, if the mind's holiness be polluted, though the body itself be untouched.   Wherefore if there be no reason, that a woman that hath already suffered another's villainy against her own will should destroy herself by voluntary death, how much less ought this course to be followed before there be any cause? and why should murder be committed, when the guilt which is feared (being feared from another) is as yet in doubt of event?   Dare they (against whom we defend the sanctity not only of the Christian women's minds, but even of their bodies in this last captivity) contradict this clear reason, wherein we affirm, that whilst the chaste resolution is unchanged by any evil consent, the guilt is wholly the ravisher's, and no part of it imputable unto the ravished?

CHAPTER XVIII

Of Lucretia, that stabbed herself because Tarquin's son had ravished her

THEY extol Lucretia, that noble and ancient matron of Rome, with all the lauds of chastity.   This woman, having her body forcibly abused by Sextus Tarquinius, son to Tarquin the Proud, revealed this villainy of the dissolute youth unto her husband Collatinus, and to Brutus her kinsman (both noble and valorous men),

binding them by oath to revenge this wicked outrage.   And then,
loathing the foulness of the fact that had been committed upon her,
she slew herself.   What? shall we say she was an adulteress, or
was she chaste? who will stand long in deciding this question?
One, declaiming singularly well and truly hereof, saith thus: 'Oh,
wonder! there were two, and yet but one committed the adultery,'
worthily and rarely spoken: intimating in this commixion, the
spotted lust of the one, and the chaste will of the other; and reaching his conclusion, not from their bodily conjunction, but from the
diversity of their minds.   'There were two,' saith he, 'yet but one
committed the adultery.'   But what was that then which she
punished so cruelly, having not committed any fault?   He was
but chased out of his country, but she was slain: if it were no un-
chasteness in her to suffer the rape unwillingly, it was no justice
in her being chaste to make away herself willingly.   I appeal to
you, you laws, and judges of Rome.   After any offence be committed, you will not have the offender put to death without his
sentence of condemnation.   Suppose then this case brought before
you, and that your judgment was, that the slain woman was not
only uncondemned, but chaste, unguilty, and innocent; would you
not punish the doer of this deed with full severity?   This deed did
Lucretia, that so famous Lucretia: this Lucretia being innocent,
chaste, and forcibly wronged, even by Lucretia's self was murdered:
now give your sentence.   But if you cannot, because the offender is
absent, why then do you so extol the murder of so chaste and
guiltless a woman? you cannot defend her before the infernal
judges, in any case, if they be such as your poets in their verses
decipher them: for according to their judgment, she is to be placed
amongst those:

> . . . qui sibi letum,
> Insontes peperere manu, lucemque perosi
> Projecere animas.[1]

> That (guiltless) spoiled themselves through black despite;
> And threw their souls to hell, through hate of light.

Whence if she now would gladly return,

> Fata obstant, tristique palus innabilis unda
> Alligat.[2]

> Fate and deep fens forbid their passage thence,
> And Styx, etc.

But how if she be not amongst them, as not dying guiltless, but
as being privy to her own sin? what if it were so, which none could
know but herself, that though Tarquinius' son offered her force,
yet see herself gave a lustful consent, and after did so grieve at

---

[1] Virg. Aen. vi. 434–6.   [2] Aen. vi. 438–9

that, that she held it worthy to be punished with death? (though
she ought not to have done so, howsoever, if she thought her repentance could be any way accepted of a sort of false gods). If it
be so, and that it be false that there were two and but one did the
sin, but rather that both were guilty of it, the one by a violent
enforcement, the other by a secret consent, then she died not innocent: and therefore her learned defenders may well say, that she
is not in hell among those that destroyed themselves being guiltless.
But this case is in such a strait that if the murder be extenuated, the
adultery is confirmed; and if this be cleared the other is aggravated:
nor is there any way out of this argument: If she be an adulteress,
why is she commended? If she be chaste, why did she kill herself?
But in this example of this noble woman, this is sufficient for us
to confute those that being themselves far from all thought of
sanctity insult over the Christian women that were forced in this
last captivity: that in Lucretia's praise, it is said that 'There were
two,' and 'but one committed adultery.' For they held Lucretia
for one that could not stain herself with any lascivious consent.
Well then, in killing herself for suffering uncleanness, being herself
unpolluted, she showed no love unto chastity, but only discovered
the infirmity of her own shame: she shamed at the filthiness that
was committed upon her, though it were without her consent: and
being a Roman, and covetous of glory, she feared, that if she lived
still, that which she had endured by violence should be thought
to have been suffered with willingness. And therefore she thought
good to show this punishment to the eyes of men, as a testimony
of her mind unto whom she could not show her mind indeed:
blushing to be held a partaker in the fact, which being by another
committed so filthily, she had endured so unwillingly. Now this
course the Christian women did not take; they live still, howsoever
violated: neither for all this did they avenge the guilt of others,
lest they should make an addition of their own guilt unto the
others', if they should go and murder themselves barbarously,
because their enemies had forced them so bestially. For howsoever, they have the glory of their chastity still within them, it
being the testimony of their conscience; this they have before the
eyes of their God, and this is all they care for (having no more
to look to but to do well) that they decline not from the authority
of the law divine, in any sinister endeavour to avoid the offence
of mortal man's suspicion.

CHAPTER XIX

*That there is no authority which allows Christians to be their
own deaths in what cause soever*

FOR it is not for nothing that we never find it commanded in the
holy canonical scriptures, or but allowed, that either for attaining
of immortality, or avoiding of calamity, we should be our own
destructions: we are forbidden it in the law: 'Thou shalt not kill': [1]
especially because it adds not 'thy neighbour'; as it doth in the
prohibition of false witness, 'Thou shalt not bear false witness
against thy neighbour': yet let no man think that he is free of this
latter crime, if he bear false witness against himself: because he
that loves his neighbour, begins his love from himself: seeing it is
written: 'Thou shalt love thy neighbour as thyself.' [2] Now, if he
be no less guiltless of false witness that testifieth falsely against
himself, than he that doth so against his neighbour (since in that
commandment where false witness is forbidden, it is forbidden
to be practised against one's neighbour, whence misunderstanding
conceits may suppose that it is not forbidden to bear false witness
against oneself), how much plainer is it to be understood, that a
man may not kill himself, seeing that unto the commandment
'Thou shalt not kill' nothing being added excludes all exception
both of others, and of him to whom the command is given.   And
therefore some would extend the extent of this precept even unto
beasts and cattle, and would have it unlawful to kill any of them.
But why not unto herbs also, and all things that grow and are
nourished by the earth? for though these kinds cannot be said
to have sense or feeling, yet they are said to be living: and therefore
they may die; and consequently by violent usage be killed.   Wherefore the apostle speaking of these kind of seeds saith thus: 'Fool,
that which thou sowest is not quickened except first it die.' [3]
And the psalmist saith: 'He destroyed their vines with hail,' [4] but
what?   Shall we therefore think it sin to cut up a twig, because the
commandment says: 'Thou shalt not kill,' and so involve ourselves
in the foul error of the Manichees?   Wherefore setting aside these
dotages, when we read this precept: 'Thou shalt not kill'; if we
hold it not to be meant of fruits or trees, because they are not
sensitive; nor of unreasonable creatures, either going, flying, swim-
ming, or creeping, because they have no society with us in reason,
which God the Creator hath not made common both to them and
us; and therefore by His just ordinance, their deaths and lives are
both most serviceable and useful unto us; then it follows necessarily, that 'Thou shalt not kill,' is meant only of men: 'Thou shalt
not kill,' namely, 'neither thyself, nor another.'   For he that kills
himself, kills no other but a man.

[1] Exod. xx. 13, 16.   [2] Matt. xxii. 39.   [3] 1 Cor. xv. 36.   [4] Ps. lxxviii. 47.

CHAPTER XX

Of some sorts of killing men which, notwithstanding, are no murder

INDEED the authority of the law divine hath set down some exceptions wherein it is lawful to kill a man, as for example those whom God commands to be slain, either by His express law, or by some particular command unto any person on any temporal occasion (and he committeth not homicide that owes his service unto him that commandeth him, being but as the sword is a help to him that useth it). And therefore those men do not break the commandment which forbiddeth killing, who do make war by the authority of God's command, or being in some place of public magistracy, do put to death malefactors according to their laws, that is, according to the rule of justice and reason. Abraham [1] was not only freed from being blamed as a murderer, but he was also commended as a godly man in that he would have killed his son Isaac, not in wickedness, but in obedience. And it is a doubtful question, whether it ought to be held as a command from God that Jephthah [2] killed his daughter that met him on his return, seeing that he had vowed to sacrifice the first living thing that came out of his house to meet him, when he returned conqueror from the wars. Nor could Samson [3] be excused pulling down the house upon himself and his enemies, but that the spirit within him, which wrought miracles by him, did prompt him unto this act. Those therefore being excepted, which either the justice of the law, or the fountain of all justice, God's particular command, would have killed; he that killeth either himself, or any other, incurreth the guilt of a homicide.

CHAPTER XXI

That voluntary death can never be any sign of magnanimity or greatness of spirit

WHOSOEVER have committed this homicide upon themselves, may perhaps be commended of some for their greatness of spirit, but never for their soundness of judgment. But indeed if you look a little deeper into the matter, it cannot be rightly termed magnanimity, when a man being unable to endure either casual miseries or other oppressions, to avoid them, destroyeth himself. For that mind discovereth itself to be of the greatest infirmity, that can neither endure hard bondage in its body, nor the fond opinion of the vulgar: and worthily is that spirit entitled great, that can rather

[1] Gen. xxii. 1–13.   [2] Judges xi. 30–9.   [3] Judges xvi. 25–30.

endure calamities than avoid them: and in respect of its own purity and enlightened conscience, can set at naught the trivial censures of mortal men, which are most commonly enclouded in a mist of ignorance and error. If we shall think it a part of magnanimity to put a man's self to death, then is Cleombrotus most worthy of this magnanimous title, who having read Plato's book of the immortality of the soul, cast himself headlong from the top of a wall, and so leaving this life, went unto another which he believed was better. For neither calamity, nor guiltiness, either true or false, urged him to avoid it by destroying himself, but his great spirit alone was sufficient to make him catch at his death, and break all the pleasing fetters of this life. Which deed notwithstanding, that it was rather great than good, Plato himself, whom he read, might have assured him; who (be sure) would have done it, or taught it himself, if he had not discerned by the same instinct whereby he discerned the soul's eternity, that this was in no case to be practised, but rather utterly prohibited.

CHAPTER XXII

Of Cato, who killed himself, being not able to endure Caesar's victory

BUT many have killed themselves for fear to fall into the hands of their foes. We dispute not here *de facto*, whether it hath been done or no, but *de jure*, whether it were to be done or no. For sound reason is before example to be sure, to which also all examples do consent, being such as by their excellence in goodness are worthily imitable. Neither patriarch, prophet, nor apostle ever did this: yet our Lord Jesus Christ, when He admonished His disciples [1] in persecution to flee from city to city, might have willed them in such cases to make a quick dispatch of themselves, and so to avoid their persecutors, had He held it fit. But if He never gave any such admonition, or command, that any to whom He promised a mansion of eternity at their deaths, should pass unto their deaths on this fashion (let the heathen that know not God produce all they can); it is plainly unlawful for any one that serveth the only true God to follow this course. But, indeed, besides Lucretia (of whom, I think, we have sufficiently argued before),[2] it is hard for them to find one other example, worth prescribing as a fit authority for others to follow, besides that Cato only that killed himself at Utica: not that he alone was his own deathsman, but because he was accounted as a learned and honest man, which may beget a belief that to do as he did were to do well. What should I say of his act more than his friends (and some of them learned men) have said who showed far more judgment in

[1] Matt. x. 23.   [2] I. xix.

dissuading the deed, and censuring it as the effect of a spirit rather
dejected than magnanimous?   And of this did Cato himself leave
a testimony in his own famous son.   For if it were base to live
under Caesar's victory, why did he advise his son to this, willing
him to entertain a full hope of Caesar's clemency?   Yea, why did
he not urge him to go willingly to his end with him?   If it were
laudable in Torquatus to kill his son that had fought and foiled his
enemy (though herein he had broken the dictator's command),
why did conquered Cato spare his overthrown son, that spared not
himself?   Was it more vile to be a conqueror against law, than to
endure a conqueror against honour?   What shall we say then, but
that even in the same measure that he loved his son, whom he both
hoped and wished that Caesar would spare, in the same did he
envy Caesar's glory, which Caesar should have got in sparing of
him also, or else (to mollify this matter somewhat) he was ashamed
to receive such courtesy at Caesar's hands.

CHAPTER XXIII

*That the Christians excel Regulus in that virtue, wherein he
excelled most*

BUT those whom we oppose will not have their Cato excelled by
our Job, that holy man, who chose rather to endure such horrible
torments in his flesh, than by adventuring upon death to avoid all
those vexations: and other saints of high credit and undoubted
faith in our scriptures, all of whom made choice rather to endure
the tyranny of their enemies, than be their own butchers.   But now
we will prove out of their own records that Regulus was Cato's
better in this glory.   For Cato never overcame Caesar, unto whom
he scorned to be subject, and chose to murder himself rather than
be servant unto him.   But Regulus overcame the Africans, and in
his generalship, returned with diverse noble victories unto the
Romans, never with any notable loss of his citizens, but always of
his foes: and yet being afterwards conquered by them, he resolved
rather to endure slavery under them, than by death to free himself
from them.   And therein he both preserved his patience under the
Carthaginians, and his constancy unto the Romans, neither depriving the enemy of his conquered body, nor his countrymen of
his unconquered mind: neither was it the love of this life that kept
him from death.   This he gave good proof of, when, without
dread, he returned back unto his foes, to whom he had given worse
cause of offence in the senate house with his tongue than ever he
had done before in the battle with his force: and therefore, this so
great a conqueror and contemner of this life, who had rather that
his foes should take it from him by any torments, than that he

should give death to himself, howsoever, must needs hold, that it was a foul guilt for a man to be his own murderer.   Rome, amongst all her worthies and virtuous spirits, cannot show one better than he was; for he, for all his great victories, continued most poor: nor could mishap crush him: for with a fixed, resolved, and an undaunted courage, returned he unto his deadliest enemies.   Now, if those magnanimous and heroical defenders of their earthly fatherland, and those true and sound servants of their indeed false gods (who had power to cut down their conquered foes by law of arms), seeing themselves afterwards to be conquered of their foes, nevertheless would not be their own butchers, but although they feared not death at all, yet would rather endure to be slaves to their foes' superiority, than to be their own executioners: how much more then should the Christians, that adore the true God, and aim wholly at the eternal dwellings, restrain themselves from this foul wickedness, whensoever it pleaseth God to expose them for a time to taste of temporal extremities, either for their trial, or for correction sake, seeing that He never forsaketh them in their humiliation, for whom He, being most high, humbled Himself so low: especially seeing that they are persons whom no laws of arms or military power can allow to destroy the conquered enemies!

CHAPTER XXIV

That sin is not to be avoided by sin

WHAT a pernicious error then is here crept into the world, that a man should kill himself, because either his enemy has injured him, or means to injure him, whereas he may not kill his enemy, whether he have offended him, or be about to offend him!   This is rather to be feared indeed, that the body, being subject unto the enemy's lust, with touch of some enticing delight do not allure the will to consent to this impurity: and therefore (say they) it is not because of another's guilt, but for fear of one's own, that such men ought to kill themselves before sin be committed upon them.   Nay, the mind that is more truly subject unto God and His wisdom than unto carnal concupiscence will never be brought to yield unto the lust of its own flesh be it never so provoked by the lust of another's: but if it be a damnable crime, and a detestable wickedness to kill oneself at all (as the Truth in plain terms saith it is), what man will be so fond as to say: Let us sin now, lest we sin hereafter; let us commit murder now, lest we fall into adultery hereafter? If wickedness be so predominant in such a one, as he or she will not choose rather to suffer in innocence than to escape by guilt, is it not better to adventure on the uncertainty of the future adultery, than the certainty of the present murder? is it not better to commit such a sin as repentance may purge, than such a one as leaves no place at all for repentance? This I speak for such as for avoiding of guilt (not in others but in themselves) and fearing to consent to the lust in themselves which another's lust inciteth, do imagine that they ought rather to endure the violence of death: but far be it from a Christian soul that trusteth in his God, that hopeth in Him and resteth on Him; far be it (I say) from such, to yield unto the delights of the flesh in any consent unto uncleanness. But if that concupiscential disobedience, which dwelleth as yet in our dying flesh, do stir itself by its own licence against the law of our will; how can it be but faultless in the body of him or her that never consenteth, when it stirs without guilt in the body that sleepeth!

CHAPTER XXV

Of some unlawful acts done by the saints, and by what occasion they were done

BUT there were some holy women (say they) in these times of persecution, who, flying from the spoilers of their chastities, threw themselves headlong into a swift river which drowned them, and so they died, and yet their martyrdoms are continually honoured with religious memorials in the Catholic Church. Well, of these I dare not judge rashly in anything. Whether the Church have any sufficient testimonies that the divine will advised it to honour these persons' memories, I cannot tell; it may be that it hath. For what if they did not this through mortal fear, but through heavenly instinct? not in error, but in obedience, as we must not believe but that Samson did? And if God command, and this command be clearly and doubtlessly discerned to be His, who dare call this obedience into question? Who dare caluminate the duty of holy love? But every one that shall resolve to sacrifice his son unto God shall not be cleared of guilt in such a resolution, because Abraham was praised for it. For the soldier, that in his order and obeisance to his governor (under whom he fighteth lawfully) killeth a man, the city never makes him guilty of homicide: nay, it makes him guilty of falsehood and contempt if he do not labour in all that he can to do it. But if he had killed the man of his own voluntary pleasure, then had he been guilty of shedding human blood, and so he is punished for the doing of that unbidden, for the not doing of which being bid he should also have been punished. If this be thus at the general's command, then why not at the Creator's? He, therefore, that heareth it said, 'Thou shalt not kill thyself,' must kill himself if He command him, whom we may in no way gainsay: only he is to mark whether this divine command be not involved in any uncertainty. By the ear we do make conjecture of the conscience, but our judgment cannot penetrate into the secrets of hearts: 'No man knows the things of a man, but the spirit of a man which is in him.' [1] This we say, this we affirm, this we universally approve, that no man ought to procure his own death for fear of temporal miseries; because in doing this he falleth into eternal: neither may he do it to avoid the sins of others, for in this he maketh himself guilty of a deadly guilt, whom others' wickedness could not make guilty: nor for his own sins past, for which he had more need to wish for life, that he might repent himself of them: nor for any desire of a better life to be hoped for after death; because such as are guilty of the loss of their own life, never enjoy any better life after their death.

CHAPTER XXVI

Whether we ought to flee from sin with voluntary death

THERE is one reason of this proposition as yet to handle, which seems to prove it commodious for a man to suffer a voluntary death: namely lest either alluring pleasures or tormenting pains should enforce him to sin afterwards. Which reason if we will give scope unto, it will run out so far, that one would think that men should be exhorted to this voluntary butchery, even then, when by the fount of regeneration [2] they are purified from all their sins. For then is the time to beware of all sins to come, when all that is past is pardoned. And if voluntary death do this, why is it not fittest then? Why doth he that is newly baptized forbear his own throat? Why doth he thrust his freed head again into all these imminent dangers of this life, seeing he may so easily avoid them all by his death; and it is written: 'He that loveth danger shall fall therein'? [3] Why then doth he love those innumerable dangers? or if he do not love them, why undertakes he them? Is any man so fondly perverse and so great a contemner of truth, that if he think one should kill himself to eschew the violence of one oppressor lest it draw him into sin, will nevertheless avouch that one should live still, and endure this whole world at all times, full of all temptations, both such as may be expected from one oppressor, and thousands besides without which no man doth nor can live? What is the reason then, why we do spend so much time in our exhortations, endeavouring to animate those whom we have baptized, either unto virginity, or chaste widowhood, or honest and honourable marriage; seeing we have both far shorter and far better ways to abandon all contagion and danger of sin; namely in persuading every one immediately after that remission of his sins which he hath

[1] 1 Cor. ii. 11.   [2] Titus iii. 5.   [3] Ecclus. iii. 26.

newly obtained in baptism, to betake him at once to a speedy death, and so send him forthwith away unto God, both fresh and fair? If any man think that this is fit to be persuaded, I say not he dotes, but I say he is plain mad. With what face can he say unto a man: Kill thyself, lest unto thy small sins thou add a greater by living in slavery unto a barbarous unchaste master? How can he (but with guilty shame) say unto a man: Kill thyself now that thy sins are forgiven thee, lest thou fall into the like again or worse, by living in this world, so fraught with manifold temptation, so alluring with unclean delights, so furious with bloody sacrileges, so hateful with errors and terrors? It is a shame and a sin to say the one, and therefore is it so likewise to do the other. For if there were any reason of just force to authorize this fact, it must needs be that which is fore-alleged. But it is not that; therefore there is none. Loathe not your lives then, you faithful of Christ, though the foe hath made havoc of your chastities. You have a great and true consolation, if your conscience bear you faithful witness that you never consented unto their sins who were suffered to commit such outrages upon you.

CHAPTER XXVII

How it was a judgment of God that the enemy was permitted to exercise his lust upon the Christian bodies

IF you ask me now why these outrages were thus permitted, I answer the providence of the Creator and Governor of the world is high, and 'His judgments are unsearchable and His ways past finding out': [1] but ask your own hearts sincerely whether you have boasted about this good of continency and chastity, or no; whether you have not been enticed by human commendations for it, and so thereby have envied it in others. I do not accuse you of that whereof I am ignorant, nor do I know what answer your hearts will return unto this question. But if they answer affirmatively, and say you have done so, then wonder not at all that you have now lost that, whereby you did but seek and rejoice to please the eyes of mortal men: and that you lost not that which could not be showed unto men. If you consented not unto the others' lust, your souls had the help of God's grace to keep them from loss, and likewise felt the disgrace of human glory, to deter them from the love of it. But your faint hearts are comforted on both sides: on this side being approved, and on that side chastised: justified on this, and reformed on the other. But their hearts that give them answer that they never gloried in the good gift of virginity, vidual chastity, or continence in marriage: but associating with

[1] Rom. xi. 33.

the meanest,[1] did with a reverend fear rejoice in this gift of God;
nor ever repined at the like excellence of sanctity and purity in
others; but neglecting the air of human fame (which always is
wont to accrue according to the rarity of the virtue that deserves it),
did wish rather to have their number multiplied, than by reason of
their fewness to become more eminent: let not those that are
such (if the barbarians' lust have seized upon some of them) allege
that this is (merely) permitted: nor let them think that God neglects
these things because He sometimes permits that which no man
ever commitsu npunished: for some aggravated evil desires are
let loose by a present and secret judgment, and are reserved to
that public and universal last judgment.   And perhaps those who
knew themselves not guilty, and that never had their hearts
puffed up with the good of this chastity (and yet had their bodies
thus abused by the enemy), had, notwithstanding, some infirmity
lurking within them which, if they had escaped this humiliation
by the war's fury, might have increased unto a fastidious pride.
Wherefore as some were taken away by death, 'lest wickedness
should alter their understandings,' [2] so these here were forced
to forgo something, lest excess of prosperity should have depraved
their virtuous modesty.   And therefore, from neither sort, either
of those that were proud, in that their bodies were pure from
all unclean touch of others, or that might have grown proud, if
they had escaped the rape done by their foes, from neither of
these is their chastity taken away, but unto them both is humility
persuaded.   The vainglory which is immanent in the one, and
imminent over the other, was excluded in them both.   Though
this is not to be overpassed with silence, that some that endured
these violences might perhaps think that continency is but a
bodily good, remaining as long as the body remains untouched,
but that it is not solely placed in the strength of the grace-assisted
will, which sanctifies both body and soul: nor that it is a good that
cannot be lost against one's will; which error this affliction brought
them to understand: for when they consider with what conscience
they honour God, and do with an unmoved faith believe this of
Him, that He will not, nay cannot in any way forsake such as thus
and thus do serve Him, and invocate His name, and do not doubt
of the great acceptation which He vouchsafes unto chastity; then
must they need perceive that it follows necessarily, that He would
never suffer this to fall upon His saints, if that by this means they
should be despoiled of that holiness which He so much loves in
them, and infuses into them.

[1] Rom. xii. 16.   [2] Wisd. of Sol. iv. 11.

CHAPTER XXVIII

*What the servants of Christ may answer the infidels, when they up-
braid them with Christ's not delivering them (in their afflictions)
from the force of their enemies' fury*

WHEREFORE all the servants of the great and true God have a comfort that is firm and fixed, not placed upon frail foundations of
momentary and transitory things: and so they pass this temporal
life in such manner, as they never need repent them of enjoying
it: because herein they are prepared for that which is eternal,
using the goods of this world but as in a pilgrimage, being in no way
entrapped in them; and so making use of the evils of this world,
as they make them serve always either to their approbation, or
their reformation.   Those that insult upon this their uprightness,
and (when they see them fallen into some of these temporal inconveniences) say unto them: Where is thy God? [1] let them tell
us where their gods are when they are afflicted with the like
oppressions; their gods, which either they worship, or desire to
worship, only for the avoiding of such inconveniences.   The family
of Christ can answer: My God is everywhere present, in all places,
whole and powerful, no space includes Him; He can be present,
unperceived, and depart away again, unmoved.   And He, when
He afflicts us with these adversities, doth it either for trial of our
perfections or reforming of our imperfections, still reserving an
eternal reward for our patient sufferance of temporal distresses.
But who are you, that I should vouchsafe to speak unto you,
especially of your gods, but most especially of mine own God who
is 'terrible and to be feared above all gods? for all the gods of the
heathen are devils, but the Lord made the heavens.' [2]

CHAPTER XXIX

*That such as complain of the Christian times desire nothing but to live
in filthy pleasures*

IF your Scipio Nasica were now alive, he that was once your
high priest, who (when in the fearful terror of the Carthaginian
wars, the most perfect man of all the city was sought for, to undertake the entertainment of the Phrygian goddess) was chosen by the
whole senate, he whose face perhaps you now durst not look on,
he would shame you from this gross impudence of yours.   For
what cause is there for you to exclaim at the prosperity of the
Christian faith in these times, but only because you would follow
your luxury uncontrolled, and having removed the impediments

[1] Ps. xlii. 3; lxxix. 10; cxv. 2.   [2] Ps. xcvi. 4, 5.

of all troublesome oppositions, swim on in your dishonest and un-hallowed dissolution? Your affections do not stand up for peace, nor for universal plenty and prosperity, to the end that you might use them when you have them, as honest men should do; that is, modestly, soberly, temperately, and religiously: no; but that hence you might keep up your unreasonable expense, in seeking out such infinite variety of pleasures, and so give birth unto those exorbitances in your prosperities, which would heap more mischiefs upon you than ever befell you by your enemies.

But Scipio, your high priest, he whom the whole senate judged the best man amongst you, fearing that this calamity would fall upon you (that I speak of) would not have Carthage, in those days the sole rival of the Roman Empire, utterly subverted, but contradicted Cato, that spoke for the destruction of it, because he feared the foe of all weak spirits, *security*; and held that Carthage would be unto his fellow citizens (as if they were young novices) both a convenient tutor, and a necessary terror. Nor did his judgment delude him: the event itself gave sufficient proof whether he spoke true or no: for afterwards when Carthage was razed down, and the greatest curber and terror of the Roman commonwealth utterly extinguished and brought to nothing; presently such an innumerable swarm of inconveniences arose out of this prosperous estate, that the bonds of concord being all rent asunder and broken, first with barbarous and bloody seditions, and next with continual giving of worse and worse causes by civil wars, such slaughters were effected, so much blood was shed by civil wars, and so much inhumanity was practised in proscribings, riots, and rapines, that those Romans that in the good time of their lives feared no hurt but from their enemies, now in the corrupt time of their lives endured far worse of their own fellows: and that lust after sovereignty, which among all other sins of the world was most appropriate unto the Romans, and most immoderate in them all, at length getting head and happy success in a few of the more powerful, overpressed all the rest, wearing them out, and crushing their necks with the yoke of wild and slavish bondage.

CHAPTER XXX

By what degrees of corruption the Romans' ambition grew to such a height

FOR when did ever this lust of sovereignty cease in proud minds, until it had by continuance of honours attained unto the dignity of regal domination? And if their ambition did not prevail, they then had no means to continue their honours. Now ambition would not prevail but amongst a people wholly corrupted with covetousness and luxury. And the people are always infected with these two contagions, by the means of affluent prosperity, which Nasica did wisely hold fit to be foreseen and prevented, by not condescending to the abolishing of so strong, so powerful, and so rich a city of their enemies; thereby to keep luxury in awful fear, that so it might not become exorbitant, and by that means also covetousness might be repressed. Which two vices once chained up, virtue, the city's supporter, might flourish, and a liberty befitting this virtue might stand strong. And hence it was, out of this most circumspect zeal unto his country, that your said high priest, who was chosen by the senate of those times for the best man, without any difference of voices (a thing worthy of often repetition), when the senate would have built a theatre, dissuaded them from this vain resolution: and in a most grave oration, persuaded them not to suffer the luxury of the Greeks to creep into their manly conditions, nor to consent unto the entry of foreign corruption, to the subversion and extirpation of their native Roman perfection, working so much by his own sole authority, that the whole bench of the judicious senate being moved by his reasons, expressly prohibited the use of those movable seats which the Romans began as then to use in the beholding of plays. How earnest would he have been to have cleansed the city of Rome of the plays themselves, if he durst have opposed their authority whom he held for gods, being ignorant that they were malicious devils: or if he knew it, then it seems he held that they were rather to be pleased than despised. For as yet, that heavenly doctrine was not delivered unto the world, which, purifying the heart by faith, changes the affection with a zealous piety to desire and aim at the blessings of heaven, or those which are above the heavens, and frees men absolutely from the slavery of those proud and ungracious devils.

CHAPTER XXXI

Of the first introduction of stage plays

BUT know (you that know not this) and mark (you that make show as if you knew it not, and murmur at Him that hath set you free from such lords) that your stage plays, those spectacles of uncleanness, those licentious vanities, were not first brought up at Rome by the corruptions of the men, but by the direct commands of your gods. It were far more tolerable for you to give divine honours unto the forenamed Scipio, than unto such kind of deities, for they were not so good as their priest was. And now do but observe, whether your minds being drunk with this continual ingurgitation of error will suffer you to taste a sip of any true consideration. Your gods, for the assuaging of the infection of the pestilence that seized on your bodies, commanded an institution of stage plays to be effected in their honours: but your priest, for avoiding the pestilence of your minds, forbade that any stage should be built for any such action. If you have so much wit as to prefer the mind before the body, then choose which of the two said parties to make your god of: for the bodily pestilence did not yet cease, because the delicate vanity of stage plays entered into the ears of this people (being then wholly given unto wars, and accustomed only to the Circensian plays); but the wily devils foreseeing (by natural reason) that this plague of the bodies should cease, by this means took occasion to thrust one far worse, not into their bodies, but into their manners, in corrupting of which lieth all their joy; and such a plague, as blinded the minds of that wretched people with such impenetrable clouds of darkness, and bespotted them with such foul stains of deformity, that even now (though this may seem incredible to succeeding ages) when this great Rome was destroyed, such as were possessed with this pestilence, flying from that sack, could come even unto Carthage, and there contend who should run maddest after stage playing.

CHAPTER XXXII

Of some vices in the Romans, which their city's ruin did never reform

O YOU senseless men, how are you bewitched, not with error but furor, that when all the nations of the east (as we hear) bewail your city's ruin, and all the most remote regions bemoan your misery with public sorrow, you yourselves run headlong unto the theatres, seeking them, entering them, filling them, and playing far madder parts now than ever you did before? This your plague of mind, this your wreck of honesty, was that which your Scipio so feared when he would not have any theatres built for you: when he saw how quickly your virtues would be abolished by prosperity, when he would not have you utterly quitted from all fear of foreign invasions. He was not of opinion that that commonwealth or city was in a happy estate, where the walls stood firm, and the good manners lay ruined. But the seducements of the damned spirits prevailed more with you, than the providence of circumspect men. And hence comes it, that the mischiefs that yourselves commit, you are so loath should be imputed to yourselves, but the mischiefs that yourselves suffer, you are ever ready to cast upon the Christian profession, for you in your security do not seek the peace of the commonwealth, but freedom for your practices of luxury. You are depraved by prosperity, and you cannot be reformed by adversity. Your Scipio would have had you to fear your foes, and so to suppress your lusts: but you, though you feel your foes, and are crushed down by them, yet will not restrain your inordinate affections. You have lost the benefit of affliction, and though you be made most miserable, yet remain you most irreformable. And yet it is God's mercy that you have your lives still: His very sparing of your lives summons you unto repentance: He it was, that (though you be ungrateful) showed you that favour as to escape your enemies' swords by calling of yourselves His servants, or flying into the churches of His martyrs.

CHAPTER XXXIII

Of the clemency of God in moderating this calamity of Rome

IT is said that Romulus and Remus built a sanctuary, whereunto whoso could escape, should be free from all assault or hurt: their endeavour in this being to increase the number of their citizens. An example making way for a wonderful honour unto Christ. The same thing, that the founders of the city did decree, the same do the destroyers of it: and what if the one did it to increase the multitude of their citizens, when the other did it to preserve the multitude of their foes? Let this then (and whatsoever besides fitly may be so used) be used as an answer of our Lord Jesus Christ's flock, and that pilgrim city of God, unto all their wicked enemies.

CHAPTER XXXIV

Of such of God's elect as live secretly as yet amongst the infidels, and of such as are false Christians

AND let this city of God remember, that even amongst her enemies, there are some concealed, that shall one day be her citizens: nor let her think it a fruitless labour to bear their hate until she hear their confession; as she hath also (as long as she is in this pilgrimage of this world) some that are partakers of the same sacraments with her, that shall not be partakers of the saints' glories with her, who are partly known, and partly unknown. Yea, such there are, that hesitate not amongst God's enemies to murmur against His glory, whose character they bear upon them: going now unto plays with them, and by and by, unto the church with us. But of the reformation of some of these we have little reason to despair, seeing that we have many secret and predestinated friends, even amongst our most known adversaries, and such as yet know not themselves to be ordained for our friendship. For the two cities (of the predestinate and the reprobate) are in this world confused together and commixed, until the general judgment make a separation: of the original progress and due limits of both which cities, what I think fit to speak, by God's help and further-ance, I will now begin, to the glory of the city of God, which being compared with her contrary, will spread her glories to a more full aspect.

CHAPTER XXXV

What subjects are to be handled in the following discourse

BUT we have a little more to say unto those that lay the afflictions of the Roman estate upon the profession of Christianity, which for-biddeth men to sacrifice unto those idols. For we must cast up a sum of all the miseries (or of as many as shall suffice) which that city, or the provinces under her subjection, endured before those sacrifices were forbidden. All which they would have imputed unto our religion, had it been then preached and taught against these sacrifices, when these miseries befell. Secondly, we must show what customs and conditions the true God vouchsafed to teach them for the increasing of their empire, that God, in whose hand are all the kingdoms of the earth: and how their false gods never helped them a jot, but rather did them infinite hurt by deceit and illusion. And lastly, we will disprove those who though they be confuted with most manifest proofs, yet will needs affirm still that their gods are to be worshipped, and that not for the benefits of this life, but for those which are belonging to the life to come. Which question (unless I be deceived) will be far more laborious, and worthier of deeper consideration, in the which we must dispute against the philosophers, not against each one, but even the most excellent and glorious of them all, and such as in many points hold as we hold, both of the immortality of the soul, and of the world's creation by the true God, and of His providence, whereby He swayeth the whole creation. But because even these also are to be confuted, in what they hold opposite unto us, we thought it our duty not to be slack in this work, but refuting all the contra-dictions of the wicked, as God shall give us power and strength to advance the verity of the city of God, the true piety and worship of God, which is the only way to attain true and eternal felicity. This therefore shall be the method of our work: and now from this second exordium we will take each thing in due order.

THE SECOND BOOK OF THE CITY OF GOD

CHAPTER I

Of the method which must of necessity be used in this disputation

IF the weak custom of human sense durst not be so bold as to oppose itself against the reasons of apparent truth, but would yield its languid infirmity unto wholesome instruction, as unto a medicine which were fittest to apply, until by God's good assistance and faith's operation it were thoroughly cured; then those that can both judge well, and instruct sufficiently, should not need many words to confute any erroneous opinion, or to make it fully apparent unto such as their desires would truly inform. But now, because there is so great and inveterate a disease rooted in the minds of the ignorant, that they will (out of their extreme blindness, whereby they see not what is most plain, or out of their obstinate perverseness, whereby they will not brook what they see) defend their irrational and brutish opinions, after that the truth has been taught them as plain as one man can teach another: hence it is that there ariseth a necessity that bindeth us to dilate more fully of what is already most plain, and to give the truth, not unto their eyes to see, but even into their heads, as it were to touch and feel. Yet, notwithstanding, this by the way: What end shall we make of altercation if we hold that the answerers are continually to be answered? For, as for those that either cannot comprehend what is said unto them, or else are so obstinate in their vain opinions, that though they do understand the truth, yet will not give it place in their minds, but reply against it, as it is written of them, 'like spectators of iniquity,' those are eternally frivolous: and if we should bind ourselves to give an answer to every contradiction that their impudence will thrust forth (how falsely they care not, for they do but make a show of opposition unto our assertions), you see what a trouble it would be, how endless, and how fruitless. And therefore (son Marcellinus) I would neither have you, nor any other (to whom this our work may yield any benefit in Jesus Christ), to read this volume with any surmise that I am bound to answer whatsoever you or they shall hear objected against it: lest you become like unto the women of whom the apostle saith, that they were 'always learning, and never able to come unto the knowledge of the truth.' [1]

[1] 2 Tim. iii. 7.

CHAPTER II

A repetition of the contents of the first book

THEREFORE in the former book, wherein I began to speak of the city of God, to which purpose all the whole work (by God's assistance) shall have reference, I did first of all take in hand to give them their answer that are so shameless as to impute the calamities inflicted upon the world (and in particular upon Rome in her last desolation wrought by the Vandals) unto the religion of Christ, which forbids men to offer service or sacrifice unto devils: whereas they are rather bound to ascribe this as a glory to Christ that, for His name's sake alone, the barbarous nations (beyond all practice and custom of wars) allowed many and spacious places of religion for those ungrateful men to escape into; and gave such honour unto the servants of Christ, not only to the true ones, but even to the counterfeit, that what the law of arms made lawful to do unto all men, they held it utterly unlawful to offer unto them. And hence arose these questions: how and wherefore these gracious mercies of God were extended unto such ungodly and ungrateful wretches as well as to His true servants; and why the afflictions of this siege fell upon the godly (in part) as well as on the reprobate. For the better dissolving of which doubts, I stayed somewhat long in a discourse of the daily gifts of God, and the miseries of man, falling out in the whole tract of this transitory life (both of which, by reason that they often light confusedly together, alike, and undistinguished both upon good livers and impious, are very powerful in moving the hearts of many): and mine especial intent herein was to give some comfort unto the sanctified and chaste women, who had their chastities offended by some incontinent acts of the soldiers; and to show them that if those accidents had not wrecked their chaste resolutions, they ought not to be ashamed of life, having no guilt in them whereof to be ashamed. And then I took occasion to speak somewhat against those that in such villainous and impudent manner do insult over the poor Christians in their adversities, and chiefly over the defloration; these fellows themselves being most unmanly and depraved wretches, altogether degenerate from the true Romans, unto whose honours (being many, and much recorded) these base creatures are so directly opposite. For it was these that made Rome, which was first founded, and after increased by the care and industry of her old worthies, to appear more filthy and corrupted in her prosperity, than she was now in her ruin: for in this, there fell but stones, walls, and houses; but in the lives of such villains as these, all the monuments, all the ornaments not of their walls, but of their manners, were utterly demolished; as then did a worse fire burn in their affections than this was now that did but burn their houses.

With the close of this, I gave an end to the first book, and now (as I resolved) will proceed to cast up a reckoning of the sundry mischiefs that this city of Rome hath suffered since she was first founded, either in herself, or in some of the provinces under her command: all of which those vile persons would have pinned upon the back of Christianity, if the doctrine of the gospel against their false and deceitful gods had in those times been revealed and preached.

CHAPTER III

Of the choice of history to show the miseries that the Romans endured, when they worshipped their idols, before the increase of Christian religion

BUT remember this, that when I handled those points, I had to do with the ignorant, out of whose blockish heads this proverb was first born: 'It will not rain because of the Christians.' For there are some others amongst them that are learned, and love that very history that makes these things plain to their understanding: but because they love to set the blind and erroneous vulgar at enmity and dissension with us Christians, they dissemble and conceal this understanding of theirs, labouring to persuade the people this— that the whole process of calamities, which at divers times and in several places fell and were still to fall upon all the world, have had their origin only and merely from the profession of Christ; grieving that it spreadeth so far, and shineth so gloriously against all their other gods and religions. But let these malicious men read but with us, with what excess of affliction the Roman estate was wrung and plagued, and that on every side, before ever this name (which they in vain do envy) did spread the glory to such note: and then if they can, let them defend their gods' goodness shown unto them in these extremities, seeing that in addition as their servants they honour them for protection from these extremities, which, if they do but suffer now in any part, they are ready to lay all the blame upon our necks. For why did their gods permit their servants to be plagued with these great afflictions (which I am now to recount) before the publishing of the name of Christ gave them cause of offence by prohibiting their sacrifices?

CHAPTER IV

That the worshippers of pagan gods never received honest instructions from them, but used all filthiness in their sacrifices

FIRST, why should not their gods have a care to see their servants well mannered? The true God doth worthily neglect those that neglect His just worship: but as for those gods whom this wicked and ungrateful crew complain that they are forbidden to worship, why do they not help to better the lives of their worshippers by giving them some good laws? It was very requisite that as they carefully attended their gods' sacrifices, so their gods should have graciously amended their imperfections. Aye (but will some say), every man may be vicious at his own will and pleasure. True; who denies that? Yet notwithstanding, it was the part of these great gods' guardians, not to conceal the forms and rudiments of good and honest life from their suppliants; but to teach them plain, and fully, and by their prophets, to correct and restrain the offenders, to restrain evildoers with public punishments, and to encourage good livers with full rewards. What temple of all this multitude of gods was ever accessory to any such teaching? We ourselves (once in our youth) went to view these spectacles, their sacrilegious mockeries; there we saw the enthusiasts, persons rapt with fury; there we heard the pipers, and took great delight in the filthy sports that they acted before the gods and goddesses, even before Berecynthia (surnamed the celestial virgin, and mother to all the gods), even before her litter, upon the feast day of her very purification. Their beastly stage players acted such ribaldry, as was a shame not only for the mother of the gods, but for the mother of any senator or any honest man, nay, even for the mothers of the players themselves to give ear to. Natural shame hath bound us with some respect unto our parents, which vice itself cannot abolish. But that beastliness of obscene speeches and actions, which the players acted in public, before the mother of all the gods, and in sight and hearing of a huge multitude of both sexes, they would be ashamed to act at home in private before their mothers, were it but for repetition sake. And as for that company that were their spectators, though they might easily be drawn thither by curiosity, yet beholding chastity so foully injured, methinks they should have been driven from thence by the mere shame that immodesty can offend honesty withal. What can sacrileges be if those were sacrifices? or what can be pollution if this were a purification? and these were called 'tables,' [1] as if they made a feast where all the unclean devils of hell might fill their bellies. For who could not know what kind of spirits these are that take pleasure in these obscenities, unless he know not that there be any such unclean spirits that thus illude men under the names of gods; or else, unless he be such a one as wisheth the pleasure and fears the displeasure of those damned powers more than he doth the love and wrath of the true and ever-living God?

[1] Latin *fercula*, meaning (1) a litter on which the images of gods were carried (2) a dish on which food was served.—ED.

CHAPTER V

Of the obscenities used in these sacrifices offered unto the mother of the gods

NOR will I abide by the judgment of those who I know do rather delight in the vicious custom of enormities than decline from it: I will have Scipio Nasica himself to be judge, he whom the whole senate proclaimed for their best man, one alone whose hands were thought fit to receive and bring in this devil's picture: let him but tell us first whether he desire that his mother's deserts were such that the senate should appoint her divine honours (as we read that both the Greeks and other Roman nations also have ordained for some particular men whose worth they held in high esteem, and whose persons they thought were made immortal, and admitted amongst the gods). Truly he would gladly wish his mother this felicity, if such a thing could be. But if we ask him then further, whether he would have such filthy presentations as Cybelus enacted as parts of his mother's honours; would he not avow (think you) that he had rather have his mother lie dead and senseless, than to live a goddess, to hear and allow such ribaldry? Yes: far be it from such a worthy senator of Rome, as would forbid the building of a theatre in a State maintained by valour, to wish his mother that worship to please her goddess-ship, which could not but offend all womanhood. Nor is it possible that he could be persuaded, that divinity could so far alter the laudable modesty of a woman, as to make her allow her servants to call upon her in such immodest terms, as being spoken in the hearing of any living woman, if she stop not her ears and get her gone, the whole kindred of her father, husband, children all would blush, and be ashamed at her shamefulness. And therefore such a mother of the gods as this (whom even the worst man would shame to have his mother alike unto) did never seek the best man of Rome (in her entrance into the people's affections) to make him better by her counsels and admonitions, but rather worse, by her deceits and illusions (like her of whom it is written: 'A woman hunteth for the precious life of a man'[1]): that his great spirit being puffed up by this (as it were divine) testimony of the senate, and he holding himself such, the best might be thus withdrawn from the truth of religion and godliness: without which, the worthiest wit is ever overthrown and extinguished in pride and vainglory. What intent then (save deceit) had she in selecting the best and most honest man, seeing she useth and desireth such things in her sacrifices as honest men abhor to use, were it but even in their sports and recreations?

[1] Prov. vi. 26.

CHAPTER VI

That the pagans' gods did never establish the doctrine of living well

HENCE it proceedeth that those gods never had care of the lives and manners of such cities and nations as gave them divine honours: but contrariwise gave free permission to such horrible and abominable evils, to enter, not upon their lands, vines, houses, or treasures, no, nor upon the body (which serves the mind), but upon the mind itself, the ruler of all the flesh, and of all the rest: this they ever allowed without any prohibition at all. If they did prohibit it, let it be proved that they did. I know their followers will talk of certain secret traditions and I know not what, some closely muttered instructions, tending to the bettering of man's life; but let them show wherever they had any public places ordained for to hear such lectures (wherein the players did not present their filthy gesture and speeches: nor where the *fugalia* were kept with all licentiousness of lust, fitly called *fugalia*, as the chasers away of all chastity and honesty): but where the people might come and hear their gods' doctrine concerning the restraint of covetousness, the suppression of ambition, and the bridling of luxury and riot: where wretches might learn that which Persius thunders unto them, saying:

> Disciteque o miseri, et causas cognoscite rerum,
> Quid sumus, aut quidnam victuri gignimur: ordo
> Quis datus, aut metae quam mollis flexus, et unde
> Quis modus argenti, quid fas optare, quid asper
> Utile nummus habet: patriae carisque propinquis
> Quantum elargiri deceat, quem te deus esse
> Jussit, et humana qua parte locatus es in re.[1]

> Learn, wretches, and conceive the course of things,
> What man is, and why nature forth him brings:
> His settled bounds, from whence how soon he strays:
> What wealths mean; that for which the good man prays;
> How to use money: how to give to friends,
> What we in earth, and God in us, intends, etc.

Let them show where these lessons of their instructing gods were ever read or rehearsed: whether ever their worshippers were wont to hear of any such matters, as we are wont to do continually in our churches, erected for this purpose in all places wheresoever the religion of Christ is diffused.

[1] *Sat.* iii. 66–72.

CHAPTER VII

That the philosophers' instructions are weak and ineffective, in that they bear no divine authority, because the examples of the gods are greater confirmations of vices in men than the wise men's disputations are on the contrary part

Do you think they will mention their philosophy schools unto us? As for them, first of all they are derived from Greece, and not from Rome: or if you say they are now Roman because Greece is become a province of the Romans, I answer again that the instructions given there are not of the teachings of your gods, but the inventions of man, whose quick wit's especial endeavour was to find by disputation what secrets were hid in the treasury of nature; what was to be desired, and what was to be avoided in our morality; and what was coherent by the laws of disputation, or not following the induction, or quite repugnant unto it. And some of these gave light to great inventions, as the grace of God assisted them, but yet they evermore erred, as the frailty of man possessed them; the divine providence justly opposing their vainglory to show the way of piety to rise from humbleness unto height, by their comparison: which we shall hereafter take an occasion to search into further by the will of the true and everlasting God. But if it were true that these philosophers invented any means sufficient to direct one to the obtaining of a happy course of life, is there not far greater reason to give them divine honours, than the other? How much more honest were it for Plato's books to be read in a temple of his, than the *galli* mutilated in the devils', or the effeminate consecrated, the lunatic gashed with cuts, and each other thing cruel or bestial, or bestially cruel, or cruelly bestial, too commonly celebrated in the solemnities of such gods? Were it not far more worthy to have some good laws of the gods rehearsed unto the youth for their instruction in integrity, than to pass the time in vain commendations of the labours of illuded antiquity? But lustful youth gazing upon a painted tablet, whereon was drawn how unto those luxurious and venomous adorations, as Persius saith, do look more after Jupiter's deeds, than either Plato's doctrine or Cato's opinions. And hereupon it is that Terence brings in the lustful youth gazing upon a painted tablet whereon was drawn how Jove sent down a shower of gold into the lap of Danae; and this was a fit precedent for this youth to follow in his lust, with a boast that he did but imitate a god. 'But what god!' said he; 'even he that shakes the temples with his thunder: since he did thus, shall I (a mean wretch to him) make bones of it? No; I did it with all mine heart.' [1]

[1] *Eun.* iii. 5, 36, 37, 42, 43.

CHAPTER VIII

*Of the Romans' stage plays, wherein the publishing of their gods'
foulest impurities did not any way offend but rather delight them*

AYE, but (will some say) these things are not taught in the institutions of the gods, but in the inventions of the poets. I will not say that the gods' mysteries are more filthy than the theatre's presentations; but this I say (and will bring history sufficient to convince all those that shall deny it) that those plays which are formed according to these poetical fictions, were not exhibited by the Romans unto their gods in their solemnities through any ignorant devotion of their own, but only by reason that the gods themselves did so strictly command, yea, and even in some sort extort from them the public presenting and dedication of those plays unto their honours. This I handled briefly in the first book.[1] For, when the city was first of all infected with the pestilence, then were stages first ordained at Rome by the authorization of the chief priest. And what is he, that in ordering of his courses, will not rather choose to follow the rudiments which are to be fetched out of plays, or whatsoever being instituted by his gods, rather than the weaker ordinances of mortal men? If the poets did falsely record Jupiter for an adulterer, then these gods, being so chaste, should be the more offended, and punish the world for thrusting such a deal of villainy into their ceremonies, and not for omitting them. Of these stage plays the best and most tolerable are tragedy and comedy; being poetical fables made to be acted at these shows: wherein notwithstanding was much dishonest matter, in actions, but none at all of words: and these the old men do cause to be taught to their children, amongst their most honest and liberal studies.

CHAPTER IX

*What the Romans' opinion was touching the restraint of the liberty of
poesy, which the Greeks, by the counsel of their gods, would not
have restrained at all*

WHAT the Romans held concerning this point, Cicero recordeth in his books which he wrote *Of the Commonwealth*, where Scipio is brought in saying thus: 'If the privilege of an old custom had not allowed them, comedies could never have given such proofs of their vileness upon theatres.'[2] And some of the ancient Greeks maintained a certain consistency in their vicious opinion,

[1] I. xxxii.   [2] *De Re Publ.* iv. 10, 33.

and made it a law that the comedian might speak what he would, of any man, by his name. Wherefore, as Africanus saith well in the same book: 'Whom did not the poet touch, nay whom did he not vex, whom spared he?' 'Perhaps so,' saith one, 'he quipped a sort of wicked, seditious, vulgar fellows, as Cleon, Cleophon, and Hyperbolus.' 'To that we assent,' quoth he again, 'though it were fitter for such citizens to be taxed by the censor than by a poet. But it was no more decent that Pericles should be maligned with verses to be recited on the stage, having so many years governed the city so well both in war and peace, than it were for our Plautus or Naevius to deride Publius or Gnaeus Scipio, or for Caecilius to mock Marcus Cato.' And again, a little after, 'Our twelve tables,' quoth he, 'having decreed the observation but of a very few things upon pain of death, yet thought it good to establish this for one of that few, that none should write or act any verse, derogatory from the good name of any man, or prejudicial unto manners. Excellently well! for our lives ought not to be the objects for poets to play upon, but for lawful magistracy and thoroughly informed justice to judge upon; nor is it fit that men should hear themselves reproached, but in such places as they may answer and defend their own cause in.' Thus much out of Cicero in his fourth book *Of the Commonwealth*, which I thought good to rehearse word for word, only I was forced to leave out somewhat, and somewhat to transpose it, for the easier understanding. For it gives great light unto the proposition which I (if so be I can) must prove and make apparent. He proceedeth further in this discourse, and in the end concludeth thus, that the ancient Romans utterly disliked that any man should be either praised or dispraised upon the stage. But as I said before, the Greeks in this, though they used less modesty, yet they followed more consistency, seeing they saw their gods so well to approve of the represented disgraces, not only of men, but even of themselves, when they came upon the stage: whether the plays were fictions of poetry, or true histories of their deeds (and I wish their worshippers had held them only worth the laughing at, and not worth imitation!), for it were too much pride in a prince to seek to have his own fame preserved, when he sees his gods before him set theirs at six and seven. For whereas it is said in their defence, that these tales of their gods were not true, but merely poetical inventions, and false fictions, why this doth make it more abominable, if you respect the purity of your religion: and if you observe the malice of the devil, what more cunning or more deceitful craftiness can there be? For when an honest and worthy ruler of a country is slandered, is not the slander so much more wicked and unpardonable, as this party's life that is slandered is clearer and sounder from touch of any such matter? what punishment then can be sufficient for those that offer their gods such foul and impious injury?

CHAPTER X

That the devils through their settled desire to do men mischief, were willing to have any villainies reported of them whether true or false

BUT those wicked spirits, whom these men take to be gods, were desirous to have such beastly stories spread abroad about them (though they themselves had never acted any such thing), only to keep men's minds inveigled in such bestial opinions, as it were in snares or nets, and by that means to draw them to predestinate damnation for company: whether it be true that such men as those whom these spirits, who rejoice in the mischiefs of men, rejoice to be considered as gods, did themselves commit any such things (for which the devils set themselves out to be adored, by a thousand several tricks of hurtful deceit): or that there were no such things done at all, but only those malicious and subtle devils do cause them to be feigned of the gods, to the end that there might be sufficient authority, derived as it were from heaven to earth, for men to commit all filthiness by. Therefore the Grecians, seeing that they had such gods as these to serve, thought it not fit to take away any liberty from the poets in using these stage-mocks and shames. And this they did either for fear lest their gods should be provoked to anger against them, in case they went about to make themselves into more honest moulds than they were, and so seem to prefer themselves before them; or else for desire to be made like their gods, even in those greatest enormities. And from this consistency came it, that they held the very actors of such plays to be worthy of honours in their cities. For in the same book *Of the Commonwealth*, [1] Aeschines of Athens, an eloquent man, having been an actor of tragedies in his youth, is said to have borne office in the commonwealth. And Aristodemus, another actor of tragedies, was sent by the Athenians upon an embassage to Philip, about especial and weighty affairs of war and peace. For they held it an unmeet thing (seeing they saw their gods approve of those actions, and arts of playing) to repute those worthy of any note of infamy, that were but the actors of them.

CHAPTER XI

That the Grecians admitted their players to bear office in their commonwealth, lest they should seem unjust in despising such men as were the pacifiers of their gods

THIS was the Grecians' practice: absurd enough, howsoever, but yet most fitly applied unto the nature of the gods. They durst not exempt the lives of their citizens from the lashes of poetical pens

[1] iv. 11, 35.

and players' tongues, because they saw their gods delighted at the
traducing of themselves: and they thought, surely, that those men
that acted such things upon the stage as pleased the gods, ought
not to be disliked in any way by them that were but servants to
those gods.   Nay, not only that, but that they ought to be absolutely
and highly honoured by their fellow citizens: for what reason could
they find, for the honouring of the priests that offered the sacrifices
which the gods accepted well, and yet allow the actors to be
disgracefully thought of, who had learnt their profession by the
special appointment of the selfsame gods, that exact these celebrations of them, and are displeased if they be not solemnized?
Especially seeing that Labeo (who they say was most exact in these
matters) distinguisheth the good spirits from the bad by this
diversity of their worships, that the bad ones are delighted with
slaughters and *tragical invocations*, and the good with *mirthful
revels* and *sportful honours*, such as *plays* (quoth he), *banquets*, and
revelling on beds are; of which hereafter (so God be pleased) we will
discourse more at large.   But to our present purpose: whether it
be so that all kinds of honours be given unto all the gods mixed and
confused, as unto only good ones (for it is not fit to say there are
any evil gods, although indeed they are all evil, being all unclean
spirits): or that according as Labeo saith, there must be a discretion
used, and that these must have such and such particular rites of
observances assigned, and those others; howsoever, the Greeks
did most consistently to hold both priests and players worthy of
honourable dignities, the priests for offering of their sacrifices, and
the players for acting of their interludes: lest otherwise, they should
be guilty of offering injury either to all their gods, if they all love
plays, or (which is worse) to those whom they account as the good
ones, if they only love them.

CHAPTER XII

*That the Romans in abridging that liberty which the poets would have
used upon men, and in allowing them to use it upon their gods, did
herein show that they prized themselves above their gods*

BUT the Romans (as Scipio boasteth in that book *Of the Commonwealth*) would by no means have the good names and manners of
their citizens liable to the quips and censures of the poets, but
inflicted a capital punishment upon all such as durst offend in that
kind: which indeed in respect of themselves was honestly and well
instituted, but in respect of their gods most proudly and irreli-
giously, for though they knew that their gods were not only patient,
but even well pleased at the representing of their reproaches and
exorbitancies, yet would they hold themselves more unworthy to

suffer such injuries than their gods, thrusting such things into their solemnities, as they avoided from themselves by all rigour of laws. Yea, Scipio, dost thou commend the restraint of this poetical liberty in taxing your persons, when thou seest it hath been ever free to calumniate your gods? Dost thou value the court alone so much more than the Capitol, than all Rome, nay, than all heaven, that the poets must be curbed by an express law, from flouting at the citizens, and yet without all control of senator, censor, prince, or priest, have free leave to throw what slander they please upon the gods? What? Was it so unseemly for Plautus or Naevius to traduce P. or Gnaeus Scipio; or for Caecilius to jest upon M. Cato? And was it seemly for your Terence to animate a youth to uncleanness by the example of the deed of high and mighty Jupiter?

CHAPTER XIII

That the Romans might have observed their gods' unworthiness by their desires of such obscene solemnities

IT might be Scipio, were he alive again, would answer me thus: How can we possibly set any penalty upon such things as our gods themselves do make sacred, by their own express induction of those plays into our customs, and by annexing them to the celebration of their sacrifices and honours, wherein such things are ever to be acted and celebrated? But why then, say I again, do not you discern them by this impurity to be no true gods, nor worthy of any divine honours at all? For if it be altogether unmeet for you to honour such men as love to see and set forth plays that are stuffed with the reproach of the Romans, how then can you judge them to be gods, how then can you but hold them for unclean spirits, that through desire to deceive others, require it as part of their greatest honours to be cast in the teeth with their own filthinesses? Indeed the Romans, though they were locked in those chains of hurtful superstition, and served such gods as they saw required such dishonest spectacles at their hands, yet had they such a care of their own honesty and dignity, that they would never vouchsafe the actors of such vile things any honour in their commonwealth, as the Greeks did: but according to Scipio's words in Cicero: 'Seeing that they held the art of stage-playing as base and unmanly, therefore they did not only detain all the honours of the city from such kind of men, but appointed the censors in their views, to remove them from being part of any tribe, and would not vouchsafe them to be counted as members of the city.' [1] A worthy decree, and well beseeming the Roman wisdom; yet this wisdom

[1] *De Re Publ.* iv. 10, 32.

would I have to imitate and follow itself. Rightly hath the council of the city in this well desiring and deserving commendation (showing itself to be in this truly Roman), appointed that whosoever will choose of a citizen of Rome to become a player, he should not only live secluded from all honours, but by the censor's censure should be made utterly incapable of living as a member of his proper tribe. But now tell me but this, why the players should be branded with inability to bear honours, and yet the plays they act inserted into the celebration of the gods' honours. The Roman valour flourished a long time, unacquainted with these theatre tricks: suppose then that men's vain affections gave them their first induction, and that they crept in by the errors of men's decayed manners, doth it hence follow that the gods must take delight in them, or desire them? If so, why then is the player debased by whom the god is pleased? And with what face can you scandalize the actors and instruments of such stage guilt, and yet adore the exactors and commanders of these actions? This now is the controversy between the Greeks and the Romans. The Greeks think that they have good reason to honour these players, seeing that they must honour them that require these plays: the Romans, on the other side, are so far from gracing them, that they will not allow them a place in a plebeian tribe, much less in the court or senate, but hold them disgraceful to all callings. Now in this disputation, this sole argument gives the upshot of all the controversy. The Greeks propound: If such gods are to be worshipped, then such actors are also to be held as honourable. The Romans assume: But such actors are in no way to be held as honourable. The Christians conclude: Therefore such gods are in no way to be worshipped.

CHAPTER XIV

That Plato, who would not allow poets to dwell in a well-governed city, showed that his sole worth was better than those gods, that desire to be honoured with stage plays

AGAIN, we ask another question: why the poets that make those comedies (and being prohibited by a law of the twelve tables to defame the citizens, yet do dishonour the gods with such foul imputations) are not reputed as dishonest and disgraceful as the players. What reason can be produced, why the actors of such poetical figments, being so ignominious to the gods, should be reputed infamous, and yet the authors be vouchsafed honours? Is not Plato more praiseworthy than you all, who disputing of the true perfection of a city would have poets banished from that society, as enemies to the city's full perfection? He had both a grief to see his gods so injured, and a care to keep out these fictions whereby the citizens' minds might be corrupted. Now make but a comparison of his humanity in expelling poets from his city, lest they should delude it with the gods' divinity that desired such plays and revels in their honours; by which the city might be deluded. He, though he did not induce or persuade them to it, yet advised and counselled the light and luxurious Greeks in his disputations to restrain the writing of such things: but these gods, by command and constraint, even forced the modest and staid Romans to present them with such things: nay, not only to present them, but even to dedicate and consecrate them in all solemnity unto their honours. Now to which of these may the city with most honesty ascribe divine worship? whether to Plato that would forbid these filthy obscenities, or to these devils that exult in deluding those men whom Plato could not persuade to the truth? This man did Labeo think meet to be reckoned amongst the demigods, as he did Hercules also, and Romulus: and he prefers the demigods before the heroes, but notwithstanding makes deities of them both: but I hold this man whom he calls a demigod, worthy to be preferred not only before the heroes, but even before all their other gods themselves. And in this the Roman laws do come somewhat near his disputations: for whereas he condemns all allowance of poets, they deprive them of their liberty to rail at any man. He excluded poets from dwelling in his city: they deprive the actors of poetical fables from the privileges of citizens: and it may be (if they durst do aught against gods that require such stage games) they would thrust them forth altogether. Wherefore the Romans can neither receive nor expect any moral instructions, either for correcting of faults or increasing of virtues, from those gods, whom their own laws already do subvert and convince. The gods require plays for increase of their honours: the Romans exclude players from partaking of theirs: the gods require their own faults to be celebrated by poets' inventions; the Romans restrain the poets' looseness from touching any of the Romans' imperfections. But Plato, that demigod, both resists this impure affection of the gods, and shows what ought to be perfected by the towardliness of the Romans; denying poets all place in a well-ordered commonwealth howsoever, whether they presented the figments of their own lusts and fancies, or related aught else as the guilt of the gods, and therefore of imitable examples: but we Christians make Plato neither whole god nor demigod; nor do we vouchsafe to compare him with any of God's angels, or His prophets, nor with any of Christ's apostles or His martyrs, nor with any Christian man; and why we will not, by God's help, in the due place we will declare. But notwithstanding, seeing they will needs have him a demigod, we think him worthy to be preferred, if not before Romulus or Hercules (though there was never historian nor poet affirmed, or feigned, that he ever killed his brother, or committed any other mischievous act), yet at least before Priapus or any Cynocephalus, or lastly any Febris; all which the Romans either had as gods from strangers, or set them up as their own. How then could such gods as these, by any counsel they could give, prevent or cure such great corruption of mind and manners (whether imminent, or already infused), seeing they regarded nothing else but to diffuse and augment this contagion of wickedness, and to have it instilled into the people's notice from the stage, as their own acts, or acts which they approve, to the end that man's lust might run the course of wickedness freely, after the gods' examples? Tully exclaimeth all in vain upon it, who when he comes to speak of poets, saith: 'The clamour and approbation of the people, when it is joined with these poetical fictions, as the testimony of some great and learned master, oh, what darkness doth it involve a man in! what fears it inflicts, what lusts it inflames!' [1]

CHAPTER XV

That flattery and not reason created some of the Roman gods

BUT what other reason in the world besides flattery have they to make choice of these so false and feigned gods, not vouchsafing Plato any little temple, whom notwithstanding they will have to be a demigod (and one who took such pains in dissuading the corruption of manners through the depravation of opinions); and yet preferring Romulus before divers of the gods, whom their most secret and exact doctrine doth but make a semi-god, and not an entire deity. And yet for him they appointed a flamen, a kind of priesthood so far above the rest as their caps did testify that they had only three of those flamens for three of their chiefest deities, the Dial or Jovial for Jupiter; the Martial, for Mars; and the Quirinal, for Romulus. For the love of his citizens having as it were hoisted him up into heaven, he was then called Quirinus, and kept that name ever after: and so by this you see Romulus here is preferred before Neptune and Pluto, Jupiter's brother, nay even before Saturn, father of them all: so that to make him great, they give him the same priesthood that Jupiter was honoured by, and likewise they give one to Mars, his pretended father, it may be rather for his sake than any other devotion.

[1] *De Re Publ.* iv. 9, 30.

CHAPTER XVI

*That if the Roman gods had had any care of justice, the city should
have had their forms of good government from them, rather than
go and borrow it of other nations*

IF the Romans could have received any good instructions of
morality from their gods, they would never have been beholden
to the Athenians for Solon's laws, as they were some years after
Rome was built: which laws notwithstanding they did not observe
as they received them, but endeavoured to better them and make
them more exact. And though Lycurgus feigned that he gave
the Lacedaemonians their laws by the authorization of Apollo,
yet the Romans very wisely would not give credence to him, and
therefore gave no admission to these laws. Indeed Numa Pompilius, Romulus' successor, is said to have given them some laws:
but all too insufficient for the government of a city. He taught
them many points of their religion, but it is not reported that he
had these institutions from the gods. Those corruptions therefore of mind, conversation, and conditions, which were so great,
that the most learned men durst affirm that these were the cankers
by which all commonwealths perished, though their walls stood
never so firm; those did these gods never endeavour to withhold
from them that worshipped them; but, as we have proved before,
did rather strive to enlarge and augment them, with all their care
and fullest diligence.

CHAPTER XVII

*Of the rape of the Sabine women, and divers other wicked acts, done
in Rome's most ancient and honourable times*

PERHAPS the gods would not give the Romans any laws, because as
Sallust saith: 'Justice and honesty prevailed as much with them by
nature as by law.' [1] Very good: out of this justice and honesty
came it, I think, that the Sabine virgins were ravished. What more
just or more honest part can be played than to force away other
men's daughters with all violence possible, rather than to receive
them at the hand of their parents? But if it were unjustly done of
the Sabines to deny the Romans their daughters, was it not far
more unjustly done of them to force them away after that denial?
There were more equity shown in making war upon those that would
not give their daughters to beget alliance with their neighbours

[1] *Catil.* 9.

and countrymen, than those that did but require back their
own, which were injuriously forced from them.   Therefore Mars
should rather have helped his warlike son in revenging the injury
of this rejected proffer of marriage, that so he might have won the
virgin that he desired by force of arms.   For there might have
been some pretence of warlike law, for the conqueror justly to bear
away those whom the conquered had unjustly denied him before.
But he, against all law of peace, violently forced them from such
as denied him them, and then began an unjust war with their
parents, to whom he had given so just a cause of anger.   Herein,
indeed, he had good and happy success.   And albeit the Circensian
plays were continued to preserve the memory of this fraudulent
act, yet neither the city nor the empire did approve such a precedent: and the Romans were more willing to err in making
Romulus a deity after this deed of iniquity, than to allow by any
law or practice this crime of his in forcing of women thus to stand
as an example for others to follow.   Out of this justice and honesty
likewise proceeded this, that after Tarquin and his children were
expelled from Rome (because his son Sextus had ravished Lucretia)
Junius Brutus being consul compelled L. Tarquinius Collatinus,
her husband, his fellow officer, a good man, and wholly guiltless,
to give over his place, and abandon the city; which vile deed of his
was done by the approbation (or at least permission) of the people,
who made Collatinus consul, as well as Brutus himself.   Out of this
justice and honesty came this also, that Marcus Camillus, that most
illustrious worthy of his time, that with such ease subdued the
warlike Veientes, the greatest foes of the Romans, and took their
chief city from them; after they had held the Romans in ten
years' war, and foiled their armies so often, that Rome herself began
to tremble, and suspected her own safety—that this man by the
malice of his backbiting enemies and the insupportable pride of
the tribunes, being accused of guilt, and perceiving the city
which he had liberated so ungrateful, that he needs must be condemned, was glad to betake himself to willing banishment: and
yet in his absence was fined at ten thousand asses, being soon after
to be called home again to free his thankless country the second
time from the Gauls.   It irks me to recapitulate the multitude of
foul enormities which that city hath enacted: the great ones seeking to bring the people under their subjection: the people again
on the other side scorning to be subject to them: and the ring-
leaders on both sides aiming wholly rather at superiority and conquest, than ever giving room to a thought of justice or honesty.

CHAPTER XVIII

*What the 'History' of Sallust reports of the Romans' conditions,
both in their times of danger and those of security*

THEREFORE I will keep a mean, and abide rather by the testimony
of Sallust himself, who spoke this in the Romans' praise (whereof
we but now discoursed), that justice and honesty prevailed as much
with them by nature as by law: extolling those times wherein the
city after the casting out of her kings grew up to such a height in
so small a space. Notwithstanding all this, this same author
confesses in the very beginning of the first book of his *History*, that
when the sway of the State was taken from the kings and given to
the consuls, within a very little while after, the city grew to be
greatly troubled with the oppressing power of the great ones,
with the division of the people from the fathers upon that cause,
and with divers other dangerous dissensions. For having recorded
how honestly and in what good concord the Romans lived together
betwixt the second war of Africa and the last, and having shown
that it was not the love of goodness, but the fear and distrust of
the Carthaginians' might and perfidiousness, that was cause of this
good order, and therefore that upon this Nasica would have
Carthage stand still undemolished, as a fit means to debar the
entrance of iniquity into Rome, and to preserve integrity by fear;
he adds presently upon this, these words: [1] 'But discord, avarice,
ambition, and all such mischiefs as prosperity is midwife unto,
grew unto their full light after the destruction of Carthage,' intimating herein, that they were sown, and continued amongst the
Romans before: which he proves in his following reason. 'For
as for the violent offensiveness of the greater persons,' saith he,
'and the division betwixt the patricians and the plebeians thence
arising, those were mischiefs amongst us from the beginning: and
the greater respect of equity and moderation found after the expulsion of the kings lasted only so long as the fear from Tarquin and
the war with Etruria persisted.' Thus you see, how that even in
that little space wherein after the expulsion of their kings they
embraced integrity, it was only fear that forced them to do so,
because they stood in dread of the wars, which Tarquin, upon
his expulsion being combined with the Etrurians, waged against
them. Now observe what Sallust adds: 'For after that,' quoth
he, 'the senators began to make slaves of the people, to judge of
heads and shoulders, as bloodily and imperiously as the kings did
to chase men from their possessions: and only they bare the
imperial sway of all. With which outrages, and chiefly with
their extreme taxes and extortions, the people being sore oppressed,
maintaining both soldiers in continual arms, and paying tribute

[1] *Hist.* i. 9.

also besides, at length stepped out, took up arms, and drew to a head upon Mount Aventine and Mount Sacer. And then they elected them tribunes, and set down other laws; but the second war of Africa gave end to these contentions on both sides.' Thus you see in how little a while, so soon after the expelling of their kings, the Romans were become such as he has described them: of whom notwithstanding he had affirmed that 'justice and honesty prevailed as much with them by nature as by law.' Now if those times were found to have been so depraved, wherein the Roman estate is reported to have been most uncorrupt and absolute, what shall we imagine may then be spoken or thought of the succeeding ages, which by a gradual alteration (to use the author's own words) of an honest and honourable city, became most dishonest and dishonourable, namely after the dissolution of Carthage, as he himself relates? How he discourses and describes these times, you may at full behold in his *History*, and what progress this corruption of manners made through the midst of the city's prosperity, even until the time of the civil wars. But from that time forward, as he reports,[1] the manners of the better sort did no more fall to decay by little and little, but ran headlong to ruin like a swift torrent, such excess of luxury and avarice entering upon the manners of the youth, that it was fitly said of Rome, that she brought forth such as would neither keep goods themselves nor suffer others to keep theirs. Then Sallust proceeds with a discourse about Sulla's villainies, and other barbarous blemishes in the commonwealth: and with him do all other writers agree in substance, though they be all far behind him in phrase. But here you see (and so I hope do all men) that whosoever will observe but this, shall easily discover the large gulf of damnable viciousness into which this city was fallen, long before the coming of our heavenly King. For these things came to pass, not only before ever Christ our Saviour taught in the flesh, but even before He was born of the Virgin, or took flesh at all. Seeing therefore that they dare not impute unto their own gods those so many and so great mischiefs, either the tolerable ones which they suffered before, or the fouler ones which they incurred after the destruction of Carthage (howsoever their gods are the engrafters of such malign opinions in men's minds, as must needs bud forth such vices), why then do they blame Christ for the evils present, who forbids them to adore such false and devilish gods by His sweet and saving doctrine, who doth condemn all these harmful and ungodly affections of man by His divine authority; and from all those miseries, withdraws His flock and family little by little out of all places of the declining world, to make of their company an eternal and celestial city, not by the applause of vanity, but by the judgment of verity?

[1] *Hist.* i. 12.

CHAPTER XIX

Of the corruptions ruling in the Roman State before Christ
abolished the worship of their idols

BEHOLD now this commonwealth of Rome, which I am not the first
to affirm, but their own writers, out of whom I speak, do aver,
to have declined from good by degrees, and from an honest and
honourable state, to have fallen into the greatest dishonesty and
dishonour possible. Behold, before ever Christ was come, how
that Carthage being once out of the way, then the patricians'
manners decayed no more by degrees, but ran headlong into corruption like a swift torrent, the youth of the city was still so defiled
with luxury and avarice.

Now let them read us the good counsel that their gods gave them
against this luxury and avarice. I wish they had only been silent
in the instructions of modesty and chastity, and had not exacted
such abominations of their worshippers, unto which by their
false divinity they gave such pernicious authority. But let them
read our laws, and they shall hear them thundering out of divine
oracles and God's clouds (as it were) against avarice and lust, by
the mouths of the prophets, by the gospel, the apostles, their acts
and their epistles, so divinely, and so excellently, all the people
flocking together to hear them; not as to a vain and jangling philosophical disputation, but as to an admonition from heaven. And
yet these wretches will not blame their gods for letting their commonwealth be so foully bespotted with enormous impieties, before
the coming of Christ: but whatsoever misery or affliction their
effeminate and unmanly pride hath tasted of since this coming,
that the Christian religion is sure to be blamed for. The good
rules and precepts whereof concerning honesty and integrity of
manners, if all the kings of the earth, and all people, princes and
all the judges of the earth, young men and virgins, old men, children,
all ages and sexes capable of reason, and even the very soldiers and
tax-takers themselves (to whom John Baptist speaks) [1] would hear
and regard well; their commonwealths would not only adorn this
earth below with present honesty, but would ascend up to heaven,
there to sit on the highest point of eternal glory. But because this
man doth but hear, and that man doth not regard, and the third
doth despise it, and far more do love the stroking hand of viciousness than the rougher touch of virtue, Christ's children are commanded to endure with patience the calamities that fall upon them
by the ministers of a wicked commonwealth. Be they kings,
princes, judges, soldiers, and governors, rich or poor, bound or
free, of what sex or sort soever, they must bear all with patience:

[1] Luke iii. 12–14.

being by their sufferance here to attain a most glorious place in
that royal and imperial city of angels above, and in that heavenly
commonwealth, where the will of Almighty God is their only law,
and His law their will.

CHAPTER XX

*Of what kind of happiness and of what conditions the accusers
of Christianity desire to partake*

BUT such worshippers, and such lovers of those vicious gods, whom
they rejoice to follow and imitate in all villainies and mischiefs,
those do never respect the goodness or the integrity of the commonwealth.   No, say they, let it but stand, let it but be rich and
victorious; or (which is best of all) let it but enjoy security and
peace, and what care we?   Yes indeed, it doth belong to our care,
that every one might have means to increase his wealth, to nourish
the expense of his continual riot, and wherewithal the greater might
still keep under the meaner.   Let the poor obey the rich, for their
bellies' sakes; and that they may live at ease under their protections.
Let the rich abuse the poor in their huge attendances, and ministering to their sumptuousness.   Let the people applaud such as afford
them delights, not such as proffer them good counsels.   Let
naught that is hard be enjoined, naught that is impure be prohibited.   Let not the king's care be how good, but how subject
his people be.   Let not subdued provinces serve their kings as
reformers of their manners, but as the rulers of their estates and
the procurers of their pleasures: not honouring them sincerely, but
fearing them servilely.   Let the laws look to him that looks after
another man's possessions, rather than him that looks not after his
own life.   Let no man be brought before the judges, but such as
has offered violence unto others' estates, houses, or persons.   But
for a man's own, let it be free for him to use it as he wills, and so of
other men's, if they consent.   Let there be good store of common
harlots, either for all that please to use them, or for those that
cannot keep private ones.   Let stately and sumptuous houses be
erected, banquets and feasts solemnized; let a man drink, eat,
game, and revel day and night, where he may or will: let dancing be
ordinary in all places: let luxurious and bloody delights fill the
theatre, with dishonest words, and shows, freely and uncontrolled.
And let him be held an enemy to the public good that is an opposite
unto this felicity.   Let the people turn away their ears from all
such as shall assay to dissuade or alter them, let them banish them,
let them kill them.   Let them be honoured for gods, that shall
procure the people this happiness, and preserve what they have
procured.   Let them have what glory or worship they will, what

plays they will or can exact of their worshippers: only let them work so that this felicity stand secure from enemy, pestilence, and all other inconveniences. Now tell me, what reasonable creature would liken such a State not unto Rome, but even to the house of Sardanapalus? which bygone king was so far given over to his pleasures that he caused it to be written upon his grave, that he only then possessed that which his luxury in his lifetime had wasted. Now if those fellows had but a king like this, that would indulge them in these impurities, and never control nor correct them in any such courses, they would be readier to erect a temple to him, and give him a flamen, than ever were the old Romans to do so unto Romulus.

CHAPTER XXI

Tully's opinion of the Roman commonwealth

But if he be scorned that said their commonwealth was most dishonest and dishonourable, and that these fellows regard not what contagion and corruption of manners do rage amongst them, so that their State may stand and continue; now shall they hear that it is not true that Sallust saith, that their commonwealth is only become vile and wicked, but that as Cicero saith, it is absolutely gone, it is lost, and nothing of it remains. For he brings in Scipio (him that destroyed Carthage) disputing of the commonwealth at such time as it was presaged that it would perish by that corruption which Sallust describes. For this disputation was at that time when one of the Gracchi was slain, from which point Sallust affirms all the great seditions to have had their origin (for in those books there is mention made of his death). Now Scipio having said (in the end of the second book)[1] that as in instruments that go with strings, or wind, or as in voices consorted, there is one certain proportion of discrepant notes unto one harmony, the least alteration whereof is harsh in the ear of the skilful hearer: and that this concord does consist of a number of contrary sounds, and yet all combined into one perfect musical melody: so in a city that is governed by reason, of all the highest, middle, and lowest estates, as of sounds, there is one true concord made out of discordant natures: and that which is harmony in music is unity in a city: that this is the firmest and surest bond of safety unto the commonwealth, and that a commonwealth can never stand without equity. When he has dilated at large of the benefit that equity brings to any government, and of the inconvenience following the absence thereof, then Pilus, one of the company, begins to speak, and entreats him to handle this question more fully, and make a larger discourse of

[1] *De Re Publ.* ii. 42.

justice, because it was then become a common report that a
commonwealth could not be governed without injustice and injury.
Hereupon Scipio agreed that this theme was to be handled more
exactly, and replied that what was as yet spoken of the commonwealth
was nothing; and that they could not proceed any farther until it
were proved not only that it is false that a commonwealth cannot
stand without injury, but also that it is true that it cannot stand
without exact justice. So the disputation concerning this point
being deferred until the next day following, in the third book it
is handled with great controversy. For Pilus undertakes the
defence of their opinion that hold that a State cannot be governed
without injustice, but with this provision, that they should not
think him to be of that opinion himself. And he argued very
diligently for this injustice against justice, endeavouring by likely
reasons and examples to show that the part he defended was useful
in the commonwealth, and that the contrary was altogether needless.
Then Laelius being entreated on all sides, stepped up, and took
the defence of justice in hand, and with all his knowledge laboured
to prove that nothing wrecked a city sooner than injustice, and that
no State could stand without perfect justice; which when he had
concluded, and the question seemed to be thoroughly discussed,
Scipio betook himself again to his intermitted discourse; and first
he rehearses and approves his definition of a commonwealth,
wherein he said it was *the estate of the commonalty*, then he determines this, that this *commonalty* is not meant of every gathering
of the multitude, but that it is a *society gathered together in one
consent of law, and in one participation of profit*.[1] Then he teaches
the profit of definitions in all disputations: and out of his definitions he gathers that there is only a commonwealth, that is,
there is only a good estate of the commonalty, where justice and
honesty have free execution, whether it be by a king, by nobles, or
by the whole people. But when the king becomes unjust (whom
he calls *tyrant* as the Greeks do), or the nobles be unjust (whose
combination he terms *faction*), or the people themselves be unjust (for which he cannot find a fit name, unless he should call
the whole company as he called the king a *tyrant*), that then this
is not a vicious commonwealth (as was affirmed the day before),
but, as the reasons depending upon those definitions proved most
directly, it is just no commonwealth at all; for it is no estate of the
people when the *tyrant* usurps on it by *faction*, nor is the commonalty a commonalty when it is not a society gathered together
in one consent of law and one participation of commodities, as he
had defined a commonalty before. Wherefore, seeing the Roman
estate was such as Sallust does decipher it to be, it was now no
dishonest or dishonourable commonwealth (as he affirmed), but it
was altogether no commonwealth at all; according unto the reasons

[1] *De Re Publ.* i. 25.

proposed in that discourse of a commonwealth before so many great princes and heads thereof; and as Tully himself, not speaking by Scipio or any other, but in his own person, doth demonstrate in the beginning of his fifth book: [1] where having first rehearsed that verse of Ennius where he saith:

> Moribus antiquis res stat Romana virisque,
> Old manners and old men upholden Rome,

'This verse,' quoth Tully, 'whether you respect the brevity, or the verity, me seemeth he spoke out as an oracle: for neither the men, unless the city had had such manners, nor the manners, unless the city had had such men, could either have founded or preserved a commonwealth of that magnitude of justice and empire. And therefore before these our days, the predecessors' conditions did still make the successors excel; and the worthy men still kept up the ordinances of honourable antiquity: but now, our age receiving the commonwealth as an excellent picture, but almost worn out with age, has not only no care to renew it with such colours as it presented at first, but never regarded it so much as to preserve but the bare draught and lineament of it: for what remainder is there now of those old manners which this poet says supported Rome? Do we not see them so clearly worn out of use, and now so far from being followed, that they are quite forgotten? What need I speak of these men? The manners perished for want of men, the cause whereof in justice we should not only be bound to give an account of, but even to answer it as a capital offence. It is not any misfortune, it is not any chance, but it is our own viciousness that has taken away the whole essence of our commonwealth from us, and left us only the bare name.'

This was Cicero's own confession, long after Africanus' death, whom he introduces as a disputant in this work of his *Of the Commonwealth*, but yet somewhat before the coming of Christ. Which mischiefs had they not been divulged until the increase of Christian religion, which of all those wretches would not have been ready to calumniate Christ for them? But why did their gods look to this no better, nor help to save the state of this commonwealth, whose loss and ruin Cicero bewails with such pitiful phrase, long before Christ came in the flesh? Nay, let the commenders thereof but observe in what case it was even then when it consisted of the ancient men and their manners, whether then it nourished true justice or no; and whether at that time it were honest indeed, or but glossed over in show! Which Cicero, not conceiving what he said, confesses in his relation thereof. But, by God's grace, we will consider that more fully elsewhere: for in the due place, I will do what I can to make a plain demonstration out of Cicero's own

[1] *De Re Publ.* v

definitions of the commonwealth and the people (spoken by
Scipio and justified by many reasons, either of Scipio's own, or
such as Tully gives him in this discourse) that the estate of Rome
was never any true commonwealth, because it never was guided by
true justice.   Indeed according to some other probable definitions,
and after a sort, it was a kind of commonwealth: but far better
governed by the antiquity of the Romans than by their posterity.
But there is not any true justice in any commonwealth whatsoever,
but in that whereof Christ is the founder and the ruler, if you
please to call that a commonwealth which we cannot deny is the
weal of the commonalty.   But if this name, being elsewhere so
common, seem too discrepant from our subject and phrase, truly
then there is true justice but in that city whereof that holy scripture
saith: 'Glorious things are spoken of thee, thou city of God.' [1]

CHAPTER XXII

*That the Roman gods never respected whether the city were
corrupted, and so brought to destruction, or no*

BUT to our present purpose: this commonwealth which they say
was so good and so laudable, before ever Christ came, was by the
judgment of their own most learned writers acknowledged to
be changed into a most dishonest and dishonourable one: nay, it
was become no commonweal at all, but was fallen into absolute
destruction by their own polluted conditions.   Wherefore to have
prevented this ruin, the gods that were the patrons thereof should
methinks have taken the pains to have given the people that
honoured them some precepts for reformation of life and manners,
seeing that they had bestowed so many temples, so many priests,
such variety of ceremonious sacrifices, so many festival solemnities,
so many and so great celebrations of plays and interludes upon them.
But these devils minded nothing but their own affairs: they respected
not how their worshippers lived: nay, their care was to see them
live like devils, only they bound them through fear to afford them
these honours.   If they did give them any good counsel, then let
it be produced to light and read, what laws given by the gods
were they that the Gracchi contemned that there should follow
turmoils and seditions in the city: show which precept of the gods
Marius or Cinna or Carbo violated, in their giving action unto the
civil wars, which they began upon such unjust causes, followed
with such cruelties and injuries, and ended in more injurious
cruelties: or what divine authorities Sulla himself broke, whose
life, deeds, and conditions to hear Sallust (and other true his-
torians) describe them, whose hair would not stand upright?   Who

[1] Ps. lxxxvii. 3.

is he now that will not confess that then the commonwealth fell absolutely? Who is he now that will dare to produce that sentence of Virgil for this corruption of manners, in the defence of their gods?

> Excessere omnes, adytis arisque relictis,
> Di, quibus imperium hoc steterat.[1]

> The gods by whom this empire stood, left all
> The temples and the altars bare.

But admit that this were true: then have they no reason to rail upon Christianity, or to say that the gods, being offended at that, did forsake them: because it was their predecessors' manners that long ago chased all their great multitude of little gods from the city altars like so many flies. But where was all this nest of deities, when the Gauls sacked the city, long before the ancient manners were contaminated? Were they present and yet fast asleep? The whole city was all subdued at that time, only the Capitol remained: and that had been surprised too, if the geese had not shown themselves better than the gods, and waked when they were all asleep. And hereupon did Rome fall almost into the superstition of the Egyptians that worship birds and beasts, for they henceforth kept a holy day, which they called the goose's feast. But this is but by the way. I come not yet to dispute of those accidental evils which are rather corporal than mental and inflicted by foes or misfortunes. I am now in discourse of the stains of the mind and manners, and how they first decayed by degrees, and afterward fell headlong into perdition: so that thence ensued so great a destruction to the commonwealth (though their city walls stood still unbattered) that their chiefest authors doubted not to proclaim it lost and gone. Good reason was it that the gods should abandon their temples and altars, and leave the town to just destruction, if it had condemned their advices of reformation. But what might one think (I pray ye) of those gods that would abide with the people that worshipped them, and yet would they never teach them any means to leave their vices and follow what was good?

CHAPTER XXIII

That the variety of temporal estates depends not upon the pleasure or displeasure of these devils, but upon the judgments of God Almighty

NAY, what say you to this, that these their gods do seem to assist them in fulfilling their desires, and yet are not able to restrain them from yielding to desires: for they that helped Marius, an unworthy base-born fellow, to originate and conduct such barbarous civil wars, to be made seven times consul, to die an old

[1] *Aen.* ii. 351-2.

man in his seventh consulship, and to escape the hands of Sulla, that immediately after bare down all before him, why did not these gods keep Marius from effecting any such bloody deeds or excessive cruelty? If his gods did not further him in these acts at all, then have we good advantage given us by their confession, that this temporal felicity which they so greatly thirst after may befall a man without the gods' furtherance; and that other men may be as Marius was, engirt with health, power, riches, honours, friends, and long life, and enjoy all these, in spite of the anger of the gods: and again, that other men may be as Regulus was, tortured in chains, slavery, misery, over-watchings, and torments, and perish in these extremities, do all the gods what they can to the contrary. And if our adversaries do acknowledge this, then must they needs confess that they do nothing to further their worshippers' interest, and consequently that all the honour given them is out of superfluity; for if they did rather teach the people the direct contraries to virtue and piety, the rewards whereof are to be expected after men's deaths, and if in these transitory and temporal benefits they can neither hinder those they hate, nor further those they love, why then are they followed with such zeal and fervency? why do you murmur as though the cause of the turbulent and lamentable times was the withdrawal of the influence of the offended gods, and hence take occasion to throw calumnious reproaches upon the Christian religion? If your gods have any power to hurt or profit men in these worldly affairs, why did they stick to that accursed Marius, and shrink from that honest Regulus? Does not this convict them of injustice and villainy? Do you think that there was any lack of their worship on the part of Regulus? Think not so: for you never read that Regulus was slacker in the worship of the gods than Marius was. Nor may you persuade yourselves that a corrupted course of life is the rather to be followed, because the gods were held more friendly to Marius than to Regulus: for Metellus, the most honest man of all the Romans, had five consuls to his sons, and lived happy in all temporal estate: and Catiline, that villainous wretch, was oppressed with misery and brought to naught in the war which his own guilt had hatched; and good men that worship that God who alone can give felicity, do shine, and are mighty in the true and surest happiness. Wherefore, when the contaminated conditions of that commonwealth did subvert it, the gods never put out their helping hands to stop this inundation of corruption into their manners, but rather made it more way, and gave the commonwealth a large pass unto destruction. Nor let them shadow themselves under goodness, or pretend that the cities' wickedness drove them away. No, no, they were all there, they are produced, they are convicted; they could neither help the city by their instructions, nor conceal themselves by their silence. I omit to relate how

Marius was commended unto the goddess Marica by the pitiful Minturnians in her wood, and how they made their prayers to her that she would prosper all his enterprises, and how he having shaken off his heavy desperation, returned with a bloody army even unto Rome itself: where what a barbarous, cruel, and more than most inhuman victory he obtained, let them, that wish to read it, look in those that have recorded it.   This as I said I omit: nor do I impute his murderous felicity unto any Marica, or I cannot tell whom, but unto the most secret judgment of the most mighty God to shut the mouths of our adversaries, and to free those from error that do observe with a discreet judgment and not with a partisan prejudice.   For if the devils have any power or can do anything at all in these affairs, it is no more than what they are permitted to do by the secret providence of the Almighty: and in this case they may be allowed to effect somewhat to the end that we should neither take too much pleasure in this earthly felicity, in that we see that wicked men like Marius may enjoy it; neither hold it as an evil, and therefore to be utterly refused, seeing that many good honest men, and servants of the true and living God, have possessed it in spite of all the devils in hell: and that we should not be so fond as to think that these unclean spirits are either to be feared for any hurt, or honoured for any profit they can bring upon man's fortunes.   For they are in power, but even as wicked men upon earth are, so that they cannot do what they please, but are mere ministers to His ordinance, whose judgments no man can either comprehend fully or reprehend justly.

CHAPTER XXIV

Of the acts of Sulla, wherein the devils showed themselves his main helpers and furtherers

Now as for Sulla himself, who brought all to such a pass, that the times before whereof he professed himself a reformer, in comparison with those that be brought forth, were wished for again; when he first of all set forward against Marius towards Rome, Livy writes that the entrails in the sacrifices were so fortunate that Postumius the soothsayer was willing to have himself kept under guard, under the penalty of losing his head, if all Sulla's intents resulted not (by the assistance of the gods) in a most wished and happy effect.   Behold now, the gods were not yet gone: they had not as yet forsaken their altars, when they did so plainly foreshow the event of Sulla's purposes: and yet they never endeavoured to mend Sulla's manners.   They refrained not from promising him great happiness; but never offered to suppress his wicked desires. Again, when he had undertaken the Asian war against Mithridates,

L. Titius was sent to him on a message, even from Jupiter himself, who sent him word that he should not fail to overcome Mithridates: no more he did indeed. And afterwards, when he endeavoured to re-enter the city, and to revenge himself and his injured friends upon the lives of the citizens, he was certified that a certain soldier of the sixth legion brought him another message from Jove, how that he had foretold him of his victory against Mithridates before, and how he promised him now the second time that he would give him power to recover the rule of the commonwealth from all his enemies, but not without much bloodshed. Then Sulla asking of what appearance the soldier was; when they had shown him, he remembered that it was he that brought him the other message in the war of Mithridates, and that he was the same man that now brought him this. What can be said to this now, that the gods should have such care to acquaint Sulla with the good events of these his wishes: and yet none of them have power to reform his foul conditions, being then about to set abroad such mischief by these domestic arms, as should not pollute, but even utterly abolish the state of the commonwealth? By this very act do they prove themselves (as I said heretofore) directly to be devils. And we do know, our scripture shows it us, and their own actions confirm it, that their whole care is to make themselves be reputed for gods, to be worshipped as divine powers, and to have such honours given them as shall put the givers and the receivers both into one desperate case, at that great day of the Lord. Besides, when Sulla came to Tarentum, and had sacrificed there, he descried in the chief lobe of the calf's liver a figure just like a crown of gold: and then Postumius, the soothsayer, answered him again, that it portended him a glorious victory, and commanded that he alone should eat of these entrails. And within a little while after, a servant of one Lucius Pontius came running in, crying out in prophetic manner: 'I bring news from Bellona, the victory is thine, Sulla': and then added, that the Capitol should be fired. Which when he had said, presently going forth of the tents, he returned the next day in greater haste than before, and said that the Capitol was now burned: and burned it was indeed. This now might quickly be done by the devil, both for ease in the knowledge of it, and speed in the relation. But now to speak to the purpose, mark but well what kind of gods these men would have that blaspheme Christ for delivering the hearts of the believers from the tyranny of the devil. The fellow cried out in his prophetic rapture: 'The victory is thine, O Sulla.' And to assure them that he spake by a divine instinct, he told them of a sudden event that should fall out soon after, in a place from which he, in whom this spirit spake, was a great way distant. But he never cried: 'Forbear thy villainies, O Sulla': those were left free to be executed by him with such horror, and committed with such outrage, as is unspeakable, after that victory which the bright sign of the crown in the calf's liver did prognosticate unto him. Now if they were good and just gods, and not wicked fiends, that had given such signs, then truly these entrails should have expressed the great mischiefs that should fall upon Sulla himself, rather than anything else: for that victory did not benefit his dignity so much, but it hurt his affections twice as much: for by it was his spirit elevated in vainglory, and he induced to abuse his prosperity without any moderation, so that these things made a greater massacre of his manners than he made of the citizens' bodies. But as for these horrid and lamentable events, the gods would never foretell him of them, either by entrails, prophecies, dreams, or soothsayings: for their fear was lest his enormities should be reformed, not lest his fortunes should be subverted. No, their endeavour was, that this glorious conqueror of his citizens might be captivated and conquered by the rankest shapes of viciousness, and by these be more strictly bound and enchained unto the subjection of the devils themselves.

CHAPTER XXV

How powerfully the devils incite men to villainies, by laying before them examples of divine authority (as it were) for them to follow in their villainous acts

WHO is he then (unless he be one of those that love to imitate such gods) that by this which is already laid open, does not see how great a grace of God it is to be separated from the society of those devils; and how strong they are in working mischief, by presenting their own examples as a divine privilege and authority, whereby men are licensed to work wickedness? Nay, they were seen, in a certain large plain of Campania, to fight a set battle amongst themselves, a little before the citizens fought that bloody conflict in the same place. For at first there were strange and terrible noises heard; and afterwards it was affirmed by many, that for certain days together one might see two armies in continual fight one against the other. And after the fight had ceased, they found the ground all trampled as with the steps of men and horses that had been made in that battle. If the deities were truly and really at war amongst themselves, why then indeed their example may give a sufficient privilege unto human conflicts (but by the way, let this be considered, that these deities in the mean space must either be very malicious, or very miserable). But if they did not fight, but only illuded the eyes of men with such a show, what intended they in this, but only that the Romans should think that they might lawfully wage civil wars, as having the practices of the gods themselves for their privileges? For presently upon this apparition the civil dissensions began to be kindled, and some bloody massacres had been effected before. And already were the hearts of many grieved at that lamentable act of a certain soldier, who in taking of the spoils of his slain foe, and discovering him by his face to be his own brother, with a thunder of curses upon those domestic quarrels, stabbed himself to the heart, and fell down dead by his brother's side. To envelop and overshadow the irksomeness of such events, and to increase the ardent thirst after more blood and destruction, did those devils (those false reputed gods) appear unto the Romans' eyes in such fighting figures, to animate the city not to be any whit in doubt to imitate such actions, as having the example of the gods for a lawful privilege for the villainies of men. And out of this cunning did these malevolent powers give command for the introduction of those stage plays, whereof we have spoken at large already, and wherein such dishonest courses of the gods were portrayed forth unto the world's eye, upon their stages and in the theatres, that all men (both those that believe that their gods did such acts, and those that do not believe it, but see how pleasing it is to them to behold such impurities) may hence be bold to take a free licence to imitate them, and practise to become like them in their lives. Lest any man therefore should imagine that the poets have rather done it as a reproach to the gods than as a thing by them deserved, when they have written of their fightings and squabbles one with another; to clear this misconstruction, they themselves have confirmed these poesies to deceive others, and have presented their combats and contentions, not only upon the stage by players, but even in the open fields by themselves. This was I enforced to lay down, because their own authors have made no doubt to affirm and record that the corrupt and rotten manners of the citizens had consumed the state of the commonwealth of Rome unto nothing, long before Christ Jesus came into the world: for which subversion of their state they will not call their gods into any question at all; but all the transitory miseries of mortality (which notwithstanding cannot make a good man perish whether he live or die) they are ready to heap on the shoulders of our Saviour Christ—our Christ, that hath so often poured His all-curing precepts upon the incurable ulcers of their damned conditions, when their false gods never put out a helping hand, never upheld this their religious commonwealth from ruining, but cankering the virtues that upheld it with their vile acts and examples, rather did all that they could to thrust it on unto destruction. No man (I think) will affirm that it perished because that

> Excessere omnes, adytis arisque relictis,
> Di . . .

The gods were gone, and left their altars bare—

as though th...
vices of the ci...
many presages fro virtue an...
they confirmed and e th m... taken at the wicked
selves as rulers of the s, soo s e ted t iro, no, there are too
and convict them to ha nd f throphecies (whereby
the Romans in these wars n pr nd extolled them-
with their own affections as d ne h wars), that prove
ver they been absent,
far transported
ds' instituations.

CHAPTER XX

*Of certain obscure instructions concerning ...nan... w...th
devils are said to have given in secret, wh e ll w ... a
taught in their public solemnities*

WHEREFORE seeing that this is so, seeing that filthines
founded with cruelties, all the gods' foulest ts and sh
(whether true or imaginary, by their wn com andments,
upon pain of their displeasure, if it were therwis), were set forth
to open view, and dedicated unto themse es in the most holy and
set solemnities, and produced as imitable spectacles to all men's
eyes: to what end is it then, that these d vils, who acknowledge
their own uncleanness by taking pleasure n such obscenities, by
being delighted with their own villainies and wickednesses as well
performed as invented; and by their exac ng thes celebrations of
modest men in such impudent manner, do onfess themselves the
authors of all pernicious and abhorred cours s; would seem (forsooth) and are reported to have given certain secret instructions
against evil manners, in their most private habitati s, and unto
some of their most selected servants? If it be so, take here then
an excellent observation of the craft and maliciousness of these
unclean spirits. The force of honesty and chastity is so great and
powerful upon man's nature, that all men, or almost all men, are
moved with the excellency of it; nor is there any man so wholly
abandoned to turpitude, but he hath some feeling of honesty left
him. Now because of the devil's depraved nature, we must note
that unless he sometime change himself into an angel of light
(as we read in our scriptures that he will do),[1] he cannot fully effect
his intention of deceit. Wherefore he spreads the blasting breath
of all impurity abroad, and in the meantime whispers a little air
of dissembled chastity within. He gives light unto the vilest
things, and keeps the best in the dark; honesty lieth hid, and
shame flies about the streets. Filthiness must not be acted but
before a great multitude of spectators: but when goodness is to be
taught, the auditory is little or none at all; as though purity were
to be blushed at, and uncleanness to be boasted of. But where

[1] 2 Cor. xi. 14.

are these rules... the devil...by be inveigled, and
the very inns... (but few)...es) remain unreformed.
such as are ho...which are... these good precepts of
such as are d...not yet... we are sure of, that before
But as for... ...even; ...stood, we beheld an in-
...elestial cha...t... where...together, and there saw a
...e very tem...of pe...sid... and a virgin goddess on the
...merable...ets o...s unto her; and there, foul and
...e rai...m ador... her. We could not see one modest
...kings...ed... actor amongst them all: but all was
...one ame... ...able filthiness. They knew well what that
...ons o...omi... and pronounced it for the nations to learn by
...y li... ...an...o carry home in their minds. Some there were
...ster...rt, that turned away their eyes from beholding
...estures of the players, and yet though they blushed to
...thi...rtificial beastliness, they gave scope unto their
disposition to learn it. ...or they durst not behold the impudent
gestures of the actors b...dly, for being shamed by the men; and
less durst they condemn the ceremonies of that deity whom they so
zealously adored. But that was presented in the temples, and in
public, which none will commit in their own private houses but in
secret. It were too great a wonder if there were any shame left
in those men of power to restrain them from acting that which their
very gods do teach them, even in their principles of religion,
telling them that they shall incur their displeasures if they do not
present them such shows. What spirit can that be, which doth
inflame bad minds with a worse instinct, which doth urge on the
committing of adultery, and feeds itself upon the sin committed,
but such a one as is delighted with such representations, filling
the temples with diabolical images, exacting the presenting of
loathsome iniquity in plays, muttering in secret I know not what
good counsels, to deceive and delude the poor remainders of
honesty, and professing in public all incitements to perdition, to
gather up whole harvests of men given over unto ruin?

CHAPTER XXVII

*What a great means of the subversion of the Roman estate the in-
troduction of those scurrilous plays was, which they surmised to be
propitiatory unto their gods*

TULLIUS, a grave man, who affected [1] to be a good philosopher, being about to be made aedile, cried out in the ears of the whole city,

[1] J. H. translated 'and a good philosopher.' St. Augustine, however, wrote
'philosophaster.'—ED.

that amongst the other duties of his magistracy he must needs go
and pacify Mother Flora [1] with the celebration of some solemn
plays: which plays, the more foully they were presented, the more
devotion was held to be shown. And in another place [2] (being then
consul) he says that when the city was in great extremity of ruin,
they were fain to present plays continually for ten days together;
and nothing was omitted which might help to pacify the gods, as
though it were not fitter to anger them with temperance than to
please them with luxury; and to procure their hate by honesty,
rather than to flatter them with such deformity. For the barbarous inhumanity of those men, for whose villainous acts the
gods were to be appeased, were it never so great, could not possibly
do more hurt than that filthiness which was acted as tending to
their appeasing, because that in this the gods will not be reconciled
unto them, but by such means as must needs produce a destruction
of the goodness of men's minds, in lieu of their preventing the
dangers imminent only over their bodies: nor will these deities
defend the city's walls until they have first destroyed all goodness
within the walls. This pacification of the gods, so obscene, so
impure, so wicked, so impudent, so unclean, whose actors the
Romans disenabled from all magistracy and freedom of city,
making them as infamous as they knew them dishonest: this pacification (I say), so beastly, and so directly opposite unto all truth
of religion and modesty, these fabulous inventions of their gods'
filthiness, these ignominious acts of the gods themselves (either
foully feigned, or more foully effected), the whole city learned both
by seeing and hearing: observing plainly that their gods were well
pleased with such presentations, and therefore they did both
exhibit them unto their idols and did imitate them themselves.
But as for that (I know not indeed well what) honest instruction,
and good counsel, which was taught in such secrecy, and unto so
few, that I am sure was not followed; if it be true that it were
taught because it was rather feared that too many would know it,
than suspected that any few would follow it.

CHAPTER XXVIII

Of the salvation attained by the Christian religion

WHY then do these men complain? think you because by the
name of Christ they see so many freed of these hellish bonds that
such unclean spirits held them in, and of the participation of the
same punishment with them? Their ungrateful iniquity hath
bound them so strongly in these devilish enormities that they
murmur and complain when they see the people flock unto the

[1] 2 *Verr.* v. 14, 36.   [2] 3 *Cat.* viii. 20.

church to these pure solemnities of Christ, where both sexes are so honestly distinguished by their several places; where they may learn how well to lead their temporal lives here, to become worthy of the eternal hereafter: where the holy doctrine of God's word is read from an eminent place, that all may hear it assure a reward to those that follow it, and a judgment to those that neglect it. Into which place if there chance to come any such as scoff at such precepts, they are presently either converted by a sudden power, or cured by a sacred fear: for there are no filthy sights set forth there, nor any obscenities to be seen, or to be followed; but there, either the commandments of the true God are propounded, His miracles related, His gifts commended, or His graces implored.

CHAPTER XXIX

An exhortation to the Romans to renounce their paganism

LET these rather be the objects of thy desires, thou courageous nation of the Romans, thou progeny of the Reguli, Scaevolae, Scipios, and Fabricii: long after these, discern but the difference between these and that luxurious, filthy, shameless malevolence of the devils. If nature have given thee any laudable eminence, it must be true piety that must purge and perfect it: impiety contaminates and consumes it. Now then, choose which of these to follow, that thy praises may arise, not from thyself that may be misled, but from the true God, who is without all error. Long ago wast thou great in popular glory: but then (as it pleased the providence of the high God) was the true religion wanting for thee to choose and embrace. But now, awake, and rouse thyself; it is now day; thou art already awake in some of thy children, in whose full virtue and constant sufferings for the truth we do justly glory: they, even these who fighting at all hands against the powers of iniquity, and conquering them all by dying undaunted, have purchased this possession for us with the price of their blood. To partake of which possession we do now invite and exhort thee, that thou wouldst become a citizen with the rest in that city wherein true remission of sins stands as a glorious sanctuary. Give no ear unto that degenerate brood of thine, which barks at the goodness of Christ and Christianity, accusing these times of badness, and yet desiring such as should be worse, by denying tranquillity to virtue, and giving security unto all iniquity: these times didst thou never approve, nor ever desiredst to secure thy temporal estate by them. Now, then, reach up at the heavenly ones; for which, take but a little pains, and thou shalt reap the possession of them unto all eternity. There shalt thou find no vestal fire, nor stone of the Capitol, but one true God, who will neither limit thy blessedness in quality, nor time, but give thee an empire, both universal, perfect, and eternal.[1] Be no longer led in blindness by these thy illuding and erroneous gods; cast them from thee, and taking up thy true liberty, shake off their damnable subjection. They are no gods, but wicked fiends; and all the empire they can give them is but possession of everlasting pain. Juno did never grieve so much that the Trojans (of whom thou descendest) should arise against the State of Rome, as these damned devils (whom as yet thou holdest for gods) do envy and repine, that mortal men should ever enjoy the glories of eternity. And thou thyself hast censured them with no obscure note, in affording them such plays, whose actors thou hast branded with express infamy. Suffer us then to plead thy freedom against all those impure devils that imposed the dedication and celebration of their own shame and filthiness upon thy neck and honour. Thou couldst remove and disenable the players of those uncleannesses from all honours: pray likewise unto the true God, to quit thee from those vile spirits that delight in beholding their own crimes, whether they be true (which is most ignominious) or feigned (which is most malicious). Thou didst well in clearing the state of thy city from all such scurrilous offscums as stage players: look a little further into it: God's Majesty can never delight in that which polluteth man's dignity. How then canst thou hold these powers, that loved such unclean plays, as members of the heavenly society, when thou holdest the men that only acted them as unworthy to be counted in the worst rank of the members of thy city? The heavenly city is far above thine, where truth is the victory, holiness the dignity, happiness the peace, and eternity the continuance. Far is it from giving place to such gods, if thy city do cast out such men. Wherefore if thou wilt come to this city, shun all fellowship with the devil. Unworthy are they of honest men's service that must be pleased with dishonesty. Let Christian reformation sever thee from having any commerce with those gods, even as the censor's view separated such men from partaking of thy dignities. But as concerning temporal felicity, which is all that the wicked desire to enjoy, and temporal affliction, which is all they seek to avoid, hereafter we mean to show, that the devils neither have nor can have any such power of either, as they are held to have (though if they had, we are bound rather to contemn them all than to worship them for these benefits, seeing that thereby we should utterly debar ourselves of that which they repine that we should ever attain). Hereafter (I say) shall it be proved, that they have no such power of those things, as these think they have, that affirm that they are to be worshipped for such ends. And here shall this book end.

[1] *Aen.* i. 278–9.

THE THIRD BOOK OF THE CITY OF GOD

CHAPTER I

Of the adverse casualties which only the wicked do fear, and which the world hath always been subject unto whilst it remained in paganism

WHAT we have already spoken I think is sufficient, concerning the depraved state of men's minds and manners, which is principally to be avoided; that in these cases these false imaginary gods did never endeavour to lighten their servants of any of these inconveniences, but rather added unto their loads and furthered their depravations. Now, I see it is time to take those evils in hand, which are the only things that these men are so loath to endure, above and beyond all others, as famine, sickness, war, invasion, thraldom, slaughter, and such other like, as we have recited in our first book: for these things alone are they, which evil men account for evils, that do not and cannot make men in any way evil. Nor are these wretches ashamed to give good things their due praise, and yet keep evil still themselves that are the praisers of good: being far more offended at the badness of their lands than of their lives; as if man were made to enjoy all things except himself. But notwithstanding all this, their gods (for all their dutiful observance) never did go about to restrain the effects of those evils which their servants are so sore afraid of, nor ever withheld them from lighting upon them; for the world was oppressed with diverse extreme and sore calamities at several times, long before the Redemption; and yet in those times what other gods but those idols were there worshipped in any part of the world except only amongst the Jews and by some other peculiar persons whom it pleased the unsearchable wisdom of the great God to illuminate? But because I study to be brief, I will not stand upon the world's miseries in general: only what is peculiar to Rome or the Roman Empire I mean to relate: that is, such inflictions as before the coming of Christ fell either upon the city itself, or upon such provinces as belonged unto it, either by conquest or society, as members of the body of that commonwealth, of those I mean to speak somewhat in particular.

CHAPTER II

Whether the gods, to whom the Romans and the Greeks exhibited like worship, had sufficient cause given them to let Troy be destroyed

FIRST therefore of Troy, or Ilium, whence the Romans claim the descent (for we may not omit nor neglect what we touched at in the first book). Why was Troy besieged, and destroyed by the

Greeks that adored the same gods that it did? The perjury of Laomedon the father (say some) was wreaked in this sack upon Priam the son. Well, then, it is true that Apollo and Neptune served as workmen under the same Laomedon, for otherwise the tale is not true that says that he promised them pay and broke his oath unto them afterwards. Now cannot I but marvel that such a great foreknower as Apollo was would work for Laomedon, and could not foretell that he would deceive him: nor is it decent to affirm that Neptune his uncle Jupiter's brother, and king of all the sea, should have no foresight at all in things to come. For Homer brings him in foretelling great matters of the progeny of Aeneas, whose successors built Rome (yet is Homer reported to have lived before the building of Rome), nay more, he saveth Aeneas from Achilles by a cloud, desiring to raise this perjured city of Troy though it were his own handiwork, as Virgil declareth of him.[1] Thus then these two gods, Neptune and Apollo, were utterly ignorant of Laomedon's intention to delude them, and built the walls of Troy for the thanks of thankless persons. Look now, whether it be a worse matter to put confidence in such gods, or to consume them. But Homer himself (it seems) did hardly believe this tale, for he makes Neptune to fight against Troy and Apollo for it; whereas the fable gives them both one cause of being offended, namely Laomedon's perjury. Let those therefore that believe such reports be ashamed to acknowledge such deities: and those that believe them not, let them never bring forward the Trojan's perjuries, nor marvel that the gods should punish perjuries at Troy and love them at Rome. For otherwise, how could it come to pass, that besides the abundance of all other corruption in the city of Rome, there should be such a great company in Catiline's conspiracy that lived only by their tongues' practice in perjury and their hands in murder? What other thing did the senators by taking bribes so plentifully and by so many false judgments? what other thing did the people by the misuse of their votes and the mishandling of the cases with which they dealt, but heap up the sin of perjury? For even in this universal corruption, the old custom of giving and taking oaths was still observed, but that was not for the restraint of wickedness by awe of religion, but to add perjury also unto the rest of their monstrous exorbitances.

[1] *Aen.* v. 810–11.

CHAPTER III

*That the gods could not justly be offended at the adultery of
Paris, using it so freely and frequently themselves*

WHEREFORE there is no reason to say that these gods who supported
the empire of Troy were offended with the Trojans' perjury, when
the Greeks did prevail against all their protections. Nor is it, as
some say in their defence, that the anger at Paris' adultery made
them give over Troy's defence, for it is their custom to practise sin
themselves, and not to punish it in others. 'The Trojans,' saith
Sallust, 'as I have heard, were the first founders and inhabitants
of Rome: those were they that came away with Aeneas, and wandered without any certain abode.' [1] If Paris' act were then to be
punished by the gods' judgments, it was either to fall upon the
Trojans, or else upon the Romans, because Aeneas' mother was
chief agent therein. But how should they hate it in Paris, when
they hated it not in Venus, one of their company, who (to omit
her other pranks) committed adultery with Anchises and by him
was begotten Aeneas. Or why should his fault anger Menelaus,
and hers please Vulcan? For I think the gods are so lacking in
jealousy of their wives as to vouchsafe mortal men to partake with
them in their loves. Some perhaps will say I scoff at these fables:
and handle not so grave a cause with sufficient gravity. Why then
if you please let us not believe that Aeneas is son to Venus; I am
content, if Romulus likewise be not held to be Mars' son. If the
one be so, why is not the other so also? Is it lawful for the gods
to meddle carnally with women, and yet unlawful for the men to
meddle carnally with goddesses? A hard, or rather an incredible
condition, that what was lawful for Mars by Venus' law should
not be lawful for Venus by her own law! But they are both
confirmed by the Roman authority; for Caesar of late believed no
less that Venus was his grandmother, than Romulus of old believed
that Mars was his father.

CHAPTER IV

*Of Varro's opinion, that it is meet in policy that some men
should feign themselves to be begotten of the gods*

BUT do you believe this? will some say; not I truly. For Varro,
one of their most learned men, doth (though faintly, yet almost
plainly) confess that they all are false. But that it is profitable for
the cities (saith he) to have their greatest men, their generals and

[1] *Catil.* 6.

governors, believe that they are begotten of gods, though it be never so false: that their minds gaining confidence from the sense of divine origin may be the more daring to undertake, more fervent to act, and so more fortunate to perform affairs of value. Which opinion of Varro (by me here laid down) you see opens a broad way to the falsehood of this belief, and teacheth us to know that many such fictions may be inserted into religion, whensoever it shall seem useful unto the state of the city to invent such fables of the gods. But whether Venus could bear Aeneas by Anchises, or Mars beget Romulus of Sylvia, Numitor's daughter, that we leave as we find it, undiscussed. For there is almost such a question arisen in our scriptures; whether the wicked angels did commit fornication with the daughters of men, and whether thereupon came giants, that is, huge and powerful men, who increased and filled all the earth.[1]

CHAPTER V

That it is altogether unlikely that the gods revenged Paris'
fornication, since they permitted Rhea's to pass unpunished

WHEREFORE now let us argue both the cases in one. If what we read of Aeneas' and Romulus' mothers be certain, how can it be that the gods should disapprove of the adulteries of mortal men, tolerating it so fully and freely in these particulars? If it be not certain, howsoever, yet cannot they distaste the dishonesties of men, that are truly acted, seeing they take pleasure in their own, though they be but feigned. Besides, if that of Mars with Rhea be of no credit, why then, no more is this of Venus with Anchises. Then let not Rhea's case be defended by producing a similar divine illustration. She was a virgin priest of Vesta, and therefore with far more justice should the gods have scourged the Romans for her offence than the Trojans for that of Paris: for the ancient Romans themselves did punish such vestals as they took in this offence by burying them alive: never sentencing others who were faulty in this kind to death (but ever to some smaller penalty), so great was their study to correct the offences of persons appertaining to religion with all severity above others.

CHAPTER VI

Of Romulus' murder of his brother, which the gods never revenged

NOW I will say more. If those deities took such grievous and severe displeasure at the enormities of men that for Paris' misdemeanour they would needs utterly subvert the city of Troy

[1] Gen. vi. 4.

by fire and sword: much more then ought the murder of Romulus'
brother to incense their furies against the Romans, than the rape
of Menelaus' wife against the Trojans. Parricide in the first
origin of a city is far more odious than adultery in the wealth
and height of it. Nor is it at all pertinent unto our purpose,
whether this murder were commanded or committed by Romulus,
which many impudently deny, many do doubt, and many do
dissemble. We will not entangle ourselves in the labyrinth of
history upon so laborious a quest. Once, sure it is, Romulus'
brother was murdered, and that neither by open enemies, nor by
strangers. If Romulus either willed it, or wrought it, so it is:
Romulus was rather the chief of Rome than Paris of Troy. Why
should the one then set all his gods against his country for but
ravishing another man's wife, and the other obtain the protection
of the same gods for murdering his own brother? If Romulus be
clear of this imputation, then is the whole city guilty of the same
crime none the less, in giving so total an assent unto such a sup-
position; and instead of killing a brother, hath done worse in
killing a father. For both the brethren were fathers and founders
to it alike, though villainy barred the one from dominion. There is
small reason to be shown (in my opinion) why the Trojans deserved
so ill that their gods should leave them to destruction, and the
Romans so well that they would stay with them to their augmentation; unless it be this, that being so overthrown and ruined
in one place, they were glad to fly away to practise their illusions
in another; nay, they were more cunning than this; they both
stayed still at Troy to deceive (after their old custom) such as
afterwards were to inhabit there; and likewise departed unto
Rome, that having a greater scope to use their impostures there,
they might have more glorious honours assigned them to feed
their vainglorious desires.

CHAPTER VII

Of the subversion of Ilium by Fimbria, a captain of Marius' faction

IN the first heat of the civil wars, what had poor Ilium done that
Fimbria, the veriest villain of all Marius' faction, should raze it
down with more fury and cruelty than ever the Grecians had
shown upon it before? For in their conquest, many escaped
captivity by flight, and many avoided death by captivity. But
Fimbria charged in an express edict that not a life should be
spared; and made one fire of the city and all the creatures within it.
Thus was Ilium requited, not by the Greeks whom her wrongs
had provoked, but by the Romans whom her ruins had propagated:
their gods in this case (alike adored of both sides) doing just

nothing; or rather, being able to do just nothing. What, were the gods gone from their shrines that protected this town since the repairing of it after the Grecian victory? If they were, show me why. For the better citizens I find, the worse are the gods. They shut out Fimbria, to keep all for Sulla; and so in his anger he set the town and them on fire, and burned them both into dust and ashes. And yet in meantime Sulla's side was better, and even now was he working out his power by force of arms; his good beginnings as yet felt no crosses. How then could the Ilians have dealt more honestly or justly or more worthily of the protection of Rome than to save a city of Romans, for better ends, and to keep out a parricide of his country's common good? But how they fared let the defenders of these gods observe. They forsook the Ilians being adulterers, and left their city to the fires of the Greeks, that from her ashes chaster Rome might arise. But why did they leave her the second time, being Rome's allies, and not rebelling against her noble daughter, but keeping her faith sincerely unto Rome's better faction? Why did they let her be demolished so utterly, not by the valorous Grecians, but by a barbarous Roman? Or, if the gods favoured not Sulla's endeavours, for whom this city kept herself, why did they attend his fortunes with such happy success elsewhere? Does not this prove them rather flatterers of the fortunate than favourers of the wretched? And therefore they had not forsaken Ilium utterly when it was utterly destroyed; no, no, the devils will still keep a watchful eye for advantage to deceive. For when all the images were burned together with the town, only Minerva was found under all the ruins of her temple, as Livy writes, untouched; not that it should be said: 'You patron gods that always Troy protect': [1] but that it should not be said: 'The gods were gone and left their altars bare' in their defence. They were permitted to save that image, not that they might thereby prove themselves powerful, but that they might thereby be proved to have been present.

CHAPTER VIII

Whether it was convenient to commit Rome to the custody of the Trojan gods

WHEREFORE seeing Troy had left so plain a lesson for all posterity to observe; what discretion was there shown in the commending of Rome to the protection of the Trojan gods? Oh, but, will some say, they were settled at Rome when Fimbria spoiled Ilium. Were they so? Whence comes the image of Minerva then? But well: it may be they were at Rome when Fimbria razed Ilium, and

[1] Virg. *Aen.* ix. 247.

at Ilium when the Gauls sacked Rome. And being quick of
hearing, and swift in motion, as soon as ever the geese called them,
they came all on a cluster, to defend what was left, the Capitol.
But they were not called soon enough to look to the rest, or else
it should not have been as it was.

CHAPTER IX

*Whether it be credible that the gods procured the peace that
lasted all Numa's reign*

IT is thought also that these are they that helped Numa Pompilius,
Romulus' successor, to preserve that continual peace that lasted
all the time of his reign, and to shut the gates of Janus' temple;
and that it was because he deserved it at their hands, in instituting
so many sacrifices for the Romans to offer unto their honour.   In
truth, the peace that this prince procured was thankworthy, could
he have applied it accordingly, and (by avoiding so pernicious a
curiosity) have taken more pains in inquiry after the true divinity.
But being as it was, the gods never gave him that quiet leisure:
but it may be they had not deluded him so foully had they not
found him so idle.   For the less that his business was, the more
time had they to entrap him: for Varro records all his courses and
endeavours to associate himself and his city with those imaginary
gods: all which (if it please God) shall be rehearsed in their due
place.   But now, since we are to speak of the benefits which are
pretended to come from those feigned deities, peace is a good
benefit: but it is a benefit given by the true God only, as the rain,
the sun, and all other helps of man's transitory life are; which are
common even to the ungracious and ungrateful persons as well as
the most thankful.   But if these Roman gods had any power to
bestow such a benefit as peace is upon Numa, or upon Rome, why
did they never do it after, when the Roman Empire was in greater
majesty and magnificence?   Were their sacrifices more powerful
at their first institution than at any time after?   Nay, many of
them then were not as yet instituted, but remained unspoken of
until afterwards, and then they were instituted indeed, and kept
for the sake of obtaining benefit.   How cometh it then to pass that
Numa's forty-three, or as some say, thirty-nine years were passed
in such full peace? and yet afterwards when those sacrifices were
instituted and celebrated, and the gods whom these solemnities
invited were now become the guardians and patrons of the State,
after so many hundred years from Rome's foundation until the
reign of Augustus, there is but one year reckoned, and that is held
as wholly miraculous, which, falling after the first African war, gave
the Romans just leave to shut up the gates of war's temple?

CHAPTER X

Whether the Romans might justly desire that their city's estate should arise to pre-eminence by such furious wars, when it might have rested firm and quiet, in such a peace as Numa procured

WILL they reply (think you) that the imperial state of Rome had no other means of augmentation but by continuance of wars, nor any fitter course to diffuse the honour thereof than this? A fit course surely! Why should any empire climb to greatness by disquiet? In this little world of man's body, is it not better to have a mean stature with an unmoved health, than a huge bigness with intolerable sickness? To take no rest at the point where thou shouldst rest, the end; but still to confound the greater growth with the greater grief? What evil had there been, nay, what good had there not been if those times had lasted that Sallust so applauded, saying: 'Kings in the beginning (for this was the first imperial name on earth) were diverse in their goodness: some exercised their corporal powers, some their spiritual, and men's lives in those times were without all exorbitance of habit or affect, each one keeping in his own compass'? [1] Why should the empire be advanced by those practices that Virgil so detests, saying:

> Deterior donec paulatim et decolor aetas
> Et belli rabies, et amor successit habendi? [2]

> Until perverse declining times succeed:
> World-frighting wars, and ill-pretended need?

But indeed the Romans had a just defence for their so continued contentions and wars: because, their foes engirding them with such universal invasions, it was sheer necessity to save themselves, and not their endeavour to become powerful over others, that put weapons into their hands. Well, be it so. For (as Sallust writes) when they had well settled their estate by laws, customs, and possessions, and seemed sufficiently potent, then, as it is in most affairs of mortality, out of their eminence arose envy in others, which armed many of their neighbour kings against them, and withheld most of their reputed friends from assisting them; the rest standing afraid, and afar off. But the Romans themselves, watchful and active, cheered up one another to encounter the foe with courage, standing in their arms as the bulwarks of their freedom, their country, and their kindred. And having made their virtue break through all mists of opposed dangers, they aided those that had helped them, returning more gain of friendship to their estate by being the agents of bounty rather than the objects, by doing good turns to others, rather than by receiving such of others.

[1] *Catil.* 2.   [2] *Aen.* viii. 326–7.

In these forms of augmenting herself, Rome kept a good decorum. But now, in Numa's reign, were there any injuries of enemy or invasions, concurring to disturb this peace of his time, or were there not? If Rome were as then molested with wars, and yet did not oppose hostility with hostility; then those means that kept the foe from being overthrown in fight, and yet without strokes compelled them to remain quiescent, those very means alone should be still of power to shut Janus' gates, and keep this peace continually in Rome. Which if it were not in their power to do, then verily the Romans had not their peace as long as it pleased the gods to allow it them, but as long as the neighbour princes were unwilling to invade and trouble them; unless those gods will dare to sell that which lies not in theirs but another's power, namely, what he has willed or not willed. These devils are indeed concerned to work upon men's infirmities as far as they are permitted by their peculiar depravity, whether they work with terrors or with incitations. But howsoever, were they of this power always, and were they not controlled by a superior sovereignty, they would still be practising their authorities in wars and slaughters: which ordinarily are rather the effects of mortal men's peculiar passions and affections, than direct practices of the damned spirits.

CHAPTER XI

Of the statue of Apollo at Cumae, that shed tears (as men thought) for the Grecians' miseries, though he could not help them

NOTWITHSTANDING that there are many of these wars and conquests that fall out quite against those gods' likings, the Roman history itself (to omit those fables that do not tell one truth for a thousand lies) shall give clear proof; for therein we read that the statue of Cumaean Apollo, in the time of the Romans' wars against the Achaians and King Aristonicus, did persist four days together in continual weeping: which prodigy amazing the soothsayers, they held it fit to cast the statue into the sea; but the ancients of Cumae dissuaded it, and showed them that it had done so likewise in the wars both against Antiochus and Perseus, testifying also, that both these wars succeeding fortunately unto Rome, the senate sent their gifts and oblations unto the statue of Apollo. And then, the soothsayers having learned wit, answered that the weeping of Apollo was lucky to the Romans, because Cumae was a Greek colony, and that the statue's tears did but portend mishap unto the country from whence it came, namely unto Greece. And soon after they heard how Aristonicus was taken prisoner, and this was the cause of Apollo's woes, shown in his tears. And as touching this point, not unfitly, though fabulously, are the devil's tricks plainly discovered in the fictions of the poets. Diana was sorry for Camilla in Virgil;[1] and Hercules wept for the death of Pallas.[2] And it may be that upon this ground Numa in his great peace given him (he neither knew nor sought to know by whom), bethinking himself in his idleness unto what gods he should commit the preservation of the Romans' fortunes (never dreaming that it is only the great and almighty God that has regard of these inferior things), and remembering himself that the gods that Aeneas brought from Troy could neither preserve the estate of the Trojans, nor that of the Lavinians founded by Aeneas, into any good continuance, thought fit to seek out some others, to join with the former which had gone with Romulus to Rome, and that were afterwards to go at the destruction of Alba, either to keep them from running away, or to help them when they saw them too weak.

CHAPTER XII

How fruitless their multitude of gods was unto the Romans, who introduced them, beyond the institution of Numa

NOR could Rome be content with those sacrifices which Numa had in such plentiful measure prescribed, for it had not as yet the great temple of Jupiter. For it was Tarquin that built the Capitol a good while after. And Aesculapius came afterwards from Epidaurus unto Rome, that he being a most expert physician, might practise in so famous a city with the greater credit. The mother of the gods also (of whence, who can tell) came thither from Pessinus, it being a thing unmeet for the son to be the chief god of the Capitol, and the mother to lie obscured I know not where: but if she be the mother of all the gods, she did not follow all her children unto Rome, but left some to follow her thither. I wonder whether she were dam unto Cynocephalus, that came out of Egypt long after or no. Whether the goddess Febris be one of her children or no, let Aesculapius, her nephew, look to that. But wheresoever she was born, I hope the stranger gods dare not call a goddess base that is a Roman citizen. Well, Rome being placed under the protection of so many gods (as who can reckon up?), both of Italians and foreigners, both of heaven, earth, hell, seas, fountains, and rivers, and, as Varro says, both certain and uncertain, and as it is in creatures, both male and female of all these several kinds—methinks that Rome having all these to be her tutors should never have tasted of such intolerable troubles as I mean to relate briefly out of their huger multitude. The great smoke she sent up was like a beacon, and called to many gods for her defence: unto all which, the priests erecting several monuments, and several

[1] *Aen.* xi. 836–49.   [2] *Aen.* x. 456–69.

mysteries, inflamed the fury of the true God in far greater measure, to whom only all these institutions rightfully belong. Truly, Rome thrived a great deal better when she had far fewer protectors: but growing greater, like as a ship calls in more sailors, so called she in more gods: doubting (I think) that those few (under whom she had passed a peaceable revolution before, in comparison of that that followed) were not now of sufficiency to defend her greatness, it being so much augmented. For at first, under the kings themselves (excepting Numa, of whom we spake before), what a mischievous beginning of dissension was that, wherein Romulus killed his one and only brother!

CHAPTER XIII

By what right the Romans attained their first wives

IN like manner, neither Juno (for all that she was now as her husband was, good friends with the Romans) nor Venus could help her son's progeny to honest and honourable marriages, but suffered this lack to grow so hurtful unto them that they were driven to get them wives by force, and soon after were compelled to go into the field against their wives' own fathers; and the wretched women being yet scarcely reconciled to their husbands for this wrong offered them, were now endowed with their fathers' murders and kindred's blood; but in this conflict the Romans had the luck to be conquerors. But oh, what worlds of wounds, what numbers of funerals, what oceans of bloodshed, did those victories cost! For one only father-in-law Caesar, and for one only son-in-law Pompey (the wife of Pompey and daughter to Caesar being dead), with what true feeling and just cause of sorrow doth Lucan cry out:

> Bella per Emathios plus quam civilia campos,
> Jusque datum sceleri canimus . . .[1]

> Wars worse than civil in the Emathian plains,
> And right left spoil to rage we sing . . .

Thus then the Romans conquered, that they might now return and embrace the daughters with arms stained with the blood of their fathers: nor durst the poor creatures weep for their slaughtered parents, for fear to offend their conquering husbands: but all the time of the battle stood with their vows in their mouths and knew not for which side to offer them. Such marriages Bellona (and not Venus) bestowed upon the Romans: or perhaps Alecto, that filthy hellish fury, now that Juno was agreed with them, had more power upon their bosoms now than she had then, when Juno

[1] *Phars.* i. 2.

entreated her help against Aeneas.   Truly Andromache's captivity was far more tolerable than these Roman marriages; for though she lived servilely, yet Pyrrhus, after he had once embraced her, would never kill Trojan more.   But the Romans slaughtered their own stepfathers in the field, whose daughters they had already enjoyed in their beds.   Andromache's estate secured her from further fears, though it freed her not from precedent sorrows: but these poor souls being matched to those stern warriors, could not but fear at their husbands going to battle, and wept at their return, having no way to freedom either by their fears or tears.   For they must either (in piety) bewail the death of their friends and kinsfolk, or (in cruelty) rejoice at the victories of their husbands.   Besides (as war's chance is variable), some lost their husbands by their fathers' swords; and some lost both, by the hand of each other. For it was no small war that Rome at that time waged.   It came to the besieging of the city itself, and the Romans were forced to rely upon the strength of their walls and gates, which being got open by a wile, and the foe being entered within the walls, even in the very market-place was there a most woeful and wicked battle, struck betwixt the fathers-in-law and the sons.   And here were the ravishers conquered, and driven to fly into their own houses, to the great stain of all their precedent (though badly and bloodily gotten) conquests: for here Romulus himself, despairing of his soldiers' valour, prayed unto Jupiter to make them stand, and hereupon got Jupiter his surname of Stator.   Nor would these butcheries have ever been brought unto any end, but that the silly ravished women came running forth with torn and dishevelled hair, and falling at their parents' feet, with passionate entreaties, instead of hostile arms, appeased their justly enraged valours. And then was Romulus, that could not endure to share with his brother, compelled to divide his kingdom with Tatius, the king of the Sabines: but how long would he tolerate them, that misliked the fellowship of his own twin-born brother?   So Tatius being slain, he, to become the greater deity, took possession of the whole kingdom.   What rights of marriage were these, what firebrands of war; what leagues of brotherhood, affinity, union, or deity! And ah, what lives the citizens lastly led, under so huge a bead-roll of gods' guardians!   You see what copious matter this subject affords, but that our intention bids us remember what is to follow, and falls to discourse on other particulars.

CHAPTER XIV

*How impious that war was, which the Romans began with the Albans,
and of the nature of those victories which ambition seeks to obtain*

BUT when Numa was gone, what did the succeeding kings? Oh,
how tragical (as well on the Romans' side as on the Albans') was
that war between Rome and Alba! Because (forsooth) the peace
of Numa was grown loathsome, therefore must the Romans and
the Albans begin alternate massacres, to so great an endamaging
of both their estates: and Alba, the daughter of Ascanius, Aeneas'
son (a more appropriate mother unto Rome than Troy), must by
Tullus Hostilius' provocation be compelled to fight with Rome
itself, her own daughter. And fighting with her, she was afflicted,
and did afflict, until the continual conflicts had utterly tired both
the parties. And then they were fain to put the final ending of
the whole war to six brethren, three Horatii on Rome's side, and
three Curiatii on Alba's. So two of the Horatii fell by the three
other: and the three other fell by the third only of the Horatii.
Thus got Rome the upper hand, yet so hardly that of six com-
batants only one survived. Now who were they that lost on both
sides? Who were they that lamented but Aeneas' progeny,
Ascanius' posterity, Venus' offspring, and Jupiter's children?
For this war was worse than civil, where the daughter city bore arms
against the mother. Besides, this brethren's fight was closed with
a horrid and abominable mischief. For in the time of the league
between both cities, a sister of the Horatii was espoused to one
of the Curiatii, who seeing her brother return with the spoils
of her dead spouse, and bursting into tears at this heavy sight, was
run through the body by her own brother in his heat and fury.
There was more true affection in this one poor woman (in my
judgment) than in all the whole Roman nation besides. She did
not deserve to be blamed for bewailing that he was slain to whom
she owed her faith (or that her brother had slain him to whom he
himself perhaps had promised his sister). For pious Aeneas is
commended in Virgil for bewailing him whom he had slain as an
enemy.[1] And Marcellus, viewing the fair city Syracuse, being then
about to be made a prey to ruin by the arms of his expedition,
revolving the inconstancy of mortal affairs, pitied it, and bewailed
it. I pray you then give thus much leave to a poor woman, in
tender affection, faultlessly to bewail her spouse, slain by her
brother, since warlike men have been praised for deploring their
enemy's estate in their own conquests. But when this one wretched
soul lamented thus that her love had lost his life by her brother's
hand, contrariwise did all Rome rejoice that she had given their

[1] *Aen.* x. 821–8.

mother so mighty a defeat, and exulted in the plenty of the allied blood that she had drawn. What face then have you to talk of your victories and your glories hereby gotten? Cast but aside the mask of mad opinion, and all these villainies will appear naked, to view, peruse, and judge. Weigh but Alba's cause and Troy's together, and you shall find a full difference. Tullus began these wars, only to renew the discontinued valours and triumphs of his countrymen. From this ground arose these horrid wars between kindred and kindred, which notwithstanding Sallust does but skim over, *sicco pede*: for having briefly recollected the precedent times, when men lived without aspiring or other desires, each man contenting himself with his own, 'But after that Cyrus,' quoth he, 'in Asia, and the Lacedaemonians and Athenians in Greece, began to subdue the countries and cities within their reaches, then desire of sovereignty grew to be a common cause of war, and opinion placed the greatest glory in the largest empire,'[1] etc. Thus far he. This desire of sovereignty is a deadly corrosive to human spirits. This made the Romans triumph over Alba, and gave the happy success of their mischiefs the style of glories. Because, as our Scripture says: 'The wicked maketh boast of his heart's desire, and the unjust dealer blesseth himself.'[2] Take off then these deluding veils from things, and let them appear as they are indeed. Let none tell me, he or he is great, because he has coped with and conquered such and such a one. Gladiators can fight and conquer, and those bloody acts of theirs in their combat do never pass unpraised. But I hold it better that a man's name should be exposed to all taint of idleness, than that he should purchase renown from such bad employment. But if two gladiators should come upon the stage, one being the father, and another the son, who could endure such a spectacle? How then can glory attend the arms of the daughter city against the mother? Do ye make a difference in that their field was larger than the gladiators' stage, and that they fought not in view of the theatre but the whole world, presenting a spectacle of eternal impiety both to the present times and to all posterity? But your great guardian gods bore all this unmoved, sitting as spectators of this tragedy, whilst for the three Curiatii that were slain, the sister of the Horatii must be stabbed by the hand of her own brother, to make even the number with her two other brethren, that Rome's conquest might cost no less blood than Alba's loss did: which as the fruit of the victory was utterly subverted; the very place which the gods (after Ilium, which the Greeks destroyed, and Lavinium, where Latinus placed fugitive Aeneas as king) had chosen to be their third place of habitation. But it may be they were gone hence also, and so it came to be razed: yes sure, all they that kept the state of it up, were departed from their shrines. Then they

[1] *Catil.* 2.   [2] Ps. x. 23.

left Alba where Amulius had reigned, having thrust out his brother,
and went to dwell at Rome, where Romulus had reigned, having
killed his brother.   Nay, but before this demolition (say they) the
people of Alba were all transported unto Rome, to make one city
of both.   Well, be it so, yet the city, that was the seat royal of
Ascanius, and the third habitation of the Trojan gods, was utterly
demolished.   And much blood was spilt before they came to make
this miserable confusion of both these peoples together.   Why
should I particularize the often renovation of these wars under so
many several kings; which when they seemed to be ended in
victory, began so often again in slaughters; and after combination
and league, broke out so fresh between kindred and kindred, both
in the predecessors and their posterity?   No vain emblem of their
misery was that continual standing open of Janus' gate: so that for
all the help of these god guardians there was not one king of them
that continued his reign in peace.

CHAPTER XV

Of the lives and deaths of the Roman kings

BUT how ended their kings still?   As for Romulus, let that flattering fable look to him, which hath sent him up into heaven.   Let
some of their own writers judge, that affirm him torn in pieces by
the senate for his pride, and that I know not who, one Julius
Proculus, was suborned to say that he appeared unto him, commanding him to bid Rome give him divine honour, and so was the
fury of the people pacified.   Besides, an eclipse of the sun falling
out at the same time, wrought so upon the ignorance of the rude
vulgar, that they ascribed all this unto Romulus' worth and glories.
As though that if the sun had mourned, as they thought it did,
they should not rather imagine that it was because Romulus was
murdered, and therefore that the sun turned his light from such a
villainy; as it did indeed when our Lord and Saviour was crucified
by the bloody and reprobate Jews.[1]   That the eclipse which befell
at our Saviour's death was quite against the regular course of the
stars is hence most plain, because it was the Jews' Easter, which is
continually kept at the full of the moon.   But the regular eclipse
of the sun never happens but in the changing of the moon.   Now
Cicero intimates plainly that this admission of Romulus into
heaven was rather imagined than performed, in the passage where,
in Scipio's words speaking of his praise, 'He attained so much,'
saith he, 'that being not to be found after the sun's eclipse, he was
accounted as admitted into the number of the gods: which opinion
no man without admirable merit of virtue can purchase.'[2]   Now

[1] Luke xxiii. 44, 45.   [2] De Re Publ. ii. 10.

whereas he says that he was not to be found, he glances doubtless either at the secrecy of the murder, or intimates the violence of the tempest.   For other writers add unto this eclipse a sudden storm, which either was the agent or the occasion of Romulus' murder. Now Tully in the same books,[1] speaking of Hostilius (third king after Romulus), who was stricken to death with thunder, says, that he was not reckoned amongst the gods, because that which was proved true (that is, that which they believed was so) in Romulus the Romans would not debase, by making it too common, in giving it to the one as well as the other.   And in his *Invectives* he says plainly: 'It is our goodwill and fame that hath made Romulus (this city's founder) a god';[2] to show that it was not so indeed, but only spread into a report by their goodwill to him for his worth and virtues.   But in his dialogue called *Hortensius*, disputing of regular eclipses, he says more plainly: 'To produce such a darkness as was made by the eclipse of the sun at Romulus' death.'[3]   Here he feared not to say directly his death, because he filled the role of a disputant, rather than of a panegyrist.   But now for the other kings of Rome, excepting Numa and Ancus Martius, that died of infirmities, what horrible ends did they all come to!   Hostilius, the subverter of Alba, as I said, was consumed, together with his whole house, by lightning.   Tarquinius Priscus was murdered by his predecessor's sons: and Servius Tullius by the villainy of his son-in-law Tarquin the Proud, who succeeded him in his kingdom. Nor yet were any of the gods gone from their shrines for all this so heinous a parricide committed upon this so good a king, though it be affirmed that they served wretched Troy in worse manner, in leaving it to the licentious fury of the Greeks only for Paris' adultery.   Nay, Tarquin having shed his father-in-law's blood, seized on his estate himself.   This parricide got his crown by his stepfather's murder, and afterwards glorying in monstrous wars and massacres, even built the Capitol up with hence-got spoils.   This wicked man the gods were so far from forsaking that they sat and looked on him, nay and would have Jupiter their principal to sit and sway all things in that stately temple, namely in that black monument of parricide.   For Tarquin was not innocent when he built the Capitol, and for his after-guilt incurred expulsion.   Foul and inhuman murder was his very ladder to that state whereby he had his means to build the Capitol.   And whereas the Romans expelled him from the State and city afterwards, the cause of that (namely Lucretia's rape) grew from his son and not from him, who was both ignorant and absent when that was done: for then was he at the siege of Ardea, and fighting for the Romans' good.   Nor know we what he would have done had he known of the crime of his son; yet without any trial or judgment the people expelled him from his empire: and having charged his

[1] *De Re Publ.* ii. 17.   [2] 3 *Cat.* 1.   [3] Frag. 39.

army to abandon him, took them in at the gates, and shut him out. But he himself after he had plagued the Romans (by their borderers' means) with extreme wars, and yet at length being not able to recover his estate, because his friends failed him, retired (as it is reported) unto Tusculum, a town fourteen miles from Rome, and there enjoying a quiet and private estate, lived peaceably with his wife, and died far more happily than his father-in-law did, who fell so bloodily by his means, and with his own daughter's consent, as it is credibly affirmed: and yet this Tarquin was never surnamed cruel nor wicked by the Romans, but the Proud; it may be because their own pride would not let them bear with his. As for the crime of killing that good king his stepfather, they showed how light they made of that, in making him murder the king, wherein I make a question whether the gods were not guilty in a deeper manner than he, by rewarding so highly a guilt so horrid, and not leaving their shrines all at that instant when it was done; unless some will say for them, that they still stayed at Rome to take a deeper revenge upon the Romans, rather than to assist them, seducing them with vain victories, and tossing them in unceasing turmoils. Thus lived the Romans in those so happy times under their kings, even until the expelling of Tarquin the Proud, which was about two hundred and forty-three years together, paying so much blood and so many lives for every victory they got, and yet hardly enlarging their empire the distance of twenty miles' compass without the walls. How far then have they to conquer, and what store of strokes to share, until they come to conquer a city of the Getulians!

CHAPTER XVI

Of the first Roman consuls; how the one expelled the other out of his country, and he himself, after many bloody murders, fell by a wound given him by his wounded foe

UNTO these times, add the other, wherein (as Sallust says [1]) things were modestly and justly carried, until the fear of Tarquin and the Etrurian war were both ended. For whilst the Etrurians assisted Tarquin's endeavours of reinstalment, Rome quaked under so burdensome a war. And therefore (says Sallust) were things carried modestly and justly, fear being the cause hereof by restraint, not justice by persuasion. In which short space, how cruel a course had the year of the two first consuls! The time being yet unexpired, Brutus degraded Collatinus, and banished him from the city: and soon after he himself perished, having interchanged many wounds with his foe, having first slain his own sons,

[1] *Hist.* 1; Frag. 9.

and his wife's brothers, because he found them actors in a plot
to recall Tarquin. Which deed, Virgil having laudably recited,
presently does in gentle manner deplore: [1] for having said:

> Natosque pater mala bella moventes
> Ad poenam pulchra pro libertate vocabit,
>
> His sons, convict of turbulent transgression,
> He kills, to quit his country from oppression,

presently in lamenting manner he adds:

> Infelix, utcumque ferent ea facta minores.
> Hapless, howe'er succeeding times shall ring.

Howsoever his posterity shall ring of the praise of such an act,
yet hapless is he that gives death's summons to his own sons.
But to give some solace to his sorrows, he adds after all:

> Vicit amor patriae laudumque immensa cupido.
> Conquer'd by country's love, and laud's high thirst.

Now in Brutus' killing of his own sons, and in being killed by
Tarquin's son, whom he had hurt, and Tarquin himself surviving
him, is not Collatinus' wrong well revenged, who being so good a
citizen was banished (only because his name was but Tarquin) as
well as Tarquin the tyrant. It was the name (you say) that was
the cause of this: well, he should have been made to change his
name then, and not to abandon his country. Again, this word
would have been but little missed in his name, if he had been called
L. Collatinus only. This therefore was no sufficient cause why
he, being one of the first consuls, should be forced to abjure both
his honours and his city. But is this injustice, being so detestable,
and so useless to the State, fit to be the foundation of Brutus'
glory? Did he these things, 'being conquered by our country's
loves, and laud's high thirst'? Tarquin being expelled, L. Tarquinius Collatinus, Lucretia's husband, was joint consul with Junius
Brutus: how justly did the people respect the character of the man
and not the name! But how unjustly did Brutus (having power
to deprive him only of his name, the cause of his offence) in
depriving him both of his country and place of honour! Thus
these evils, thus these ill effects fell out even then when things
were said to be carried so modestly and so justly. And Lucretius,
that had Brutus' place, died ere this year ended; so that P. Valerius
that succeeded Collatinus, and M. Horatius that had Lucretius'
place, ended that hellish and murderous year, which saw itself pass
by five consuls. This was the year wherein Rome devised her
platform of new government, their fears now beginning to diminish,
not because they had no wars, but because those they had were but

[1] *Aen.* vi. 820-3.

light ones. But the time being expired wherein things were
modestly and justly managed, then followed those which Sallust
does thus briefly delineate: 'Then began the patricians to oppress
the people with servile conditions, to judge of life and death as
imperiously as the kings had done before; to thrust men from their
possessions; to put by all others, and to sway all themselves; with
which outrages, and chiefly with their extorted taxes, the people
being too much vexed (being bound both to maintain an army and
also to pay contributions besides), they rushed up to arms, and
entrenched themselves upon Mounts Sacer and Aventine; and
there they made them tribunes, and divers laws; but these
discords and tumultuous contentions ended not till the second
African war.' [1]

CHAPTER XVII

*Of the vexations of the Roman estate, after the first beginning of the
consuls' rule: and of the little good that their gods all this while
did them.*

BUT why should I spend so much time in writing of these things,
or make others spend it in reading them? How miserable the
state of Rome stood all that long time until the second Punic war,
how sorely shaken by foreign wars and intestine discord, Sallust
has already made a succinct demonstration. And so their victories
never brought any true felicity to the good, but only vain solaces
to the wretched, and inductions and enticements to the turbulent
to continue disquiet's progress. Let no wise Roman then be
angry with us for saying this; but we need not entreat, we are
already assured, they will not. For we use but the words of their
own writers, and that with far less gall than they themselves meant
it, and in less elaboration than they spoke it. Yet those do they
learn, and those they make their children learn. Then why are
they angered with me for saying as Sallust says: 'Many troubles,
seditions, and lastly, civil wars burst out, whilst a few of the
greatest, under the honest style of fathers, used the licence of
tyrants, nor did the citizens attain the title of good and bad, according to their deserts in the State (all being foul alike), but he that
had most wealth and power to injure, because he defended the
present government (as fittest for his turn), he was the only good
man'? [2] If these writers now held it as pertinent to an honest
man's liberty to be so free-tongued against their own city's corruptions, which elsewhere they have been often enforced to commend, because they had no knowledge of any better state, wherein
they might become denizens eternal; what then shall we do, seeing

that to the extent that our trust in God is firmer, so much ought our tongues to be the freer in repelling the scandal they cast upon our Saviour Christ, with intent to seduce unsettled and unsound minds from that city, where happiness is man's possession unto all eternity? Neither do we load their gods with any more horrid guilt than their own writers do, whom they read and reverence; what we say, we say it from them, being unable to recite all, or all that they have of this kind. Where then were these gods (which men hold so venerable for the attaining of worldly vanities) when the Romans, whose services they angled for so cunningly, were afflicted so extremely? Where were they when Consul Valerius was slain in defence of the Capitol, when it was scaled by slaves and exiles? It was rather in his power to protect the temple of Jupiter, than in the power of all that crowd of gods, and their great king, to yield him any help at all. Where were they when the city, being so overborne with seditions, was fain to send to Athens to borrow laws, expecting a brief period of quietness, and was unpeopled by such a sore famine and pestilence? Where were they besides, when the people in this great famine elected their first prefect of the provisions, and when in the increase of this dearth Sp. Aemilius, for distributing corn overbountifully amongst the starved people, was brought under the suspicion of affecting monarchy, and at the instance of the said prefect, by the means of L. Quintius, dictator, an aged, weak man, he was slain by the hand of Q. Servilius, the general of the horsemen, not without a most dreadful and dangerous tumult in the whole city. Where were they when, at the beginning of a wasteful pestilence, the people, being wholly tired with frustrate invocations, thought it fit to appease them with new 'bed-spreadings,' a thing never done before? Then were there beds brought into the temples and spread in honour of the gods, and hence this sacrifice (nay sacrilege) took the name. Where were they when for ten full years together the Romans never fought against the Veians but they had the worse, until Furius Camillus was fain to help them, whom they unkindly banished afterwards for his good service? Where were they when the Gauls took Rome, sacked it, spoiled it, burned it, and made a very shambles of it? Where were they when that great plague destroyed almost all the city, and Camillus amongst the rest, who had saved his thankless country from the Veians, and after from the Gauls? In this pestilence they first brought up their stage plays, a greater plague than the other to their conditions though not to their carcasses. Where were they when another sad contagion arose (as it is said) from the poisoning tricks of the matrons, yea of the most and noblest, whose conditions herein proved worse than all those pestilent airs? Or when the two consuls with their army being shut in the Caudine Forks by the Samnites, were glad to make a base treaty with them? And delivering six hundred gentlemen for hostages, went away with all the rest, without arms, without baggage, without anything but their very upper garments? Or when the army perished almost wholly, part by the plague, and part by thunders? Or when in another great mortality the city was forced to fetch Aesculapius (as a physician for her) from Epidaurus, because Jupiter, the king of the Capitol, had ever been so employed in his youth in rapes and adulteries that these exercises gave him no time to learn physic. Or when the Brutians, Lucans, Samnites, Etrurians, and Senonian Gauls, conspiring all together, first slew their ambassadors, and then a whole army with the praetor, ten tribunes, and thirteen thousand soldiers? Or then, when the long and fatal sedition was in the city, wherein the people at last encamped themselves on Janiculum, having plundered the whole city? Which mischief grew to such a lamentable pass, that they were glad (for the last refuge in all desperate cases) to create a dictator, Hortensius, who having reunited the people, and recalled them, died in his office, as no dictator had done before, which was a great shame to the gods, now that Aesculapius was come amongst them. And then grew wars so fast upon them, that their *proletarii* (to whom they gave this name because of their leisure for the getting of children, being so needy that they could not follow the wars themselves) were now, for want of soldiers, compelled to serve themselves. For now did Pyrrhus, that famous and warlike Epirot (being called in by the Tarentines), become Rome's heavy foe: and asking the oracle of his success, truly Apollo answered him very neatly, in such ambiguous manner, that which way soe'er it happened, his deity might stand unblemished: *Aio te Aeacida Romanos vincere posse*, said he: so that whether Pyrrhus or the Romans had the upper hand, the oracle need not care, for Apollo speaks true anyhow. After this followed a sore and bloody fight, wherein notwithstanding Pyrrhus was conqueror, so that now he might justly esteem Phoebus a true foreteller, as he understood him; but that in the next conflict the Romans had the better; and in this great hostility arose as great a plague amongst the women: for, ere they could be delivered, being big with child, still they died. Now here Aesculapius had an excuse; he professed himself the prince of physic and not of midwifery. Cattle died also so sore, that one would have thought the world's utter devastation had entered. And then there was a winter how strangely unseasonable! the snow lying in the market-place forty days together in a monstrous depth; all Tiber being frozen quite over. If this had happened in our times, Lord, how it would have been scanned upon! And what of that great pestilence, which took so many thousand hence and which (in spite of all Aesculapius' drugs) lasted till the next year, so that they were fain to betake themselves to the books of the sibyls: in which kind of oracles (as Tully says well in his book *De Divinatione* [1]) the expounders of them are oftener trusted than otherwise, guess they never so unlikely! And then it was said that the pestilence raged so because many of the temples were put unto private men's uses: hereby freeing Aesculapius either from great ignorance or negligence. But why were these temples turned unto private habitations without prohibition, but only because they saw they had lost too much labour in praying to such a crew of gods so long; and so becoming wiser by degrees, had left haunting those places little by little, and at length abandoned them wholly for the private uses of such as would inhabit them! For those houses which then, for avoiding of this pestilence, were so diligently repaired—if they had not been afterwards utterly neglected, and so encroached upon by private men as before, Varro should be to blame for saying (speaking of temples) that many of them were unknown. But in the meantime this attention to the temples was a pretty excuse for the gods, but no cure at all for the pestilence.

CHAPTER XVIII

The miseries of the Romans in the African wars, and the small stead their gods stood them therein

BUT now in the wars of Africa, victory still hovering doubtfully betwixt both sides, and two mighty and powerful nations using all their might and power to reciprocal ruin, how many petty kingdoms perished herein! How many fair cities were demolished, or afflicted, or utterly lost! How far did this disastrous contention spread, to the ruin of so many realms and great estates! How often were the conquerors on either side conquered! What store of men (armed and naked) was there that perished! How many ships were sunk at sea by fight and tempest! Should we particularize, we should become a direct historiographer. Then Rome being in these deep plunges, ran headlong unto those vain and ridiculous remedies: for then were the secular plays renewed by the admonition of the sibyl's books: which institution had been ordained a hundred years before, but was now worn out of all memory in those so happy times. The high priests also renewed the sacred plays to the hell-gods which the better times had in like manner abolished before. Nor was it any wonder to see them now revenged, for the hell-gods desired now to become revellers, being enriched by this continual supply of dying men: who (like wretches) in following those bloody and unrelenting wars, did nothing but act the devils' revels, and prepare banquets for the

[1] ii. 54, 110–12.

infernal spirits. Nor was there a more laudable accident in all this whole war, than that Regulus should be taken prisoner: a worthy man, and before that mishap a scourge to the Carthaginians: who had ended the African war long before, but that he would have bound the Carthaginians to stricter conditions than they could bear. The most sudden captivity and the most faithful oath of this man, and his most cruel death, if the gods do not blush at, surely they are brazen-faced, and have no blood in them. Nay, for all this, Rome's walls stood not safe, but tasted of some mischief, and all those within them; for the river Tiber overflowing, drowned almost all the level parts of the city: turning some places as it were into torrents, and some others into fens or lakes. This plague ushered in a worse one of fire, which beginning in the market-place burned all the higher buildings thereabouts, sparing not the asylum and temple of Vesta, where it was so duly kept alight by those not so honourable as damnable votaresses. Now it did not only continue here burning but raging: with the fury whereof the virgins being panic-stricken, Metellus, the high priest, ran into the fire, and was half burned in fetching out of it those fatal relics, which had been the ruin of three cities where they had been resident. The fire either did not recognize him for all he was the priest: or else the goddess of fire was not there; for if she had been she would not have fled from the flames. But here you see how a mortal man could do Vesta more good than she could do him: for if these gods could not guard themselves from the fire, how could they guard the city which they were thought to guard from burnings and inundations? Truly not a whit, as the thing showed itself. Herein we would not raise these objections against the Romans, if they would affirm that all these their sacred observances only aim at eternity, and not at the goods of this transitory world; and that therefore when those corporal things perished, there was yet no loss of that for the promotion of which they were ordained, because they might soon be made fit for the same uses again. But now such is their miserable blindness that they think that those idols, that might have perished in this fiery extremity, had power to preserve the temporal happiness of the city: and now though it can be shown that even while they remained unconsumed such ruins of their safeties and such great mischiefs befell the city, this makes them ashamed to change that opinion which they see they cannot possibly defend.

CHAPTER XIX

Of the sad accidents that befell in the second African war, wherein the powers on both sides were wholly consumed

BUT all too tedious were it to relate the slaughters of both nations in the second African war. They had so many fights both far and near, that by their own confessions who were rather Rome's commenders than true chroniclers, the conquerors were ever more like to the conquered than otherwise. For when Hannibal arose out of Spain, and broke over the Pyrenean hills, all France, and the very Alps; gathering huge powers, and doing horrible mischiefs in all this long tract, rushing like an inundation into the face of Italy, what bloody fields were there pitched, what battles struck! How often did the Romans abandon the field, how many cities fell to the foe, how many were taken, how many were razed! What victories did Hannibal win, and what glories did he build himself upon the ruined Romans! In vain should I speak of Cannae's horrible overthrow, where Hannibal's own excessive thirst of blood was so fully glutted upon his foes that he himself bade hold: whence he sent three bushels of rings unto Carthage, to show how huge a company had fallen at that fight that they were easier to be measured than numbered; and hence might they conjecture what a massacre there was of the meaner sort, that had no rings to wear, and that the poorer they were, the more of them perished. Finally, such a lack of soldiers followed this overthrow, that the Romans were fain to get malefactors to go to war for quittance of their guilt; to set all their slaves free; and out of this graceless crew, not to supply their defective regiments, but even to make up a whole army. Nay, these slaves (but let us not wrong them, they are freemen now) so wanted even weapons to fight for Rome withal, that they were fain to fetch them out of the temples, as if they should say to their gods: Come, pray let these weapons go, you have kept them long enough to no end: we will see whether our bond-slaves can do more good for us with them than you our gods could yet do. And then the treasury failing, the private estate of each man became public, so that each one giving what he was able, their rings, nay their very *bullae*[1] (the wretched marks of their dignities) being all bestowed, the senate themselves (much more the other companies and tribes) left not themselves any money in the world. Who could have endured the rages of those men, if they had been driven to this poverty in these our times, seeing we can barely endure them as it is, although they have store now to bestow upon stage players, which then they were full fain, for their uttermost means of safety, to spend upon the soldiers?

[1] Ornaments of gold worn by freedmen on the neck.—ED.

CHAPTER XX

*Of the ruin of the Saguntines, who perished for their confederacy
with Rome, the Roman gods never helping them*

BUT in all the disasters of the second African war, there was none
more lamentable than the dissolution of the Saguntines. These,
inhabiting a city in Spain, being sworn friends to the Romans,
were destroyed for keeping their faith to them. For Hannibal,
breaking the league with Rome, gave here the first occasion of war,
engirting the city of Saguntum with a cruel and strait siege:
whereof the Romans having intelligence, sent an embassage to
wish Hannibal to raise his siege: but the legates being despised
by him, went to Carthage, whence (having done nothing) they
returned without any redress for the breach of the league, and in
the meantime this city (once so stately) was now brought to such
misery, that about eight or nine months after the beginning of the
siege the Africans took it and razed it to the very ground. To
read how it perished were a horror; much more to write it: yet I
will run over it briefly, seeing it is very pertinent to the argument
we prosecute. First it was eaten down with famine: for some say
it was driven to feed upon the carcasses which it harboured. And
then being in this labyrinth of languors, yet rather than take in
Hannibal as a conqueror, the citizens made a huge fire in the
market-place, and therein entombed all their parents, wives,
children, and friends (after they had slain them first), and lastly
themselves. Here now these gluttonous, treacherous, wasteful,
cheating, dancing gods should have done somewhat: here they
should have done somewhat to help these distressed faithful
friends of the Romans, and to save them from perishing, for their
loyalty's sake. They were called as witnesses between both, when
the league was made between Rome and these poor men; who
keeping that faith which they had willingly passed, solemnly
sworn, and sacredly observed, under their protections, were
besieged, afflicted, and subverted by one that had broken all faith,
all religion. If the gods with thunder and lightning could frighten
Hannibal from Rome's walls, and make him keep aloof from them,
they should first have practised this here: for I dare aver, that with
far more honesty might they have helped the Romans' friends,
being in extremes for keeping their faith to them, and having then
no means nor power, than they did the Romans themselves, that
fought for themselves, and had very good forces and purses able
to repel Hannibal's powers. If they had been careful guardians
of Rome's glory, they would never have left it stained with the
sufferance of this sad calamity of the Saguntines. But now how
sottish is their belief that think these gods kept Rome from perishing by the hand of victorious Hannibal and the Carthaginians,

that could not save Saguntum from perishing for keeping her faith sworn so solemnly to the Romans? If Saguntum had been Christian and had suffered such an extremity for the gospel (though it ought not in that case to have wrecked itself by fire nor sword), yet had it endured such for the gospel, it would have borne it stoutly, by reason of that hope which it would have held in Christ to have been after all crowned by Him with an eternal guerdon. But as for these false gods, that desire to be and are worshipped only for the assurance of this transitory term of our mortality, what can their attorneys, their orators, say for them in this ruin of the Saguntines, more than they said in that of Regulus? He was only one man, this a whole city, but perseverance in faith was cause of both calamities. For this faith would he return to his foes, and for this would not they turn to their foes. Doth loyalty then grieve the gods? Or may ungrateful cities (as well as men) be destroyed, and yet stand in their gods' liking still? Let them choose which they like: if the gods be angry at men's keeping of their faith, let them seek faithless wretches to serve them. But if they that serve them and have their favours, be nevertheless afflicted and spoiled, then to what end are they adored? Wherefore let them hold their tongues that think they lost their city because they lost their gods: for though they had them all, they might nevertheless not only complain of misery, but feel it at full, as Regulus and the Saguntines did.

CHAPTER XXI

Of Rome's ingratitude to Scipio, that freed it from imminent danger, and of the conditions of the citizens in those times that Sallust commends to have been so virtuous

FURTHERMORE, in the space between the first and second Carthaginian war when, as Sallust says,[1] the Romans lived in all concord and content (the remembrance of my theme makes me omit much): in those times of concord and content, Scipio, that 'protector and raiser of his country,' the rare, admirable ender of that so extreme, so dangerous, and so fatal a war as that of Carthage was, the conqueror of Hannibal, the tamer of Carthage, whose very youth is graced with all praises of religiousness and divine conversation: this man, so great and so gracious, was forced to give place to the accusations of his enemies, to leave his country, which but for him had been left to destruction; and after his high heroical triumph, to bequeath the remainder of his days to the poor town of Linternum: banishing all affection for his country so far from him, that it is said that he gave express charge at his death, that his body

[1] *Hist.* 1; Frag. 8 and 22.

should not in any case be buried in that so ungrateful soil of Rome.
Afterwards, in the triumph of Cn. Manlius (vice-consul) over
the Gallo-Grecians, the luxury of Asia entered, the worst foe
Rome ever felt. Gilded beds and precious coverings got then
their first ingress. Then began they to have wenches to sing at
their banquets, and many other licentious disorders. But I am
to speak of the calamities that they suffered so unwillingly, not of
the offences that they committed so lavishly. And therefore what
I spake of Scipio, that left his country for his enemies (having first
preserved it from utter ruin) and died a willing exile, that was to
our purpose, to show that the Roman gods, from whose temples
he drove Hannibal, did never requite him with any the least touch
of temporal felicity, for which only they are adored. But because
Sallust says that Rome was so well mannered in those days, I
thought good to touch on this Asian luxury, that you might understand that Sallust spoke in comparison of the after-times, wherein
discord was at the highest flood, and good manners at their lowest
ebb. For then (that is, between the second and last African war),
the Voconian law was promulgated, that none should make a woman
his heir, not even were she his only daughter; than which decree
I can see nothing more barbarous and unjust. But indeed the
mischiefs that the city suffered were not so many nor so violent in
the space betwixt the two Punic wars as they were at other times:
for though they felt the smart of war abroad, yet they enjoyed the
sweets of victory; and at home they agreed better than they did in
the times of security.

But in the last African war, by the only valour of that Scipio, that
therefore was surnamed Africanus, that city, that compared and
contended with Rome, was utterly razed to dust and ruined; and
then broke in such an inundation of depravity, drawn into the
state by security and prosperity, that Carthage might justly be
said to have been a more dangerous enemy to Rome in her dissolution, than she was in her opposition. And this continued
until Augustus' time, who (methinks) did not abridge the Romans
of their liberty, as of a thing which they loved and praised, but as
though they had utterly despised it and left it for the taking.
Then reduced he all things unto an imperial command, renewing
and repairing the commonwealth, that was become all moth-eaten
and rusty with age, vice, and negligence. I omit the divers and
diversely arising contentions and battles of all this whole time:
that league of Numantia, stained with so foul an ignominy, where
the chickens flew out of their cages, as presaging some great ill
luck (they say) unto Mancinus, then consul: so that it seemed the
little city that had plagued the Roman army who besieged it so
many years, did now begin to be a terror to the Romans' whole
estate, and boded misfortune unto such of her forces as came
against it.

CHAPTER XXII

Of the edict of Mithridates commanding every Roman that was to be found in Asia to be put to death

BUT as I said, these shall pass: yet not that of Mithridates, King of Asia, who gave direct command, that whatever Roman was to be found trafficking or travelling anywhere in all Asia, upon one certain day, should be immediately slain; and it was effected. How dolorous a sight was this, to see men slain in such numbers, wheresoever they were taken, in field, road, town, house, street, court, temple, bed, or table, or wheresoever, so suddenly and so wickedly! What sorrows would possess the standers-by, and perhaps the very doers of the deeds themselves, to hear the sad groans of the dying men! Unto what extremity were the hosts of lodgings brought now, when they must not only behold those murders committed in their houses, but even help to perform them themselves! To turn so suddenly from gentle humanity unto barbarous cruelty! To do the act of an enemy in peace, and that on his friend, interchanging indeed wounds with the murdered, the murdered being stricken in the body, and the murderer in the mind! And did all these that were thus slain neglect auguries? Had they no gods public or private to ask counsel of, before they betook them unto this travel from whence they were never to return? If this be true, then have they of our times no cause to complain of us, for the neglect of those things which the Romans of old contemned as vanities. But if they did not, but used to ask counsel of them, then tell me (I pray) to what end was it when other men's powers fell so heavy upon these wretches without any prohibition or means to avoid them?

CHAPTER XXIII

Of the more private and interior mischiefs that Rome endured, which were presaged by that prodigious madness of all the creatures that served the use of man

BUT now let us do what we can to recite those evils which the more domestic they were to Rome, the more miserable they made it: I mean the civil or rather uncivil discords, being now no more seditions but open wars, and those in the very bowels of the city, wherein so much blood was spilt: where the senators' powers were now no more bent to altercations and wranglings, but directly to arms and weapons. What rivers of Romans' blood flowed from the social, servile, and civil wars! How sore a waste fell upon the breast of all Italy from hence! For before that Latium (being

associate and confederate with the rest) arose against Rome, all the
creatures that were useful unto man, dogs, horses, asses, oxen, and
all others besides, that served human occasions, growing suddenly
stark mad, and losing all their meekness, ran wild out of the towns
into the deserts, fields, and forests, flying the company not only of
all others, but even of their own masters, and endangering any
man that offered to come near them.   What a prodigious sign was
here!   But if this, being so great a mischief of itself, were but the
presage of another, what a mischief must that be then, that was
ushered in by such a mischievous presage!   If this had befallen in
our times, we should be sure to have had these faithless miscreants
a great deal madder than the other dogs were.

CHAPTER XXIV

Of the civil discord that arose from the seditions of the Gracchi

THE sedition of the Gracchi about the agrarian laws gave the first
vent unto all the civil wars; for the lands that the nobility wrong-
fully possessed, they would needs have shared amongst the people;
but it was a dangerous thing for them to undertake the righting of
a wrong of such continuance, and in the end it proved indeed
their destruction.   What a slaughter was there, when Tiberius
Gracchus was slain; and when his brother followed him within a
while after!   The noble and the base were butchered together in
tumults and uproars of the people, not in formal justice nor by
order of law but all in hugger-mugger.   After the latter Gracchus'
slaughter, followed that of L. Opimius, consul, who taking arms in
the city against this Gracchus, and killing him and all his fellows,
had made a huge slaughter of citizens, by this means having caused
three thousand to be executed that he had condemned by law.
By which one may guess what a massacre there was of all in that
tumultuous conflict, since three thousand were marked out by law,
as orderly condemned, and justly slain.   He that killed Gracchus
had the weight of his head in gold, for that was his bargain before.
And in this fray was M. Fulvius slain, and all his children.

CHAPTER XXV

*Of the temple of Concord built by the senate in the place where
these seditions and slaughters were effected*

A FINE decree surely was it of the senate, to give charge for the
building of Concord's temple, just in the place where those outrages
were acted: that the monument of Gracchus' punishment might
be still in the eye of the pleaders, and stand fresh in their memory.

But what was this but a direct scoffing of their gods! They built
a goddess a temple, who had she been amongst them, would never
have suffered such gross breaches of her laws as these were;
unless Concord being guilty of this crime, by leaving the hearts of
the citizens, deserved therefore to be imprisoned in this temple.
Otherwise, to keep in line with their deeds, they should have built
Discord a temple in that place. Is there any reason that Concord
should be a goddess and not Discord? or that (according to Labeo's
distinction) she should not be a good goddess and Discord an evil
one? He spoke in this manner because he saw that Fever had a
temple built her, as well as Health. By the same reason should
Discord have had one as well as Concord. Wherefore the Romans
were not wise to live in the displeasure of so wicked a goddess:
they have forgotten that she was the destruction of Troy, by
causing strife amongst the three goddesses by sending amongst
them the golden apple because she was not bidden to their feast:
whereupon the goddesses fell to scolding; Venus got the apple,
Paris, Helen, and Troy utter destruction. Wherefore if it were
through her anger because she had no temple there with the rest,
that she set the Romans at such variance, how much more angry
would she be to see her chiefest enemy have a temple built in that
place, where she had shown such absolute power! Now their
greatest scholars are angered with us for deriding these vanities;
and yet worshipping those promiscuous gods, they cannot for their
lives clear themselves of this question of Concord and Discord,
whether they let them alone unworshipped and prefer Febris and
Bellona before them (to whom their most ancient temples were
dedicated), or that they do worship them both as well as the rest.
Howsoever, they are in the briers, seeing that Concord got her
gone, and left Discord to play havoc amongst them by herself.

CHAPTER XXVI

Of the divers wars that followed after the building of Concord's temple

Now they all thought that this new temple of Concord, and
memorial of Gracchus, would be an excellent restraint unto all
seditious spirits. But how far they shot wide, let the subsequent
times indicate. For from that time forth, the pleaders never went
about to avoid the examples of the Gracchi, but laboured to exceed
them in their projects. L. Saturninus, tribune, C. Caesar Servilius, praetor, and not long after that, M. Drusus, all these began
more bloody seditions, whence there arose not only civil slaughters,
but at last they broke openly out into the Confederates' war, which
brought all Italy unto most miserable and desperate extremities.
Then followed the Slaves' war, and other civil wars, wherein it is

strange to record what fields were pitched, what bloodshed and
what murder stuck upon the face of all Italy, as far as the Romans
had any power or sovereignty.   And how small a company, less
than seventy gladiators, began this Slaves' war, which mounted to
that terror and danger!   What multitudes of generals did this
rascal crew overthrow!   What numbers of Roman cities and provinces they destroyed, it is more than work enough for a professed
historian to declare.   For the war held out not only in Italy, but
these slaves overran all Macedonia, Sicily, and the sea-coasts.
And then what outrageous robberies at first, and what terrible wars
afterwards were managed by the Pirates, what pen is sufficient to
recapitulate?

CHAPTER XXVII

Of the civil wars between Sulla and Marius

WHEN Marius being now tainted with his countrymen's blood, and
having slain many of his adversaries, was at length foiled and forced
to fly the city, it now got time to take a little breath; presently (to
use Tully's words) [1] upon the sudden Cinna and Marius began to
be conquerors again.   And then out went the heart bloods of the
most worthy men, and the lights of all the city.   But soon after
came Sulla, and revenged this barbarous massacre; but with what
damage to the state and city it is not my purpose to utter; for
that this revenge was worse than if all the offences that were
punished had been left unpunished, let Lucan testify in these
words:

> Excessit medicina modum, nimiumque secuta est
> Qua morbi duxere manus: periere nocentes.
> Sed cum jam soli possent superesse nocentes,
> Tunc data libertas odiis resolutaque legum
> Frenis ira ruit. [2]

> The medicine wrought too sore, making the cure
> Too cruel for the patient to endure:
> The guilty fell: but none yet such remaining,
> Hate riseth at full height, and wrath disdaining
> Laws' reins brake out.

For in that war of Sulla and Marius (besides those that fell in the
field) the whole city, streets, market-places, theatres, and temples
were filled with dead bodies: so that it was a question whether the
conquerors slaughtered so many to attain the conquest, or because
they had already attained it.   In Marius' first victory, at his return
from exile, besides infinite other slaughters, Octavius' head (the
consul's) was poled up in the pleading-place: Caesar and Fimbria

---

[1] 3 *Cat.* x. 24.   [2] *Phars.* ii. 142–4.

were slain in their houses; the two Crassi, father and son, killed in one another's sight; Baebius and Numitorius trailed about upon hooks till death: Catulus poisoned himself to escape his enemies; and Merula, the flamen of Jupiter, cut his own veins and so bled himself out of their danger; Marius having given order for the killing of all those whom he did not re-salute, or proffer his hand unto.

CHAPTER XXVIII

How Sulla revenged Marius' murders

Now as for Sulla's victory, the revenger of all this cruelty, it was not got without much store of citizens' blood; and yet the wars only ended and not the grudges: for this victory broke out into a far more cruel waste in the midst of all this peace. For after the butcheries that the elder Marius had made (being yet but fresh and bleeding), there followed worse by the hands of the younger Marius and Carbo, both of the old faction of Marius. These two perceiving Sulla come upon them, being desperate both of safety and victory, filled all with slaughters both of themselves and others: for besides the massacre they made elsewhere in the city, they besieged the senate in the very court, and from thence as from a prison, dragged them out to execution. Mucius Scaevola, the priest, was slain just as he had hold of the altar of Vesta, the most reverend relic of all the city, almost quenching with his blood that fire which the virgins' care kept always burning. Then entered victorious Sulla into the city, and in the common street (war's cruelty now done, and peace's beginning) put seven thousand unarmed men to the sword, not in fight, but by an express command. And after that he put even whom he willed to death, throughout the whole city, insomuch that the slaughters grew so innumerable that one was glad to put Sulla in mind that he must either let some live, or else he should have none to be lord over. And then indeed this ravenous murderer began to be restrained by degrees; and a list was published (with great applause) which proscribed but 2,000 of the patriots and gentlemen, appointing them all to be killed forthwith. The number made all men sad, but the manner cheered them again: nor were they so sad that so many should perish, as they rejoiced that the rest should escape. Nevertheless, this cruel carelessness of theirs groaned at the exquisite torments that some of the condemned persons suffered in their deaths. For one of them was torn in pieces by men's hands without touch of iron, where the executioners showed far more cruelty in rending this living man thus, than they use ordinarily upon a dead beast. Another having first his eyes plucked out, and then all the parts of his body cut away joint by joint, was forced to live, or rather to die, thus long in such intolerable torment. Many also of the noblest cities and towns were put unto the sack: and as one guilty man is wont to be led out to death, so was one whole city then laid out and appointed for execution. These were the fruits of their peace after their wars, wherein they hasted not to get the conquest, but were swift to abuse it when got. Thus this peace competed in blood with that war, and quite exceeded it; for that war killed but the armed, but this peace never spared the naked. In the war he that was stricken, if he could, might strike again: but in this peace he that escaped the war must not live, but took his death with patience perforce.

CHAPTER XXIX

A comparison of the Goths' corruptions with the calamities that the Romans endured either by the Gauls, or by the authors of their civil wars

WHAT barbarousness of other foreign nations, what cruelty of strangers, is comparable to this conquest of one of their citizens? What foe did Rome ever feel, more fatal, inhuman, and outrageous? Which were more horrible or more detestable—the irruptions first of the Gauls, and since of the Goths, or the inundations that Sulla, Marius, and other great Romans made with the blood of their own citizens? The Gauls indeed killed the senate, and spoiled all but the Capitol, that was defended against them. But they notwithstanding sold the besieged their freedom for gold, whereas they might have extorted it from them by famine, if not by force. But as for the Goths, they spared so many of the Senate, that it was a marvel that they killed any. But Sulla, when Marius was yet alive, sat on the very Capitol (which the Gauls entered not), to behold from thence the slaughters which he commanded to be performed. And Marius, being but fled to return with more power and fury, keeping still in the Capitol, deprived numbers of their lives and states, colouring all this villainy by the decrees of the senate. And when he was gone, what did the Marian faction respect or spare, when they would not forbear to kill old Scaevola, a citizen, a senator, the chief priest, embracing that very altar, whereon they say the fate of Rome itself was adored? And that last list of Sulla's (to omit the innumerable deaths besides) cut the throats of more senators than the Goths' whole army could find in their hearts but to spoil.

CHAPTER XXX

Of the great and pernicious multitude of the Romans' wars a little before the coming of Christ

WITH what face then, with what heart, with what impudence, folly, nay madness do they impute these later calamities unto our Saviour, and yet will not impose the former upon their idols? Their civil discords by their own writers' confessions have been ever more extremely bloody than their foreign wars. The means which did not only afflict but utterly subvert their State arose long before Christ, by the combination of these wicked causes arising from the war of Sulla and Marius, unto those of Sertorius and Catiline; the one of whom Sulla proscribed, and the other he nourished: and then downwards to the wars of Lepidus and Catulus, whereof the one would confirm Sulla's ordinances, and the other would disannul them: then to the war of Pompey and Caesar: whereof Pompey was a follower of Sulla, and either equalled, or even exceeded him in state and power; and Caesar was one that could not bear the greatness of Pompey because he lacked it himself: which notwithstanding, after he had overthrown him and made him away, he went far beyond. From hence they come down to the other Caesar, called Augustus, in whose reign our Saviour Christ was born. This Augustus had much civil war, wherein were lost many excellent men, and Tully, that excellent commonwealth's man, was one amongst the rest. For C. Caesar, the conqueror of Pompey, though he used his victory with mercy, restoring their states and dignities to all his adversaries: notwithstanding all this, by a conspiracy of the noblest senators he was stabbed to death in the court, for the defence of their liberty, who held him to aim at a monarchy. After this Anthony (a man neither like him in means, nor manners, but given over to all sensuality) seemed to aim at his power: whom Tully did stoutly withstand in defence of the said liberty. And then stepped up that younger Caesar, the other Caesar's adopted son, afterwards styled (as I said) Augustus: him did Tully favour and confirm against Anthony, hoping that he would be the man, who having demolished Anthony's pretences and powers, would re-erect the liberty of his country. But far mistaken was he and short-sighted in this matter, for this young man whose power he had augmented, first of all suffered Anthony to cut off Cicero's head, as if it had been a bargain between them, and then brought that liberty which the other so pleaded for, into his own sole command, and under his own particular subjection.

CHAPTER XXXI

*That those men that are not allowed any longer to worship idols, do
show themselves fools in imputing their present miseries unto Christ,
seeing that they endured the like when they did worship the devils*

BUT let them blame their own gods for such mischiefs, that will
not thank our Saviour Christ for any of His benefits. For whensoever they befell, their gods' altars steamed with Sabaean per-
fumes, and fresh flowers, their priests were gallant, their temples
shone, plays, sacrifices, and furies were all on foot amongst men;
yea even when there was such an effusion of civil blood that the
altars of the very gods were besprinkled with it. Tully chose
no temple for refuge, because he saw it availed not Scaevola.
But those that are now so ready with their saucy insults against
Christianity, of late either fled themselves into such places as
were dedicated to Christ, or else were brought thither by the
barbarians.

This I know, and every impartial judge may know as well as I,
that if mankind had received Christianity before the African wars
(to omit the other that I have rehearsed, and that is too long to
rehearse), and withal that such a desolation should have happened
as fell upon Europe and Africa in the said wars; there is none of
those infidels that oppose us now, but would have laid the sole
cause of it all upon the back of Christendom. But much more intolerable would their railings be, if either the irruption of the
Gauls, or the inundation of Tiber, and that great spoil by fire, had
immediately followed upon the first preaching and receiving of
Christian religion; but worst of all, if the civil wars, that exceeded
all, had followed thereupon. And those evils which fell out so
incredibly, so far beyond all belief that the world reputed them as
prodigies, had they come to pass in Christian times, who should
have borne the blame thereof but the Christians? For those things
which were rather strange than pernicious, as the speaking of the
ox, the exclamations of children in their mothers' wombs, the
flying of serpents, and the alteration of female creatures, both hens
and women, into masculine forms, and such as these I willingly
omit; those things are recorded in their histories, not in their
fables, but be they true or false, they do not bring so much affliction
unto man as admiration. But when it rained earth, and chalk, and
stones (not concrescences, that might be called hail, but actual
stones), this verily might endamage the earth's inhabitants. In
the said authors we read that the fires of Etna broke out so far
that the sea boiled therewith, the rocks were burned, and the
pitch dropped off the ships. This was no light hurt, but an incredible wonder. Again, Sicily was so overwhelmed another time

with the ashes thereof, that the houses of Catina were all turned over into the dust; whereupon the Romans pitying their calamity, released them of that year's tribute. It is recorded also, that the number of the locusts in Africa was most wonderful and prodigious, it being as then a province of the Romans; and that having consumed all the fruits and leaves of the trees, they fell all into the sea like a most huge and immeasurable cloud. And being dead, and cast upon the shore again, there arose such a pestilence of their stink that thereof died eighty thousand men in Masinissa's kingdom alone, and many more in other countries thereabouts, and of the thirty thousand Roman soldiers that remained at Utica there were only ten that survived. And so this foolery of theirs, which we must both endure and answer, what wrong would it not offer to the profession of the gospel, had it been preached before the birth of these prodigious accidents? Yet it will not call the meanest of their gods to account for any of these misfortunes whatsoever, and yet these fools will worship them still in hope to be protected by them from these inconveniences, when they see nevertheless, how those that worshipped the same gods before have been oppressed, and overborne with the same burdens of calamity, nay with loads of miseries, far more ponderous and intolerable than ever these latter times produced.

THE FOURTH BOOK OF THE CITY OF GOD

CHAPTER I

Of the contents of the first book

AT my first entrance upon this discourse of the city of God, I held it convenient, first of all, to stop their mouths, who, in their extreme desire of only temporal bliss and greediness after worldly vanities, hurl the blame upon Christianity (the true and only means of salvation) whensoever it pleases God in His mercy to correct and admonish them (rather than in His justice to punish them or afflict them) with any temporal inconvenience. And because the unlearned and vulgar sort of those persons are incited against us the more by the endeavours and examples of those whom they hold learned, thinking (upon their assertions) that such calamities as have befallen them of late never befell in times past; and being confirmed in this error by such as know it for an error and yet dissemble their knowledge; we thought it fit to show how far this their opinion swerved from the truth, out of such books as their own authors have left unto posterity, for the better understanding of the state of precedent ages; and to make it plain and apparent that those imaginary gods, which they either did worship as then in public, or as now in secret, are nothing but most foul, unclean spirits, and most deceitful and malignant devils, so that their only delight was to have most bestial and abominable practices, either published as their true exploits, or feigned of them by poetical inventions, which they commanded to be publicly presented in plays and at solemn feasts, to the end that man's infirmity, presuming upon these patterns as upon divine authorities, might never be withdrawn from acting the like wickedness. This we confirmed, not by mere conjectures, but partly by what of late times ourself hath beheld in the celebration exhibited unto such gods, and partly by their own writings, that left those reports recorded, not as in disgrace, but as in honour to their gods: so that Varro (a man of the greatest learning and authority amongst them of any, writing of divinity and humanity, and giving each object its proper attribute according to the worth and due respect thereof) hesitates not to affirm, that those stage plays are not matters of human invention, but divine things, since if the city were quit of all but honest men, stage plays should have no place in human activities. Nor did Varro affirm this of himself, but set it down as he had seen the use of these plays in Rome, being there born and brought up.

CHAPTER II

The contents of the second and third books

AND having propounded a method of our discourse in the end of the first book, whereof we have dealt with some parts in the books following, now we know that we are to proceed with those things which our order obliges us to relate. We promised therefore to say somewhat against those that impute the Romans' calamities unto Christianity; and to make a special record of the evils that we should find their city, or the provinces thereof, to have endured ere their sacrifices were prohibited: all which without doubt they would have blamed us for, had our religion and its prohibition of such sacrifices been known to them. This we performed sufficiently (I think) in the two last books, in the former of them reciting the evils which were either the only ones, or the sorest and most extreme (I mean those corruptions of manners); in the latter those which these fools fear mostly to suffer, such as afflictions of body and goods, which the best men oftentimes partake of, as well as the worst. But the things that make them evil and deprave their souls they cling to not so much with patience as with extremity of desire. Then I touched a little on the city, and so came down speedily to Augustus. But if I would have dilated not upon these reciprocal hurts that one man doth to another, as wars, desolations, etc., but upon the things that befall them by the very elements, and from nature, which Apuleius briefly speaks of in one place of his book *De Mundo*, saying that all earthly things have their changes, revolutions, and dissolutions (for he saith that by an exceeding earthquake, the ground opened at a certain time, and swallowed up whole cities, and all that were in them; showers and inundations overwhelmed whole countries; continents were cut into by strange tides, and made islands; and the sea elsewhere subsiding made the ground passable on foot; storms and tempests overturned whole cities; lightning consumed many of the eastern countries, and deluges as many of the west; fire sprang from the cauldrons of Etna, as from a torrent, and ran down the hills)—if I should have collected all examples of this kind that I could, which happened long before the name of Christ beat down those ruins of salvation, what end should I ever make? I promised also to make demonstration of the Romans' conditions, and why the true God did vouchsafe them that increase of their empire, even He in whose hand are all kingdoms, when their own puppet gods never did them a pennyworth of good, but deceived them as much as they could. Now then am I to discourse of their deception, but chiefly of the empire's increase. For, as for their devils' deceits, the second book opened them reasonably fully.

And in all the three books past, as occasion served, we noted how much aid and comfort the great God did vouchsafe both the good and bad in these afflictions of war only by the name of Christ, which the barbarians so highly reverenced beyond all use and custom of hostility. Even He did this, that 'maketh the sun to shine both upon good and bad, raineth both upon the just and the unjust.' [1]

CHAPTER III

Whether happy and wise men should account it as part of their felicity to possess an empire that is enlarged by no means but war

Now then let us examine the nature of this spaciousness and continuance of empire, which these men give their gods such great thanks for; to whom also they say they exhibited those plays (that were so filthy both in actors and the action) without any offence to honesty. But first, I would make a little inquiry, seeing you cannot show such estates to be anyway happy, as are in continual wars, and constantly in terror, trouble, and guilt of shedding human blood, though it be their foes'; with what reason or wisdom any man doth wish to glory in the largeness of empire, since all their joy is but as a glass, bright and brittle, and evermore in fear and danger of breaking. To dive the deeper into this matter, let us not give the sails of our souls to every air of human breath, nor suffer our understanding's eye to be smoked up with the fumes of vain words concerning kingdoms, provinces, nations, or such. No, let us take two men (for every particular man is a part of the greatest city and kingdom of the world, as a letter is a part of a word); and of these two men, let us imagine the one to be poor, or but of a mean estate, the other potent and wealthy; but withal, let my wealthy man take with him fears, sorrows, covetousness, suspicion, disquiet, contentions, making immense additions to his estate only by adding to his heap of most bitter cares; and let my poor man take with him sufficiency with little, love of kindred, neighbours, friends, joyous peace, peaceful religion, soundness of body, sincereness of heart, abstinence of diet, chastity of carriage, and security of conscience. Where should a man find any one so sottish as would make a doubt which of these to prefer in his choice? Well then, even as we have done with these two men, so let us do with two families, two nations, or two kingdoms. Test them both by the standard of equity; which done, and duly considered when it is done, here doth vanity lie bare to the view, and there shines felicity. Wherefore it is more convenient that such as fear and follow the law of the true God should have the swaying of such empires not so much for themselves, as for those over

[1] Matt. v. 45.

whom they are emperors. For themselves, their piety, and their honesty (God's admired gifts) will suffice them, both to the enjoying of true felicity in this life, and the attaining of that eternal and true felicity in the next. So that here upon earth, the rule that is given to the good man does not return him so much good as it does those that are under his rule. But contrariwise, the government of the wicked harms themselves far more than their subjects, for it gives themselves the greater liberty to exercise their lusts; but for their subjects, they have none but their own iniquities to answer for; for what injury soever the unrighteous master does to the righteous servant, it is no scourge for his guilt, but a trial of his virtue. And therefore he that is good is free though he be a slave, and he that is evil, a slave though he be a king. Nor is he slave to one man, but that which is worst of all, unto as many masters as he affects vices; according to the scripture, speaking thus hereof: 'Of whatsoever a man is overcome, to that he is in bondage.' [1]

CHAPTER IV

Kingdoms without justice, how like they are unto thievish purchases

SET justice aside then, and what are kingdoms but fair thievish purchases? For what are thieves' purchases but little kingdoms, for in thefts the hands of the underlings are directed by the commander, the confederacy of them is sworn together, and the pillage is shared by the law amongst them? And if those ragamuffins grow up to be able enough to keep forts, build habitations, possess cities, and conquer adjoining nations, then their government is no more called thievish, but graced with the eminent name of a kingdom, given and gotten, not because they have left their practices, but because now they may use them without danger of law. Elegant and excellent was that pirate's answer to the great Macedonian Alexander, who had taken him: the king asking him how he durst molest the seas so, he replied with a free spirit: 'How darest thou molest the whole world? But because I do it with a little ship only, I am called a thief: thou, doing it with a great navy, art called an emperor.'

CHAPTER V

Of those fugitive gladiators whose power grew parallel with a regal dignity

I WILL therefore omit to review the crew that Romulus called together, by proclaiming freedom from fear of punishment to all

[1] 2 Pet. ii. 19.

such as would inhabit Rome; hereby both augmenting his city, and getting a band of fellows about him that were fit for any villainous or desperate act whatsoever. But this I say, that the very empire of Rome, albeit now grown so great and so powerful by subduing so many nations, and so become sole terror of all the rest, was nevertheless extremely daunted, and driven into a terrible fear of an invasion very hardly to be avoided, by a small crew of rascally gladiators that had fled from the training school in Campania, and were now grown to such a mighty army that under the conduct of three captains they had made a most lamentable and cruel waste and spoil of the most part of the country. Let them tell me now, what god it was that raised up these men from a few poor contemptible thieves to a government so terrible to the state and strength of Rome itself. Will it be answered that they had no help at all from the gods, because they continued but a while, as though every man's life must of necessity be of long continuance? Why then the gods help no king to his kingdom, because most kings die very soon. Nor is that to be accounted as a benefit which every man loses in so little a time, and which vanishes (like a vapour) so soon after it is given. For what is it unto them that worshipped these gods under Romulus, and are now dead, that the Roman empire be ever so much increased since, seeing they are now pleading their own particular causes in hell, the character of which it belongs not to this place to dispute? And this may be understood likewise of all that have ended their lives in a few years, and bear the burdens of their deeds with them, howsoever their empire be afterwards augmented and continued through the lives and deaths of many successors. But if this be not so, and if those benefits (though of so short spare) are to be ascribed to the gods' goodness, then assuredly the gladiators had much to thank them for, who by their help did cast off their bonds of slavery, and fled and escaped, and got an army of such strength and good discipline together, that Rome itself began to be terribly afraid of them, and lost divers fields against them. They got the upper hand of divers generals; they used what pleasures they would; they did just what they chose; and until their last overthrow, which was given them with extreme difficulty, they lived in all pomp and regality. But now unto matter of more consequence.

CHAPTER VI

Of the covetousness of Ninus, who made the first war upon his neighbours through the greedy desire he had to increase his kingdom

JUSTIN, that wrote the Greek or rather universal history after Trogus Pompeius, not only in Latin (as did he), but in a similar succinct manner, begins his book thus: 'The sway and rule of nations at the first was in the hands of kings, who got their heights of majesty, not by courting popular favour, but by their own moderate carriage, approved by good men. The people had no law but the king's will. Their care and custom was the keeping, not the augmenting, of their dominion's limits. Every man's kingdom was bounded within his own country. Ninus of Assyria was the first that followed the lust of sovereignty in breaking the old hereditary law of nations. He first warred on the adjoining countries, subduing the people (as yet unacquainted with arts military) as far as Libya.' And a little after: 'Ninus confirmed his conquest by continuing the possession of it. And having subdued the neighbouring nations, from them he levied stronger powers, and set farther footing into the world, until by making one victory the continual means of another, he had made an entire conquest of all the east.' How truly soever he or Trogus wrote this (for I have found them both elsewhere erroneous by true proofs), yet it is certain by the record of other writers that Ninus enlarged the Assyrian's monarchy exceedingly, and that it continued longer than the Romans' hath done as yet. For as the chroniclers do deliver up account, it was one thousand two hundred and forty years after Ninus' reign to the translation of this monarchy to the Medians. Now to war against one's neighbours, and to proceed to the hurt of such as hurt not you, for greedy desire of rule and sovereignty, what is this but flat thievery in a greater excess and quantity than ordinary?

CHAPTER VII

Whether the pagan gods have any power either to further or hinder the progress, increase, or defects of earthly kingdoms

IF this kingdom continued so long, and so spacious, without the assistance of any of those gods, why are they reputed as the enlargers and preservers of Rome's monarchy? There must be the like reason for both. But if Assyria were bound to thank the gods, I demand which gods? For the nations that Ninus conquered had none. And if the Assyrians had any peculiar ones, that were better state-builders and preservers, were they dead then when the monarchy was translated to the Medes? Or were they unpaid, or had the Medians promised them better wages, that they would needs migrate thither and from them again into Persia at the invitation of Cyrus, as promising them somewhat that suited them better? The Persians ever since a little after the short (though spacious) monarchy of Alexander the Great, confirmed their estate in that large country of the East, and are a kingdom at this day. If this be so, then either the gods have no faith, in that they keep

flitting from the friend to the foe (which Camillus would not do,
though Rome were most unthankful to him for his most serviceable
conquest of the Veians, but burying the wrong, freed it the second
time from the Gauls). Or else they are not so valiant as gods
should be: but may be conquered and chased away by human
strength and cunning. Or when they do fight, it is the gods on
the one side that beat the gods on the other, and not the men.
It follows then they are foes amongst themselves. If so, the city
should never give them any more worship than it held to be due
to any other people or nation whatsoever that helpeth them. But
howsoever this flight, or this removal, or this killing of these gods
fell out, the name of Christ was not yet known in those times and
places, when and wherein these changes of states did thus follow
the effects of war. For if after those twelve hundred years, and
the overplus, when the Assyrian monarchy was removed, the
Christian religion had come in, and preached of another, an eternal
monarchy, and condemned all their gods for false and feigned, and
their sacrifices for sacrilegious fooleries; what would the vain men
of that nation have replied, but that the kingdom was overthrown
because they had left their old religion and received this of ours?
In which foolish answer let these our later antagonists behold
themselves as in a glass: and blush (if they be not past grace) to
follow so fond a precedent: though indeed the Roman Empire be
rather afflicted than altered or translated, as it was often before
Christ's coming: and as it recovered from those afflictions before,
so we ought not to despair of its recovery in the present. Who
knows the will of God herein?

CHAPTER VIII

*What precious gods those were by whose power the Romans held their
empire to be enlarged and preserved, seeing that they durst not trust
them with the defence of mean and particular matters*

LET us now make inquiry, if you will, which god (or gods) of all
this swarm that Rome worshipped was it that did enlarge and protect this their empire. In a world of such worth and dignity,
they durst not secretly commit any dealing to the goddess Cloacina,
nor to the goddess Volupia, the lady of pleasure, nor to Libentina,
the goddess of lust, nor to Vaticanus, the god of children's crying,
nor to Cunina, the goddess of their cradles. But how can this one
little book possibly have room to contain the names of all their gods
and goddesses, when their great volumes will not do it, seeing they
have a several god to see to every particular act they take in hand?
Durst they trust one god with their lands, think you? No,
Rusina must look to the country, Jugatinus to the hill tops:

Collatina to the whole hills besides, and Vallonia to the valleys. Nor could Segetia alone be sufficient to protect the corn: but while it was in the ground, Seia must look to it: when it was up, and ready to mow, Segetia: when it was mown and laid up, then Tutilina took charge of it, who did not like that Segetia alone should have charge of it all the while before it came dried unto her hand. Nor was it sufficient for those wretches, that their poor seduced souls, that scorned to embrace one true God, should become prostitute unto this meaner multitude of devils; they must have more: so they made Proserpina goddess of the corn's first leaves and buds; the knots Nodotus looked unto, Volutina to the blades, and when the ear began to look out, it was Patelana's charge; when the ear began to be even bearded (because *hostire* was taken of old for 'to make even') Hostilina's work came in; when the flowers bloomed, Flora was called forth; when they grew white, Lacturcia; being ripe Matuta, being cut down Runcina. Oh, let them pass; that which shames not them I loathe. These few I have reckoned, to show that they durst in no way affirm that these gods were the ordainers, adorners, augmenters, or preservers of the empire of Rome, having each one such peculiar charges assigned them, as they had no leisure in the world to deal in any other matter. How should Segetia guard the empire, that must not meddle but with the corn; or Cunina look to the wars, that must deal with naught but children's cradles; or Nodotus give his aid in the battle, that cannot help so much as the blade of the corn, but is bound to look to the knot only? Every house hath a porter to the door: and though he be but a single man, yet he is sufficient for that office: but they must have their three gods, Forculus for the door, Cardea for the hinge, and Limentinus for the threshold. Forsooth Forculus could not possibly keep both door, hinges, and threshold.

CHAPTER IX

Whether it was Jove, whom the Romans held the chief god, that was this protector and enlarger of their empire

WHEREFORE setting aside this nest of inferior gods for a while, let us look into the offices of the greater; and see which of them brought Rome to such a pre-eminence over the other nations. This surely was Jove's work. For him they made the king over all their gods besides, as his sceptre and his seat on the highest part of all the Capitol do sufficiently testify. And of him they have a very convenient saying (though it be from a poet): 'All is full of Jove.' [1] And Varro is of opinion that those that worship but one God, and that without any statue, do mean this Jove, though they call him

[1] Virg. *Eclog*. iii. 60.

by another name. Which being so, why is he so badly used at
Rome, and by others also in other places, as to have a statue made
him? This so displeased Varro, that although he were overborne
with the custom of so great a city, yet he hesitated not both to
affirm and record that in making those statues they both banished
all fear and brought in much error?

CHAPTER X

*What opinion they followed, that set diverse gods to rule in diverse
parts of the world*

BUT why had he Juno added to him, both as his 'sister and wife'? [1]
Because we place Jupiter in the sky (say they) and Juno in the air;
and these two are contiguous, one immediately next above the
other. Very well, then all is not full of Jove as you said but now,
if Juno do fill a part. Does the one fill the other (being man and
wife), and are they distinct in their several elements, and yet conjoined in them both? Why then hath Jove the sky assigned him
and Juno the air? Again, if only these two sufficed for all, what
should Neptune do with the sea, and Pluto with the earth? Nay,
and for fear of lack of brood, Neptune must have a Salacia, and
Pluto a Proserpina for wives to breed upon. For as Juno possesses
the lower part of the heavens, the air (say they); so does Salacia the
inner parts of the sea, and Proserpina the bowels of the earth.
Alas, they would fain stitch up their lies handsomely, and cannot
find which way. For if this were true, the world should have but
three elements (and not four as their ancient writers have recorded),
if every couple of gods should have their element. But they themselves have there affirmed that the sky is one thing and the air
another. But the water, within and without, is all water (there
may be some diversity, but never any alteration of the essential
form): and earth is earth, however it be severally distinguished.
Now the world being complete in these four, where is Minerva's
share? She has a share in the Capitol though she be not daughter
to Jove and Juno both. If she dwell in the highest part of the
sky, and therefore the poets feigned her to be the birth of Jove's
own brain, why is not she then made the absolute empress of
heaven, seeing that she sits above Jove? Because it is not meet to
make the child lord over the parent? Why then was not that
equity kept between Saturn and Jupiter? Because Saturn was
conquered? Did they fight then? No, say they; that is but a
poetical fiction, a fable. Well, thus you see they will trust no
fables, and think better of their gods than so. But how chances it
then that Saturn (seeing he might not sit above his son Jove) had

[1] Virg. *Aen.* i. 47.

not a seat equal with him? Because Saturn (say they) is nothing but the 'length of time.' Well then, they that worship Saturn, worship Time and Jove; the king of all the gods is said to be born of Time! And what wrong do we to Jove and Juno in saying they are born of Time, seeing that by the pagans' own confessions they signify heaven and earth, both of which were created in time; for this the greatest scholars and wisest of them all commend to our memory. Nor did Virgil speak out of fiction, but out of philosophy, when he said:

> Tum pater omnipotens fecundis imbribus Aether
> Conjugis in gremium laetae descendit.[1]

> Almighty Aether in a fattening shower,
> Dropped in the lap of his glad spouse.

That was into the earth. In which they make a difference also, for herein Terra and Tellus and Tellumo are all different things, they say. And all these they have as gods, distinct in name, office, and ceremonial rites. Terra is also called the mother of the gods, that the poets may now feign with far more toleration (seeing that their very books of religion affirm it), that Juno is not only wife and sister but mother also unto Jove. The same earth they style both Ceres and Vesta, yet Vesta they say most commonly is 'the fire,' and guards that which the city cannot lack. And therefore the virgins kept it, because fire and virginity do never bring forth anything. All which vanity it was fit He only should abolish that was born of a virgin. But who can endure to hear them ascribe so much honour and chastity to the fire, and yet not shame to call Vesta, Venus, that her virgins might have the less care of the honour of virginity? For if Venus were Vesta how should the virgins do her good service in abstaining from venery? Or are there two Venuses, the one a virgin, the other a wanton? Or three rather, one of the virgins (Vesta), one of the wives, and one of the whores? To such a one as this last is, the Phoenicians consecrated the prostitution of their daughters, before they married them. Now which of these is Vulcan's wife? Not the virgin, since she has a husband. Not the whore, for let not Juno's son, and Minerva's forger, be wronged. Well then, it was Venus the wife: yet we would have her to stand as a pattern to be imitated for her tricks that she played with Mars. Oh now (say they) you run to the fables again. Why what reason is there that you should grieve oɪ hear those things from our lips, and yet applaud them on your own stages? Why does it vex you that we should say (a thing utterly incredible, but that it is so fully proved) that those foul and open crimes of their gods were instituted and celebrated in their public honours, and by their own commands?

[1] *Georg.* ii. 325–6.

CHAPTER XI

Of the multitude of gods which the pagan doctors avouch to be but one and the same Jupiter

WHEREFORE let them flourish with their physical arguments as long as they like. Let Jupiter be one while the soul of this terrene world, filling the whole fabric of the four elements, more or less, as they please; and another while but a quarter-ruler with his brethren and sisters: let him be the sky now, embracing Juno, which is the air under him; and let him by and by be both sky and air, filling the lap of the earth, his wife and mother, with fertile showers and seeds. This is no absurdity in their divinity. And (to omit the long and tedious catalogue of his removes and strange transmutations) let him forthwith be that one and only god, of whom the famous poet was thought to say:

> . . . Deum namque ire per omnes
> Terrasque tractusque maris coelumque profundum.[1]

> . . . For God His spirit imparts
> To the earth's, the sea's, and heaven's profoundest parts.

Let him be Jupiter in the sky, Juno in the air, Neptune in the sea, Salacia in the sea's depth, Pluto in the earth, Proserpina in the earth's lowest part, Vesta in the household's fire, Vulcan in the smith's shop, Sol, Luna, and the stars in the spheres, Apollo in divination, Mercury in traffic, Janus in the porter, in the bounds Terminus, in time Saturn, in war Mars and Bellona, in the vineyards Bacchus, in the corn Ceres, in the woods Diana, in men's wits Minerva; let him rule the seed of man as Liber, and of women as Libera; as he is father of the day, let him be Diespiter; as ruler of the monthly disease of women, let him be the goddess Mena; and Lucina that helps in their childbirth. And helping the fruits which increase, let him take the name of Ops. Let him be Vaticanus, that opens the child's mouth first to cry, and Levana, that raises it from the ground to rear it; and Cunina, that guards the cradle. Let none but him sing the destinies of the new-born child, and be called Carmentis; let him sway chance, and be styled Fortuna; or women's paps, and be called Rumina (because the ancients called a pap *ruma*); let him be Potina and suckle the young babes; or Educa and feed them; or Paventia for frighting them; or Venilia for sudden hope; Volupia for pleasure, Agenoria for action, Stimula for provocation, Strenua for confirming man's courage, Numeria for teaching children to count twenty, and Camena for singing. Nay let us make him Consus for his

[1] Virg. *Georg.* iv. 221–2.

counsel, Sentia for his sententious inspirations, Juventas for the guiding of our passage from youth to fuller age.   For our chin's sake (which, if he love us, he clothes in hair) let him be Fortuna Barbata: nay rather, because he is a male god, let him either be Barbatus, as Nodotus is, or because he has a beard, let him not be Fortuna, but Fortunius.   Later, let him be Jugatinus, the joiner in marriage; and at the loosing of a virgin's nuptial girdle let him be invoked by the name of Virginensis: let him be Mutinus, which amongst the Greeks was Priapus, but that (it may be) he will be ashamed of.   Let Jupiter alone be all these that I have reckoned, and that I have not reckoned (for I have thought fit to omit a great many), or as those hold which make him the soul of the world (many of whom are learned men), let all these be but as parts and virtues of him.   If it be so, as I do not yet inquire how it is, what should they lose if they took a shorter course, and adore but one God?   What one thing belonging unto His power were despised, if Himself entirely were duly worshipped?   If they fear that some of his parts would be angry for being neglected, why then it is not as they say, that all this is but as the life of one soul, containing all those gods as the parts, powers, virtues, and faculties thereof; but every part hath a life, really and distinctly separate from the other.   This must needs be true, if one of them may be offended, and another be pleased, and both with one act.   And to say that the whole of Jove would be offended, if all his parts were not severally worshipped, this were foolish; for there were not one of them left out, if the person were adored in whom they are all jointly included.   For to omit the rest (being innumerable), when they say that the stars are all and every one real parts of Jove, and live, have reasonable souls, and therefore are absolute gods, they say they know not what, and see not how many of them they leave without altars and without worship, both of which notwithstanding they have exhibited themselves and commanded others to exhibit unto a certain small number of them.   Wherefore if they doubt the anger of the rest, why are not they afraid to live in the displeasure of the most part of heaven, having given content but unto so few?   Now if they worshipped all the stars inclusively in Jupiter's particular person, they might satisfy them all by this means in the adoration of him alone: for so, none of them would be displeased, seeing they all were worshipped in him; nor should any have cause to think they were contemned.   Whereas otherwise the greater part may conceive just anger for being thus omitted by those that give all the honour unto a very few: and their anger may well be the greater, in that they shine above as unregarded, and behold filthy Priapus stand naked below, in great respect and credit.

CHAPTER XII

Of their opinion that held God to be the soul, and the world to be the body

WHAT of this? Ought not this to move the sharpest wits, nay, all in general? For indeed there is no great sharpness of wit required to the laying aside of all wrangling, and to inquire whether God be the world's soul or no, and whether the world be His body or no, both making one creature, whether He be nature's storehouse containing all things in Himself, and whether out of His soul, that animates all this whole mass, the lives and beings of all living creatures be taken or no, each one according to their natures, and whether there be nothing on earth which is not part of God. If this were true, mark but the irreligious consequence thereof. A man, if it were so, should not tread, without treading part of God under his feet; and in every creature that he killed, he should kill a part of the Deity. I will not relate what others may think of it. I cannot speak it without exceeding shame.

CHAPTER XIII

Of such as hold that the reasonable creatures only are parts of the divine essence

IF they say indeed, that all things in the whole world do not share in God's nature, but yet all reasonable creatures do, truly I cannot see how that can stand. Then the world is not God; for otherwise how can they keep brute beasts from being part of Him? But why need we contend about this? Let us go but unto this reasonable creature, man. Can there be a more damnable absurdity, than to believe that part of God's essence is beaten, when an offending child is beaten? To make the component parts of almighty God as lascivious, unjust, wicked, and damnable, as divers men are—what man can endure to hear it but he that is absolutely mad? Lastly, how can God be justly angry with those that do not worship Him, when they are parts of His own self that are guilty? So then, they are forced to say that every particular god hath his life and subsistence by himself, and that they are not pieces of one another, but that each one that is particularly known must have his peculiar worship: that is known I say, because they cannot all be known. And Jupiter being king over them all is the reason why (as I imagine) they believe him to be the sole erecter and protector of Rome's monarchy. For if it were not he that did it, whom should they think able to perform so great a work; each one having his peculiar task already so distinctly assigned, that one must by no means meddle with that which was under the charge of another? So then the conclusion is, it must needs be only the king of gods that erected and preserved this kingdom of men.

CHAPTER XIV

That the augmentations of kingdoms are unfitly ascribed to Jove; Victory (whom they call a goddess) being sufficient of herself to give a full dispatch to all such businesses

Now here is a question. Why may not sovereignty itself be a god? What should hinder it more than hinders Victory? Or what need is there for men to trouble Jove, if Victory be but favourable enough, and will stay with such as she means to make conquerors? If she be but propitious, let Jove mind his own business, the nations shall come under. Yea, but it may be they are good men and loath to wrong their neighbours that wrong not them, or to provoke them to war, without a juster cause than mere desire to enlarge their kingdom. Nay, be they of that mind, I commend them with all mine heart.

CHAPTER XV

Whether an honest man ought to entertain any desire to enlarge his empire

WHEREFORE let them observe whether it befit a good and upright man to rejoice in the enlarging of his dominions. For it was the badness of those against whom just wars were undertaken that hath advanced earthly sovereignties to that state they now hold: which would have still been little, if no enemy had given cause or provocation to war by offering his neighbour wrong. If men had always been thus conditioned, the kingdoms of the earth would have continued little in quantity, and peaceful in neighbourly agreement. And then many kingdoms would have been in the world, as many families are now in a city. So that the waging of war, and the augmentation of dominions by conquest, may seem to the bad as a great felicity, but the good must needs hold it a mere necessity. But because it would be worse if the bad should get all the sovereignty, and so overrule the good, therefore in that respect the honest men may esteem their own sovereignty a felicity. But doubtless, he is far more happy that has a good neighbour by him in quiet, than he that must be forced to subdue an evil neighbour by contention. It is an evil wish, to wish for one that thou hatest or fearest, or for one to trouble thee so that thou mightest have one to conquer. Wherefore if the Romans attained to so great an empire by honest, upright, and just wars, why should they not reverence their enemy's iniquity, and take it as one of their goddesses? For we see that iniquity hath given good assistance to the increase of this empire by making others so bad that they provoke just wars, that so the Romans might have just cause to subdue them, and so consequently to enlarge their own dominions. And why should not Iniquity be a goddess (at least that of foreign nations) as well as Fear and Paleness and Fever at Rome? So that by these two deities, Iniquity and Victory, the first beginning the wars, and the latter ending them with the conquest, Rome's empire was enlarged infinitely, whilst Jove kept holiday in the Capitol. For what hath Jupiter to do here where those (which they may say are but merely his benefits) are worshipped, invocated, and accounted for deities and parts of his essence? Indeed he should have had a fair good hand in this business, if that he were called Sovereignty as well as she is called Victory. But if that Sovereignty be but a mere gift of Jove's, then why may not Victory be so too? Both would be held to be so if the Romans did not worship a dead stone in the Capitol, but the true King of kings and Lord of all domination both in earth and heaven.

CHAPTER XVI

The reason why the Romans, in their appointment of several gods for every thing and every action, would needs place the Temple of Rest or Quiet without the gates

BUT I wonder much that the Romans, appointing particular gods over everything, and almost every motion—Agenoria, that stirred men to action; Stimula, that forced them forward; Murcia, that never went out of her place, and, as Pomponius says, made men slothful, and disabled them from action; Strenua, that made men resolute: unto all which gods and goddesses they offered public sacrifices, and kept solemn feasts—should have vouchsafed to Quies, the goddess of Rest, only a temple without Porta Collina, but allowed her no public honours at all in the city. Was this a sign of their unquiet and turbulent spirits, or that those who had such a rabble of devil-gods to worship and reverence, should never come to enjoy that Rest, whereunto the true Physician invites us, saying: 'Learn of Me that I am meek, and lowly in heart, and you shall find rest unto your souls'? [1]

[1] Matt. xi. 29.

CHAPTER XVII

Whether, if Jove is the chief god of all, Victory ought to be accounted as one of the number

WILL they say (think you) that Jupiter sends this goddess Victory whither he pleases, and she obeying him, sets up her abode on that side that he commands? It is true indeed: but not of that Jove which their fondness dreams is king of the gods; but of Him that is the true King of all times and all things, that can send not victory, which is no substance, but His angels, and make them conquer whom He pleases; whose counsels may be unknown, but never unjust. For if Victory be a goddess, why is not Triumph a god and husband unto her, or her brother, or son, or somewhat? For they believe such absurdities of the gods, that if the poets should feign them, or we cast them in their teeth, they would answer that it was a ridiculous figment, not to be attributed to the true gods. And yet they laugh not at themselves, who did more than read those dotages in the poets, when they adored them in their temples. Wherefore they should worship and adore only Jupiter indeed, and let all this multitude pass. For if Victory be a goddess and subject unto that king, she dares not resist him, but must be ready to fulfil his pleasure whithersoever he send her.

CHAPTER XVIII

Why Fortune and Felicity were made goddesses

NAY, Felicity is a goddess also now. She has got her an altar, a temple, sacrifices, and everything fit. Why should not she have all the worship to herself? Wheresoever she is, there should all good be. But why is Fortune preferred to the honour of a deity? Is Felicity one thing and Fortune another? Yes, Fortune may be both good and bad; but if Felicity once grow bad, she loses her name. Truly I think we should have all the gods of both sexes (if they have sexes) to be good ones: and so thought Plato and other excellent philosophers and statesmen. How then can the goddess Fortune be now good and now evil? Is she no goddess when she is not good, but is turned immediately into a devil? Why then how many goddesses are there? Even as many as there be fortunate men, that is of good fortune. For since there are many others who at one and the same time are men of evil fortune, Fortune should be both good and evil at once, if she could: good to these and bad to the others. But she that is the goddess, is she always good? If so, she is Felicity herself. Why changes she her name then? Yet that may be tolerated. For many things have two or three names. But why then hath she different temples, altars, and ceremonies? Because (say they) that is Felicity that does follow a man's deserts: that good fortune which lights casually upon good and evil, without any respect of deserts, and is therefore called Fortune. How can she then be good, coming with no discretion as well to evil men as good? And why is she adored, being so blind that she commonly deserts those that honour her, and stays with those that scorn her? If her servants obtain grace at her hands, and get her to stay with them, then she follows merit, and is Fortune no more. Where is her definition then? How then doth she receive her name from chance circumstances? If she be Fortune, in vain is all her worship: but if she discern and help her servants, then she is Fortune no more. But does not Jupiter send her also whither his pleasure is? Well, if he do, then let him have all the worship to himself: for she cannot gainsay him, if he bid her depart to such or such a man. Or it may be that the evil do honour her, to get themselves some merit whereby they may purchase Felicity, and so enjoy her company instead of Fortune's.

CHAPTER XIX

Of a goddess called Fortuna Muliebris

NAY, they are in such dotage upon this same Fortune, that they do steadfastly affirm that the image which the matrons dedicated and named 'Fortuna Muliebris,' 'the woman's fortune,' did speak particular words; and that not once but often, saying that they had dedicated her very properly: which if it were true, we ought not to wonder at. For the devils can use this deception with ease; which was the more discoverable, in that it was she that spoke, who follows chance, and not desert. Fortune spoke, but Felicity was silent: unto what other end was this, but only to make men neglect living well, seeing that without any desert this Lady Fortune might make them fortunate? But yet if Fortune did speak, the man's fortune (methinks) should have spoken, and not the woman's, because otherwise, the women that consecrated the statue might be thought to feign that the image spoke, because they love so well to be heard speak themselves.

CHAPTER XX

Of the deification of Virtue and Faith by the pagans, and of their omission of the worship that was due to divers other gods, if it be true that these were gods

THEY made a goddess also of Virtue: which if she were such, should take precedence over a great many of the rest. But being no goddess, but a gift of God, let it be obtained of Him that alone has power of the gift of it, and farewell all the crowd of these counterfeit gods. But why is Faith made a goddess, and graced with a temple and an altar? Whosoever knows Faith well, makes his own bosom her temple. But how know they what Faith is, when her chief office is to believe in the true God? And why may not Virtue suffice? Is not Faith there where Virtue is? They divide Virtue into four parts, Prudence, Justice, Fortitude, and Temperance; and because every one of these has several subdivisions, therefore Faith falls to be part of justice, and is of chief power with us, that know that the 'just shall live by faith.'[1] But I wonder at these men that do so thirst after an abundance of gods, that having made Faith a goddess, they will so neglect a great many goddesses more of her nature, to whom they should afford temples and altars as well as to her? Why is not Temperance made a goddess, having given such lustre to divers Roman princes? Nor Fortitude that held Scaevola's hand in the fire, and went with Curtius into the spacious gulf for the love of his country, and stood by the two Decii, the father and the son, when they vowed their lives to their nation? If, by the way, this were true valour in them (which is a question not under discussion here), why are not Prudence and Wisdom made deities as well as the rest? Is it because they are all worshipped under the general name of Virtue? So might all the supposed parts of one God be entirely worshipped in His sole and particular worship. But in Virtue there are Faith and Chastity, as parts indeed, and yet those must have peculiar altars and sacrifices. But it is vanity and not verity that turns such qualities into deities.

CHAPTER XXI

*That such as knew not the true and only God had better have
been contented with Virtue and Felicity*

FOR these are the gifts of God, not gods themselves. But where Virtue and Felicity are, what needeth any more? What will satisfy him whom these two cannot satisfy? Virtue embraceth all good acts, and Felicity all good desires. If it were for these that Jupiter was worshipped (and what is the extent and continuance of dominion, but an appurtenance of Felicity?), why perceived they not that these were but his gifts, and not deities themselves? But if they were deities, what need any beside them? For let them cast over all the sum of their gods' and goddesses' functions, as their inventions have distributed them, and find if they can that he that has Virtue and Felicity needs any of their helps, or has any use of them? Why need he trouble Mercury or Minerva for learning virtue, when Virtue includes all in herself? For virtue is but an art of living well and justly, as all the old writers do define it. And

[1]Hab. ii. 4.

therefore some say that the word art comes of ἀρετή in Greek, which
is virtue.   But if none but clever men could be virtuous, what use
then is there of Father Catius, a god that maketh men acute, when
Felicity can do all this?   For to be born clever is a felicity.   Wherefore, though the child being yet unborn could not merit this
felicity, yet she bestows cleverness upon the child as a benefit unto
the parents that honoured her.   But why need the women in travail
call on Lucina, Felicity being able with her presence both to make
their labour easy and their offspring happy?   Why need Ops be
troubled with the children when they are new born, Vaticanus
when they cry, Cunina when they sleep, Rumina when they suck,
Statilius when they learn to stand, Adeona and Abeona when they
come and go, Mens for a good mind for them, Volumnus and
Volumna for a good will for them, the nuptial gods for their marriage, the field gods for their harvest, and chiefly Fructesia; Mars
and Bellona for their fights, Victoria for their victories, Honor for
their honours, Pecunia for their riches, Aesculanus and his son
Argentinus for coin enough both of brass and silver?   The first is
the father, because brass money was in use before silver: I wonder
that Argentinus begot not Aurinus, for gold followed soon after.
If they had had Aurinus, sure as death he should have had place of
father and grandfather, as well as Jove had above Saturn.   Why
need men run unto so many for this good or that (to such a crew as
neither I can reckon nor themselves discern, having a god for every
little act and accident of men), when Felicity would have bestowed
all in far less time and with far less toil; nor need any other be
troubled, either for bestowing of good, or diverting of bad?   Why
should Fessonia be called unto the weary, Pellonia to chase away the
foe, Apollo or Aesculapius to the sick, or both, and few enough in a
disease of danger?   Nor needed Spinensis to meddle with the
thorns, nor any entreaty to keep away Rubigo.   Felicity's present
aid alone would keep all mischiefs away, and repulse them at their
first approach.   But now to shut up this discourse of these two,
Virtue and Felicity; if Felicity be the reward of Virtue, then is it
no goddess, but a gift of God, but if it be a goddess, it must needs
be the producer of Virtue, seeing that to attain to virtue is the
greatest felicity.

CHAPTER XXII

*Of the knowledge of these pagan gods, which Varro boasts he
taught the Romans*

WHAT great good turn then does Varro boast that he has done unto
his citizens, in the particularizing of the gods and their worships
that the Romans must observe?   For what boots it (says he) to
know a physician by name and by face, and yet to be ignorant what

a physician is? So likewise it boots not (says he) to know Aesculapius unless you know that he cures diseases: otherwise you know
not what to pray to him for. And this he confirms in another
simile, saying: 'A man cannot live well, nay he cannot live at all, if
he know not the smith, the painter, the carpenter, etc., distinctly;
where to have this necessary, where that, where to be taught this
or that. So it is plain, that to know what power every god hath,
and for what object, is wonderfully useful. For thence may we
gather to whom to plead for every need we have, and not follow
the mimes, in begging water of Bacchus, and wine of the Nymphs.'
Who would not give this man thanks now, if his doctrine were
true, and did show the worship of the true God, of whom alone
we are to ask all things?

CHAPTER XXIII

*Of the absolute sufficiency of Felicity alone, whom the Romans (who
   worshipped so many gods) did for a great while neglect, and gave no
   divine honours unto*

BUT if their books be true, and Felicity be a goddess, how comes
it to pass that she has not all the worship unto herself, being of
herself sufficient for all needs? Who wishes anything but happiness? And why was it not till the days of Lucullus that the
Romans thought it fit to erect her a temple? Why did not Romulus, that wished the city so well, provide a place for her, seeing that
her presence might have saved him all his labour in praying to the
other gods? He had never been king, nor ever come to have
been a god, had not she stuck to him. Why then did he clog the
Romans with such a load of gods, Janus, Jove, Mars, Picus,
Faunus, Tiberinus, Hercules, and all the rest? And what did
Tatius, bringing in Saturn, Ops, Sol, Luna, Vulcan, Lux, and
to crown all, sweet Cloacina, leaving Felicity in the dust? And
what was in Numa's mind, that he should gather such a host of he-
gods and she-gods, and leave her out? Could he not find her for
the multitude? Verily Hostilius would never have brought Fear
and Pallor to be propitiated, if he had had any knowledge of this
Felicity. For had she come there, Fear and Pallor must needs
have been sent packing.

Again, in all the increase of the empire, she was not thought of,
no man served her. What was the reason of this? Was the
empire more great than happy? Perhaps so: for how can true
Felicity be there where true Piety is not? And Piety is the true
worship of the true God, not the adoration of that multitude of
false gods, or devils if you will. But afterwards, when Felicity
was introduced, and had got a place with the rest, the great infelicity of the civil wars followed presently upon it. Was not

Felicity angry (think you) that she was let pass so long, and then taken in at last, not to her honour but to her disgrace, being ranked with Priapus, and Cloacina, and Fear, and Pallor, and Fever, and others that were no gods to be worshipped, but defects in the worshippers? Lastly, seeing she must be fain to share honours with so unworthy a rabble, why had she not at least a better part of honours than the others? Who could endure that the goddess Felicity should stand by and neither be reckoned amongst the 'superior gods,' that were of Jove's council, nor amongst the 'select gods' either; nor yet have a temple that should have excelled all the rest in height of posture and magnificnece of fabric? Why should she not have a better one than Jupiter? For she herself gave him his kingdom, if ever he were a happy king. And that happiness is of better worth than sovereignty is most plain. For many men doubtless may be found that would not be kings, but none that would not be happy. So that if the gods were asked their minds, by augury, or otherwise, whether they would give place to Felicity or no, I will undertake, that even if all the room besides were filled with other gods' altars so that Felicity could not have a fit place built, Jupiter himself would give place and let Felicity have his own seat upon the top of the Tarpeian hill. Nor is there one of them that would not do as much, unless (which is impossible) some of them would be so mad as to lose her favour and grow miserable. Jupiter would never use her as he was used by Mars, Terminus, and Juventas, who by no means could be persuaded to give their king place. For (as they write) Tarquin being desirous to build the Capitol, and seeing the place he thought fittest already taken up by other strange gods, durst not act against their will, but thought that good manners would teach them to give place unto their king: and seeing that there was a great fort there, where he meant to build, he asked them by augury whether they were willing to resign the place to their king or no. All were content, except Mars, Terminus, and Juventas: and so the Capitol was built, and they for their sauciness had such small monuments left that the Romans' greatest divines did scarcely know where they stood. But Jove would never deal so uncivilly with Felicity as Mars, Terminus, and Juventas dealt with him. And then those that would not yield to him, assuredly would yield to her, that made him their king. Or if they would not, why then it were because they had rather abide in obscurity in Felicity's house than sit in eminence without her company; so that had she but the highest place, the citizens would soon learn where to pray for good gifts, and in time, by the very persuasion of nature, put away that swarm of gods, and pray only to Felicity, offer sacrifice only to her, and frequent her temple only, if they desired to be happy, as all would do; and so all men would come and offer all prayers for her to herself; for who would beg anything but Felicity of any god? And so Felicity having power to be abiding with whom she will (as she may if she be a goddess), what man were so foolish as to go and entreat her company of another god, when he might obtain it of herself? And so the dignity of place also should of right be hers above all the other gods. For they write that the ancient Romans did worship one Summanus, one that ruled the thunder of the night, above Jupiter that ruled the day thunder. But after Jupiter had gotten him such a sumptuous house, the company came in so fast unto him, that within a while one could scarce find one that had heard, nay more, that had read so much as the name of Summanus. But now if Felicity be no goddess, being (in truth) but a gift of God; then is it fit to find out that God that can bestow it, and to throw aside this dangerous crowd of counterfeit deities, which a vain pack of fools do run thus headlong after, taking God's gifts for God Himself, and by their obstinacy giving Him continual cause of offence, whose gifts they are; for so shall he never want infelicity that honours Felicity as a goddess, and neglects Him that is the giver of all felicity: even as he shall never lack hunger that licks the picture of a crust, and never asks bread of him that hath it to give him.

CHAPTER XXIV

What reasons the pagans bring for their worshipping of gods' gifts for gods themselves

LET us examine their reasons. Do you think (say they) our ancestors were such fools that they knew not those to be gods' gifts, and not gods? No truly; but because they knew that they could not have them but from some god, they called the gods which they thought had the gift of them by the names of the things themselves; sometimes deriving words from thence (as Bellona of *bellum*, war, not Bellum itself; Cunina of *cunae*, cradles, not Cuna; Segetia of *seges*, corn, not Seges itself; Pomona of *pomum*, an apple, not Pomum; and Bubona of *bos*, an ox, not Bos); and sometimes never altering the word at all, but calling them just as the thing is called: as Pecunia the goddess, that gives money (not holding money itself for a goddess), and Virtus, that gives virtue, Honor for honour, Victoria for victory, Concordia for concord; and so Felicity being called a goddess, is not meant of the thing given, but of the power that giveth it. Well, out of this reason will we find an easy way to persuade all such as have not hardened their hearts to be of our opinion.

CHAPTER XXV

Of the worship of one God only, whose name although they knew not,
yet they took him for the giver of felicity

FOR if man's weakness observed thus much, that felicity could not
come but from some god, and if this was perceived by those that
worshipped so many gods, who therefore would call him that they
thought could give something by the name of the thing itself,
knowing no other name he had; this proves sufficiently that Jupiter,
whom they worshipped already, could not give felicity, but only
he whom they worshipped under the name of Felicity.   So then,
it is confirmed that they thought felicity could not be given but
by a god that they knew not well: seek but him out then and give
him his due worship and it sufficeth.   Cashier this rabble of
innumerable and unnecessary gods, nay devils: let not that god
suffice the worshipper, whose gift is not sufficient: hold not (I say)
that god for a sufficient giver of felicity whose felicity is wholly
insufficient.   But let him for whom felicity is sufficient (and man
has nothing more to wish for than this) serve the one and only God,
the giver of felicity.   It is not he that they call Jove.   For if it
were he, they would never stand seeking this gift of another, who
goes under the name of Felicity: besides, they would not do Jove's
honour that wrong, as to count him as Jove is counted, an adulterer
with other men's wives, and an unchaste lover and ravisher of fair
boys.

CHAPTER XXVI

Of the stage plays which the gods exacted of their servants

'BUT these were fictions of Homer,' quoth Tully, 'transferring
human desires unto the gods.   I had rather they had transferred
divine desires unto us.' [1]   This grave man indeed was much displeased with the unseasonable fictions of those times.   But why
then did the wisest and most learned men of all the Romans present
stage plays, writing them and acting them to the honour of their
gods, and as parts and points of their religion?   Here Tully
exclaims not against poetic fictions but against the old ordinances.
And would not the ordainers exclaim too, and say, Why what do
we?   Our gods entreated us, nay forced us upon pain of destruction, to offer them such things as honours: punishing the neglect
thereof with severity, and showing themselves pleased in the
amendment of that neglect.   That which I will now relate is
reckoned as one of their most virtuous and memorable deeds.

[1] *Tusc. Disp.* i. 26, 65.

Titus Latinus, a rustic housekeeper, was warned in a dream to bid the Roman senate restore the stage plays, because upon their first day of presentation an offender carried out and whipped to death before all the people had sore displeased the gods that do not love such sad spectacles, but are all for mirth and jollity. Well, he neglected to tell the senate this, but was warned again the next night. Neglecting it again, suddenly his son died. And the third night he was warned again upon pain of a greater mischief. He not daring as yet to reveal it, fell into a sore and horrible disease. And then having imparted it to his friends, they counselled him to open it to the senate. So he was carried to them in his coach, and having told his dream, grew well in an instant, and went home on his feet. The senate being amazed with his miracle renewed the plays at fourfold charges. Who sees not now (that sees at all) how villainously these devils abuse those men that are their slaves, in forcing these things from them as honours which an upright judgment would easily discern to be obscenities. From this slavery can nothing deliver man but the grace of God through Jesus Christ our Lord. In those plays, the gods' crimes that the poets feign are presented: yet by the gods' express charge were they by the senate renewed. And there did the stage players act, produce, and present Jove for the veriest whoremaster in the world. Had this been false, he would have been offended at it; but taking delight (as he did) to have villainies invented upon him, who would serve him that would not serve the devil? Is this the founder, enlarger, and establisher of the Roman Empire? Is he not more base and abject than any Roman that beheld him thus presented? Can he give happiness that loved this unhappy worship, and would be more unhappily angry if it were not afforded him?

CHAPTER XXVII

Of the three kinds of gods whereof Scaevola disputed

IT is at least in memory that Scaevola, their learned priest, disputed of three kinds of gods that were taught by authors; one by the poets; one by the philosophers; one by the princes of the city. The first sort, he says, were but fooleries, much of their doctrine being fictions: the second, ill-suited to a politic state, having much superfluity and divers inconveniences. For the superfluity is no great matter, for it is a saying amongst men, 'Superfluity hurteth not.' But what are the inconveniences? To deny openly that Hercules, Aesculapius, Castor, and Pollux are gods; for the philosophers teach that they were men, and died as other men do. To what end is this, but that the cities should be filled with statues of such as are no true gods, the true god having neither sex, age, nor body? But this Scaevola would not have the people to know, because he did not think it was false himself. So that he holds it fit that cities should be deluded in religion, which indeed Varro hesitates not plainly to affirm in *De Rebus Divinis*. A godly religion, whereto when weak minds go for refuge, and seek to be freed by the truth, they must be told that it is fit that they be illuded! Nor does the same book conceal the cause why Scaevola rejects the poets' gods. It is because they do so deform them with their stories that they are not fit to keep good men company, one being said to steal, and another to commit adultery: and also to do and say so filthily and foolishly, as that two of the three goddesses striving for eminence of beauty, being conquered by Venus destroyed Troy; that Jove was turned to a bull, or a swan, to have the company of some wench or other; that a goddess married a man, and that Saturn ate up his sons. No wonder, no vice, but there you have it set down, quite against the natures of the deities. O Scaevola, abolish those plays if it be in thy power! Tell the people what absurd honours they offer the gods, gazing on their guilt, and remembering their pranks, as a licence for their own practice! If they say, You priests brought them us, entreat the gods that commanded them to suffer their abolishment. If they be bad, and therefore nowise credible with reverence to the gods' majesties, then the greater is the injury that is offered unto them, about whom they are so freely invented. But they are devils, Scaevola, teaching guiltiness, and joying in filthiness; they will not hear thee. They think it no injury to have such black crimes imputed unto them, but rather hold themselves wronged if they be not imputed and exhibited. Now if thou callest on Jove against them, were there no other cause for it but the most frequent presenting of his enormities (though you call him the god and king of the world), would he not think himself the most highly wronged by you, for ranking him in worship with such filthy companions, and making him governor of them?

CHAPTER XXVIII

Whether the Romans' diligence in this worship of those gods did their empire any good at all

BY no means then could these gods preserve the Roman Empire, being so criminal in their own filthy desiring of such honours as these are, which rather serve to condemn them than appease them. For if they could have done that, the Greeks should have had their help before, who afforded them far better store of such sacrifices as these, with far more stage plays and shows. For they, seeing the poets tear their gods to pieces so freely, never thought shame to let them tear themselves to pieces, but allowed them free leave to traduce whom they pleased, and held the stage players worthy of the best honours of their state. But even as Rome might have had golden coins, even if they never worshipped Aurinus for it, so might they have had silver and brass ones without Argentinus or his father Aesculanus, and all other necessaries. So it is clear that they could not possess their kingdom against the will of the true God, and that, even if all the other gods were unrecognized and unworshipped, nevertheless that one God, being known and well and duly worshipped, would have kept their kingdom on earth in better estate than ever, and afterward have bestowed a kingdom on each of them in heaven (had they a kingdom before or had they none) that should endure for ever.

CHAPTER XXIX

Of the falseness of that augury that presaged courage and stability to the state of Rome

FOR what a goodly presage was that which I spake of but now,[1] of the obstinacy of Mars, Terminus, and Juventas in not giving place to Jove the king of the gods; that it should signify that Mars' nation, the Romans, should yield place to no man: that no man should remove the limits of their empire, because of Terminus, and that their youth should yield to none, because of Juventas! Now mark how they misused the king of gods, daring to give these auguries as in his defiance, and as glorying in not yielding to him, though if these antiquities were true, they need fear nothing. For they are not going to confess that the gods must give place to Christ that would not give place to Jove: and they might give Christ place without prejudice to the empire's limits, a place taken both out of the temples and the hearts of their worshippers. Nevertheless long before Christ came in the flesh and the recording in writing of that augury, yet after that presage in Tarquin's time, the Romans lost many a battle, and proved Juventas a liar in his prophecy, and Mars' nation was cut in pieces even within the very walls, by the conquering Gauls; and the limits of the empire were brought to a narrow compass in Hannibal's time when most of the cities of Italy fell from Rome to him. Thus was this fine augury fulfilled, and the obstinacy of the presages remained to prove them rebellious devils. For it is one thing not to give place, and another to give place and regain it afterwards. And yet afterwards the bounds of the empire were altered in the east by Hadrian's means, who lost Armenia, Mesopotamia, and Syria unto the Persians, to show the god Terminus, who would not give place to Jove himself, but guarded the Roman limits against all

[1] IV. xxiii.

men, to show him, I say, that Hadrian a king of men could do more
than Jove the king of gods. The said provinces being recovered
afterwards, now almost in our times, the god Terminus has given
ground again, Julian (that was given so to the oracles) desperately
commanding all the ships to be burned that brought the army vic-
tuals, so that the soldiers fainting, and he himself being slain by his
foes' hands, there was no means for one man to escape, but by
yielding to the foe so much of the empire as now to this day they
possess: making a bargain not altogether so bad as Hadrian's was,
but taking a middle course between two extremes. And so Terminus' standing out with Jove was but an unlucky sign and foolish
augury, seeing that Hadrian's will, Julian's rashness, and Jovian's
necessity all made him give room to them. The Romans that were
of discretion observed this well, but they could not overturn the
inveterate idolatry wherein the devils had bound the city so fast:
and they themselves, though holding these things vain, thought
notwithstanding nature should have that divine worship allowed
her, which indeed is the prerogative of the true God alone, under
whom she is at command. 'These served the creature, rather than
the Creator,' as the apostle says, 'who is blessed for evermore.' [1]
This God's help was needed, to send some godly men to suffer
death for the true religion, and thereby to take away these erroneous
illusions from the world.

CHAPTER XXX

*The confessions of such as do worship those pagan gods, from
their own mouths*

CICERO being augur derided the auguries, and blames men for
letting their actions rely upon the voice of a crow or a daw. Oh, but
this academic faith, that all things are uncertain—he that holds it
is not worthy to be trusted in any of these mysteries. Q. Lucil.
Balbus in Tully's second book *De Natura Deorum* [2] disputes hereof;
and having proved these superstitions to be physical in nature,
yet condemns the institution of images and their fables, in these
words: 'Perceive you not then that from the useful observations
of these things in nature, reason was found to bring in those
imaginary and forged gods? Hence came all the false opinions,
errors, and old wives' tales: for now are we acquainted with the
shapes, ages, apparel, kinds, marriages, kindreds, and all are
squared out by human fancies: nay they are presented in a condition of mental disturbance. We have heard of their desires,
sorrows, and passions. Nor lacked they wars, if all tales be true:
they fought in parties, not only in Homer, but all on a side also

---

[1] Rom. i. 25.   [2] ii. 28, 70.

against the Titans and Giants: and hence arises a sottish belief of
their vanity, and extreme inconstancy.' Behold now what they
themselves say that worship these forgeries: he affirms that these
things belonged to superstition, but he treats of religion as the
Stoics do. 'For,' quoth he, 'not only the philosophers, but all our
ancestors made a difference between religion and superstition.
For such as prayed whole days together, and offered for their
children's lives, those were called superstitious.' Who perceives
not now that he, standing in awe of this city's custom, did notwithstanding commend the religion of his ancestors, and would fain
have severed it from superstition, but that he cannot tell how?
For if the ancients called those superstitious, that prayed and
sacrificed whole days together, were not they worthy of that name
also, whom he reprehends for inventing so many distinct ages,
images, and sexes, etc., for the whole number of the gods? If
worshippers of those be culpable, it implies guilt also unto these
ancients that invented and adored such idle fooleries: and unto
him also (for all his eloquent evasions) that must be tied by necessity
to this absurd worship, and dares not speak in a public oration
what he delivers here in a private disputation. Thanks therefore
be given to our Lord Jesus Christ, by all us Christians; not to
heaven and earth (as he would have it) but unto Him that made
heaven and earth, who has overturned and abolished those superstitions (which Balbus durst scarcely mutter at) by His heavenly
humility, His apostles' preaching, and His martyrs' faith, that died
for the truth and lived in the truth, having by these means rooted
all errors not only out of the hearts of the religious, but even out
of the temples of the superstitious.

CHAPTER XXXI

Of Varro's rejecting the popular opinion, and of his belief of one God,
though he knew not the true God

AND what say you about Varro (whom we are sorry should consider
plays as an honour to the gods in religion, though not in his own
judgment, seeing he exhorts men to the adoration of the gods so
religiously)? Does not he confess that he is not of the opinion
of those that left the Romans their religion, and that if he were to
leave the city any institutions, he would rather give them their
gods after the prescript of nature? But seeing that the former
has been of so long continuance, he says that it was but his duty
to prosecute his discourse hereof from the oldest antiquities, to the
end that the people should be induced rather to honour than to
contemn them; wherein this judicious writer shows that he does
not disclose everything, because they would be contemptible not

only to himself but to the rabble if revealed. I should perhaps be thought to have but conjectured this, but that he himself says in many places that there is much truth which the people ought not to know: nay and if it were falsehood, yet it were fit the people should nevertheless think that it were truth: and therefore the Grecians shut up their *teletae* [1] and their most secret mysteries in walls. Here he has made a discovery of all the politic governments of the world. But the devils take great delight in this playing double: making themselves the masters both over the deceivers and the deceived, from whose dominion nothing frees us but the grace of God, through Jesus Christ our Lord. This acute and learned man says further, that he thinks only those discern God who teach that He is a soul, moving and swaying the whole world: and hereby, though he yet have no firm hold of the truth (for God is no soul, but the soul's Maker), yet if the city's custom had permitted him, assuredly he would have taught them the worship of one sole God, and the Governor of the world: so that we should but have this one controversy with him, whether God were a soul, or the soul's Maker. He says also that the old Romans were a hundred threescore and ten years without idols: and had they been so still (quoth he) religion had been kept the purer. To prove which, he produces (amongst others) the Jews, and concludes, that whosoever they were that first invented images, they took from the city all awe and added unto error: being well advised that the senselessness of the idols would make the gods themselves seem contemptible. But whereas he saith they added unto error, that proves that there was some error there, before images came in. And therefore his saying, that those only discerned God which called Him a soul governing the world; and his opinion that the gods' honours would have been purer without images—these positions declare how near the truth he draws. For could he have done any good against such an overgrown error, he would have showed them that one God alone should have been adored, even He that governs the world, and that He is not to be pictured: and might the youth of the city being set in a path so near to the truth, might easily have been persuaded afterwards that God was an unchangeable nature, creating the soul also. These things being thus, whatever fooleries those men have discovered of their gods in their books, they have been laid open by the immediate hand of God (compelling them to confess them), rather than by their own desire to dissuade them: wherefore what we allege from them is for the purpose of confuting those that will not see from what a damned slavery to the devil that same singular sacrifice of so holy blood and the gift of the spirit have delivered us.

[1] = sacrifices.

CHAPTER XXXII

What reason the kings of the world had for the permitting of those false religions in such places as they conquered

HE says also that in the gods' genealogies, the people followed the poets more than the philosophers, and thence the old Romans their ancestors had their belief in so many sexes, marriages, and lineages of the gods. The reason of this (I suppose) was, because the politic and wise men did especially endeavour to deceive their people in this illusive manner, and to make them not only worshippers, but even imitators of the devils that delighted to delude them. For even as the devils cannot possess any but such as they have deceived; so unjust and devil-like princes persuaded their people to their own vain inventions, under the name of religion, thereby to bind their affections the firmer to their service, and so to keep them under their sovereignties. And what ignorant and weak man can avoid both the charms of princes and devils?

CHAPTER XXXIII

That God has appointed a time for the continuance of every state on earth

WHEREFORE God, that only and true author of felicity, Himself giveth kingdoms to good and to bad; not rashly, nor casually, but as the time is appointed, which is well known to Him, though hidden for us; unto which appointment notwithstanding He does not serve, but as a lord sways it, never giving true felicity but to the good. For this both subjects and kings may either have or lack, and yet be as they are, servants and governors. The fullness indeed of it shall be in that life where no man shall serve. And therefore here on earth He gives kingdoms to the bad as well as to the good, lest His servants that are but yet proselytes should covet them as great matters. And this is the mystery of the Old Testament, wherein the New was hidden: that there all the gifts and promises were of this world, and yet of the world to come also to those that understood them, even though the eternal good that was meant by those temporal ones was not as yet manifested: nor in what gifts of God the true felicity was resident.

CHAPTER XXXIV

Of the Jews' kingdom, which one God alone kept unmoved as long as they kept the truth of religion

To show therefore that all those temporal goods which those men gape after, that can dream of no better, are in God's hands alone, and in none of their idols, therefore multiplied He His people in Egypt from a very few, and then delivered them from thence by miraculous wonders. Their women never called upon Lucina when their children multiplied upon them incredibly; and when He preserved them from the Egyptians that persecuted them and would have killed all their children. They sucked without Rumina's help; slept without Cunina, ate and drank without Educa and Potica, and were brought up without any of these puppy gods' help: married without the nuptial gods, begot children without Priapus, crossed through the divided sea without calling upon Neptune, and left all their foes drowned behind them. They dedicated no goddess Mannia, when heaven had rained manna for them: nor worshipped the Nymphs when the rock was cleft and the waters flowed out. They used no Mars nor Bellona in their wars, and conquered, not without victory, but without making Victory a goddess. They had corn, oxen, honey, apples, without Segetia, Bobona, Mellona, or Pomona. And to conclude, all things that the Romans begged of so many false gods, they received of one true God in far happier measure. And had they not persisted in their impious curiosity in running after strange gods, as if they had been enchanted, and lastly in killing Christ; in the same kingdom had they lived happily still, if not in a larger. And that they are now dispersed over the whole earth, is God's especial providence, that what altars, groves, woods, and temples of the false gods He reproves, and what sacrifices He forbids, might all be discerned by their books as their fall itself was foretold them by their prophets: lest haply the pagans reading them in ours might think we had feigned them. But now to our next book, to make an end of this tedious one.

THE FIFTH BOOK OF THE CITY OF GOD

CHAPTER I

That neither the Roman Empire nor any other kingdom had any establishment from the power of fortune or from the stars

WHEREAS it is apparent to all men's discretion that felicity is the hope of all human desires, and that she is no goddess, but merely the gift of a god, and consequently that there is no god worthy of worship, but He in whose power it lies to bestow this felicity upon men; so that if she were a goddess herself, the worship of all the rest should be entirely hers: now let us look into the reasons why God that can give those earthly goods, as well to the good as the evil (and consequently to such as are not happy), should vouchsafe the Roman Empire so large an extension, and so long a continuance: for we have already partly proved, and hereafter in convenient place will prove more fully, that it was not their rabble of false gods that kept it in the state it was in. Wherefore the cause of this was neither fortune, nor fate, as they call them, holding fortune to be an event of things beyond all reason and cause: and fate an event from some necessity of order, excluding the will of God and man. But the God of heaven, by His only providence, disposes of the kingdoms of earth, which if any man will say is swayed by fate, and mean by that fate the will of God, he may hold his opinion still, but yet he must amend his phrase of speech; for why did he not learn this of him that taught him what fate was? The ordinary custom of this has made man imagine fate to be a power of the stars, so or so placed in nativities or conceptions; which some do separate from the determination of God, and others do affirm to depend wholly thereupon. But those that hold that the stars do manage our action, or our passions, good or ill, without God's appointment, are to be silenced and not to be heard, be they of the true religion, or be they bondslaves to idolatry of what sort soever; for what does this opinion do but flatly exclude all deity? Against this error, we profess not any disputation, but only against those that calumniate the Christian religion, in defence of their imaginary gods. As for those that make these operations of the stars in good or bad to depend upon God's will, if they say that they have this power given them from Him to use according to their own wills, they do heaven much wrong, in imagining that any wicked acts or injuries are decreed in so glorious a senate, such deeds as if any earthly city had but instituted them the whole generation of man would have conspired the subversion of it.   And what part has God left him in this disposing of human affairs, if they be swayed by a necessity from the stars, whereas He is Lord of stars and men?   If they do not say that the stars are causes of these wicked arts, through a power that God has given them, but that they effect them by His express command; is this fit to be imagined for true of God, that is unworthy to be held true of the stars?   But if the stars be said to portend this only and not to procure it, and if their positions be but signs, not causes of such effects (for so hold many great scholars; though the astrologers are not wont to say 'Mars in such a position signifies this, or that': no, but 'makes the child born a homicide,' and though we grant them this error of speech, which they must learn from the philosophers to correct in all their presages derived from the stars' position): yet how comes it to pass that they could never show the reason for that diversity of life, actions, fortune, profession, art, honour, and such human accidents, that has befallen two twins; nor why there is a great difference, both in those aforesaid courses and in their death, so that in this case, many strangers have come nearer them in their courses of life, than the one has done the other, though both be born within a little space of time the one from the other, and though both be conceived in one instant and from one act of generation?

CHAPTER II

Of the similitude and dissimilitude of health of body, and many other accidents in twins of one birth

CICERO says that Hippocrates, that excellent physician, wrote that two children that were brethren, falling sick, and the sickness waxing and waning in both alike, were hereupon suspected to be twins.   And Posidonius, a Stoic, and one much addicted to astrology, labours to prove them to have been born both under one constellation and conceived both under one.   So that which the physician ascribes to the similitude of their temperatures of body, the astrologer attributes to the power and position of the stars in their nativities.   But truly in this question, the physician's conjecture stands upon more probability, because their parents' constitution might be easily transfused into them both alike at their conception: and their first growth might participate equally of their mother's disposition of body, and then being nourished both in one house, with one nourishment, in one air, country, and other things corresponding, this now might have much power in the proportioning of both their natures alike, as physic will testify. Besides, use of one exercise equally in both might form their bodies into a similitude, which might very well admit all alterations of health alike, and equally in both. But to draw the figure of heaven and the stars into this parity of passions (it being likely that a great company of the greatest diversity of effects that could be might have originated in diverse parts of the world at one and the same time) were a presumption unpardonable. For we have known two twins that have had both diverse fortunes and different sicknesses both in time and nature: whereof (methinks) Hippocrates gives a very good reason, namely the diversity of nourishment and exercise, which might be the cause of different health in them; yet that diversity was effected by their will and inclination, and not by their bodily constitution. But neither Posidonius, nor any patron of this fate in the stars, can tell what to say in this case, if he will not delude the simple and ignorant with a discourse of that they know not. As for their talk of the space of time between the twins' nativities, due to a particular spot in the heavens where the hour of birth is signified, which they call the horoscope—it is either not so significant as the diversity of will, act, manners, and fortune of the twins born doth require; or else it is more significant than their difference of honours, state, nobility, or meanness will permit: both which diversities they place only in the hour of the nativity. But if they should be both born before the horoscope were fully varied, then would I require a unity in each particular of their fortunes which cannot be found in any two twins that ever yet were born. But if the horoscope be changed before both be born, then for this diversity I will require a difference of parents, which twins cannot possibly have.

CHAPTER III

Of Nigidius the astrologer's argument, in this question of the twins, drawn from the potter's wheel

FRUSTRATE therefore is that notable fiction of the potter's wheel, which Nigidius (they say) answered to one that plunged him in this controversy, whereupon he was called Potter. Turning a potter's wheel twice or thrice about as fast as he could, he took ink, and in the turning made two marks (as it seemed) in one place of the wheel's edge: and then, staying the wheel, the marks were found far asunder one from another upon the edge of the wheel. 'Even so,' said he, 'is the swift course of heaven, though one child be born after another in as short a time as I gave these two marks, yet in the heavens will be passed a great space. And that,' quoth he, 'is the cause of the diversity of conditions and fortunes betwixt two twins.' Here is a figment now far more brittle than the pots that were made by that wheel; for if there be so much power in heaven (which cannot be comprehended by the constellations), that one of the twins may be an heir and inherit, and not the other, how dare those astrologers give such presages unto others that are not twins, seeing they are included in those secret points in nativities which none can comprehend? But if they say they do prognosticate this to others, because they know that it belongs unto the known and more distant spaces that pass in nativities; while those moments that may come between the birth of two twins do but concern slight things, and such as the astrologer is not accustomed to be troubled with (for no one will ask the calculator when he should sit, walk, or dine); how can this be said when we show such diversity in the manners, states, actions, and fortunes of two twins?

CHAPTER IV

Of Esau and Jacob, two twins, and of the diversity of their conditions and qualities

IN the memory of our forefathers (to speak of men of note) there were two twins born [1] so near together that the second held the first by the heel; yet in their lives, manners, and actions, was such a main disparity, that that very difference made them enemies one to another. I mean not this, that the one sat when the other stood, nor that the one slept when the other waked. These belong to those first marks and moments which they cannot comprehend who erect those figures of nativity for the astrologers to judge upon. One of them bound himself to serve for wages, the other served not at all: the one was loved by his mother, so was not the other: the one lost his honour and inheritance (a matter of great moment amongst them), and the other obtained it. And how great a diversity was there in their marriages, wives, children, and goods? Exceeding much.

CHAPTER V

How the mathematicians may be convicted of professing vanity

WHEREFORE if these things belong to those spaces of time that pass betwixt the births of twins, and are not wrought upon by the constellations, why then are they presaged out of the horoscopes in the case of others? But if they be presaged as pertinent unto the larger spaces of time that fall under the notice of astrologers, and not under these momentary minutes that are indistinguishable; then what use is there of the potter's wheel, but only to turn leaden heads about till they become brain-sick, and past discerning

[1] Gen. xxv. 26.

those mathematicians' vanities? And those whose diseases (so similar in all circumstances) made Hippocrates, by the rules of physic, judge to be twins, do not they sufficiently put down those that will needs make that proceed from the stars which arises out of the temperature of their body? For why did they not sicken as they were born, one after another (for born together they could not be)? Or if their different times of birth be no cause of different times of sickness, why do they allege it to be the cause of other accidents? Why should they travel, marry, beget children, and do suchlike at diverse times, only because they were born at diverse times, and yet not be sick at diverse times by the same reason? If their difference of birth changed their horoscope and all other matters thereon depending, why then did that equality remain with the times of their sickness, that was found in the time of their conception? Or if they say that the course of sickness only follows the conception, and all the rest the nativity, then ought they not to prognosticate anything concerning sickness at nativities, unless they have the hour of conception. But if the astrologer presage sickness without seeing the figure of the conception, because the said presage is included in those interposed moments of the birth, how would he tell either of those twins when he should be sick, who having each a diverse horoscope, yet must nevertheless fall sick both at one time? Finally, I ask again, if the intermission in the birth of two twins be so much that it alters their whole fortunes, because of their horoscopes: and in altering of the four angles (wherein they put all the power), alters also their whole destinies, how can this come to pass, when the time of their conceptions was both at one instant? Or if two that are both conceived at one point of time may have the fortune to be born the one before the other, why may not two that are born both in one moment of time have the fortune to die the one before the other? For if that one and the same moment of their conception hindered not the succession of their birth, why should the same moment that is one in both the births hinder the successive time of their death? If their conception, being in one minute, permit these to have diverse fortunes in their mother's womb; why should not their nativity, being of the same state, permit them to have diverse fortunes while they live upon earth? And let us take away all the fictions of this art (or rather vanity) of theirs, in this one question. What is the cause, that such as are conceived both in one moment of time, both under one constellation, should nevertheless have different destinies in their mother's womb to be born at several times; and yet, two being born of two mothers, both in one moment of time, cannot have diverse destinies, whereby the one may die before the other, or outlive the other? Did not their destiny enter upon their conception, or could they not have it unless they were first born? Why is it said then that if the hour of conception be known, they can presage many things most oracularly? And hereupon it is said of some, that a certain wise man did make choice of an hour of copulation with his wife, whereby to beget a son whose after-worth should be admired? And lastly, whereof comes it that Posidonius the astrologer gave this reason for the two brethren's participated sickness, that it was because they were born and conceived both together? He added 'conceived,' so that it should not be objected to him that it was not certain that such as were conceived together should be born both at the same instant: and that he might draw this mutual sickness of theirs, not from their parity of constitutions, but from the power of the stars. But if there be such a power of equalizing the destiny of twins in their conception, then verily the diversity of time in their birth ought not to alter it. If the destinies of twins be changed by their several times of birth, why may we not rather conceive that before their birth they were appointed by destiny to several births? Shall not then the will of the living man change the fate of his nativity, when his order of birth can change the fate of his conception?

CHAPTER VI

Of twins of different sexes

IT often falls out, notwithstanding, that in these concurrences and unions of time, conception, and constellation, the children conceived are the one a male, the other a female. I know two twins of diverse sexes, both of them alive and lusty at this day. They are as like in favour one to another as their difference of sex can permit: but in their fashion, and order of life, so unlike that (besides the actions which must of necessity distinguish between men and women), he is continually at war, being a staff-officer, and never comes home: she is continually in her country where she was born, and never goes abroad. Nay, which is more incredible (respecting the powers of the stars and not the wills of God and men), he is a married man, and she is a holy virgin; he has many children, and she was never married. Oh, but their horoscopes had a great sway in all those things. Tush, I have shown the power of that to be just nothing, already. Aye (they say), but whatsoever it does, it is there in the nativity that it must do it. But why not in the conception, wherein it is manifest that there was but one generative act concurrent? For nature's power is such that a woman having once conceived, cannot achieve a second conception, until she be delivered of the first, and therefore it is necessary that the twins' conceptions fall both in one moment. Were their diverse horoscopes (think you) the cause that in their birth he became a man-child, and she a woman? Wherefore though it is no such absurdity to say that there are some planetary influences that have effect only upon diversity of forms in bodies, as we see the alteration of the year by the sun's access and departure, and divers things to increase and decrease, just as the moon does (crabs for example and all shell-fish: besides the wonderful course of the sea): yet it is absurd to say that the mind of man is subject unto any of these powers of the stars. Those who strive to make us connect our actions with the stars do but urge us to inquire whether the differences that exist even in bodies themselves can be attributed to that source. For what is so pertinent unto the body as the sex thereof? And yet we see that two twins of diverse sexes may be conceived both under one constellation. Wherefore what more stupid absurdity can there be, than to say that that figure of heaven which was one in the conception of them both had not power to keep the sister from differing in sex from her brother, with whom she shared the same constellation; and yet that that figure of heaven which ruled at their nativity had power to make her differ so far from him in her virginal sanctity.

CHAPTER VII

Of the election of days of marriage, of planting and of sowing

BUT who can endure this foolery of theirs, to invent a new destiny for every action a man undertaketh. That wise man aforesaid, it seems, was not born to have an admirable son, but rather a contemptible one; and therefore elected he his hour wherein to beget a worthy one. So thus did he work himself a destiny, more than his stars portended, and made that a part of his fate which was not signified in his nativity. Oh, fondness most fatal! A day must now be chosen for marriage: because otherwise one might light on an unlucky day, and so make an ill marriage. But where then is the destiny of your nativity? Can a man change what his fate has appointed, by choosing this day or that; and cannot the fate of that day which he chooses be altered by another fate? Again, if men alone of all the creatures of earth be under this starry power, why do they choose days to plant, and days to sow, and so forth; days to tame cattle, days to put to the males for increase of oxen, or horses, and suchlike? If the election of those days be good, because the stars have dominion over all earthly bodies, living creatures and plants, according as the times do change; let them but consider how many creatures have their origin at one and the same instant, and yet have such diverse ends, so that he that but noteth will deride those observations as children's toys. For what dolt will say that all herbs, trees, beasts, birds, serpents, worms, and fishes, have each one a particular moment of time to be brought forth in? Yet men are wont to try the mathematicians' skill, by bringing them the constellations of the births of beasts, which they have for this end diligently observed at home; and him they hold the most skilled mathematician that can say by the constellation, This portends the birth of a beast and not of a man. Nay, they dare to show what beast it is; whether fit for bearing wool, for carriages, for the plough, or the custody of the house; for they are often asked counsel of the destinies of dogs, and give answers breeding great admiration. Nay, men are now grown to that grossness of brain, that they think when a man is born, creation is tied to such an order, that not so much as a fly is brought forth in that region at that time; for if they give us but birth-room for a fly, we will draw them by gradation till we come to an elephant. Nor have they wit to consider this, that in their selected day of sowing corn, it springs and grows up altogether, and being grown to the height it ripens altogether; and yet the canker spoils one piece and the birds another, and men pull up the third of all this corn, that nevertheless grew up altogether. How will they deal with the constellation of this, that has partaken so many kinds of ending? Or does it not repent them of electing days for these things, denying them to belong to heaven's disposing, and putting men only under the stars, to whom alone of all the creatures upon earth God has given free and unconstrained wills! These being considered, it is no evil belief to think that the astrologers do presage many things wonderfully and truly, but that is by a secret instinct of evil spirits (whose care it is to infect, deceive, and confirm men's minds in this false and dangerous opinion of fate in the stars), and not by any art of discerning the horoscope, for such is there none.

CHAPTER VIII

Of their opinion that give not the name of fate to the position of the stars, but unto the dependence of causes upon the will of God

As for those that do not give the position of the stars in nativities and conceptions the name of fate, but reserve it only for that connection of causes, whereby all things come to pass, we need not use many words to them: because they conform this coherence of causes to the will of God, who is well and justly believed both to foreknow all things before the event, and to leave no event undisposed of ere it be an event: from whom are all powers, though from Him arise not all wills. For that it is the will of that great and all-disposing God, which they call fate, these verses (of Annaeus Seneca's I think) will prove:

> Duc me, summe pater, altique dominator poli,
> Quocunque placuerit, nulla parenda mora est.
> Adsum impiger: fac nolle, comitabor gemens:
> Malusque patiar facere quod lucuit bono.
> Ducunt volentem fata, nolentem trahunt.[1]

> Lead me, great Lord, king of eternity,
> Even where Thou wilt, I 'll not resist Thee.
> Change Thou my will yet still I vow subjection,
> Being led, to that that is in the good election.
> 'Fate leads the willing, draws the obstinate.'

Thus in the last verse, he directly calls that fate which in the former he called the 'will of the great Lord,' to whom he promises obedience, and to be led willingly, lest he be drawn on by force, because, 'Fate leads the willing, draws the obstinate.' And Homer's verses translated into Latin by Tully are as these are:

> Tales sunt hominum mentes qualis pater ipse,
> Jupiter auctiferas lustravit lumine terras.[2]

> Such are the minds of men as Jove the great
> Vouchsafes, that fills the earth with light, and heat.

We would not bring poetic sentences for confirmation of this question; but because Tully says that the Stoics, standing up for this power of fate, are wont to quote this place of Homer, we now allege them, not as his opinion, but as theirs, who by these verses of fate showed in their disputations what they thought of fate, because they call upon Jove, whom they held to be that great god upon whose directions these causes did depend.

CHAPTER IX

*Of God's foreknowledge and man's freedom of election; against
the opinion of Cicero*

AGAINST those men Tully thinks he cannot hold argument, unless he overthrow divination, and therefore he labours to prove that there is no prescience, nor foreknowledge of things to come, either in God or man; there is directly no such matter. Thus denies he God's foreknowledge, and idly seeks to subvert the radiant lustre of true prophecies, by propounding certain ambiguous and fallible oracles, whose truth notwithstanding he does not confute. But these conjectures of the mathematicians he lays flat, for indeed they are of the kind to destroy themselves. But for all that, their opinion is more tolerable, that ascribe a fate unto the stars, than his, that rejects all foreknowledge of things to come. For to acknowledge a God, and yet to deny that, is monstrous madness: which he observing, went about to prove even that which 'the fool hath said in his heart; there is no God.'[1] Not, however, in his own person, for he saw the danger of malice too well; and therefore when making Cotta dispute against the Stoics upon this theme, in his books *De Natura Deorum*, he seems more willing to hold with Lucilius Balbus, that defended the Stoics, than with Cotta, that argued against the divine essence. But in his books *De Divinatione*, he directly opposes the foreknowledge of things, of himself and in his own person; all which it seems he did lest he should yield unto fate, and so lose the freedom of election: for he supposed that in yielding to this foreknowledge, fate should follow necessarily thereupon, without any denial. But howsoever the philosophers wind themselves in webs of disputations, we, as we confess the great and true God, so do we acknowledge His high will, power, and foreknowledge. Nor let us fear that we do not perform all our actions by our own will, because He, whose foreknowledge cannot err, knew before that we should do thus or thus: which Tully feared, and therefore denied foreknowledge; and the Stoics, that held not all things to be done by necessity, thought that they were done by fate. What then did Tully fear in this prescience, that he framed such detestable arguments against it? Verily this, that if all events were known before they came to pass, they should come to pass according to that foreknowledge. And if they come so to pass, then God knows the certain order of things beforehand, and consequently the certain order of the causes; and if He know a certain order of causes in all events, then are all events disposed by fate: which if it be so, we have nothing left in our power, nothing in our will: 'which granted,' says he, 'the whole course of humanity is overturned: law, correction, praise, disgrace, exhortation, prohibition, all are to no end: nor is there any justice in punishing the bad and rewarding the good.' For avoiding of which inconveniences (so absurd and so pernicious) he utterly rejects this foreknowledge of things, and draws the religious mind into this strait, that either there must be somewhat in the power of our will, or else that there is a foreknowledge of things to come; but that the granting of the one is the subversion of the other: choosing the foreknowledge, we must lose the freedom of election, and choosing this we must deny the other. Now this learned and devout man, of the two makes choice of freedom of election: and to confirm it, denies the foreknowledge utterly, and so instead of making men free, makes them blasphemous. But the religious mind chooses them both, confesses and confirms them both. 'How,' says he? 'For granting this foreknowledge, there follow so many consequences that they quite subvert all power of our will: and holding this free will, by the same degrees of reasoning we ascend, till we find there is no prescience of future things at all; for these are the steps in our argument.   If there be any freedom of the will, all things do not follow destiny: if all things follow not destiny, then is there no set order in the causes of things: now if there be no set order in the causes of all things, then is there no set order of the things themselves in God's foreknowledge, since they come from their causes.   If there be not a set order of all things in God's foreknowledge, then all things fall not out according to the said knowledge.   Now if all things fall not out as he had His fore-knowledge of them, then is there in God no foreknowledge of things to come.'   To these sacrilegious and wicked opposers, thus we reply: God doth both know all things ere they come to pass, and we do all things willingly, which we do not feel ourselves and know ourselves directly enforced to.   We hold not that all things, but rather that nothing follows fate; and whereas fate is wont to be taken for a position of the stars in nativities and conceptions, we hold this a vain and frivolous assumption: we neither deny an order of causes wherein the will of God is all in all, neither do we call it by the name of fate, unless fate be derived of *fari*, 'to speak,' for we cannot deny that the scripture says: 'God spake once, these two things I have heard, that power belongeth unto God, and to Thee, O Lord, mercy, for Thou wilt reward every man according to his works.' [1] For whereas He says: 'God spake once,' it is meant that He spoke unmovably and unchangeably, that all things should fall out as He spoke, and meant to have them.   In this respect we may derive fate from *fari*, 'to speak,' but we must needs say withal that it is used in another sense than we should have men to think upon.   But it does not follow that nothing should be left free to our will, because God knows the certain and set order of all events.   For our very wills are in that order of causes, which God knows so surely and hath in His prescience; human wills being the cause of human actions: so that He that keeps a knowledge of the causes of all things, cannot leave men's wills out of that knowledge, knowing them to be the causes of their actions.   For Tully's own words: 'Nothing comes to pass without an efficient cause,' [2] is sufficient alone to sway down this matter quite against himself: for what avails the subsequence: 'Nothing is without a cause, but every cause is not fated, because there are causes of chance, nature, and will'?   It is sufficient that nothing is done but by precedent cause. For those causes that are casual, giving origin to the name of fortune, we deny not: we say they are secret, and ascribe them either to the will of the true God, or of any other spirit.   The natural causes we do never divide from His will, who is nature's Creator: but the voluntary causes, God, angels, men, and divers other creatures have often in their will and power; if we may call

that power a will by which the brute beasts avoid their own hurt
and desire their good by nature's instinct.   That there is a will in
angels, I do absolutely affirm; be they good whom we call God's
angels, or evil whom we call the devil's angels, fiends, or devils
themselves.   So men good and bad have all their wills: and hereby
it is apparent that the efficient causes of all effects are voluntary
causes and nothing but the decrees of that nature, which is 'the
spirit of life.'   For air or wind is called a spirit; but because it is a
body, it is not the spirit of life.   But the spirit of life that quickens
all things is the Creator of all bodies and all created spirits: this is
God, 'a Spirit from eternity, uncreated': in His will there is that
height of power which assists the wills of the good spirits, judges
the bad, disposes of all, giving power to whom He pleases, and
holding it from whom He wills.   For as He is a Creator of all
natures, so is He of all powers: but not the giver of all wills; for
wicked wills are not of Him, being against that nature which is of
Him.   So the bodies are all subject unto diverse wills: some to
our own wills (that is, the wills rather of men than of beasts), some
to the angels, but all to the will of God: unto whom all wills are
subject, because they have no power but what He gives them.
The cause then that makes all, and is not made itself, is God.   The
other causes do both effect and are effected: such are all created
spirits, chiefly the reasonable ones.   The corporal causes, which
are rather effects than otherwise, are not to be counted as efficient
causes, because they came but to do that which the will of the
spirit within them doth enjoin them: how then can that set order
of causes in God's foreknowledge deprive our wills of power, seeing
our wills bear such a sway amongst the very causes themselves?
But let Cicero wrangle, and his fellows, that say this order is fated,
or rather fate itself; which we abhor, because of the word's being
chiefly used in a false sense: but whereas he denies that God knows
assuredly the set order of those causes, we detest his assertion,
worse than the Stoics do: for he either denies God (which he
endeavours under a false person in his books *De Natura Deorum*, or
if he do acknowledge Him, yet in denying Him this foreknowledge
he says but as the fool said in his heart, 'There is no God'; for if
God lack the prescience of all future events He is not God.   And
therefore our wills are of as much power as God would have them,
and knew before that they should be; and the power that they have
is theirs free, to do what they shall do truly and freely: because He
foreknew that they should have this power, and do these acts,
whose foreknowledge cannot be deceived.   Wherefore if I wish
to use the word fate in anything, I would rather say that it belonged
to the weaker, and that will belonged to the higher who has the
other in his power, rather than grant that our liberty of will were
taken away by that set order which the Stoics (after a peculiar
phrase of their own) call fate.

CHAPTER X

Whether necessity has any dominion over the will of man

NOR need we fear that necessity which the Stoics were so afraid of, that in their distinctions of causes, they put some under necessity and some not under it; and in those that they did not subject unto it they put our wills also, lest they should lose their freedom by being subject to necessity. But if that be necessity in us which is not in our power, but will be done, do what we can against it, as the necessity of death; then is it plain that our wills are subject to no such necessity, use we them howsoever, well or badly: for we do many things which we could not do against our wills. And first of all to will itself: if we will a thing, there is our will; if we will not, it is not. For we cannot will against our wills. Now if necessity be defined to be 'that whereby such a thing must needs fall out thus, or thus,' I see no reason we should fear that it could hinder the freedom of our wills in anything. For we neither subject God's being nor His prescience unto necessity, when we say God must needs live eternally, and God must needs foreknow all things; no more than His honour is diminished in saying He cannot err, He cannot die, He cannot do this. Why? Because His power were less, if He could do it, than now it is in that He cannot. Justly is He called almighty, yet may He not die nor err. He is called almighty because He can do all that is in His will, not because He can suffer what is not His will; which if He could He were not almighty. So that He cannot do some things, because He can do all things. So when we say that if we will anything, we must of necessity will it with a freedom of will, that is true: and we do not put our will under any such necessity as deprives it of the freedom. So that our wills are ours, willing what we will; and if we will it not, neither do they will it: and if any man suffer anything by the will of another against his own will, his will has its own power still, and his sufferance comes rather from the power of God than from his own will: for if he willed that it should be otherwise, and yet could not have it so, his will must needs be hindered by a greater power: yet his will should be free still, and not in any other's power but his that willed it, though he could not have his will performed: wherefore whatsoever a man suffers against his will, he ought not to attribute it unto the wills of angels, men, or any other created spirits, but even to His who gave their wills this power. So then, our wills are not useless, because God foresees what will be in them: He that foresaw it whatever it be, foresaw somewhat: and if He did foreknow somewhat, then by His foreknowledge there is something in our wills. Wherefore we are neither compelled to leave our freedom of will by retaining God's foreknowledge, nor by holding our will's freedom to deny God's foreknowledge. God forbid that we should. We believe and affirm them both constantly and truly, the latter as a part of our good faith, the former as a rule for our good life: and badly does he live that believes not aright of God. So God forbid that to be free we should deny His foreknowledge, by whose help we either are or shall be free. Therefore law, correction, praise, disgrace, exhortation, and prohibition are not in vain: because He foreknew that there should be such. They have that power which He foreknew they should have; and prayers are powerful to attain those things which He foreknows that He will give to such as pray for them. Good deeds has He predestinated to reward, and evil to punishment. Nor does man sin because God foreknew that he would sin: nay it is doubtless he that sins, when he does sin, because God, whose knowledge cannot be mistaken, foresaw that neither fate nor fortune, nor anything else, but the man himself would sin, who if he had not been willing, he had not sinned: but whether he should be unwilling to sin or no, that also did God foreknow.

CHAPTER XI

Of God's universal providence, ruling all, and comprising all

WHEREFORE the great and mighty God with His Word and His Holy Spirit (which three are one), God only omnipotent, Maker and Creator of every soul and of every body, in participation of whom all such are happy that follow His truth and reject vanities: He that made man a reasonable creature of soul and body, and He that did neither let him pass unpunished for his sin, nor yet excluded him from mercy: He that gave both unto good and bad existence with the stones, power of production with the trees, senses with the beasts of the field, and understanding with the angels; He, from whom is all being, beauty, form, and order, number, weight, and measure; He, from whom all nature, mean and excellent, all seeds of form, all forms of seed, all motion both of forms and seeds derive and have being: He that gave flesh its original beauty, strength, propagation, form and shape, health and symmetry: He that gave to the unreasonable soul sense, memory, and appetite, and to the reasonable besides these, mind, understanding, and will: He (I say) having left neither heaven, nor earth, nor angel, nor man, no, nor the most base and contemptible creature, neither the bird's feather, nor the herb's flower, nor the tree's leaf, without the true harmony of their parts, and peaceful concord of composition; it is no way credible that He would leave the kingdoms of men and their bondages and freedoms loose and uncomprised in the laws of His eternal providence.

CHAPTER XII

How the ancient Romans obtained this increase of their kingdom at the true God's hand, seeing that they never worshipped Him

Now let us look what desert of the Romans moved the true God to augment their dominion, He in whose power all the kingdoms of the earth are. For the better performance of this we wrote our last book before, to prove that their gods whom they worshipped in such ridiculous manner had no such power; and thus far have we proceeded in this book, to take away the question of destiny and fate, lest some man being persuaded that it was not the deed of the gods, should rather ascribe it unto fate than to God's will, so mighty and so omnipotent. The ancient Romans therefore (as their histories report) though like all other nations (excepting the Hebrews) they worshipped idols and false gods, offering their sacrifices to the devils, not to the true Deity, yet 'their desire of praise made them bountiful of their purses; they loved glory and wealth honestly gotten':[1] honour they dearly loved, and honesty, offering willingly both their lives and their states for them. The zealous desire of this one thing suppressed all other inordinate affections: and hence they desired to keep their country in freedom, and then in sovereignty, because they saw how baseness went with servitude, and glory with dominion. Whereupon they rejected the imperiousness of their kings, and set down a yearly government between two heads,[2] called consuls from *consulendo*, of providing; not kings nor lords, of reign and rule (though *rex* do seem rather to come from *regendo*, of governing, and *regnum*, the kingdom, of *rex*, than otherwise): but they held the state of a king to consist more in this imperious domination, than either in his discipline of governance or his benevolent providence. So having expelled Tarquin and instituted consuls, then (as Sallust says well in their praise) the city getting their freedom thus memorably, grew up in glory as much as it did in power: the desire of which glory wrought all these world-admired acts which they performed. Sallust praises also M. Cato and C. Caesar, both worthy men of his time, saying that the commonwealth had not had a famous man for a long time before, but that then it had a couple of illustrious virtue, though of diverse conditions. He praises Caesar for his desire of empire, arms, and war, whereby to exemplify his valour, trusting so in the fortune of a great spirit that he roused up the poor barbarians to war, tossing Bellona's bloody ensign about, that the Romans might thereby give proof of their vigours. This wrought he for desire of praise and glory. Even so in the precedent ages, their love, first of liberty and afterward of sovereignty and glory,

---

[1] Sallust, *Catil.* 7.   [2] *Catil.* 6.

whetted them to all hard attempts. Their famous poet gives
testimony of both, saying:

> Nec non Tarquinium ejectum Porsenna jubebat
> Accipere, ingentique urbem obsidione premebat:
> Aeneadae in ferrum pro libertate ruebant, etc.[1]

> Porsenna girts them with a world of men,
> Commands that Tarquin be restored, but then
> To arms the Romans for their freedom run.

For then was it honour to die bravely, or to live freely. But
having got their freedom, then succeeded such a greediness of
glory in them, that freedom alone seemed nothing without domination, in accord with that which the same poet makes Jove
to speak in prophetic wise:

> . . . Quin aspera Juno
> Quae mare nunc terrasque metu coelumque fatigat,
> Consilia in melius referet, mecumque fovebit
> Romanos, rerum dominos, gentemque togatum.
> Sic placitum.   Veniet lustris labentibus aetas,
> Cum domus Assaraci Phthiam clarasque Mycenas
> Servitio premet, ac victis dominabitur Argis.[2]

> . . . And Juno though she yet
> Fill heaven and earth with her disquiet fit,
> Shall turn her mind at length, and join with me,
> To guard the Romans' gownèd progeny.
> It stands.   Succeeding times shall see the day,
> That old Assaracus's stock shall sway
> Phthia, Mycenae, and all Argos round, etc.

Which Virgil makes Jupiter speak prophetically, it being fallen
out true before he wrote these verses. But this by the way to
show that the Romans' affection of liberty and domination was a
parcel of their most principal glory and lustre. Hence it is that
the same poet, in distributing the arts amongst the nations, gives the
Romans the art of domination and sovereignty over others, saying:

> Excudent alii spirantia mollius aera,
> Cedo equidem, vivos ducent de marmore vultus.
> Orabunt causas melius, caelique meatus
> Describent radio et surgentia sidera dicent:
> Tu regere imperio populos, Romane, memento,
> (Hae tibi erunt artes), pacique imponere morem;
> Parcere subjectis et debellare superbos.[3]

> Others can better carve in brass perhaps,
> 'Tis true: or cut the stone to human shapes:
> Others can better practise law's loud jars,
> Or teach the motions of the fulgid stars.
> But, Romans, be your arts, to rule in wars,
> To make all knees to sacred peace be bowed,
> To spare the lowly and pull down the proud.

[1] Virg. *Aen.* viii. 646–8.   [2] *Aen.* i. 279–85.   [3] *Aen.* vi. 847–53.

These arts they were the more perfect in, through their abstinence from pleasures, from covetousness after riches (the corrupters both of body and mind), from extorting from the poor citizen, and from bestowing on beastly players. So that in the dominion of those corruptions which befell afterwards, when Virgil and Sallust did both write, the Romans used not the foresaid arts, but deceits and tricks to raise their glories. And therefore Sallust says: 'At first men's hearts gave place to ambition, rather than covetousness, because that was more near to virtue; for the industrious and the slothful have both one desire of honour, glory, and sovereignty; but the first,' says he, 'goes the true way to work, the latter by craft and false means, because he has not the true course. The true way is to come to honour by virtue, not by ambition; which honour, empire, and glory, good and bad wish both alike. But the good goes the true way, that is, by virtue leading him directly to his possession of honour, glory, sovereignty.'[1] That this was the Romans' course, their temples showed, Virtue's and Honour's being so close together (though herein they took God's gifts for gods themselves): wherein you might easily see that their end was to show that there was no access to honour but by virtue, whereunto all they that were good referred it; for the evil had it not, though they laboured for honour by indirect means, namely, by deceit and illusion. The praise of Cato excels, of whom Sallust says that 'The more he shunned glory the more it pursued him.'[2] For this glory that they seek is the 'good opinion of men concerning such or such.' And therefore that is the best virtue, that stands not upon others' judgments, but upon one's own conscience, as the apostle says: 'Our glory is this, the testimony of our conscience';[3] and again: 'Let every man prove his own work, and so shall he have glory in himself only, and not in another.'[4] So that glory and honour which they desire so, and aim so after by good means, must not go before virtue, but follow it: for there is no true virtue but aims at man's chiefest good. And therefore the honours that Cato required he should not have required, but the city should have returned him them as his due desert. But whereas there were but two famous Romans in that time, Caesar and Cato, Cato's virtue seems far nearer the truth of virtue than Caesar's. And let us take Cato's opinion of the state of the city as it was then, and as it had been before. 'Think not,' says he, 'that our ancestry brought the city into this height by arms. If it were so, we should make it far more admirable than ever. But they had other means which we lack; industry at home, equity abroad, freedom in consultation, and purity of minds in all men, free from lust and error. For these have we gotten riot and avarice, public beggary and private wealth: riches we praise, and sloth we follow: good and bad are now undistinguished, ambition

[1] *Catil.* 11.   [2] *Catil.* 54.   [3] 2 Cor. i. 12.   [4] Gal. vi. 4.

I—* H 98²

devouring all the guerdon due to virtue. Nor wonder at it, when each one consults his own private interests, when you serve your lusts at home, and your profit or favour in public. This is that that lays the State open to every incursion of others.' [1] He that reads these words of Cato in Sallust, may think that the old Romans were all such as those whom we have shown to be so praiseworthy before. It is not so; for otherwise his words which we related in our second book [2] should be false, where he says that the city grew troubled with the oppressing power of the great ones, and that the people grew to a division from the fathers upon this cause: that there were divers other dangerous dissensions, and that they agreed in honesty and concord no longer than they stood in fear of Tarquin, and of the great war of Etruria: which being ended, the senators began to make slaves of the people, to chastise them as imperiously as the kings had done; to chase men from their possessions; and their faction alone bare the sway of all. Unto which discords (the one desiring to rule, and the other refusing to obey) the second African war gave end, because a fear began then to return upon them, and called their turbulent spirits from those altercations to look to the good of the whole, and establish a concord. But all the great affairs were managed by a few that were as honest as the times afforded, and so by mitigating and making tolerable those evils, the State grew up well, through the providence of a few good governors. For as this writer says, [3] having heard and read of many memorable military deeds of the Romans by sea and land, he had a great desire to know what it was that supported those great businesses, wherein the Romans very often with a handful of men have held out in war against most powerful, rich, and victorious kings: and having looked well into it, he finds that the outstanding virtue of a very few citizens has been cause of this happy success of all the rest: surmounting wealth by poverty, and multitude by scarcity. 'But after corruption had eaten through the city,' says he, 'then the greatness of the commonwealth supported the viciousness of her magistrates.' So the virtue of a few aiming at glory, honour, and sovereignty, by a true line—that same virtue is that which Cato so prefers. This was the industry at home that he so commended, which made their public treasury rich, though the private were but mean. And the corruption of manners he brings in as just the contrary, producing public beggary through private wealth. Wherefore, whereas the monarchies of the east had been a long time glorious, God resolved to erect one now in the west also, which although it were after them in time, yet should be before them in greatness and dignity. And this he left in the hands of such men as swayed it, especially to punish the vicious states of other nations: and those men were such, as for honour and domina-

[1] Sallust, *Catil*. 52.   [2] II. xviii.   [3] Sallust, *Catil*. 53.

tion's sake would have an absolute care of their country, whence they received this honour: and would not hesitate to lay down their own lives for their fellows, suppressing covetousness and all other vices, except the desire of honour alone.

CHAPTER XIII

Of ambition, which being a vice, is notwithstanding herein held a virtue in that it doth restrain vices of worse natures

BUT he is better sighted that can see this desire of glory to be a vice. Horace saw it, and therefore said:

> Laudis amore tumes: sunt certa piacula quae te
> Ter pure lecto poterunt recreare libello.[1]

> You swell with thirst of praise; but I can tell
> A medicine: read this book thrice over well.

And in his *Odes* he sung this to the same purpose of suppressing ambitious thoughts:

> Latius regnes avidum domando
> Spiritum, quam si Libyam remotis
> Gadibus jungas, et uterque Poenus
>   Serviat uni.[2]

> He that can conquer his desires rebelling,
> Hath larger monarchy, than he that sways
> The Libyans, Gades, and both Africas,
>   And more excelling.

However, those that do not bridle their exorbitant desires by faith, by the power of the Holy Spirit, and the love of that intellectual beauty, though they cannot be holy, yet they may be less base, because of their love of human glory. Tully could not dissemble this, in his book *Of the Commonwealth*, where speaking of the education of a prince for a city, he says 'he must be nourished with glory';[3] and so thereupon infers what worthy deeds this glory had drawn from his ancestors. So that they were so far from resisting this vice, that they did wholly give themselves to augment and excite it, thinking it useful to the State: though in his books of philosophy, Tully never dissembles this contagion, but confesses it as clear as day. For speaking of studies aiming at the true good and contemning the vain blasts of human praises, he infers this axiom: 'Honour nourishes arts, and glory keeps all men at work on studies, and what men approve not, lies unregarded.'[4]

[1] *Epist.* i. 1, 36–7.   [2] *Carm.* ii. 2, 9–12.   [3] v. 75.   [4] *Tusc. Disp.* i. 2, 4.

CHAPTER XIV

*That we are to avoid this desire of human honour, the glory of the
righteous being wholly in God*

WHEREFORE without doubt, we had better resist this desire than
yield to it.   For so much the nearer are we to God, as we are purer
from this impurity: which although in this life it be not fully
rooted out of the heart, because it is a temptation that troubles
even the most proficient in religion, yet let the love of righteousness suppress the thirst of ambitiousness.   And thus if some things
lie unrespected because men approve them not, and yet be good
and honest; then let the love of human praise blush and give place
to the love of truth.   For this is a great enemy to our faith, if the
desire of glory have more room in our hearts than the fear or love
of our God; and therefore He says: 'How can you believe that
expect honour one from another and seek not the honour that
cometh of God?' [1]   And likewise it is said of some that believed
in Him and yet durst not profess it: 'They loved the praise of
men more than the praise of God.' [2]   Which the holy apostles
did not: for they preached the name of Christ, where it was not
only not approved of (as Tully says, 'and what men approve not,
lies unregarded'), but where it was even detested, holding the rule
that their Master (the mind's physician) had taught them: 'Whosoever shall deny Me before men, him will I also deny before my
Father which is in heaven,[3] and before the angels of God': [4]
so that all their reproaches by their cruel persecutions, their extreme
pains, could not drive them from preaching this salvation, let
the madness of man oppose what it could.   And when this divine
life, conversation, and doctrine of theirs having suppressed all
hardness of heart, and erected the peace of righteousness, was
crowned with an unbounded glory in Christ's Church; in this did
not they rest, as in the expected guerdon of their virtues, but
referred it all unto Christ's glory, by whose grace they were what
they were.   And the same did they transfuse into such as they
converted unto the love of Him, whereby they might become such
as they were before them: for to keep them from touch of human
ambition their Master taught them this: 'Take heed that you do
not your good deeds before men, to be seen of them, or else ye
shall have no reward of your Father which is in heaven.' [5]   But
lest they should misconceive this, and fear to do well before men;
and so become less profitable by striving to keep their virtuous acts
in secret, than otherwise; He says again: 'Let your light so shine
before men, that they may see your good works and glorify your
Father which is in heaven.' [6]   Do not well with an intent that men

[1] John v. 44.   [2] John xii. 43.   [3] Matt. x. 33.
[4] Luke xii. 9.   [5] Matt. vi. 1.   [6] Matt. v. 16.

should see you do so, and so turn to behold you, who by yourselves
are nothing: but do so that they may glorify your Father in heaven,
unto whom if they turn they may be such as you are.   Thus did
the martyrs, that excelled the Scaevolas, Curtii, and Decii (not by
punishing themselves, but by bearing the inflictions of others) in
true virtue, piety, and innumerable multitude.   But the others,
living in an earthly city, wherein the end of all their endeavours
was by themselves propounded to themselves, the fame and
domination of this world and not the eternity of heaven; not in the
everlasting life, but in their own ends, and the mouths of their
posterity: what should they love, but glory, whereby they desired
to survive after death in the memories and mouths of such as
commended them.

CHAPTER XV

Of the temporal rewards that God bestowed upon the Romans' virtues and good conditions

IF God did neither mean to bless such as we have spoken of with
eternity in His heavenly city, amongst His angels (to which society
that true piety brings men, which affords that true divine worship,
which the Greeks call λατρεία, to none but only the true God),
nor to vouchsafe them an earthly glory or excellence of imperial
dignity; then should their virtues, the good acts whereby they endeavoured to ascend to this glory, pass unrewarded.   But the
Lord says even of such as do good for human glory: 'Verily I say
unto you they have their reward.' [1]   These therefore that neglected their private estates for the commonwealth and public
treasury, opposing covetousness, having a full care of their country's
freedom, and living according to their laws, without touch of lust
or guilt, these seemed to go the right way to get themselves honour,
and did so; honoured they are almost all the world over; all nations
very near received their laws; honoured were they then in all
men's mouths, and now in most men's writings through the world.
Thus have they no reason to complain of God's justice; they have
their reward.

CHAPTER XVI

Of the reward of the eternal citizens of heaven, to whom the examples of the Romans' virtues were of good use

BUT as for their reward that endure reproaches here on earth for
the city of God (which the lovers of the world do hate and deride),
that is of another nature.   That city is eternal: no man is born in
it, because no man dies in it.   Felicity is there fully, yet no goddess,
but the gift of God.   Of this habitation have we a promise by

[1] Matt. vi. 2, 5.

faith, as long as we are here in pilgrimage on earth, and long for
that rest above. The sun arises not there both upon good and
bad,[1] but the Son of righteousness shines only over the good.
There shall there be no need to respect the common treasury more
than the private; truth is all the treasure that lies there. And
therefore the Roman Empire had that glorious increase, not only to
be a fit guerdon to the virtues of such worthies as we forenamed,
but also that the citizens of heaven in their pilgrimages upon earth
might observe those examples with a sober diligence, and thence
gather how great care, love, and respect ought to be carried to the
heavenly country for life eternal, if those men had such a dear
love of their earthly country for glory so temporal.

CHAPTER XVII

*The fruits of the Romans' wars both to themselves and to those with
whom they warred*

FOR what doth it matter in respect of this short and transitory life,
under whose dominion a mortal man doth live, as long as he be not
compelled to acts of impiety or injustice. But did the Romans
ever hurt any of the nations whom they conquered and gave laws
unto, but in the very fury and war of the conquest? If they could
have given those laws by agreement, it had been better (but then
there had been no place for triumph), for the Romans lived under
the same laws themselves that they gave to others. This had been
sufficient for the State, but that Mars, Bellona, and Victory should
then have been displeased, and displaced also, if they had had no
wars and no victories. Would not then the state of Rome and
other nations have been all one, especially if that had been done
which was most gravely and worthily performed afterwards, every
man that belonged to the Roman Empire receiving the freedom of
the city, as though they were now all citizens of Rome, whereas
before there were but a very few, so that such as had no lands
had to live at the public expense? This sustenance would have
been supplied more readily unto good governors by men who were
sharers in the commonwealth than it would have been had it been
extorted from them as a conquered people. For how does the
fact that some conquer and others are conquered promote men's
safety, manners, or dignities either? I see no good it does, but
only that it adds unto their intolerable vainglory, who aim at such
matters, and war for them, and lastly receive them as their labour's
reward. Does not their land pay tribute to the State as well as
others? Yes. May they learn anything that others may not?
No. And are there not many senators that never saw Rome?
True. Take away vainglory and what are men but men? And

[1] Matt. v. 45.

if the perverseness of the age would permit the very best men to
bear away the greatest honours, even then should not this human
honour be so prizeworthy, being but a breath and a light smoke.
But let us use these things, to do ourselves good towards God.
Let us consider what obstacles these men have scorned, what pains
they have taken, what desires they have suppressed, and only for
this human glory which afterwards they received as the reward of
their virtues; and let this serve to suppress our pride also, that
seeing the city wherein we are promised habitation and kingdom is
as far different from this in excellence as heaven from earth, life
eternal from mirth temporal, firm glory from fuming vainglory,
angels' company from men's, and His light that made the sun and
moon from the light of the sun and moon; we may feel that the
citizens of this heavenly region have done just nothing for attaining
this celestial dwelling, seeing that the others have taken such pains
in that habitation of earth which they had already attained.
Especially does the remission of sins call us as citizens to that
eternal dwelling; and this has a kind of resemblance to Romulus'
sanctuary, by which he gathered a multitude of people into his
city through hope of impunity.

CHAPTER XVIII

*How far the Christians should be from boasting of their deeds for their
eternal country, the Romans having done so much for their temporal
city and for human glory*

WHY is it then so much to despise all this world's vanities for
eternity whereas Brutus could kill his sons for fear his country
should lose bare liberty, a deed which the heavenly country compels no one to do?   Truly it is a more difficult matter to kill one's
children, than to let go those things which we do but gather for
our children, or to give them to the poor when faith or righteousness bids us.   Earthly riches can neither bless us nor our children
with happiness; we must either lose them in this life or leave them
to be enjoyed after our death by one, we cannot tell whom, perhaps
by those we would not should have them.   No, it is God, the
mind's true wealth, that makes us happy.   The poet rears Brutus
a monument of unhappiness for killing his sons, though otherwise
he praises him:

> . . . Natosque pater fera bella moventes,
> Ad poenam patriae pro libertate vocabit
> Infelix, utcumque ferent ea facta minores.[1]

> His sons, convict of turbulent transgression,
> He kills, to free his country from oppression,
> Hapless howe'er succeeding times shall ring.

[1] Virg. *Aen.* vi. 820–2.

But in the next verse he gives him comfort: 'Vicit amor patriae laudumque immensa cupido.' 'Conquer'd by his country's love, and thirst of praise'—the two things that set all the Romans upon admirable action. So then if the father could kill his own sons, for mortal freedom and thirst of praise (both transitory desires), what great matter is it, if we do not kill our sons, but count the poor of Christ our sons, and for that eternal liberty, which frees us from sin, death, and hell, not for human cupidity, but for Christian charity, to free men, not from Tarquin, but from the devils and their king? And if Torquatus, another Roman, slew his own son, not for fighting against his country, but only for going against his command, being general (he being a valorous youth and provoked by his enemy, yea and getting the victory); because there was more hurt in his contempt of authority than good in his conquest: why should they boast, who for the laws of that never-ending country do forsake only those things which are never so dear as children, namely earthly goods and possessions? If Furius Camillus, after his banishment by his ungrateful country, which he had saved from being oppressed by the valorous Veians, yet would deign to come to free it the second time, because he had no better place to show his glory in: why is he extolled as having done great matters, who having perhaps suffered some great disgrace and injury in the Church by his carnal enemies, has not departed to the Church's enemies, the heretics, or invented some heresy against it himself, but rather has guarded it, as far as in him lay, from all the pernicious invasions of heresy, because there is no other place to live in unto eternal life, though there be others enough to attain human glory in? If Scaevola, when he saw he had failed to kill Porsenna (a sore foe to Rome), and killed another for him, to make a peace with him, put his hand into the fire that burned on the altar, saying that Rome had a multitude such as he that had conspired his destruction, and by this speech so terrified him that he made an instant peace with them and got him packing: why shall any man talk of his merits in respect of the kingdom of heaven, if he lose not his hand but his whole body in the fire for it, not by his own choice but by the power of the persecutor? If Curtius (to satisfy the oracle that commanded Rome to cast the best jewel it had into a great gulf, and the Romans being resolved that valour and men of arms were their best jewels) took his horse and armour, and willingly leaped into that gaping gulf; why shall a man say he has done much for heaven that shall not cast himself to death but endure death at the hands of some enemy of his faith, seeing that God, his Lord, and the King of his country, has given him this rule as a certain oracle: 'Fear not them that kill the body, but are not able to kill the soul'? [1] If the two Decii consecrated themselves to their country's good and sacrificed their blood (as

[1] Matt. x. 28.

with prayers) unto the angry gods for the deliverance of the Roman army, let not the holy martyrs be proud of doing anything for the partaking of their eternal possessions, where felicity has neither error nor end, if they do contend in charitable faith and faithful charity, even unto the shedding of their blood both for their brethren for whom, and also for their enemies by whom, it is shed. If Marcus Pulvillus, in his dedication of the temple to Jove, Juno, and Minerva, false news being brought by those that envied his honour of his son's death, that so he might leave all the dedication to his fellow, and go perturbed away, did nevertheless so contemn the news, that he bade them cast him forth unburied, his desire of glory utterly conquering his grief of being childless: why should that man say he has done much for the preaching of the gospel (which frees and gathers God's citizens out of so many errors) to whom being careful of his father's funeral the Lord said: 'Follow me, and let the dead bury their dead'?[1] If M. Regulus, not to deal falsely with his most cruel enemies, returned back to them from Rome itself, because (as he answered the Romans who would have stayed him) he could not live in the dignity of an honest citizen in Rome, since he had been a slave in Africa: and if the Carthaginians put him to a horrible death for speaking against them in Rome's senate: what torments are not to be scorned for the faith of the country unto whose eternal happiness faith itself conducts us? Or what reward had God for all His benefits, if, for the faith which every one owes to Him, a man should suffer as much torment as Regulus suffered for the faith which he owed to his bloodiest foes? Or how dare any Christian boast of voluntary poverty (the means to make his travel unto his country, where God the true riches dwelleth, more light and easy) when he shall hear or read of L. Valerius, who, dying a consul, was so poor that his burial was paid for out of the common purse, or of Q. Cincinnatus, who having but four acres of land, and tilling it himself with his own hands, was fetched from the plough to be dictator, an office more honourable than the consul's, and having conquered his foes, and gotten great honour, returned to his old state of poverty? Or why should any man think it a great matter not to be seduced from the fellowship of celestial powers by this world's vanities, when he reads how Fabricius could not be drawn from the Romans by all the promises of Pyrrhus the king of Epirus, though they extended even to the fourth part of his kingdom, but would live there still in his accustomed poverty? For if, though they had a rich and powerful commonwealth, those men were so poor themselves, that one that had been twice consul was put out of that senate of poor men by the censors' decree, because he was found to be worth ten pound in silver—if those men that enriched the treasury by their triumphs were so poor themselves, then much

[1] Matt. viii. 22.

more ought the Christians (whose riches are for a better intent all in common, as the apostles' Acts record, to be distributed to every man according to his need: 'neither any of them said that anything he possessed was his own, but all was in common'[1])—much more, I say, ought they to know that this is no just thing to boast upon, seeing that they do for gaining the society of the angels that which the others did or nearly did for the preserving of the glory of the Romans. These now, and other suchlike deeds recounted in their books, how should they have been so known and so famous, had not Rome's empire had this great and magnificent exaltation and expanse? Wherefore that empire, so spacious and so continual and renowned by the virtues of those illustrious men, was given both to stand as a reward for their merits, and to produce examples for our uses, that if we observe not the laws of those virtues for attaining the celestial kingdom, which they did for preserving one but terrestrial, we might be ashamed: but that if we do, then we be not exalted, for as the apostle says: 'The afflictions of this present time are not worthy of the glory which shall be showed unto us.'[2]   But their lives seemed worthy of that present temporal glory. And therefore the Jews, that executed Christ (the New Testament revealing what the Old concealed, that God was not to be worshipped for the earthly benefits which He bestows upon bad as well as good, but for life eternal, and the perpetual blessing of that supernal city), were justly given to be the slaves and instruments of the Romans' glory: that those that sought earthly glory by any virtue soever, might overcome and subdue those that refused and murdered the giver of true glory and eternal felicity.

CHAPTER XIX

The difference between the desire of glory and the desire of rule

THERE is a difference between desire of glory and desire of rule: for though the first do incline to the second, yet such as seek the true human glory have a desire to be pleasing unto good judgments; for there is much good in manners whereof many can judge well, although many again have not this good, nor go that honest way to glory, honour, and sovereignty that Sallust speaks of: 'He goeth the true way.'[3]   But whosoever desires to rule without that desire of glory which keeps men in awe of good judgments, he cares not by what villainy he compass his desire, and so his going about it will show. And therefore the hunter of glory either follows the true track or covers his courses so well, that he is held to be still in the true track, and thought to be good when he is not

[1] Acts ii. 44, 45; iv. 32.   [2] Rom. viii. 18.   [3] *Catil.* 11.

so. Wherefore to the virtuous, contempt of glory is a great virtue:
because God beholds it, and not the judgment of man; for whatsoever he does before men to show this contempt, he has no means
of showing to those, who suspect him of so behaving in order to
win greater glory, that their suspicions are unfounded. But he
that contemns their opinionative praise, contemns also with it their
unadvised suspicion: yet not their salvation (if he be good),
because he that has his goodness from God is of that justice that
he loves his very enemies, and so loves them that he wishes his
slanderers and backbiters to be reformed, and to become his companions, not here but in his eternal country. For as he respects not
the praises of his commenders, so he neglects not their loves, desiring neither to falsify their praises nor delude their loves: and
therefore urges them to the praise of Him from whom every one
hath all his praiseworthy endowments. But the man that despising
glory dotes on domination, is worse than a beast, both in manners,
barbarism, and lust's extremity. Such men Rome has had: for
though they had lost the care of esteem, yet they retained still the
desire for sovereignty: nay Rome (says history) had many such.
But Nero Caesar was he that got first of all to the top turret of all
this enormity, whose luxury was such that one would not have
feared any manly act of his; and yet was his cruelty such, as one
ignorant of him would not have thought any effeminate spark
resident in him; yet even such as this man was have no dominion
but from the great God's providence, holding man's vices sometimes worthy of such plagues. The scripture about him is plain:
'By me kings reign and princes: tyrants by me govern the earth.'[1]
But lest *tyrannus* here should be taken for wild and wicked kings,
and not (as it is meant) for all the old worthies, hear Virgil:

> Pars mihi pacis erit dextram tetigisse tyranni.[2]
>
> Some peace I hope, by touching your king's hands.

But elsewhere it is more plainly spoken of God, that He makes a
'hypocrite to reign, because the people are snared in perverseness.'[3]
Wherefore though I have done what I can to show the cause why
the true and just God gave the Romans such assistance in erecting
their empire's and city's earthly glory upon such a frame of
monarchy, yet there may be a more secret cause than yet we see;
namely, the diverse merits of the world, open to God, though not
to us: it being plain to all godly men, that no man can have true
virtue without true piety, that is, the true adoration of the one and
true God: nor is that virtue true either, when it serves but for
human ostentation. But those that are not of the eternal city
called in the scriptures[4] the city of God, are more useful to their
earthly city in possessing that purely world-respecting virtue, than

<hr />

[1] Prov. viii. 15, 16.   [2] *Aen.* vii. 266.   [3] Job xxxiv. 30.
[4] Ps. xlvi. 4; xlviii. 1; lxxxvii. 3.

if they lacked that also. But if those that are truly godly and
upright of life come to have the government of estates, there can
no greater happiness befall the world than through the mercy of
God to be governed by such men. And they do attribute all their
virtues (be they never so admired) unto the grace of God only, who
gave them in answer to their desires, their faith and prayers.
Besides, they know how far they are from true perfection of justice;
I mean such as is in the angelical powers, for whose fellowship they
make themselves fit. But let that virtue that serves human glory
without piety be never so much extolled, it is not comparable even
with the imperfect beginnings of the saints' virtues, whose assured
hope stands fixed in the grace and mercy of the true God.

CHAPTER XX

*That virtue is as much disgraced in serving human glory as in obeying
the pleasures of the body*

THE philosophers that make virtue the end of all human good,
are wont in order to shame such as approved virtue and yet applied
it all to bodily delight (holding this to be desirable for itself, and
virtue to be sought only in respect to this pleasure) to delineate a
picture (as it were with their tongues) wherein Pleasure sits on a
throne, like a delicate queen, and all the Virtues about her, ready
at a beck to do her command. There she commands Prudence to
seek out a way whereby Pleasure may reign in safety: Justice must
go and do good turns to attain friends, for the use of corporal delights, and wrong none: Fortitude's task is that if any hurt (not
mortal) invade the body, she must hold Pleasure so fast in the mind
that the remembrance of delights past may dull the touch of the pain
present. Temperance must so temper the nourishment, that im-
moderation come not to trouble the health, and so offend Lady
Pleasure, whom the Epicureans do say is chiefly resident in the
body's soundness. Thus the Virtues, being in their own dignities
absolute commanders, must pull all their glories under the feet of
Pleasure and submit themselves to an imperious and dishonest
woman. Than this picture there cannot be a sight more vile,
deformed, and abominable to a good man, say the philosophers;
and it is true. Nor think I that the picture would be so fair as it
should be, if human glory were painted in the throne of Pleasure:
for though it be not a nice piece,[1] as the other is, yet it is turgid, and
full of empty air, so that ill should it beseem the substantial Virtues
to be subject to such a shadow; that Prudence should foresee
nothing, Justice distribute nothing, Fortitude endure nothing,
Temperance moderate nothing, but that which aimeth at the

[1] Lat. *luxuriosa femina!*—ED.

pleasing of men and the serving of windy glory.   Nor are they quit from this blot, who contemning the judgments of others (as scorners of glory) yet in their own conceit hold their wisdom at a high price; for their virtue (if they have any) serves human glory in another manner.   For he that pleases himself is but a man; but he that hopes and believes truly and piously in God, whom he loves, applies his thoughts more upon that which he displeases himself in, than upon those things, which if they be in him do rather please the truth than him.   Nor does he ascribe the power he has to please unto any other but unto His mercy whom he fears to displease; giving thanks for the cure of this, and praying for the cure of that.

CHAPTER XXI

That the true God, in whose hand and providence all the state of the world consists, did order and dispose of the monarchy of the Romans

THIS being thus, the true God that gives the heavenly kingdom only to the godly, but the earthly ones both to good and bad as Himself likes, whose pleasure is all justice; He is to have all power of giving or taking away sovereignty ascribed unto Himself alone, and no other.   For though we have shown some things that He pleased to manifest unto us, yet far, far is it beyond our powers to penetrate into men's merits, or scan the deserts of kingdoms aright.   This one God, therefore, that neither stays from judging nor favouring of mankind, when His pleasure was, and whilst it was His pleasure, let Rome have sovereignty: so did He with Assyria and Persia who (as their books say) worshipped only two gods, a good and a bad: to omit the Hebrews, of whom I think sufficient is already spoken, both of their worship of one God, and of their kingdom.   But He that gave Persia corn without Segetia's help, and so many gifts of the earth without any of those many gods that had each one a share in them, or rather were three or four to a share, He also gave them their kingdom without their helps, by whose adoration they thought they kept their kingdom.   And so for the men: He that gave Marius rule, gave Caesar rule; He that gave Augustus it, gave Nero it: He that gave Vespasian rule, or Titus his son, both sweet-natured men, gave it also to Domitian, that cruel bloodsucker. And to be brief, He that gave it to Constantine the Christian, gave it also to Julian the Apostate, whose worthy character was wholly blinded by sacrilegious curiosity, and all through the desire of rule: whose heart wandered after the vanity of false oracles, as he found, when upon their promise of victory he burned all his ships that victualled his army: and then being slain in one of his many rash adventures, he left his poor army in the jaws of their enemies without any means of escape, so that the god Terminus (of whom we spake before) [1] was fain to yield, and to remove the bounds of the empire.   Thus did he give place to Necessity that would not give place to Jupiter.   All these did the true, sacred, and only God dispose and direct as He pleased; and if the causes be unknown why He did thus, or thus, is He therefore unjust?

CHAPTER XXII

That the origins and conclusions of wars are all at God's disposal

So likewise does He with the times and ends of war, be it His pleasure justly to correct or mercifully to pity mankind, ending them sooner or later as He wills.   Pompey's pirate war, and Scipio's third African war, were ended with incredible celerity. The slaves' war also, though it cost Rome two consuls and many captains, making all Italy feel the smart of it, yet in the third year after it was begun, it was finished.   The Picenes, Marsians, Pelignians (Italians all) sought to pluck their necks from their long and strict servitude unto Rome, though it now had subdued huge dominions, and razed Carthage.   In this war the Romans were sorely foiled, two consuls killed, and many a tall soldier and worthy senator left dead: yet this war had continuance but unto the fifth year.   But the second African war lasted a great while, eighteen years, to the great weakening of the commonwealth, and almost the utter ruin thereof, seventy thousand soldiers falling in two battles. The first African war held three-and-twenty years; Mithridates' war forty years.   And lest any one should think that in the ancient laudable times the Romans had any better rules to dispatch war sooner than the rest, the Samnites' war lasted almost fifty years, wherein the Romans were conquered even unto slavery.   But because they loved not glory for justice, but justice for glory, they broke the peace and league which they had made.   These things I write, because some being ignorant of antiquities, and some others being dissemblers of what they know, might otherwise upon discovery of a long war since the time of Christianity, fly in the face of our religion, and say if it were not for that, and if the old adorations were restored, that war would have been ended by the Romans' virtues and the assistance of Mars and Bellona, as soon as the rest were.   Let them that read of their wars but recollect what uncertain fortune the ancient Romans had in the wars with the whole world, being tossed like a tempestuous sea with a thousand storms of invasions and arms: and then let them needs confess, what so fain they would conceal, and cease in this opposition against God's power, to possess others with errors, and be the butchers of their own souls.

[1] IV. xxiii and xxix.

CHAPTER XXIII

Of the battle wherein Radagaisus, an idolatrous king of the Goths, was slain with all his army

NAY, that wonderful mercy of God's, in an act done within our memories, they will not so much as mention with thanksgiving, but endeavour, as much as in them lies, to smother in eternal oblivion; which should we do, we should be as graceless and ungrateful as they. Radagaisus, king of the Goths, having brought a huge army even before the walls of Rome, and holding his sword even over their necks (as it were), upon one day was overthrown so suddenly, that not so much as one Roman being slain, nor yet wounded, his whole army, consisting of about ten thousand men, was utterly defeated, he himself and his sons being taken and justly beheaded. If this wicked barbarian had entered Rome with those forces, whom would he have spared? What places would he have honoured, what God would he have feared? Whose blood, whose chastity should have escaped him? But oh, how these wretches boasted of his precedent conquests, that he had been so victorious, that he had gotten such and such fields, only because he was a daily sacrificer to those gods which Christianity had chased from Rome! For at his approach thither, where by the beck of God's majesty he was crushed to nothing, his fame was so spacious that it was told us here at Carthage that the pagans believed, reported, and boasted that he could not be conquered by any of those that would not suffer the Romans to adore those gods, whose good favours he had obtained by the daily sacrifices he offered. Thus they never gave thanks for the merciful goodness of God, who having resolved to chastise the world's corruption with a greater barbarian irruption, yet did moderate His justice with such mercy, that at first He gave their leader into the hands of his enemies, because the devils whom he served should gain no souls by the persuasion of the glory of his conquests. And then when such barbarians had taken Rome, which against all custom of hostility defended such as fled into the holy places, only in reverence of Christianity, professing themselves far greater enemies for the name of Christ unto the devils and sacrilegious sacrifices (in which the other reposed his trust), than unto the opposed soldiers themselves: thus God did give the Romans this merciful correction, and by destroying the devils' adorers, showed them that there was neither any help in those sacrifices for the state of this present life (as they may see that will be attentive and not obstinate), nor that the true religion is to be refused because of earthly necessities, but rather held fast, in hope and expectation of the heavenly glories.

CHAPTER XXIV

The state and truth of a Christian emperor's felicity

FOR we Christians do not say that Christian emperors are happy, because they have a long reign, or die leaving their sons in quiet possession of their empires, or have been ever victorious, or powerful against all their opposers. These are but gifts and solaces of this laborious joyless life. Idolaters, and such as belong not to God (as these emperors do), may enjoy them; because God in His mercy will not have these that know Him to believe that such things are the best goods He gives. But happy they are (say we) if they reign justly, free from being puffed up with the flattering exaltations of their attendants, or the cringes of their subjects; if they know themselves to be but men, and remember that; if they make their power their trumpeter to divulge the true adoration of God's majesty; if they love, fear, and honour Him; if they long the most for that empire where they need not fear to have partners; if they be slack to revenge, quick to forgive; if they use correction for the public good, and not for private hate; if their pardons promise not liberty of offending, but indeed only hope of reformation; if they counterpoise their enforced acts of severity with the like weight of bounty and clemency; if their lusts be the lesser because they have the larger licence; if they desire to rule their own desires, rather than others' estates; and if they do all things, not for glory, but for charity, and with all, and before all, give God the due sacrifice of prayer for their imperfections: such Christian emperors we call happy, here in hope, and hereafter, when the time we look for comes, in deed.

CHAPTER XXV

Of the prosperous estate that God bestowed upon Constantine, a Christian emperor

FOR the good God, lest those that worship Him for the life of eternity should think that no man can attain to this earthly glory but such as adore the devils (whose power in those things bears a great sway), bestowed such store of those earthly benefits as no other man durst wish for, upon Constantine the emperor, one that worshipped no devils, but only the said true God. To him did He grant the building of a new city, partaker of the Roman Empire, as the daughter of Rome herself; but excluding all diabolical temples, or idols. Long did he reign therein, and alone swayed the whole Roman world: he was in war most victorious; in suppressing tyrants most fortunate. He died an aged man, and left his sons all emperors. But lest any emperor after him should turn Christian for hope of attaining Constantine's felicity (the end of Christianity being not that, but life eternal), He cut off Jovinian far sooner than He did Julian, and suffered Gratian to be slain by his enemies' sword; yet with far more respect than Pompey was killed, that worshipped the Roman gods. For Cato, whom he left as his successor in the war he waged, could never revenge his death; but Gratian (though the souls of the godly regard not such solaces) was fully revenged by Theodosius, with whom he shared the empire, though he had a younger brother: being more regardful of a faithful friend than of a too extensive power.

CHAPTER XXVI

Of the faith and devotion of Theodosius Augustus

So he did not only keep the faith which he owed him in his lifetime, but like a Christian indeed, received his little brother Valentinian into his protection and defence, when Maximus his murderer had chased him from his State: and held the care of a father over him, which he need not have done, but might easily have taken all to himself, had his ambition overpoised his religion. But he preserved his imperial State for him, and gave him all the comfort honest courtesy could bestow. And when the good fortune of Maximus begot him a terrible name, Theodosius did not creep into a corner of his palace, with wizards and conjurers, but sent to John, that lived in a wilderness of Egypt, who he had heard was graced from God by the spirit of prophecy: to him sent he and received a true promise of victory. So soon after having killed the tyrant Maximus he restored the child Valentinian to his empire from whence he was driven, showing him all the reverent love that could be. And when this child was slain (as he was soon after, either by treachery, or by some other casualty), and that Eugenius another tyrant was unlawfully set up in his place, receiving another answer from the prophet, his faith being firm, he fetched him down from his usurped place, rather by prayer than power; for the soldiers that were in the battle on the usurper's side told it unto us, that there came such a violent wind from Theodosius' side, that it smote their darts forth of their hands, and if any were thrown, it took them presently in an instant, and forced them upon the faces of those that threw them. And therefore Claudian (though no Christian) sings this well of his praise:

O nimium dilecte deo cui militat aether,
Et conjurati veniunt ad classica venti.[1]

O God's belov'd, whom powers aerial,
And winds come arm'd to help, when thou dost call!

[1] *De Tert. Consul. Honor. August.* 97–8.

And being victor (according to his faith and presage) he threw down
certain images of Jupiter which had been consecrated (I know not
with what ceremonies) against him, and mirthfully and kindly gave
his footmen their thunderbolts; who (as they well might) jested
upon them, because they were glad, and said they would abide
their flashes well enough; for the sons of his foe, some of them fell
in the fight (not by his command): others being not yet Christians,
but flying into the church, by this means he made Christians, and
loved them with a Christian charity; not diminishing their honours
a whit, but adding more to them.   He suffered no private grudges
to be held against any one after the victory.   He used not these
civil wars, as Cinna, Marius, and Sulla did, that would not have
them ended when they were ended; but he rather sorrowed that
they were begun, than ended then to any man's hurt.   And in all
these troubles, from his reign's beginning, he forgot not to assist
and succour the labouring Church, by all the wholesome laws
which he could promulgate against the faithless; Valens an Arian
heretic having done much hurt therein, whereof he rejoiced more
to be a member than an earthly emperor.   He commanded the
demolition of all idols of the Gentiles, knowing that not so much as
earthly blessings are in the devils' power, but that all and each particular are in God's.   And what was there ever more memorable than
that religious humility of his, when being even forced by his
attendants to revenge the injury offered him by the Thessalonians
(unto whom notwithstanding at the bishop's entreaties he had
promised pardon) he was excommunicated and showed such repentance, that the people entreating for him, rather did lament to
see the imperial majesty so abased, than feared his wrath when
they had offended.   These good works, and a tedious roll of
suchlike, did he bear away with him out of this transitory smoke
of all kind of human glory: their reward is eternal felicity, given by
the true God, only to the good.   For the rest, be they honours, or
helps of this life, as the world itself, light, air, water, earth, soul,
sense, and spirit of life, these He gives promiscuously to good and
bad; and so He doth also with the greatness and continuance of
the temporal empires of all men, which He bestows on either sort,
as He pleases.

CHAPTER XXVII

*Augustine's invective against such as wrote against the books
already published*

BUT now I see I must take those in hand, that seeing they are convicted by just plain arguments in this, that these false gods have
no power in the distribution of temporal goods (which fools desire
only), now go on to affirm that they are worshipped, not for the

helps of this life present, but of that which is to come. For in these five books past, we have said enough to such as (like little babies) cry out that they would fain worship them for those earthly helps, but cannot be suffered. The first three books I had no sooner finished, and let them pass abroad into some men's hands, but I heard of some that prepared to make some kind of an answer to them, or a reply upon them. Afterward I heard that they had written it, and did but watch for a time when to publish it securely. But I advise them not to wish a thing so inexpedient: it is an easy thing for any man to seem to have made an answer that has not wished to keep silent; but what is more talkative than vanity, which cannot have the power of truth, by reason it has more tongue than truth? But let these fellows mark each thing well: and if their impartial judgments tell them that their tongue-ripe satirism may more easily disturb the truth of this world than subvert it, let them keep in their trumperies, and learn rather to be reformed by the wise than applauded by the foolish. For if they expect a time not for the freedom of truth but for the licensing of reproach, God forbid that that should be true of them, which Tully spoke of a certain man, that was called happy, in having free leave to offend: 'Oh, wretched he that hath free liberty to offend!' [1] And therefore whoever he be that thinks himself happy in his freedom of reproaching others, I give him to understand that far happier should he be in the lack of that licence, seeing that now he may in form of consultation contradict or oppose what he will, setting aside the desire for vain applause; and hear what he will, and what is fit, in honest, grave, free, and friendly disputation.

[1] *Tusc. Disp.* v. 19, 55.

THE SIXTH BOOK OF THE CITY OF GOD

CHAPTER I

Of those that affirm they do worship these gods for eternal life and not for temporal respects

IN the five precedent books I think they be sufficiently confounded that hold that that worship ought to be given unto these false gods, which is peculiar only to one true God, and in Greek is called λατρεία, and that this worship ought to be offered unto them for temporal commodities; all of which gods Christianity proves either to be frivolous and unprofitable images, or damned spirits, or at least and at best no creators but creatures. But who knows not that neither those five books, nor all that a man could make, would stay and satisfy excess of obstinacy? For it is some men's glory (vain indeed) never to yield to the truth, but to oppose it to their own perdition, in whose bosoms sin has so large an empire; for their disease exceeds all cure, not through the physician's want of skill, but the patient's impatient frowardness. But as for such as read the said books without any obstinate intent, or with little, and ponder the things they read in an impartial discretion, those shall approve that our labour in their satisfaction has rather performed more than the question required than otherwise: and that all the malice, wherein they make Christianity the cause of all the afflictions falling upon this transitory world (the best learned of them dissembling their knowledge against their own consciences), is not only void of all reason and honesty, but fraught with light rashness and pernicious impudence.

Now, therefore (as our method exacts), are they to be dealt with that make eternity the end of this erroneous worship, which the Christian religion so rejects. Let us take our beginning from the holy and oracular psalmist, that says: 'Blessed is the man that maketh the Lord his trust, and regardeth not the proud nor such as turn aside to lies.'[1] But of all such as do go astray in those errors the philosophers are least faulty, that could never abide the fond opinions of the vulgar, who made their gods images, and fabled divers things of them, most false and unworthy of the deities; or else believed them from the reports of others, and from that belief intruded them into the ceremonies, and made them parts of their worship. Wherefore with such as though they durst not openly, yet secretly disliked those things, this question may be fitly

[1] Ps. xl. 4.

disputed: whether it be fit to worship for the life to come not the one God the maker of all bodies and spirits but many gods, being all (by their best philosophers' confessions) both created and set in their positions by Him. But who can endure to hear it said that the gods which I reckoned up in part in the fourth book,[1] and which have peculiar charges, can give one life eternal? And those sharp-witted men that boast of the good they do by writing these things, in instructing the people what to entreat at each of their hands, would they commit such a gross absurdity as that which the mimes do in jest, asking water of Bacchus and wine of the Nymphs? For example: would they teach a man that prayed unto the Nymphs for wine, if they answered him, We have no wine, go to Bacchus for that: then to reply, If you have no wine, I pray you then give me life eternal? What grosser foolery could there be than this? Would not the Nymphs fall a laughing (for they are prone to laughter when they do not affect deceit as the devils are wont to do), and say to him, Why, fond man, dost thou think we have life eternal at command, that have not a cup of wine at command as thou hearest? Such fruitless absurdity should it be to ask eternal life, or hope for it of such gods as are so bound to peculiar charges in things respecting this frail and transitory life, that it were like scurrilous buffoonery to demand anything of any one of them which rests under the disposing of another. Which when the mimes do, men do very worthily laugh at them in the theatre; and when ignorant fools do it, they are far more worthily derided in the world. Wherefore the peculiar positions that we ought to make unto every god, ordained by the governors of cities, their learned men have compiled, and left unto memory: which must be made to Bacchus, which to the Nymphs, Vulcan, etc., part whereof I recited in the fourth book, and part I willingly omitted. Now then, if it be an error to ask wine of Ceres, bread of Bacchus, water of Vulcan, and fire of the Nymphs: how much more were it an error to ask life eternal of any one of them? Wherefore if in our disputation about the earthly kingdoms, and in whose power they should be, we showed that it was directly false to believe that they consisted in the power of any one of those imaginary gods; were it not outrageous madness then to believe that the life eternal, with which the kingdoms of the earth are in no way worthy to be compared, should be in the gift of any of them? Nor can their state, and height, compared with the baseness of an earthly kingdom in respect of them, be a sufficient cloak for their defect in not being able to give it: because (forsooth) they do not respect it. No, whoever he be that considering the frailty of man's nature makes a scorn of the momentary state of earthly dominion, he will think it an unworthy injury to the gods to have the giving and guarding of such vanities imposed upon them. And by this, if (according

[1] Chapters viii, xi, and xxi.

as we proved sufficiently in the last two books) no one god of all this catalogue of noble and ignoble gods were fit to be held the bestower of earthly states, how much less fit were they all to make a mortal man partaker of immortality? Besides (because now we dispute against those that stand for their worship in respect of the life to come) they are not to be worshipped for those things which these men's erroneous opinion (far from all truth) have put as their proprieties, and things peculiarly in their power: as they believe that hold the honouring of them very useful in things of this present life, against whom I have spoken to the best of my power in the five precedent volumes. Which being thus, if such as adore Juventas flourish in vigour of youth, and those that do not either die under age, or pass it with the griefs of decrepit sickness: if the chins of Fortuna Barbata's servants grow full of hair, and all other be beardless: then justly might we say that thus far these goddesses are limited in their offices: and therefore it were no good asking life eternal of Juventas, that could not give one a beard, nor were any good to be expected of Fortuna Barbata after this life, that had not power to make one live till he had a beard. But now, their worship being of no use for those things in their power, seeing many have worshipped Juventas that lived not to be youths; and as many honoured Fortuna Barbata that never had good beards: and many without beards that worshipped her were mocked by them that had beards and scorned her: is any man then so mad, that knowing the worshipping of them to be ineffectual in those things whereto their pretended power extends, yet will believe it to be effectual in the obtaining of life eternal? Nay, even those that did share out their authority for them (lest being so many, there should some sit idle), and so taught their worship to the rude vulgar, not even these themselves durst affirm that the life eternal was a gift comprised in any of their powers.

CHAPTER II

What may be thought of Varro's opinion of the gods, who deals so with them in his discovery of them and their ceremonies, that with more reverence unto them he might have held his peace

WHO was ever a more curious inquisitor of these matters, a more learned discoverer, a more diligent judge, a more elegant divider, or a more exact recorder, than Varro? And though he be not eloquent, yet is he so instructive and sententious, that to read his universal learning will delight one that loves matter as much as Tully will one that loves words. Yea Tully himself[1] leaves this testimony of him, that the same disputation that he handles in his Academic dialogues, he had (he says) with Marcus Varro, a man the most acute, and doubtless the most learned of his time. He

[1] Cf. *Acad. Quaest.* i. 1.

says not the most 'eloquent,' because herein he had his betters: but, most 'acute': and in his *Academics* where he made doubts of all things, he calls him 'doubtless the most learned': being so assured hereof that he would take away all doubt which he used to introduce into all questions, only in this academical disputation forgetting himself to be an Academic.   And in his first book, having commended his works, 'We,' saith he, 'in the city were but as wandering pilgrims, thy books brought us home, and taught us to know what and who we were. Thy country's age, time, religious and political discipline, habitations, order, all the forms, causes, and kinds of divine and civil discipline, by these are fully discovered.' [1]   So great was his learning, as Terentian also testifies of him in the verse, *Vir doctissimus undecunque Varro*, [2] 'Varro, a man of universal skill,' who has read so much that we wonder how he has had time to write, and has written so much that we wonder how any man should read so much. This man (I say), so learned and so witty, had he been a direct opposer of that religion he wrote for, and held the ceremonies in no way religious, but wholly superstitious, could not (I imagine) have recorded more detestable absurdities thereof than he has already. But being a worshipper of the same gods, and a teacher of that worship, so that he professes he fears that his work should be lost, not by the enemies' incursion, but by the citizens' negligence, and affirms that with a more worthy and profitable care were they to be preserved, than that wherewith Metellus fetched the Palladium from the flames, and Aeneas his household gods from the sack of Troy: yet for all this, does he leave such things to memory, as all, both learned and ignorant, do judge most absurd and unworthy to be mentioned in religion. What ought we then to gather, but that this deeply 'skilled man' (being not freed by the Holy Spirit) was overburdened with the custom of his city, and yet under show of commending their religion gave the world notice of his opinion.

CHAPTER III

The division of Varro's books which he styles ' The Antiquity of Divine and Human Affairs'

HE wrote one-and-forty books of antiquities, dividing them into affairs divine and human: the human he handled in five-and-twenty of them, the divine in sixteen, so following the division that every six books of humanity he divided into four parts, prosecuting the persons, place, time, and nature of them all. In his first six he wrote of the men, in the second six of the places, in his third six of the times, in his last six of the actions: one separate book, as the

[1] *Acad. Quaest.* i. 3, 9.   [2] *De Litteris, Syllabis, Pedibus, et Metris*, iv. 2846.

argument of them all, he placed before them all. In his handling of divine affairs he also follows the same method (for divine rites are performed by men in time and place). The four heads I rehearsed he comprises in three special books. In the first three he writes of the men, the next three of places, the third of the times, the last of the sacrifices, herein also handling who offered, where, when, and what they offered with acuteness and judgment. But because the chief expectation was to know to whom they offered, of this followed a full discourse in his three last books, which made them up to fifteen, but in all sixteen, because a book went as an argument by itself before all that followed: which being ended, consequently out of that fivefold division the three first books did follow of the men, so subdivided that the first was of the priests, the second of the augurs, the third of the fifteen rite-observers. His second three books, of the places, handled (1) the chapels; (2) the temples; (3) the religious places. The three books of the times handled (1) their holy days; (2) the Circensian games; (3) the stage plays. Of the three concerning the sacrifices, the first handled consecrations; the second, the private offerings; the third, the public. All these being the parts of their precedent pomp, the gods themselves follow in the three last, they on whom all this cost is bestowed: in the first the gods known; in the second, the gods uncertain; in the third, the whole company of them; in the fourth, the selected principals of them. Now in this goodly frame and fabric of a well-distinguished work, it is apparent to all that are not obstinately blind that vain and impudent are they that beg or expect eternal life of any of these gods: both by that we have spoken and that we will speak. These are but the institutions of men, or of devils: not good devils, as he says, but to be plain, wicked spirits, that out of their strange malice, instil such pernicious opinions into men's phantasies, by abusing their senses, and illuding their weak capacities, thereby to draw their souls into vanity more deep, and unloose the hold they have, or might have, on the unchangeable and eternal verity. Varro professes himself to write of humanity before divinity, because first, says he, there were cities and societies, which afterwards gave being to these institutions. But the true religion has no origin from earthly societies: God the giver of eternal comfort inspires it into the hearts of such as honour Him.

CHAPTER IV

That by Varro's disputations, the affairs of those men that worshipped the gods are of far more antiquity than those of the gods themselves

THIS therefore is the reason Varro gives why he writes first of the men and after of the gods who had their ceremonial institutions from men: 'Even as,' says he, 'the painter is older than the picture, and the carpenter than the house, so are cities before their ordinances.' But yet, he says, if he were to write of the full nature of the gods, he would have begun with them, and have dealt with men afterwards: as though here he were writing but of part of their natures, not of all: or as though some part of the gods' nature (though not all) should not always be preferred before men? Nay, what say you to his discourse in his three last books of gods certain, gods uncertain, and gods selected? Here he seems to omit no nature of the gods. Why, then, should he say that if we were to write of all the nature of gods and men, we would have done with the gods ere we would begin with the men? Either he writes of the gods' natures in whole, in part, or not all: if in whole, then should the discourse have had first place in his work: if in part, why should it not be first nevertheless? Is it unfit to prefer part of the gods' nature before the whole of man's? If it be much to prefer it before all mankind, yet it is not so to prefer it before all the Romans. And the books were written only in Rome's respect, not in the world's. Yet (says he) the men are fittest before, as the painter to the picture, and the carpenter to the building: plainly intimating that the deities' affairs had (as pictures and buildings have) their origin directly from man. So then it remaineth that he wrote not all of the gods' nature, a truth which he would not speak plainly out, but leave to the reader's intelligence. For where he says 'not all' ordinarily it is understood 'some,' but may be taken for 'none.' For 'none' is neither 'all' nor 'some.' For as he says, if it were all the gods' nature that he wrote of, he would have handled it before the men's. But truth (hold he his peace) cries out, it should nevertheless have precedence over the Romans in particular, though it be but a part itself. But it is rightly placed as it is, the last of all, therefore it is none at all. His desire therefore was not to prefer humanity before divinity, but truth before falsehood. For in his dissertation on humanity he follows history: but in that on divinity nothing but vain relations and idle opinions. This is the aim of his subtle intimation, in preferring the first, and giving the reason why he does so: which had he not given, some other means perhaps might have been invented for the defence of his method. But giving it himself, he neither leaves others place for other suspicions, nor fails to show that he does but prefer men before men's institutions, not man's nature before the deities': herein confessing that his books of divinity are not of the truth pertaining to their nature, but of their falsehood effecting others' error: which (as we said in our fourth book [1]) he professed by saying that if he were to found a city he would conform nearer to the rule of nature: but finding one established already, he could not choose but follow the established customs.

[1] Chapter xxxi.

CHAPTER V

Of Varro's three kinds of divinity, fabulous, natural, and politic

AGAIN, what means his threefold distinction of the doctrine concerning the gods, into mythical, physical, and civil? And (to give him a Latin tongue) the first is *fabulare*, but we will call it fabulous, for μῦθος in Greek is a fable or tale. The second is 'natural' in the common use of the word. The third he names in Latin, civil. And then proceeds: mythical, the poets use principally; physical, the philosophers; civil, the vulgar. For the first (says he) is fraught with fictions most disgraceful to the deities; as this, that this god is born of one's head, that of one's thigh, that of drops of blood; and this, that some of the gods were thieves, adulterers, and servants to man; and finally, they attribute such things to the gods as cannot be resident but in the most contemptible wretch of all mortality, nor happen but unto such slavish natures. Here now as far as fear permitted, he makes a fair discovery of the injury offered to the gods by such ungodly fables: and here he might, seeing he speaks not of the natural nor civil divinity, but of the fabulous which he thought he might reprehend freely. But now to the next. The second, says he, is that wherewith the philosophers have filled their volumes: wherein they dispute what, whence, and when the gods were; whether from eternity of fire, as Heraclitus held, or of numbers, as Pythagoras taught; or of atoms, as Epicurus believed; and such as are far more tolerable within the schools than without in the open forum. Here he blames nothing in this kind, but only relates the controversies which divided them into sects and factions. Yet this kind he excludes from the people's ears, but not the other which was so filthy and so frivolous. Oh, the religious ears of the people, and even with them of Rome! The philosophers' discourses of the gods they cannot anyway endure; but the poets' fictions, and the players' actions, being so much dishonourable to the divine essences, and fit to be spoken by none but the most abject persons, those they abide and behold with patience, nay, with pleasure. Nay, these the gods themselves do like, and therefore have them decreed as expiations. Aye but, say some, we distinguish these two kinds, the mythical and the physical, from the civil, whereof you now are to speak; and so does he distinguish them also. Well, let us see what he says to that. I see good cause why the fabulous should be separate from the rest, because it is false, foul, and unworthy. But in dividing the natural and the civil, what does he in this but approve that the civil is faulty also? For if it be natural, why is it excluded? And if it be not natural, why is it admitted? This is that that makes him handle the human things before the divine, because in the latter he followed that which men had ordained, not that which the truth exacted. But let us see his civil divinity. The third kind, says he, is that which men of the city, chiefly the priests, ought to be cunning in: as, which gods to worship in public, and with what peculiar sort of sacrifices each one must be served. But let us go on with him. The first kind of divinity, says he, was adapted to the stage. The second to the world. The third to the city. Who sees not which he prefers? Even his second philosophical kind. This belongs (he says) to the world, than which they hold nothing more excellent. But the other two, the first and the third, them he distinguishes and confines to the stage and the city; for we see that the appertaining of them to the city has no consequence why they should pertain to the world, though there be cities in the world; for false opinion may get that believed as truth in a city which has not any nature or place in any part of the world. And for the stage, where is that but in the city? There was it ordained by the city; and for what end but stage plays? And what stage plays but of their gods, of whom these books are penned with so much pains?

CHAPTER VI

Of the fabulous and politic divinity, against Varro

VARRO, seeing thou art most acute, and doubtless most learned, yet but a man, neither God, nor assisted by God's spirit in the discovery of truth in divinity, thou seest this, that the divine affairs are to be excluded from human vanities; and yet thou fearest to offend the people's vicious opinions and customs in these public superstitions, being notwithstanding, as both thyself held and thy written works affirm to be, directly opposite to the nature of the deities, or such as men's infirmity surmised was included in the elements. What doth this human (though excelling) wit of thine in this place? What help doth thy great reading afford thee in these straits? Thou art desirous to honour the natural gods, and forced to worship the civil. Thou hast found some fabulous ones whom thou darest speak thy mind against; giving the civil some part of their disgrace whether thou wilt or no; for thou sayest the fabulous are for the theatre, the natural for the world, the civil for the city; the world being the work of God, the theatre and city of men: nor are they other gods that you laugh at, than those you worship; nor be your plays exhibited to any but those you sacrifice unto. How much more subtly were they divided into some natural, and some instituted by men? And of these latter, the poets' books taught one part, and the priests' another; yet notwithstanding with such a coherence in untruth that the devils that like no truth approve them both. But setting aside your natural divinity (whereof hereafter) pleases it you to ask or hope for life eternal of your poetic ridiculous stage gods? No, on no account. God forbid such sacrilegious madness! Will you expect it of those gods whom these presentations do please and appease, though in them their crimes be the things presented and acted! I think no man so brainlessly sottish. Therefore neither your fabulous divinity nor your politic can give you everlasting life. For the first sows the gods' turpitude, and the latter, by favouring it, reaps it. The first spreads lies, the latter collects them. The first haunts the deities with outrageous fictions, and the latter imputes these fictions to the honour of the deities. The first makes songs of the gods' lascivious pranks, and the latter sings them on the gods' feast days. The first records the wickedness of the gods, and the latter loves the rehearsal of those records. The first either shames the gods or feigns of them: the latter either witnesses the truth or delights in the fiction. Both are filthy and both are damnable. But the fabulous professes turpitude openly, and the politic makes that turpitude her ornament. Is there any hope of life eternal where the temporal suffers such pollution? Or do wicked company and acts of dishonest men pollute our lives, and not the society of those false-adorned and filthily adored fiends? If their faults be true, how vile are the worshipped? If false, how wicked the worshippers? But some ignorant person may gather from this discourse that it is the poetical fictions only and stage presentments that are derogatory from the deity's glory, but not the doctrine of the priests at all; that is pure and holy. Is it so? No; if it were, they would never have given order to erect plays for the gods' honour, nor would the gods ever have demanded it. But the priests feared not to present such things for the gods' honour in the theatres, because they had practised the like in the temples. Lastly, our said author endeavouring to make politic divinity a third nature distinct from the natural and fabulous, makes it rather to be produced from them both, than separate from either. For he says that the poets write not so much as the people observe, and the philosophers write too much for them to observe: both of which, notwithstanding, they do so eschew, that they extract no small part of their civil religion from either of them. Wherefore we will write of such things as the poetic and the politic divinities have in common. Indeed we should acknowledge a greater share from the philosophers, though some we must thank the poets for. Yet in another place of the gods' generations, he says the people rather follow the poets than the philosophers. For here he teaches what should be done, there what was done: that the philosophers wrote for use, the poets for delight: and therefore the poesies that the people must not follow describe the gods' crimes, yet delight both gods and men: for the poets (as he said) write for delight, and not for use, yet write such things as the gods desire, and the people present them with.

CHAPTER VII

The coherence and similitude between the fabulous divinity and the civil

THEREFORE this fabulous, scenical, filthy, and ridiculous divinity is all merged in the civil. And part of that which all condemn in its entirety all must be bound to reverence. Nor is it a part incongruent (as I mean to show) or but slightly depending upon the body of the other, but as conformed and consonant as a member is unto the fabric of the whole body. For what are all those images, forms, ages, sexes, and habits of the gods? The poets have Jove with a beard, and Mercury with none; have not the priests so? Have the players made Priapus with such huge privities, and not the priests? Does the temple expose him to be honoured in one form, and the stage to be laughed at in another? Do not the statues in the temples as well as the players on the stage present Saturn old, and Apollo youthful? Why are Forculus and Limentinus, gods of doors and thresholds, of the masculine sex, and Cardea, goddess of hinges, of the feminine? Because those are found so in the book of priests which the grave poets held too base to have places in their poems. Why is the stage Diana armed, and the city's a weaponless virgin? Why is the stage Apollo a harper, and Apollo of Delphos none? But these are honest as compared with the worse. What held they of Jove, when they placed his nurse in the Capitol? Did they not confirm Euhemerus that wrote truly (not idly) that all these gods were mortal men? And those that placed a sort of glutton parasite goddess at Jove's table, what intended they but to make the sacrifices ridiculous? If the player had said that Jove bade his parasites to a feast, the people would have laughed at it. But Varro spoke it not in the gods' derision but their commendation, as his divine, not his human works do keep the record. He spoke it not in explaining the stage laws, but the Capitol's. These and suchlike bind him to this confession, that as they made the gods of human shapes, so they believed them prone to human pleasures; for the wicked spirits lost no time in instilling those illusions into their phantasies. And thence it came that Hercules' sexton being idle, fell to dice with himself, making one of his hands stand for Hercules and another for himself: and played for this: that if he got the victory of Hercules, he would provide himself a rich supper, and a wench of the temple stock: and if Hercules overcame, he would provide such another supper for him of his own purse: having thereupon won of himself by the hand of Hercules, he provided a rich supper, and a delicate courtesan called Larentina. Now she lying all night in the temple, in a vision had the carnal company of Hercules, who told her that the first man she met in the morning after her departure should pay her for the sport that

Hercules owed her for. She departing accordingly met with one Tarutius, a rich young man, who falling acquainted with her and using her company long, at last died and left her his heir. She having got this great estate, not to be ungrateful to the deities whose reward she held this to be, made the people of Rome her heir: and then being gone (none knew how), a writing was found that affirmed that for these deeds she was deified. If poets or players had given first life to this fable, it would quickly have been packed up among fabulous divinity, and quite secluded from the politic society. But since the people not the poets, the ministers not the players, the temples not the theatres are by this author taxed of such turpitude, the players do not vainly present the gods' bestiality, it being so vile, but the priests do in vain attempt to feign their honesty, which is none at all. There are the sacrifices of Juno, kept in her beloved island Samos, where Jove married her. There are sacrifices to Ceres, where she sought her daughter Proserpina whom Pluto had ravished her: to Venus, where her sweet delicate Adonis was killed by a boar: to Cybele, where her sweetheart Atys, a fair and delicate youth, being castrated by chaste fury, was bewailed by the rest of the wretched castrated *galli*. These sacrifices being more beastly than all stage absurdities (yet by them professed and practised), why do they seek to exclude the poets' figments from their politic divinity, as unworthy to be ranked with such an honest kind? They are rather beholden to the players that do not present all their secret sacrileges unto the people's view. What may we think of their sacrifices done in covert, when the public ones are so detestably profane? How they use the eunuchs and their Ganymedes in holes and corners, look they to that: yet can they not conceal the bestial hurt done unto such by forcing them. Let them persuade any man that they can use such ministers to any good end: yet are such men part of their sacred persons. What their acts are we know not, their instruments we know. But what the stage presents we know, and what the whores present: yet there is no use of eunuch nor pathic: yet of obscene and filthy persons there is: for honest men ought not to act them. But what sacrifices are these (think you) that require for the more sanctity such ministers as are not admitted, no, not even in theatrical bawdry?

CHAPTER VIII

Of the natural interpretations which the pagan doctors pretend for their gods

AYE, but these things (say they) are all to be interpreted naturally and physiologically. Good, as though we were in quest of physiology and not of theology, as if we sought nature and set God aside.

For though the true God be God in nature and not in opinion only, yet is not all nature God; for men, beasts, birds, trees, and stones have each a nature that is no deity. But if your interpretation of the mother of the gods be that she is the earth, what need we seek further? What do they say more that say all your gods were mortal men? For as the earth is the mother, so are they earth's children. In true theology, however, the earth is the work not the mother of God. But refer her sacrifices to what nature you can, for men to suffer women's desires is not according but contrary to nature. Thus this crime, this disease, this shame is professed in her sacrifices, that the vilest wretch living would scarcely confess by tortures. Again if these ceremonies, so much fouler than all stage obscenity, have their natural interpretations for their defence; why should not the like pretended excuse be sufficient for the poetical fictions? They interpret much in the same manner: so that whereas it is counted so horrid a thing to say that Saturn devoured his sons, they have expounded it thus: that length of time, signified by Saturn's name, consumes all things it produces: or as Varro interprets it, that Saturn belongs to the seeds which, being produced by the earth, are entombed in it again. Others give other senses, and so of the rest. Yet is this called fabulous theology, and cast out, scorned, and excluded from all the expositions; and because of the unworthy fictions, expelled both from coherence with the natural and philosophical kind, as also with the civil and political. Because indeed, the judicious and learned compilers hereof saw both the fabulous and the politic worthy of reprehension; but they durst not reprove the latter as they might do the former. The former they made culpable, and the latter they made comparable with it, not to prefer one before the other, but to show them both fit to be rejected alike: and so having turned them both out of credit without incurring the danger of openly condemning the latter, the third, the natural kind, might have a place in better men's minds. For the civil and the fabulous are both fabulous and both civil; both fabulous, witness he that observes their obscenities; both civil, witness he that observes their confusing them together in plays and sacrifices. How then can the power of eternity lie in their hands whom their own statues and sacrifices do prove to be like those fabulous rejected gods, in form, age, sex, habit, descent, ceremonies, etc.? In all of which they either are convicted of mortality, and attaining those erroneous honours by the devils' assistance, in or after their life or death; or else of being true devils themselves that could catch all occasions of filling men's hearts with error's contagion.

CHAPTER IX

Of the offices of each peculiar god

WHAT say you to the absurd and base division of the gods' charges, where each one must have prayers made to him for that which he commands? Of these we have recited part but not all. Is it not more like a scene of scurrility than a lecture of divinity? If a man should set two nurses to look to his child, one for the meat and another for the drink, as they do two goddesses, Educa and Potina, he should be taken for an ass, or a mimical fool. And then they have a Liber that lets loose the masculine sperm in men at carnal copulation, and one Libera for the women, whom they hold Venus (for women, they say, do let forth sperm also), and therefore they dedicate a man's privy member to Liber, and a woman's to Libera; besides wine and the women assigned unto Liber as the provokers of lust. And in such mad manner keep they their Bacchanalian feasts; where Varro confesses that the Bacchantes could not possibly do such things unless they were mad; yet the Senate being grown wiser, disliked and abolished these sacrifices. It may be here they discerned the power of the devils in such men's minds as held them to be gods. Truly this could not have been upon the stage. There the players are never mad, though it be a kind of madness to honour the gods that delight in such gracelessness. But what a strange distinction has he of the religious and the superstitious, that the latter do stand in fear of the gods, and the first do but reverence them as parents, not fearing them as foes: and to call all the gods so good that they will far sooner spare the guilty than hurt the guiltless: and yet for all this the woman in childbed must have three gods to look to her after her deliverance, lest Sylvanus come in the night and torment her: in signification whereof, three men must go about the house in the night, and first strike the thresholds with an hatchet, then with a pestle, and then sweep them with besoms, that by these signs of worship they may keep Sylvanus out: because the trees are not pruned without iron, nor corn made into meal without pestles; nor the fruits swept up together without besoms. From these three acts, three gods got names: Intercidona, from the hatchet's cutting, *intercisio*; Pilumnus, from *pilum*, the pestle or mortar: Deverra, from *verro*, to sweep. And these kept Sylvanus from the woman in bed. Thus were they fain to have three good against one bad, or all had been too little: and these three must with their handsome neat culture oppose his rough, savage brutishness. Is this your gods' innocence? Is this their concord? Are these your saving city deities, far more ridiculous than your stage gods? When man and woman are wed together, god Jugatinus has to function: nay, that is tolerable. When the bride must be led home, god

Domiducus look to your charge. Now who must protect her at home? God Domitius. Aye, but who must make her stay with her husband? Why that can goddess Manturna do. Oh, why proceed we further! Spare, spare man's chaster ears: let carnal effect and shamefaced secrecy give end to the rest! What does all that crew of gods in the bridal chamber upon the departure of the *paranymphi*, the feast-masters. They are there, not to make the woman more shamefaced by their being present but, because she is weak and timorous, to help her to lose her virginity with less difficulty. For there is goddess Virginensis, god Subigus, goddess Prema, goddess Partunda, and Venus, and Priapus. If the man stood in need of help in this business, why were not one of them sufficient to help him? Would not Venus' power serve, who they said was so called because virginity could not be lost without her help? If there be any shame in man that is not in the gods, when the married couple shall think that so many gods of both sexes do stand by at their carnal conjunction, and have their hands in this business, will not he be less forward and she more reluctant? If Virginensis be there to loose the virgin girdle, Subigus to subject her under the man, and Prema to press her down from moving after the act, what shall Partunda have to do but blush and get her out of doors, and leave the husband to do his business. For it were very dishonest for any one to fulfil her name upon the bride but he. But perhaps they allow her presence because she is a female. If she were a male and called Partundus, the husband would call more protectors of his wife's honesty against him than the child-bearing woman doth against Sylvanus. But why talk I of this, when Priapus (that unreasonable male) is there, upon whose huge and beastly member the new bride was commanded (after a most honest, old, and religious order observed by the matrons) to get up and sit! Now let them go, and subtly distinguish their fabulous theology from the political, the theatre from the city, the stage from the temple, the poets' verses from the priests' documents, as turpitude from honesty, falsehood from truth, lightness from gravity, foolery from seriousness! Now let them use all the subtle art they can in it! We know what they do that understand the dependence of the fabulous theology upon the civil, and that from the poets' verses it rebounds to the city again as an image from a glass; and therefore they, not daring to condemn the civil kind, present the image thereof, which they spare not to spit true disgrace upon, that as many as can conceive them may loathe the thing that shape presents and resembles. Which the gods notwithstanding behold with such pleasure, that that very delight of theirs betrays their damned essences; and therefore by terrible means have they wrung these stage honours from their servants in the sacrifices: manifesting hereby that themselves were most unclean spirits, and making that abject, reprobate, and absurd stage divinity a part of this civil kind that was held selected and approved, that all of it being naught but a lump of absurdities framed of such false gods as never were, one part of it might be preserved in the priests' writings, and another in the poets'. Now whether it have more parts is another question. As for Varro's division, I think I have made it plain enough that the divinities of the stage and the city belong both to that one political kind: and seeing they are both markable with the like brands of foul, false, and unworthy impiety, far be it from religious men to expect eternal life from either of them. Lastly, Varro himself reckons his gods from man's origin, beginning with Janus, and so proceeds through man's life to his age and death, ending with Naenia, a goddess whose verses were sung at old men's funerals. And then he mentions gods that concern not man but his accidents, as apparel, meat, and such necessaries of life, showing what each alone could do, and consequently what one should ask of each one. In which universal diligence of his he never showed whom to ask eternal life of; for which only it is that we are Christians. Who is therefore so dull, that he conceives not that this man in his diligent discovery of political divinity, and his direct and apparent comparison of it with the fabulous kind, and his plain affirmation that this fabulous kind was a part of the civil, desired only to get a place for the natural kind (which he called the philosophers' kind) in the mind of men: fully reprehending the fabulous kind, but not daring meddle with the civil, only showing it subject to reprehension, so that it being excluded together with the fabulous, the natural kind might have sole place in the elections of all good understandings? Of which kind, God willing, I mean to speak more particularly and fully in a convenient place.

CHAPTER X

Of Seneca's freer reprehension of the civil theology than Varro's was of the fabulous

BUT the liberty that this man lacked in reprehending that civil divinity which was so like to the stage's, Annaeus Seneca (whom some proofs confirm to have lived in the apostles' times) lacked not fully, though in part he did. In his works written he had it, but in his life he lacked it. For in his book against superstitions, far more free is he in beating down the political kind of theology, than Varro was against the poetical. For speaking of images, the immortal and sacred gods (says he) do they consecrate in a vile, dead, and base substance, confining them to shapes of men, beasts, fishes, and ambiguous monster-like creatures; calling them deities, which if one should meet alive were monsters and prodigies.

And a little after, speaking of natural divinity, having rejected some opinions, he proposes himself a question thus: Shall I believe (says one) that heaven and earth are gods, that there are some under the moon, and some above it? Shall I respect Plato, or Strato the Peripatetic, while this makes God without a soul, and that without a body? Answering then to the question, What then? says he. Dost thou think there is more truth in the dreams of Romulus, Tatius, or Tullus Hostilius? Tatius dedicated the goddess Cloacina; Romulus, Picus and Tibernius; Hostilius, Fear and Paleness, two extreme affections of man; the one being a perturbation of an affrighted mind, the other of the body; not a disease but a colour. Are these more like gods, inhabitants of heaven? And of their cruel and obscene ceremonies, how freely did he strike at them! One castrates himself, another cuts off his limbs; and this is their propitiation for the gods' anger: but no worship at all ought they to have that delight in such as this is. The fury and disturbance of mind in some is raised so high by seeking to appease the gods, that not the most barbarous and fable-renowned tyrants would desire to behold it. Tyrants indeed have rent off the parts of some men, but never made them their own tormentors. Some have been castrated for their princes' lust: but never commanded to be their own castrators. But these kill themselves in the temples, offering their vows in blood and wounds. If one had time to take a view of their actions, he should see them do things so unbeseeming honesty, so unworthy of freedom, and so unlike to soberness, that none would make question of their madness, if they were fewer: but now their multitude is their privilege. And then the Capitolian tricks that he records, and fearlessly inveighs at, who would not hold them mad ones, or mockeries? For first in the losing of Osiris in the Egyptian sacrifices, and then in the finding him again, first the sorrow and then their great joy—all this is a puppetry and a fiction; yet the fond people though they find not nor lose anything, weep for all that, and rejoice again as heartily as if they had. Aye, but this madness has its fixed time. It is tolerable (says he) to be but once a year mad. But come into the Capitol, and you will be ashamed at the mad acts of public furor. One sets the gods under their king, another tells Jove what o'clock it is, another is his sergeant, and another makes a rubbing of him as if he anointed him. Others dress Juno and Minerva's hair, standing afar off from the temple, not only from their images, and making movements with their fingers as if they were combing and crisping it: another holds the glass, and another bids the gods to be his advocates. Some present them with scrolls, and propound their causes to them. One old archplayer played the mime continually in the Capitol, as if the gods had found great sport in him whom the world had rejected. Nay there you have all trades work for the gods. And a little after: But these though

they be idle before the gods, yet they are not bawdy, or offensive.
But some sit there that think Jove is in love with them: never respecting Juno's poetically supposed terrible aspect.   This freedom
Varro durst not assume.   He durst go no farther than poetical theology: but not to the civil which this man crushes in sunder.   But if
we mark the truth, the temples where these things are done are
worse than the theatres where they are but feigned.   And therefore
Seneca selected those parts of this civil theology for a wise man to
observe in his actions, but not to make a religion of.   'A wise man,'
says he, 'will observe these as commands of the laws, not as the
pleasures of the gods'; and again: 'We can make marriages, nay and
those unlawful ones, amongst the gods, joining brother and sister;
Mars and Bellona, Vulcan and Venus, Neptune and Salacia: yet
some we leave single, as wanting means of the bargain, chiefly
being widows, as Populonia, Fulgura, and Rumina; nor do I wonder
that these want suitors.'   But this rabble of base gods forged by inveterate superstition, we will adore (says he) rather for law's sake
than for religion's, or any other respect.   So that neither law nor
custom gave induction to those things either as grateful to the gods
or useful unto men.   But this man whom the philosophers made
as free, yet being a great senator of Rome, worshipped what he
disavowed, professed what he condemned, and adored what he
accused: because his philosophy had taught him this great matter,
not to be superstitious in the world, but for law and custom's sake
to imitate those things in the temple, but not act them in the
theatre: so much the more damnably, because that which he
counterfeited, he did it so that the people thought he had not
counterfeited: but the player rather delighted them with sport
than wronged them with deceit.

CHAPTER XI

Seneca's opinion of the Jews

THIS man amongst his other invectives against the superstitions of
politic theology condemns also the Jews' sacrifices, chiefly their
sabbaths: saying that by their seventh day interposed, they spend
the seventh part of their lives in idleness, and hurt themselves by
not attending to divers things in time.   Yet dares he not meddle
with the Christians (though then the Jews' deadly foes) on either
account, lest he should praise them against his country's old custom,
or dispraise them perhaps against his own conscience.   Speaking
of the Jews, he says: 'The custom of that wicked nation getting
head through all the world, the vanquished gave laws to the vanquishers.'   This he wondered at, not knowing the work of the Godhead.   But his opinion of their sacraments he sets down.   They

know the cause of their ceremonies (says he), but most of the people do they know not what. But of the Jewish sacrifices, how far God's institutions first directed them, and then how, by the men of God that had the mystery of eternity revealed to them, they were by the same authority abolished, we have both elsewhere spoken chiefly against the Manichees, and in this work in a convenient place mean to say somewhat more.

CHAPTER XII

That it is plain by this discovery of the pagan gods' vanity, that they cannot give eternal life, not having power to help in the temporal

Now for the three theologies, mythical, physical, and political: or fabulous, natural, and civil—that the life eternal is neither to be expected from the fabulous, for that the pagans themselves reject and reprehend; nor from the civil, for that is proved but a part of the other: if this be not sufficient to prove, let that be added which the former books contain, chiefly the fourth [1] concerning the giver of happiness. For if felicity were a goddess, to whom should one go for eternal life but to her? But being none but a gift of God, to what god must we offer ourselves but to the giver of that felicity, for that eternal and true happiness which we so entirely desire? But let no man doubt that none of those filth-adored gods can give it; those that are more filthily angry unless that worship be given them in that manner, and herein proving themselves downright devils: what is said I think is sufficient to prove this. Now he that cannot give felicity, how can he give eternal life? Eternal life we call endless felicity; for if the soul love eternally in pains, as the devils do, that is rather eternal death. For there is no death so sore nor sure as that which never ends. But the soul being of that immortal nature that it cannot but live in some way, therefore the greatest death it can endure is the deprivation of it from glory, and constitution in endless punishment. So he only gives eternal life (that is, endlessly happy) that gives true felicity. Which since the politic gods cannot give, as is proved, they are not to be adored for their benefits of this life, as we showed in our first five precedent books; and much less for life eternal, as this last book of all by their own helps has convinced. But if any man think (because old customs keep fast roots) that we have not shown cause sufficient for the rejecting of their politic theology, let him peruse the next book, which by the assistance of God I intend shall immediately follow this former.

[1] Chapter xxvi.

THE SEVENTH BOOK OF THE
CITY OF GOD

CHAPTER I

Whether divinity be found in the select gods, since it is not extant in the politic theology

WHEREAS I employ my most diligent endeavour about the extirpation of inveterate and depraved opinions which the continuance of error has deeply rooted in the hearts of mortal men: and whereas I work by that grace of God (who as the true God is able to bring this work to effect) according to my poor talent: the quick and apprehensive spirits that have drawn full satisfaction from the works precedent must bear my proceedings with pardon and patience; and not think my subsequent discourse to be superfluous unto others because it is needless unto them. The affirmation that divinity is not to be sought for terrestrial uses (though thence we must desire all earthly supplies that we need) but for the celestial glory which is alone eternal, is a great matter. This divinity, or let me say deity (for this word our Christians have now in use as expressly translated from the Greek θειότης)—this divinity therefore or deity is not in that politic theology which M. Varro discourses of in his sixteen books: that is, the worship of any god there expressed will not yield to man eternal life. He that will not be persuaded that this is true out of our sixth book last finished, when he has read this, I believe shall not find any point of this question left undiscussed: for some perhaps may think that the selected gods of Varro's last book (whereof we said somewhat) and none but they are to be honoured for this eternal beatitude. I say not herein as Tertullian said,[1] with more wit perhaps than truth: If the gods be chosen like onions, then the rest are counted as wicked. This I say not, for I see that out of an elected body another particular election may be made: as out of a company of elected soldiers one is elected for this office in arms and another for one not so weighty: and in the church, when the elders are elected, the others are not held reprobate, being all God's good faithful elect. In architecture, corner and foundation stones are chosen, yet the rest are not refused but will fit other places. Grapes are chosen to eat; but they are not worth naught which we leave for wine. The matter is plain and needs no farther process. Wherefore neither the gods nor their servants are faulty, in that they are selected from many: but let us rather look what the selected are, and what is the end of their selection.

[1] *Ad Nation.* ii. 9.

CHAPTER II

*The selected gods, and whether they be exempted from the baser
gods' functions*

THOSE selected gods Varro commends in one whole book, and
these are Janus, Jove, Saturn, Genius, Mercury, Apollo, Mars,
Vulcan, Neptune, Sol, Orcus, Liber Pater, Tellus, Ceres, Juno,
Luna, Diana, Minerva, Venus, and Vesta. In these twenty
are twelve males and eight females. Now are they called select
for their principal charges in the world, or because they were
more known and adored than the rest? If because of their
greater charges, then may they not come to meddle in the petty
businesses of the baser gods. But at the conception of the child,
whence all those petty gods' charges arise, Janus is making fit
reception for the seed; Saturn has business in the seed also; Liber is
making the man's seed flow abundantly; and Libera, who they
say is Venus, is working the like in the woman: all these are of your
selected gods. But then there is Mena, the goddess of the female
flux, a daughter of Jove but yet a base one. And this sway over the
flux he gives to Juno also, in his book of the select ones amongst
whom she is queen: and here as Juno Lucina, together with her
stepdaughter Mena, rule both one blood. And then there are
two obscure fellows (of gods), Vitumnus and Sentinus; one gives
vital breath, and another sense to the child begotten. These two
base gods do more service here than all the other great selected
gods; for what is all that they heap together in the woman's womb,
without life and sense, but as a lump of clay and dust?

CHAPTER III

*That these gods' elections are without all reason, since baser gods have
nobler charges*

BUT why does he call so many of the selected gods to this charge
and then Vitumnus and Sentinus get the principal offices of all the
rest? Select Janus, he makes way for the seed; select Saturn, he
brings it; select Liber, he puts it freely forth; and so does Libera,
be she Ceres or Venus, to the women; select Juno, with her
daughter Mena's help, brings flux of blood to nourish the birth.
But base Vitumnus, he brings life to it: obscure Sentinus, he gives
it sense; which two gifts are as far above the rest, as they are short
of reason. For as the reasonable creature excels that which is but
only sensitive as the beast: so the sensitive must needs excel that
which has neither sense nor life. So that Vitumnus the quickener
and Sentinus the sense-giver had more reason to be selected than

either Janus the seed-giver, Saturn the giver, or Liber and Libera the loosers: which seed it were unworthy to imagine, unless it were animated and made sensitive: which select gifts the select gods give not, but only a couple of poor obscure fellows that must stand at the door when these are let in. If they reply, Janus is god of all beginnings, and therefore justly opens the womb: Saturn, of all seed, and therefore justly works in the man's sowing of it: Liber and Libera, of the distillation of seed in all spermatical creatures, and therefore must work in this dispersing of man's: Juno, of all births and purgations, and therefore justly must have a hand in the woman's at this time—well, what of Vitumnus and Sentinus? Have they dominion over all things living and sensitive? If it be granted, then see how these two are advanced. For seeds to grow on earth is earth's nature: but to live and have sense, that comes from the gods of the stars, they say. But if they say that these two have sway only over fleshly senses; why then could not he that gives sense to fishes and all things else, give flesh sense also, and extend his general power through each particular? What need then of Vitumnus and Sentinus? If he that rules life and sense, rule all things else, and gave the charge of fleshly sensitives to these his two servants, as a place of no credit: kept these selected gods so few attendants, that they could not commit the said base offices to some of their followers, but must debase all (their nobility the cause of their selection) to be joined as fellow workmen with such a base couple? Nay, Juno, the selected queen of all the selected, Jove's wife and sister, yet is Interduca to the children, and works with a couple of base goddesses, Adeona and Abeona. And there is goddess Mens, that sends the child a good mind; she is not select, and yet no greater gift can be given to man. Now Juno plays Interduca and Domiduca, as though it were any matter to make a journey or to come well home, if one be not in his right mind: yet the goddess of this good gift was none of the select. Truly she deserved it before Minerva that had charge of the child's memory in this distribution of duties. For who doubts that it is better to have a good mind than a memory ever so capable? For he that has a good mind is never evil. But many wicked men have admirable memories, and are so much worse because they cannot forget their evil cogitations. Yet is Minerva selected. And for Virtue and Felicity (of whom our fourth book treats),[1] those goddesses they had, but never selected them, whilst Mars and Orcus, the one the causer of death, and the other the receiver, these were selected. Seeing therefore that in these worthless affairs, shared amongst so many, the patrician and plebeian gods work all together in hugger-mugger: and that some gods that were not held worthy of selection had more honourable charges in the business than the selected: it remains to believe, that their being

[1] Chapters xxi and xxiii.

known to the vulgar more than the others, and not their bearing charge above the others, put in their names into this bill of selection. And therefore Varro himself says, that many father-gods and mother-goddesses were grown ignoble, like mortal men. If therefore Felicity is not to be placed amongst those selects, because they got their places rather by chance than by desert: yet surely Fortune should be one amongst them, or rather above them, who gives not her gifts by reason, but ever casually, as it falls out. She of right should have been their chief, as showing her power chiefly upon them; whereas we see it was no virtue nor reasonable felicity of theirs but only the power of fortune (as all their adorers do believe) that made them be selected. For witty Sallust (it may be) excluded not the gods when he said: 'Fortune ruleth in everything: disposing them according to her will than unto truth.' [1] For they can show no reason why Venus should be famous and Virtue obscure, seeing both are made goddesses, and their merits are not comparable. If Venus deserved her enhancement in this, that more desire her than Virtue, why then is Minerva famous and Lady Money obscure, seeing that in all sorts of men there is more love for coin than knowledge? And even in the arts, you shall not find one but it is set to sale, and still there is more respect to that which respects other ends than to that which other ends do most respect. If therefore the fond vulgar were the selectors, why was not Money put before Minerva, since all their trades aim at money? But if the wise men selected them, why was Venus preferred before Virtue, which all reason will of right prefer? Certainly, as I said, if Fortune, who (as they think that think her so powerful) rules in everything, disposing them rather according to her lust and liking than to right or reason, had so much power over the gods that she could advance and obscure whom she wished, then should the first place of the selected of right have been hers, that had such authority over the state of the gods. But may we not think that Fortune was Fortune's own foe, and so kept her from the place? Sure it was so: she was her own foe, that could give advancements to others, and took none herself.

CHAPTER IV

That the meaner gods being buried in silence were better used than the select, whose faults were so shamefully traduced

Now any one that longed after honour might gratulate those selected gods, and say their selection had been good, if it had not rather been used to their disgrace than their honours: for the baseness of the meaner sort kept them from scorn. Indeed, we do laugh when we see how fond opinion has parted them into

[1] *Catil.* 8.

squadrons, and set them to work upon trifles like collectors of petty
taxes, or the goldsmiths in Silver Street, where the cup goes
through so many hands ere it be done, whereas one good workman
might do all himself. But I think they had each such little shares,
to learn their work the sooner, lest the whole should have been too
long in learning. But we can scarcely find one of the unselected
gods that is become infamous by doing any foul act; but scarcely
one of the select who has not become so. The latter came down
to the base works of the first, but the first ascended not to the high
crimes of the latter. Indeed, of Janus I find nothing blameworthy:
perhaps he lived honestly and out of the rank of villains. He
received Saturn courteously, being expelled from his kingdom,
and shared his state with him; and they built two cities, the one
Janiculum, the other Saturnia. But those senseless adorers of
idolatry and filthiness have made him a very monster: sometimes
with two faces, sometimes with four. Did they desire that since
the other gods had lost all honesty of face by their foul act, his
innocence should be the more apparent by his many foreheads?

CHAPTER V

Of the pagans' more abstruse physical doctrine

BUT let us rather hear their natural expositions, wherewith they
would seem to cloak their piteous errors as in cloudy mysteries.
First, Varro so commends them, that he says the pictures, shapes,
and vestures of the gods were erected of old for the devout, therein
to contemplate the world's soul, and the parts thereof, that is, the
true gods, in their minds; whereof such as erected human shapes
seemed to compare the immortal essence unto the soul in man,
as if the vessel should be put for the thing itself, and a flagon set in
Liber's temple, to signify wine, taking the container for the contained: so by that human shape the reasonable soul might be
expressed; for that human shape contains like a vase that nature,
of which they say that God or the gods are. These are the mystical
doctrines which his sharp wit went deep into, and so delivered.
But tell me, thou acute man, hast thou lost that judgment in these
mysteries that made thee say that they that first made images let
loose the city from all awe, and added error to error, and that the
old Romans served the gods in better order without any statues at
all? They were what caused thee to speak against their successors.
For had they had statues also, perhaps fear would have made thee
have suppressed thy opinion of abolishing images, and have made
thee have sought further for these vain mythologies and figments.
For thy soul so learned and so ingenious (which we much bewail
in thee), by being ungrateful to that God by whom, not with whom
it was made; and not being a part of Him but a thing made by

Him, who is not the life of all things, but all life's maker, could never come to His knowledge by these mysteries. But of what nature and worth they are, let us see. Meantime this learned man affirms the world's soul entirely to be truly God, so that all his theology being natural, extends itself even to the nature of the reasonable soul. Of this natural kind he speaks briefly in his book whence we have this: wherein we must see whether all his mystical wrestlings can bring the natural to the civil, of which he discourses in his last book of the select gods. If he can, all shall be natural. And then what need he to be so careful in their distinction? But if they be rightly divided, seeing that the natural that he likes so is not true (for he comes but to the soul, not to God that made the soul), how much more is the civil kind untrue and abject, that is all corporal and concerned with the body; as his own interpretations being diligently called out shall by my rehearsal make most apparent.

CHAPTER VI

Of Varro's opinion that God was the soul of the world, and yet had many souls under Him in His parts, all of which were of the divine nature

THE same Varro, speaking further of this physical theology, says, that he holds God to be the soul of the world, which the Greeks call κόσμος, and that this world is God. But as a whole man, body and soul, is called wise of the soul only, so is the world called God in respect of the soul only, being both soul and body. Here (seemingly) he confesses one God, but it is to bring in more; for so he divides the world into heaven and earth: heaven into the air and the sky, earth into land and water: all which four parts he fills with souls; the sky highest, the air next, then the water, and then the earth. The souls of the first two he makes immortal, the latter mortal. The space between the highest heaven and the moon he fills with souls ethereal and stars, affirming that they both are and seem celestial gods. Between the moon and the tops of the winds he bestows airy souls, but invisible (save to the mind), calling them Heroes, Lares, and Genii. This he briefly records in his prologue to his natural theology, which pleased not him alone, but many philosophers more: whereof with God's help we will discourse at full, when we handle the civil theology as it respects the select gods.

CHAPTER VII

Whether it stand to reason that Janus and Terminus should be two gods

JANUS, therefore, whom I begun with, what is he? The world. Why this is a plain and brief answer. But why has he the rule of beginnings then, and another (one Terminus) of the ends? For

therefore they have two months dedicated to them, January to
Janus, and February to Terminus. And so the *terminalia* are then
kept, when the purgatorial sacrifice called *februum* was also kept,
whence the month has the name. Doth then the beginning of
things belong to the world, to Janus, and not the end, for that is
assigned to another? Are not all things beginning in the world
to have their end also therein? What foolishness is this, to give
him in his work but half a power, and yet in his image a double
face? Were it not better to call that double-faced statue both
Janus and Terminus, and to give the beginnings to one face and the
ends to another, because he that does an act must regard both?
For in all actions he that regards not the beginning foreseeth not
the end. So that a retrospective memory and a prospective intention must of force go together. But if they imagine that blessedness of life is but begun and not ended in this world, and that
therefore the world (Janus) is to have but power over the beginnings:
why then they should put Terminus amongst the selected gods
before him: for though they were both employed about one
subject, yet Terminus should have the better place; for the glory
is in the conclusion of every act, and the beginnings are full of
doubt and fear till they be brought to perfection, which every one
at the beginning of an act does desire, intend, and expect; nor joys
he in the beginning, but in the consummation of his intentions.

CHAPTER VIII

*Why the worshippers of Janus made him two faces, and yet would
have him set forth with four also*

BUT now to the meaning of Janus' two faces. Two he had (say
they), one before, another behind, because when we gape our
mouth is like the world, and therefore the Greek called the palate
ουρανός, heaven. And some Latin poets have called the palate
caelum, heaven also: from whence is a way outward, to the teeth,
and inward to the throat. See now to what a pass the world is
come, for your Greek or poetical name of the palate! What is all
this to life eternal, or the soul? Here is God's worship all bestowed for a little spittle to spit out, or swallow down, as the gates
shall open or shut. But who is so foolish that cannot find in the
world two contrary passages, whereat one may enter in or out, but
of our mouth and throat (whose like is not in the world) must
frame the similitude of the world in Janus, only for the palate,
whose similitude is not in Janus? And whereas they make him
four faces, calling his statue double Janus, these they attribute to
the four corners of the world, as if the world's four corners looked
all forward, as his four faces do. Again, if Janus be the world,

and the world consist of four parts, then the picture of two-faced Janus is false (for though he be four-faced sometimes, yet he never hath four gates). Or if the two-faced picture be true, because east and west include usually all the world, will any man when we name the north and the south call the world double, as they do Janus with his four faces? Nor have they any similitude in the world correspondent to their four gates of ingress and egress; as they have found for the two faces in the mouth of a man: unless Neptune come with a fish; there indeed in his mouth is a passage in and a passage out, and ways forth on either side his gills. But of all these ways there is none leads any soul from vanity, but such as hear the Truth say: 'I am the door.'[1]

CHAPTER IX

Of Jove's power and Janus' compared together

BUT let them tell us now whom they mean by Jove or Jupiter. He is a god (quoth they) that rules the causes of all effects in the world. This is a great charge. Let Virgil's excellent verse bear witness:

Felix qui potuit rerum cognoscere causas.[2]

Oh, blessed he, and excellent, that kens the cause of each event.

But why then is Janus preferred before him? Let the great absolute scholar speak. Because, says he, 'Janus rules the first things, and Jove the greatest.' Why then Jove is still worthy of the superiority: the greatest things control the first; and excel them in dignity though they be short of them in time. If the beginnings and the excellences of all acts be compared together, this is true. To go is the beginning of an act; but to finish the journey is the perfection. To begin to learn, is the first stage, but the habit of learning is the excellence; and so in all things, the beginning is the first, and the end the best. But the cause of Janus and Terminus is already heard. But the causes that Jove sways are not effects, but efficients: nor can the things begun or ended be before them, for the agent is always before the act. Wherefore let Janus have sway in beginnings of acts, Jove yet has dominion in things before his. For nothing is either ended or begun without a precedent efficient cause. Now as for this great nature's master and cause-disposing god, if the vulgar call him Jove, and adore him with such horrible imputations of villainy as they do, they had better and with less sacrilege believe in no god at all. They had better call any other Jove that were worthy of these horrid and hateful horrors, or set a stock before them and call it Jove, with intent to blaspheme him (as Saturn had a stone given him, to devour in his son's stead), than to

[1] John x. 9.   [2] Georg. ii. 490.

call him 'both thunderer and adulterer, the world's ruler and the
women's ravisher, the giver of all good causes to nature and the
receiver of all bad in himself.' Again, if Janus be the world, I ask
where Jove's seat is. Our author has said that the true gods are
but parts of the world's soul, and the soul itself: well then, he that
is not such is no true god. How then? Is Jove the world's soul,
and Janus the body, that is, this visible world? If it be so, Janus
is no god, for the world's body is none: but the soul and its parts
only, on their showing. So Varro says plainly that God is the
world's soul, and this soul is God. But as a wise man has body and
soul, and yet his name 'wise' is only in respect of his soul, so the
world has soul and body, yet is called God only in reference to the
soul. So then the world's body alone is no god: but the soul, either
separate or combined with the body, yet so that the godhead rest
only in itself. If Janus then be the world and a god, how can Jove
be a part of Janus only, and yet so great a god? For they give
more to Jove than Janus; *Jovis omnia plena*,[1] 'all is full of Jove,'
say they. Therefore if Jove be a god, and the king of gods, they
cannot make any but him to be the world, because he must reign
over the rest, as over his own parts. To this purpose Varro in his
book of the worship of the gods, which he published separate from
these other, set down a distich of Valerius Soranus' making: it
is this:

> Jupiter omnipotens regum, rex ipse deusque,
> Progenitor, genetrixque deum, deus unus et omnis.

> High Jove, kings' king, and parent general
> To all the gods: God only, and God all.

These verses Varro expounds, and calling the giver of seed the
male, and the receiver the female, accounted Jove the world, that
both gives all seed itself, and receives it unto itself. And therefore
Soranus (says he) calls Jove *progenitor*, *genetrixque*, father and
mother, 'full parent general, to all,' etc., and by the same reason
is it that he was called one and all: for the world is one, and all
things are in that one.

CHAPTER X

Whether Janus and Jove be rightly distinguished or no

WHEREFORE Janus being the world, and Jove the world also, and
yet the world but one, why then are not Janus and Jove one? Why
have they several temples, several altars, rites and statues all
several? Because the origin is one thing and the cause another,
and therefore their names and natures are distinct herein? Why,

[1] Virg. *Eclog.* iii. 60.

how can this be? If one man have two spheres of authority or two arts, because they are distinct, is he therefore two officers, or two tradesmen? So then if one god have two powers over causes, and over origins, must he needs therefore be two gods, because they are two things? If this may be said, then let Jove be as many gods as he has surnames for his several authorities, for all his powers, whence they are derived, are truly distinct. Let us look at a few of them, and see if this be not true.

CHAPTER XI

Of Jove's surnames, referred all unto him as to one god, not as to many

THEY called him Victor, Invincible, Helper, Inciter, Supporter, Hundredfooted, Overthrower, the Rafter, the Nourisher, the Giver of suck, and innumerable other names too long to rehearse. All the names they gave one god for divers qualities and powers, yet did they not make him a god for each particular, because he conquered, was unconquered, helped the needy, had power to enforce, to stay, to establish, to overturn, because he bore up the world like a rafter, because he nourished all, and as it were gave all the world suck. Mark these powers conferred with the epithets: some are of worth, some idle; yet one god's work they are all, as they say. I think there is more nearness of nature between the causes and the beginnings of things, for which they make one world two gods, Janus and Jove, who (they say) both contain all, and yet give creatures suck: yet for these two works of such different qualities, Jove is not compelled to become two gods, but plays the one part as he is Tigillus the Rafter, and the other as he is Ruminus, the Breast that gives suck. I will not say that it were more fit for Juno to suckle the world's creatures than Jupiter, especially having power to make a waiting-maid of goddess Rumina: for it may be they will reply: Why, Juno is nothing but Jupiter, as Soranus says:

> Jupiter omnipotens regum, rerumque deumque
> Progenitor, genetrixque deorum . . .

He is God only and God all: but why is he called Ruminus then, when if you look a little further into him, you shall find him to be Rumina the goddess. For if it seem justly unworthy of the majesty of the gods, to set one to look to the knot of the corn, and another to the blade, how much more is it irreverently ridiculous to put a base office, the suckling of whelps, lambs, calves, or so, unto the performance of two gods, the one whereof is lord of the whole universe: aye, and not this either with his wife, but with a base goddess, some ignoble Rumina, unless he be both Ruminus and Rumina, this for the females, and that for the males? For I dare say that they would not have given Jove a female name, but that he is called a father and a mother, or a full parent generally in the said verses. Nay, I find him also named Pecunia, a name of one of the paltry goddesses in our fourth book.[1] But since men and women both have money, why is he not Pecunius and Pecunia as well as Ruminus and Rumina? but let them look to that.

CHAPTER XII

That Jupiter is called Pecunia also

BUT do you hear their reason for this name? He is called Pecunia (say they), coin, because he can do all things. Oh, fine reason for a name of a god! Nay, he that does all things is basely injured that is called Pecunia, coin. For what is that which all mortal men possess under the name of coin, or money, in comparison with the things contained in heaven and earth? But avarice gave him this name, that he that loved money might say his god was not any sort of god, but the king of all the rest. Far more reason therefore had they to call him riches: for riches and money are two different things. Wise, just, and honest men we call rich, though they have little or no money, for they are the richer in virtues; which make them content with what they have for the satisfying of their bodily necessities; whereas the greedy, covetous man that always gapes after money, him we count ever poor and needy. Such may have store of money, but therein they shall never lack store of want. And God, we say well, is rich, not in money, but in omnipotency. So likewise, moneyed men are called rich, but be they greedy, they are ever needy; and moneyless men are called poor, but be they contented, they are inwardly wealthy. What stuff then shall a man consider that theology, whose chief god has a name which no wise man in the world would make choice of! How much likelier were it (if their religion in any point concerned eternal life) to call their chief universal god Wisdom, the love of which cleans one from the stains of avarice, that is, the love of money.

CHAPTER XIII

That the interpretations of Saturn and Genius prove them both to be Jupiter

BUT why should we speak any more of Jupiter; to whom all the other gods have such relation, that the opinion of many gods will by and by prove a Babel, and Jove stand for them all, whether they be taken as his parts and powers, or whether the soul that they

[1] Chapters xxi and xxiv.

hold is diffused through all the world got itself so many diverse names by the manifold operations which it effected in the parts of this huge mass, whereof the visible universe has the fabric and composition? For what is this same Saturn? A chief god (says he) and one that is lord of all seeds and sowing. But does not the exposition of Soranus' verses say that Jove is the world, and both creator and conceiver of all seeds? He therefore must needs rule the sowing of them. And what is Genius? God of generation (says he). Why tell me, has any one that power, but the world, to whom it was said: 'High Jove, full parent general of all'? Besides, he says in another place that the Genius is the reasonable soul, peculiar in each particular man; and that the soul of the world is a god of the same nature, reducing it to this—that that soul is the universal Genius to all those particulars. Why then it is the same that they call Jove. For if each Genius be a god, and each reasonable soul a Genius, then is each reasonable soul a god by all consequence; which if absurdity urges them to deny, it results that they make the world's singular soul their selected Genius, and consequently make their Genius directly Jove.

CHAPTER XIV

Of the functions of Mars and Mercury

But in all the world's parts they could find never a corner for Mars and Mercury to practise in the elements, and therefore they gave them power in men's actions, the latter of eloquence, and the other of war. Now as for Mercury, if he have power over the gods' language also, then is he their king, if Jupiter borrow all his phrase from him: but this were absurd. But if his power stretches but unto man's only, it is unlikely that Jove would take such a base charge in hand as suckling not only children, but cattle also, calves or foals, whence he has his name Ruminus, and leave the rule of our speech (so glorious a thing and that wherein we excel the beasts) unto the sway of another, his inferior. Aye, but how if Mercury be the speech only itself, for so they interpret him: and therefore he is called Mercurius, *quasi medius currens*, the mean current, because to speak is the only current means for one man to express his mind to another; and his Greek name ἑρμῆς is nothing but interpreter, and speech, or interpretation, which is called in Greek also ἑρμηνεία; and thence is he lord of merchants, because buying and selling is all by words and discourses. Hereupon they wing his head and his feet, to signify the swift passage of speech, and call him the messenger, because all messages and thoughts whatsoever are transported from man to man by speech. Why, very well. If Mercury then be but speech, I hope he is no god then, by their own confessions. But they make gods of no gods; and offering to unclean spirits, instead of being inspired with gods, are possessed with devils. And because the world and elements had no room for Mars to work in nature, they made him god of war, which is a work of man not to be desired. But if Mars be war as Mercury is speech, I would it were as sure that there were no war to be falsely called god, as it is plain that Mars is no god.

CHAPTER XV

Of certain stars that the pagans called their gods

PERHAPS these stars are their gods that they call by their gods' names. For one they call Mercury, another Mars: nay and there is one Jove also, though all the world be but Jove. So is there a Saturn, yet Saturn has no small place besides, being the ruler of all seed. But then there is the brightest of all, Venus, though they will needs make her the moon also: though in their opinion she and Juno contend as much for that glorious star as they did for the golden apple. For some say that Lucifer is Venus: others, Juno, but Venus (as she does ever) wins the day. For many more call it Venus than Juno; there are few or none of the latter opinion. But who will not laugh to have Jove named the king of gods and yet see Venus have a far brighter star than his? His splendour should have been as supereminent as his power: but it seems less, they reply, and hers more, because one is nearer the earth than the other. But if the highest place deserve the honour, why has not Saturn a higher place in the heavens than Jupiter? Or could not the vanity that made Jove king, mount so high as the stars, so that Saturn obtains that in heaven which he could neither attain in his kingdom nor in the Capitol? But why has not Janus a star as well as Jove, being all the world, and comprehending all as well as Jove? Did he fall to a compromise, and for one star in heaven was content to take many faces upon earth? And if two stars only made them count Mars and Mercury for deities, being notwithstanding nothing but war and speech, no parts of the world, but acts of men: why have not Aries, Taurus, Cancer, Scorpio, etc., that are in the highest heaven, and have more certain motions—why have they not temples, altars, and sacrifices, nor any place either among the popular gods or the selected?

CHAPTER XVI

Of Apollo, Diana, and other select gods, called parts of the world

AND though they make Apollo a wizard and a physician, yet to make him a part of the world they say he is the sun, and Diana, his sister, is the moon, and goddess of journeys. So is she a virgin also, untouched, and they both bear shafts, because these two stars only do send rays to the earth. Vulcan, they say, is the world's fire; Neptune the water; Father Dis the earth's foundation and depth; Bacchus and Ceres seed gods, he of the masculine, she of the feminine; or he of the moisture, and she of the dry part of the seed. All this now has reference to the world, to Jove, who is called the 'full parent general,' because he both begets and brings forth all things seminal. And Ceres, the great mother, her they make the earth and Juno besides. Thus the second causes of things are in her power, though Jove be called the full parent, as they affirm him to be all the world. And Minerva, because they had made her the arts' goddess, and had never a star for her, they made her also the sky, or the moon: Vesta they accounted the chief of all the goddesses, being taken for the earth; and yet gave her the protection of the world's fire, more light, and not so violent as that of Vulcan's was. And thus by all these select gods they intend but the world: in some total, and in others partial: total, as Jove is: partial, as Genius, the great mother, Sol and Luna, or rather Apollo and Diana. Sometimes one god stands for many things, and sometimes one thing presents many gods. The first is true in Jupiter; he is all the world, he is heaven only, and he is only a star in heaven: so is Juno, goddess of all second causes, yet the air only, and yet the earth, though she might get the star from Venus. So is Minerva the highest sky, and the moon in the lowest sky, as they hold. The second is true in the world, which is both Jove and Janus: and in the earth, which is Juno, the great mother, and Ceres.

CHAPTER XVII

That Varro himself held his opinions of the gods to be ambiguous

BUT even as these cited examples do, so all the rest rather make the matter intricate than plain: and following the manner of matters of opinion, sway this way and that way, so that Varro himself likes better to doubt them than to deliver this or that positively. For of his three last books, having ended the first about the certain gods, then he came into that of the uncertain ones, and there he

says: 'If I set down ambiguities about these gods, I am not blameworthy. He that thinks I ought to judge of them, or might, let
him judge when he reads them. I had rather call all my former
assertions into question than propound all that I am to handle in
this book positively.' Thus does he make doubts of his doctrine
of the certain gods as well as of the rest. Besides, in his book of
the select ones, having made his preface out of natural theology,
entering into these politic fooleries and mad fictions, where truth
both opposed him and antiquity oppressed him, 'Here' (says he)
'I will write of the gods to whom the Romans have built temples
and diversity of statues; but I will write, as Xenophanes Colo-
phonius writes, what I think, not what I will defend; for man may
think, but God is He that knoweth.' Thus timorously he promises
to speak of things not known nor firmly believed, but only matters
of opinion, and doubted of, being men's institutions. He knew
that there was the world, heaven, earth, stars, and all those together
with the whole universe subject unto one powerful and invisible
King: this he firmly believed; but he durst not say that Janus was
the world, or that Saturn was Jove's father and yet his subject, nor
of the rest of this nature durst he affirm anything confidently.

CHAPTER XVIII

The likeliest cause of the propagation of paganism

OF all these gods the most credible reason is this; that these gods
were men, that by the means of such as were their flatterers had
each of them rites and sacrifices ordained for them correspondent
unto some of their deeds, manners, fortunes, wits, and so forth:
and that other men (rather devils) sucking in these errors, and
delighting in their ceremonies' novelties, so gave them their
propagation, being furthered with poetical fictions and diabolical
illusions. For it were a likelier matter that an ungracious son
did fear killing by as ungracious a father, and so expelled him from
his kingdom, than that which Varro says, that Jove is above Saturn,
because the efficient cause which is Jove's is before the seed which
is Saturn's. For were this true, Saturn should never have been
before Jove, nor consequently his father. For the cause goeth
always before the seed, but the seed never generates the cause.
But in this endeavour to honour the vain fables or impious acts of
men with natural interpretations, their most learned men are
brought into such quandaries that we cannot choose but pity their
misguided folly as well.

CHAPTER XIX

The interpretations of the worship of Saturn

SATURN (say they) devoured all his children, that is, all seeds return to the earth from whence they came: and a clod of earth was laid instead of Jove for him to devour, by which is meant that men did use to bury their corn in the earth before ploughing was invented. So then should Saturn be called the earth itself, and not the seeds, for it is the earth that doth as it were devour its own offspring, when the seeds it produces are all returned into it again. But what correspondence has men's covering of corn with clods, unto the laying before Saturn of a clod instead of Jove? Is not the corn which is covered with the clod returned into the earth's womb as well as the rest? For they speak as if he that laid the clod took away the seed. Thus, say they, by the laying of this clod was Jove taken from Saturn, whereas the laying of a clod upon a seed makes the earth to devour it the sooner. This being so, Jove is the seed, not the seed's cause, as was said but now. But these men's brains run so far astray with those fond interpretations, that they know not well what to say. A sickle he bears for his husbandry, they say. Now in his reign husbandry was not invented, and therefore (as our author interprets) the first times were called his, because then men did live upon the earth's voluntary increase and fruits. Perhaps he took the sickle upon the loss of his sceptre as one that having been an idle king in his own reign might become a diligent labourer in his son's. Then he proceedeth, and saith that some people, as the Carthaginians, offered infants in sacrifice to him, and others, as the Gauls, offered men, because mankind is chief of all things produced of seed. But what need I say more of this most cruel folly? This is the observation of it all, that none of these interpretations have reference to the true, living, incorporeal, changeless God, from whom the eternal life is to be craved: but all their ends are in all things corporal, temporal, mutable, and mortal. And whereas Saturn, they say, did castrate his father Caelus, that is (quoth he) to be understood thus, 'that the divine seed is in Saturn's power and not in heaven's': that is, 'nothing in heaven hath its origin from seed.' Behold here is Saturn made heaven's son, that is, Jove's. For they affirm steadfastly that Jove is heaven. Thus does falsehood without any opposer overthrow itself. He says further, that he was called Κρόνος, that is, space of time, without which no seed can come to perfection. This and much like is spoken of Saturn in reference to the seed. Surely Saturn with all this power should have been sufficient alone to have governed the seed. Why should they call any more gods to this charge, as Liber, and Libera, or Ceres, of whose power over seed he speaks as if he had not spoken at all of Saturn?

CHAPTER XX

Of the sacrifices of Ceres Eleusina

OF Ceres' sacrifices, those of Eleusina, used at Athens, were the
most noble. Of them does Varro say little or nothing; only he
talks a little of the corn that Ceres found out, and of her loss of
Proserpina that was carried off by Pluto. And she (he says) does
signify fruitfulness of seed; which one time failing, and the earth
seeming to bewail that lack of fertility, there arose an opinion that
Hell or Pluto had taken away the daughter of Ceres, the said fruitfulness, which from *proserpere*, to creep forward, is called Proserpina; which thing they deplore in public manner. But because
fertility came again, all their joy returned at the return of Proserpina, and so had Ceres' feasts institution. Furthermore, he says
this, that she has many things in her sacrifices which have no
reference but to the corn.

CHAPTER XXI

Of the obscenity of Bacchus' sacrifices

BUT now for Liber's sacrifices, who rules not only all moisture of
seeds and fruits, whereof wine seems principal, but of creatures
also. To describe their full turpitude, it irks me for loss of time,
but not to demonstrate these men's foolish pride. Amongst a
great deal of necessary omission, let me recount this. He says
that Liber's sacrifices were kept with such licence in the high-
ways in Italy, that they adored men's privities in his honour:
their beastliness exulting, and scorning any more secrecy. This
beastly sight upon his feast days was honourably mounted upon a
wagon, and first rode thus through the country, and then was
brought into the city in this pomp. But at Lavinium they kept a
whole month holy to Liber, using during that space all the beastly
words they could devise, until the beastly spectacle had passed
through the market-place, and was placed where it used to stand.
And then must the most honest matron of the town crown it with
a garland. Thus for the seed's success was Liber adored: and to
expel witchcraft from the fields, an honest matron must do that in
public which a whore should not do upon the stage if the matrons
looked on. For this was Saturn accounted insufficient in this
charge—that the unclean soul finding occasion to multiply the
gods, and by this uncleanness being kept from the true God, and
being prostitute unto the false, through more unclean desires
might give holy names to these sacrileges, and entangle itself in
eternal pollution with the devils.

CHAPTER XXII

Of Neptune, Salacia, and Venilia

Now Neptune had one Salacia to wife, governess (they say) of the lowest parts of the sea. Why is Venilia joined with her, but to keep the poor soul prostitute to a multitude of devils? But what says this rare theology to stop our mouths with reason? Venilia is the flowing tide; Salacia the ebbing. What! Two goddesses, when the water ebbing and the water flowing is all one? See how the soul's lust flows to damnation! Though this water going be the same returning, yet by this vanity are two more devils invited, to whom the soul goes, and never returns. I pray thee, Varro, or you that have read so much, and boast what you have learned, explain me this, not by the eternal unchanging nature which alone is God, but by the world's soul, and the parts, which you hold true gods. The error wherein you make Neptune to be that part of the world's soul that is in the sea, that is somewhat tolerable: but are the water ebbing and the water flowing two parts of the world, or of the world's soul? Which of all your wits contains this unwise credence? But why did your ancestors ordain you those two goddesses, but that they would provide that you should not be ruled by any more gods, but by many more devils, that delighted in such vanities. But why has Salacia, that you call the inmost sea, being there under her husband, lost her place? For you bring her up above when she is the ebbing tide. Has she in anger thrust her husband down into the bottom for entertaining Venilia as his harlot?

CHAPTER XXIII

Of the earth, held by Varro to be a goddess, because the world's soul (his god) does penetrate his lowest part, and communicates his essence therewith

We see one earth, filled with creatures: yet being a mass of elemental bodies and the world's lowest part, why call they it a goddess? Because it is fruitful? Why then are not men gods that make it so with labour, not with worship? No, the part of the world's soul (say they) 'contained in her, maketh her divine.' Good: as though that soul were not more apparent in man, without all question, though men are no gods; and yet, which is most lamentable, are subjected so that they adore the inferiors as gods, such is their miserable error. Varro, in his book of the select gods, puts three degrees of the soul in all nature. One, living in all bodies unsensitive, only having life: this, he says, we have in our bones, nails, and hair; and so have trees living without sense.

Secondly, the power of sense diffused through our eyes, ears, nose, mouth, and touch. Thirdly, the highest degree of the soul, called the mind, or intellect, confined unto man: wherein are that part in the world he calls a god, and in us a genius. So divides he the world's soul into three degrees. First, stones and wood, and this insensible earth which we tread on, which are as it were its bones and nails. Secondly the sun, moon, and stars, of which we are sensible, and which are its senses. Thirdly the ether, which is its mind and which penetrates the stars, making them gods; and which through them descends to the earth so that it becomes goddess Tellus, and thence reaches the sea as god Neptune. Stay, now back a little from this natural theology, whither he went to refresh himself after his toil in these straits: back again I say to the civil; let us plead in this court a little. I say not yet, that if the earth and stones be like our nails and bones, they are as lacking in intellect as in sense. Or that if our bones and nails be said to have intellect, because we have it, he is as very a fool that calls them gods in the world, as he that should term them men in us. But this perhaps must be disputed with the philosophers. Let us to our civil theme. For it may be though he lift up his head a little to the freedom of this natural theology, yet coming to this book and knowing what he had to do, he looks now and then back, and says this, lest his ancestors and others should be held to have adored Tellus and Neptune to no purpose. But this I say, seeing earth only is that part of the world's soul that penetrates earth: why is it not made entirely one goddess, and so called Tellus? Which done, where is Orcus, Jove's and Neptune's brother, Father Dis? And where is Proserpina his wife that other opinions, there recorded, hold to be the earth's depth, not her fertility? If they say the soul of the world that passes in the upper part is Dis, and that in the lower, Proserpina, what shall then become of Tellus? For thus is she entirely divided into halves: so that where she should be third, there is no place, unless some will say that Orcus and Proserpina together are Tellus, and so make not three but one or two of them: yet three they are held to be, and worshipped by three several sorts of rites, by their altars, priests, and statues, and are indeed three devils that do draw the deceived soul to damnable whoredom. But one other question. What part of the world's soul is Tellumo? No, says he, the earth has two powers, a masculine to produce, and a feminine to receive; this is Tellus, and that Tellumo. But why then do the priests (as he shows) add other two and make them four—Tellumo, Tellus, Altor, Rusor? For the two first, you are answered. Why Altor? From *alo*, to nourish; earth nourishes all things. Why Rusor? From *rursus*, again; all things turn again to earth.

CHAPTER XXIV

Of earth's surnames and significations, which though they arose of diverse origins, yet should they not be accounted diverse gods

THEREFORE earth for her four qualities ought to have four names, yet not to make four gods. One Jove is assigned many surnames, and so is one Juno: in all which the multitude of their powers belong to one god and one goddess, not producing a multitude of gods. But as the vilest women are sometimes ashamed of the company that their lust calls them into, so the polluted soul, prostitute unto all hell, though it loved multitudes of false gods, yet it sometimes loathed them. For Varro, as if feeling shame at this crew, would have Tellus to be but one goddess. They call her (says he) the great mother, and her timbrel is a sign of the earth's roundness: the turrets on her head, of the towns: the seats about her, of her eternal stability when all things else are moved: her *galli*, priests, signify that such as lack seed must follow the earth that contains all: their violent motions about her do advise the tillers of earth not to sit idle, for there is still work for them. The cymbals signify the noises with plough-irons, etc., in husbandry; they are of brass, for so were these instruments before iron was found out. The tame lion signified that the roughest land might by tillage be made fertile. And then he adds, that she was called mother earth, and many other names, which made them think her several gods. They held earth to be Ops (says he) because work makes her more fruitful; mother, for her general production; great, for giving meat; Proserpina, because the fruits do creep (*proserpunt*) out of her; Vesta, for that the herbs are her vesture: and so, says he, are other deities fitly reduced unto her by several respects. But if she be one goddess (as in truth she is not), why run ye to so many? Let one have all these names, and not be many goddesses. But error's power prevailed to draw Varro fearfully after it: for he says, neither does this control their opinions that take these for many gods. There may be one thing (says he) and many things therein. Well, suppose that many things are in a man? Are there therefore many men? Many things are in a goddess, therefore many goddesses? But let them divide, combine, multiply, duplicate, and implicate what they will. These are the mysteries of great mother earth, all referred to seed and husbandry. But do your timbrels, turrets, eunuchs, ravings, cymbals, and lions in all this reference promise eternal life? Do your gelded *galli* serve her to show that seed-lackers must follow the earth, and not rather that the following of her brought them to this lack? For does the service of this goddess supply their lack or bring them to lack? Is this to explain, or to explode rather? Nor is the devils' power herein ever a jot observed, that could exact such

cruelties, and yet promise naught worth the wishing. If earth
were held no goddess, men would lay their hands upon her and
strengthen themselves by her, and not upon themselves, to castrate
themselves for her: if she were no goddess, she would be made so
fertile by other hands that she should never make men barren by
their own hands. And whereas in Liber's sacrifices an honest
matron must crown that beastly member, her husband perhaps
standing by blushing and sweating (if he have any shame), and
whereas in marriages the bride must ride upon Priapus, these are
far more light and contemptible than that cruel obscenity, and
obscene cruelty: for here the devils illude both sexes, but make
neither of them their own murderers. There they fear the be-
witching of their corn, here they fear not the unmanning of themselves. There the bride is not so shamed that she either loses
chastity or virginity; here the massacre of manhood is such, that
the castrated person is left neither man nor woman.

CHAPTER XXV

What exposition the Greek wise men give of the castrating of Atys

BUT we have forgotten Atys and his meaning all this while, in
memory of whose love the *galli* are castrated. But the wise Greeks
forgot not this goodly matter. Because of the earth's front in the
spring being fairer then than ever, Porphyry, a famous philosopher,
says: Atys signifies the flowers, and was therefore castrated, because the flower falls off before the fruit. So then, not Atys, the
man or manlike, but his privy parts only were compared to the
flowers, for they fell off in his spring; nay, many fell not off, but
were cut off; nor followed any fruit upon this, but rather lasting
sterility. What then does all that which remained of him after his
castration signify? To what is that referred? What is the meaning of that now? Or because they could find no reference for this
remainder, do they think that he became that which the fable shows,
and as is recorded? Nay, Varro is ours against them in that justly,
and will not affirm it, for his learning told him it was false.

CHAPTER XXVI

Of the filthiness of this great mother's sacrifices

NO more would Varro speak of the Ganymedes that were consecrated unto the said great mother, against all shame of man and
woman, who with anointed heads, painted faces, relaxed bodies, and
lascivious paces, went even until yesterday up and down the streets
of Carthage, basely begging of the people wherewithal to sustain
themselves. Of these have not I (to my knowledge) read anything: their expositions, tongues, and reasons were all ashamed to

deal with them.   Thus the great mother exceeded all her son-gods, not in greatness of deity, but of obscenity.   Janus himself was not so monstrous as this monster; he was but deformed in his statue, but this was both bloody and deformed in her sacrifice.   He had members of stone given him, but she takes members of flesh from all her attendants.   This shame all Jove's lecheries came short of; he, besides his female rapes, defamed heaven but with one Ganymede; but she has both shamed heaven and polluted earth with multitudes of professed and public sodomites.   It may be thought that Saturn, that castrated his father, comes near or exceeds this filthiness: oh, but in his religion men are rather killed by others than castrated by themselves.   He ate up his sons, say the poets.   Let the natural theologians say what they will, history says he killed them, yet did not the Romans learn to sacrifice their sons to him from the Africans.   But this great mother brought her eunuchs even into the Roman temple, keeping her bestial cruelty even there, thinking to help the Romans to strength, by cutting away their strength's fountains.   What are Mercury's theft, Venus' lust, the whoredom and the turpitude of the rest (which, were they not commonly sung upon stages, we would relate), what are they all to this foul evil, that the mother of the gods only had as her peculiar, especially as the rest are held to be but poetical fictions, as if the poets had invented this too, that they were pleasing to the gods? So then it was the poets' audaciousness that recorded them, but whose is it to exhibit them at the gods' urgent exacting, but the gods' downright obscenity, the devils' confessions, and the wretched souls' illusions?   But this adoration of Cybele by castrating oneself the poets never invented, but did rather abhor it than mention it.   Is any one to be dedicated to these select gods for blessedness of life hereafter, that cannot live honestly under them here, but lies in bondage to such unclean filthiness, and so many damned devils? But all this (say they) hath reference to the world; nay, look if it be not to the wicked.   What cannot be referred to the world that is found to be in the world?   But we do seek a mind that trusting in the true religion does not worship the world as his god, but commends it for His sake, as His admired work; and, being purified from all the stains of the world, so approaches to Him that made the world.   We see these selected gods more notorious than the rest, not to the advancement of their merits, but the divulging of their shames.   This proves them men, as not only poems but histories also do explain; for that which Virgil says:

> Primus ab aetherio venit Saturnus Olympo,
> Arma Jovis fugiens, et regnis exsul ademptis,[1]

> Whence Saturn came Olympus was the place,
> Flying Jove's arms, exil'd in wretched case,

[1] *Aen.* viii. 319-20.

and that which follows, the same has Euhemerus written in a continuous history, translated into Latin by Ennius; whence because much is taken both in Greek and also in Latin that has been spoken against these errors by others before us, I cease to urge them further.

CHAPTER XXVII

Of the naturalists' figments that neither adore the true Deity, nor use the adoration thereto belonging

WHEN I consider the physical theories which learned and quick-witted men have endeavoured to turn into divine matters, I discover as plain as day that they cannot have reference to aught but natural and terrestrial (though invisible) objects, all which are far from the true God. If this extended no further than the congruence of symbol and fact which true religion permitted, then though their want of the knowledge of the true God were to be deplored, yet would their abstinence from acting or authorizing obscenity be in part approved. But since it is wickedness to worship either body or soul for the true God (whose dwelling in the soul alone makes it happy), how much more vile is it to adore these things with a worship neither attaining salvation nor temporal renown! And therefore if any worldly element be set up for adoration with temple, priest, or sacrifice, which are the true God's peculiar, or any created spirit, although good and pure; it is not so ill a thing because the things used in the worship are evil, as because they are such as are due only to His worship, to whom all worship is due. But if any one say he worships the true God in monstrous statues, sacrifices of men, crowning of privities, castration, payments for sodomy, wounds, filthy and obscene festival games, he does not offend because He that he worships is not to be worshipped, but because He is not to be worshipped so as he does worship Him. But he that with these filthinesses, worships not God the Creator of all, but a creature, be it harmless or no, animate or dead; double is his offence to God: once for adoring that for Him which is not He; and once for adoring Him with such rites as are not to be afforded unto either. But the foulness of these men's worship is plain: but what or whom they worship would be obscure, were it not for their own history that records the gods that exacted those bestialities so terribly: so therefore doubtless they were devils, called by their politic theology into idols, and passing from thence into men's hearts.

CHAPTER XXVIII

That Varro's doctrine of theology hangeth in no way together

THEREFORE to what purpose is it that so learned a man as Varro has endeavoured to reduce all these gods to heaven and earth, and cannot? They slip from his fingers and fall away, do what he can: for being about to speak of the goddesses: 'Seeing that as I said,' quoth he, 'in my first book about places of origin, there are observed two beginnings of the gods, heaven and earth producing deities celestial and terrestrial; as before when about to speak of the masculine gods we began with heaven, concerning Janus called heaven or the world, so now of the feminine we begin with the earth, Tellus.' I see how sorely so good a wit is already troubled. He is drawn by a sense of likeness to make heaven the agent and earth the patient, and therefore gives the first the masculine form, and the latter the feminine: and yet understands not that He that gives those unto both these two, made them both. And hereupon he interprets the Samothracians' celebrated mysteries so, saying that he will lay open such things thereof to his nation as it never knew: this he promises most religiously. For he says he hath observed in images that one thing signifies earth, another heaven, another the abstracts of forms, Plato's 'ideas.' He will have Jove to be heaven, Juno earth, Minerva the ideas: heaven the efficient, earth the substance, idea the pattern of each effect. Now here I omit to say that Plato ascribed so much to these ideas that he says heaven does nothing according to them, but itself was made by them. This, I say, that Varro in his book of the select gods, has utterly overthrown this distinction of those three: heaven he places for the masculine, for the feminine earth: amongst which he puts Minerva, that but now was above heaven. And Neptune, a masculine god, is in the sea, therefore rather in earth than heaven. Father Dis, or Pluto, a male god and their brother, he is also in earth uppermost, and Proserpina, his wife, under him. How can those heaven gods now be earth gods, or these earth gods have place above or reference to heaven? What sobriety, solidity, or certainty is in this discourse? And earth is mother of them all, that is served with nothing but sodomy, cutting, and frantic ravings. Why then does he call Janus the gods' chief, and Tellus the goddesses', where error neither allows one head, nor fury a sane one? Why go they vainly about to refer these to the world, as if it could be adored for the true God, the work for the maker? That these can have no reference thither, the truth has convinced: refer them but unto dead men, and devils, and the controversy is at an end.

CHAPTER XXIX

That all that the naturalists refer to the world's parts should be referred to God

FOR this their natural theology refers all these things to the world, which (would they avoid scruple of sacrilege) they should of right refer to the true God, the world's Maker and Creator of all souls and bodies. Observe but this. We worship God, not heaven nor earth (of which two parts the world consists), nor a soul or souls diffused through all the parts thereof, but a God that made heaven and earth and all therein. He made all creatures that live, brutish and senseless, sensitive and reasonable. And now let us run through the operations of this true and high God, briefly, on account of which, in order to explain absurd and obscene mysteries, they have introduced many devils. We worship that God that has given motion, existence, and limits to each created nature, that knows, contains, and disposes all causes, that gave power to the seeds, and reason to such as He vouchsafed: that has bestowed the use of speech upon us, that has given knowledge of future things to such spirits as He pleases, and prophecies by whom He pleases: that for man's due correction, orders and ends all wars and worldly tribulations: that created the violent and vehement fire of this world, for the even temperature of this great and huge mass: that framed and guided all the waters: that set up the sun as the world's clearest light, and gave it congruous act and motion: that takes not His power from the spirits infernal: that affords nourishment moist or dry unto every creature according to its nature: that founded the earth and makes it fertile: that gives the fruits thereof to men and beasts: that knows and orders all causes, principal and secondary: that gives the moon her motion: and has set down ways in heaven and earth to direct our change of place: that has graced the wit He created, with arts and sciences, as ornaments to nature: that instituted copulation for propagation sake: that gave men the use of the earthly fire to meet by and use in their conventions. These are the things that learned Varro either from others' doctrine or his own conjecture strives to ascribe unto the selected gods by a multitude of I wot not what natural interpretations.

CHAPTER XXX

The means to discern the Creator from the creatures, and to avoid the worshipping of so many gods for one, because there are so many powers in one

BUT these are the operation of one only and true God: yet as one and the same god in all places, all in all, not included in place, not confined to local quantity, indivisible and immutable, filling heaven and earth with His present power, His nature needing no help.   So does He dispose of all His works of creation, that each one has the peculiar motion permitted it.   For though it can do nothing without Him, yet is not anything that which He is.   He doth much by His angels, but only He makes them also blessed.   So that though He do send His angels to men for some causes, yet He makes not the men blessed by His angels, but by Himself as He does the angels.   From this true and everlasting God, and from none other, hope we for life eternal.

CHAPTER XXXI

The peculiar benefits (besides His common bounty) that God bestows upon His servants

FOR of Him, besides these benefits whereof we have spoken partly, such as are left to the administration of nature and bestowed both upon good and bad, we have a particular bounty of His love peculiar only to the good.   For although we can never yield Him sufficient thanks for our being, life, sense, and understanding of Him, yet for that He has not forsaken us when we were involved in sin, when we turned away from His contemplation, and were blinded with love of black iniquity; for that He has sent us His Word, His only Son, by whose incarnation and passion for us we might conceive how dearly God esteemed us, and by that singular sacrifice be purged from our guilt, and by the illumination of His Holy Spirit in our hearts, tread down all difficulties, and ascend to that eternal rest, and ineffable sweetness of His contemplation— what heart, how many tongues, can suffice to return sufficient thanks for this last benefit?

CHAPTER XXXII

That the mystery of our redemption by Christ was not obscure in the precedent times, but continually intimated in divers significations

THIS mystery of eternal life, even from the first origin of mankind, was first by the angels declared unto such as God vouchsafed by divers signs and mystical shadows congruent to the times wherein they were shown.   And then the Hebrews being gathered into a commonwealth to keep the memory of this mystery had divers that prophesied the things that should fall out from the coming of Christ unto this very day; some of which prophets understood the prophecies, and some did not.   Afterwards they were dispersed amongst the Gentiles to leave them the testimony of the scriptures which promised eternal salvation in Jesus Christ. For not only all the prophecies, which were in words, and all the precepts which had reference to actions and manners, were therein contained, but all their sacrifices also, the priesthoods, temple or tabernacle, altars, ceremonies, feasts, and whatever has reference to that divine worship of God, were all presages and prophetical significations of that eternal life bestowed by Christ, all which we now either believe are fulfilled, or see are now being fulfilled, or trust shall be fulfilled hereafter in Him.

CHAPTER XXXIII

That Christianity alone is of power to lay open the devils' subtlety and delight in illuding ignorant men

THIS true religion alone is of power to lay open that the gentiles' gods are most unclean spirits, desiring upon the occasion of some departed souls, or under the shapes of some earthly creatures, to be accounted gods, and in their proud impurity taking pleasure in those obscenities as in divine honours, maligning the conversion of all men's souls unto the true God. From whose beastly and abominable tyranny a man then gets free, when he lays his belief upon Him, who has by His rare example of humility given us a means of rising no less great than that pride by which the demons fell. Hence arose those troops of gods, whereof partly we have spoken, and others of other nations, as well as those we now are in hand with, the senate of selected gods: selected indeed, but for villainy, not for virtue: whose rites Varro, seeking by reason to reduce to nature, and to cover turpitude with an honest cloak, can by no means make square together: because indeed the causes that he held (or would have others hold) for their worship, are not such as he takes them to be, nor the causes of their worship. For if they or their like were so, though they had nothing to do with the true God, nor life eternal which true religion must afford, yet their colour of reason would be some mitigation for the absurd acts of ignorance: which Varro did endeavour to bring about in regard to certain of their theatre fables, or temple mysteries. But he did not free the theatres for their correspondence with the temples, but condemned the temples for their correspondence with the theatres; yet he endeavoured with natural reasons to wipe away the filthy shapes that those presentments imprinted in the senses.

CHAPTER XXXIV

*Of Numa's books, which the senate, for keeping their mysteries in
secret, did command should be burned*

BUT contrariwise, we do find (as Varro himself said of Numa's
books) that these natural reasons given for these ceremonies could
in no way be allowed of: and not only was it considered unworthy
that their priests should read them, but also that the written statements of them should lie in concealment. For now I will tell you
what I promised in my third book [1] to relate in convenient place.
One Terentius (as Varro has it in his book *De Cultu Deorum*)
had some ground near to Mount Janiculum; and as his servants
were ploughing near to Numa's tomb, the plough turned up some
books containing the ceremonies' institutions. Terentius brought
them into the city to the praetor, who having looked in them,
brought this so weighty an affair before the senate: where having
read some of the first causes why he had instituted this and that
in their religion, the senate agreed with dead Numa, and like
religious fathers, gave order to the praetor for the burning of them.

Every one here may believe as he wills: nay, let any contentious
mad patron of absurd vanity say here what he wills. Sufficeth it,
I show that the causes that Numa their king gave for his own institutions, ought neither to be shown to people, senate, no, nor to
the priests themselves: and that Numa by his unlawful curiosity
came to the knowledge of such devilish secrets as he was worthy
to be reprehended for writing of. Yet though he were a king that
feared no man, he durst not for all that either publish them or
abolish them: publish them he would not for fear of teaching
wickedness: burn them he durst not for fear of offending the
devils: so he buried them where he thought they would be safe,
not fearing the turning up of his grave by a plough. But the
senate, fearing to reprove their ancestors' religion, and so agreeing
with Numa's doctrine, yet held these books too pernicious either
to be buried again (lest men's madder curiosity should seek them
out) or to be put to any use but burning: to the end that seeing
they must needs stick to their old superstition, they might do it
with less blame by concealing the causes of it, whose knowledge
would have disturbed the whole city.

CHAPTER XXXV

Of hydromancy, whereby Numa was mocked with apparitions

FOR Numa himself, being not instructed by any prophet or angel
of God, was fain to fall to hydromancy: making his gods (or rather
his devils) to appear in water, and instruct him in his religious

[1] Chapter ix.

institutions. Which kind of divination, says Varro, came from Persia, and was used by Numa, and afterwards by Pythagoras, wherein they used blood also, and called forth spirits infernal. Necromancy the Greeks call it, but necromancy or hydromancy, whatever you like to call it, is where the dead seem to speak. How they do these things, look they to that: for I will not say that their laws prohibited the use of such things in their cities before the coming of our Saviour. I do not say so; perhaps they were allowed it. But hence did Numa learn his ordinances which he published without publishing their causes: so afraid was he of that which he had learned, and which afterwards the senate burned. But why then does Varro give them such a number of other natural reasons, which, had they been in Numa's books, they had not been burned. For otherwise Varro's books, that were dedicated to Caesar the priest, should have been burned in like manner? So that Numa's taking nymph Egeria to his wife was (as Varro says) nothing but his use of water in hydromancy. For so actions are wont to be spiced with falsehood and turned into fables. So by that hydromancy did this curious king learn his religious laws that he gave the Romans, and which the priests have in their books; also their causes he learned also, but kept to himself: and so to speak entombed them in death with himself, such was his desire to conceal them from the world. So then either were these books filled with the devil's bestial desires, and thereby all the politic theology that presented such filthinesses made altogether execrable; or else the gods were shown by them to be none but men departed whom worn-eaten antiquity persuaded the world to be gods, whereas they were devils that delighted in those obscene ministries, and under the names of those whom the people held divine, got place to play their impostures, and by illusive miracles to captivate all their souls. But it was by God's eternal secret providence that they were permitted to confess all to Numa, who by his hydromancy was become their friend, and yet not to warn him rather to burn them at his death, than to bury them: for they could neither withstand the plough that found them, nor Varro's pen, that unto all memory has recorded them. For the devils cannot exceed their direct permission, which God allows them for the merits of those that in His justice seem either worthy to be only afflicted, or wholly seduced by them. But the horrible danger of these books, and their distance from true divinity, may by this be gathered, that the senate chose rather to burn them that Numa had but hidden, than to fear what he feared that durst not burn them. Wherefore he that will neither have happiness in the future life, nor godliness in the present, let him use these means for eternity. But he that will have no society with the devil, let him not fear the superstition that their adoration exacts, but let him stick to the true religion which unmasks and confounds all their villainies and abominations.

THE EIGHTH BOOK OF THE CITY OF GOD

CHAPTER I

Of the questions of natural theology to be handled with the most excellent philosophers

Now had we need to call our wits together in far more exact manner than we used in our precedent discourses; for now we are to have to do with the theology called natural. Nor deal we against all and sundry (for this is neither the civil, nor stage theology, the one of which records the gods' filthy crimes, and the other their more filthy desires, and both show them devils and not gods), but against philosophers whose very name, truly interpreted, professes a love of wisdom. Now if God be wisdom, as truth and scripture testify, then a true philosopher is a lover of God. But because the thing thus called is not in all men that boast of that name (for all that are called philosophers are not lovers of the true wisdom), we must select those whose opinions we can learn from their writings, and with them dispute of this question in due fashion. I undertake not here to refute all the philosophers' assertions that concern other matters, but such only as pertain to this theology (which word in Greek signifies speech of divinity), nor all of that kind either, but only such as holding that a deity is concerned with matters terrestrial, yet affirm that the adoration of one unchangeable God suffices not unto eternal life, but that many such are made and ordained by Him, to be adored also for this respect. For these do surpass Varro's opinion in their aim at the truth: for he could carry his natural theology no further than the world and the world's soul: but these beyond all living nature acknowledge a God, Creator not only of this visible world (usually called heaven and earth), but of every living soul also: and One that makes the reasonable soul blessed, by the participation of His incorporeal and unchangeable light. That these philosophers were called Platonists, of their first founder Plato, I think that none that has heard of these opinions is ignorant.

CHAPTER II

Of the two kinds of philosophers, Italian and Ionian, and of their authors

WHEREFORE concerning this Plato, as much as shall concern our purpose, I will speak in brief, with a remembrance of such as before him held the same positions. The Greek records (a language

the most famous of all the nations) do record two kinds of philosophers: the Italian, out of that part of Italy which was once called
Magna Graecia: and the Ionian, in the country now called Greece.
The Italian had their origin from Pythagoras of Samos, who also
was the first author (they say) of the name of philosophers. For
whereas they were before called wise men, that professed a reformed
course of life above the rest, he being asked what he professed
answered: 'He was a philosopher, that is a lover and a longer after
wisdom': but to call himself a wise man seemed to him of too great
arrogance. But the Ionics were they whose chief was Thales
of Miletus, one of the seven sages. The other six were distinguished by their several courses of life, and the rules they gave
for order of life. But Thales, to propagate his doctrine through
successors, searched into the secrets of nature, and committing his
propositions unto monuments and letters, grew famous: but most
admired he was, because he got the knowledge of astrological computations, and was able to prognosticate the eclipses of sun and
moon, yet did he think that all the world was made of water and
that water was the beginning of all the elements, and all was
composed thereof. Nor did he teach that this fair admired
universe was governed by any divine or mental power. After
him came Anaximander, his scholar, but he changed his opinion
concerning the natures of things: holding that the whole world was
not created of one thing (as Thales held, of water), but that everything had origin from its own beginnings, which singular beginnings he held to be infinite, and that infinite worlds were
thereby gotten, all of which had their successive origin, continuance, and end: nor did he mention any divine mind as ruler
of any part hereof. This man left Anaximenes, his scholar and
successor, who held all things to have their causes from the infinite
air: but he professed there were gods; yet made them creatures of
the air, not creators thereof. But Anaxagoras, his scholar, first
held the divine mind to be the efficient cause of all things visible,
out of an infinite matter consisting of unlike parts in themselves,
and that every kind of thing was produced according to its species,
but all by the work of the divine essence. And Diogenes, another
of Anaximenes' followers, held that the air was the substance producing all things, but that it was aided by the divine essence
without which of itself it could do nothing. To Anaxagoras
succeeded Archelaus, and he also held all things to consist of this
dissimilitude of parts, yet in such a way that there was a divine
essence energizing them, by dispersing and compacting this con-
sonance and dissonance. This man's scholar was Socrates, Plato's
master, for whose sake I have made this short recapitulation of
these others.

CHAPTER III

Of the Socratical discipline

SOCRATES therefore was the first that reduced philosophy to the reformation of manners, for all before him aimed at natural speculation rather than practice of morality. I cannot surely tell whether the tediousness of these obscurities moved Socrates to apply his mind unto some more clear and certain invention, for an assistance unto beatitude; which was the good of all the other philosophers' intents and labours: or (as some do favourably surmise) he was unwilling that men's minds, being suppressed with corrupt and earthly desires, should attempt to rise unto the height of understanding these physical causes, whose total and whose origin depended solely (as he held) upon the will of one God omnipotent and true. Wherefore he held that no mind but a purified one could comprehend them: and therefore first urged a reformed course of life, which effected, the mind unladen of terrestrial distractions might tower up to eternity, and with the one intellectual purity stick firm in contemplation of the nature of that incorporeal, and unchangeable, and incomprehensible light, which contains the causes of all creation. Yet sure it is that in his moral disputations he did with most elegant and acute urbanity tax and detect the ignorance of these overweening fellows that build castles on their own knowledge, either confessing his own ignorance, or dissembling his understanding, whereupon envy taking hold of them, he was wrecked by a calumnious accusation, and so put to death. Yet did Athens that condemned him, afterward publicly lament for him, and the wrath of the commonalty fell so sore upon his two accusers that one of them was trodden to death by the multitude, and another forced to avoid the like by a voluntary banishment. This Socrates (so famous in his life and death) left many of his scholars behind him, whose study and emulation was ever about morality and that *summum bonum*, that greatest good, which no man lacking can attain beatitude. Which being not evident in Socrates' controversial questions, each man followed his own opinion, and made that the final good. The final good is that which, attained, makes man happy. But Socrates' scholars were so divided (strange, having all one master) that some (Aristippus) made pleasure this final good: others (Antisthenes) virtue. So each of the rest had his choice: too long to particularize.

CHAPTER IV

Of Plato, the chief of Socrates' scholars, who divided philosophy into three kinds

BUT of all Socrates' scholars, there was one whose glory worthily obscured all the rest: Plato. He was an Athenian, born of noble parentage, and endowed with perfection of understanding far more than all his fellows. So he, thinking that his invention and Socrates' instructions were all too short of the true aim of philosophy, therefore would needs travel to any place where fame told him he might drink of the fount of noble sapience. So went he into Egypt, and there learnt all that he held to be worth learning, and from thence into Italy, where the Pythagoreans were famous, and there did he drain from the most eminent teachers all the philosophy of Italy. And because he dearly loved his master Socrates, he makes him in all his dialogues express that which either he had learned of others, or invented of himself, with his delicate urbanity and morality. So whereas the study of wisdom is either concerning action or contemplation, and thence assumes two several names, active and contemplative, the active consisting in the practice of morality in one's life, and the contemplative in penetrating into the abstruse causes of nature, and the nature of divinity; Socrates is said to excel in the active, Pythagoras in the contemplative. But Plato conjoined them into one perfect kind, which he subdivided into three sorts: the *moral*, consisting chiefly in action; the *natural*, in contemplation; the *rational*, in distinction of true and false: which though it be useful in both the others, yet it pertains more particularly to contemplation. And therefore this *trichotomy*, or triple division, does not contradict the other, *dichotomy*, that includes all in action and contemplation. But as for Plato's opinion herein as to what should be the end of all actions, the cause of all natures, and the light of all reasons, it would be tedious to discuss, and rash affirmations cannot be made. For delighting in his master Socrates' dissembling of his knowledge (whom he makes disputant in all his dialogues), and affecting that method, he left his own opinions in these great questions as ambiguous (very near) as his master's. Yet do we intend out of his own discourses, and his quotations from others, to repeat some of his propositions, either such as do square with the truth of that religion, which our faith professes and defends, or such as oppose it: as far as shall concern the singularity or multitude of gods, whom we must worship for the obtaining of eternal felicity in the life to come. For it may be that such as knew Plato to excel all the other philosophers of all nations, and understood him far better than others, do think that in God is the cause of natures, the light of reason, and the rule of life: which have reference to the three philosophies, natural, rational, and moral. For if a man were created, by the excellent part of his nature, to aspire to that which excels all, that is, the One, True, Almighty God, without whom nothing has being, no reason instructs, and no use assists: then let Him be searched out, in whom we have all security; let Him be beheld, in whom is all our certainty; let Him be beloved, in whom is all our morality.

CHAPTER V

That the chief controversy with the Platonists is about theology, and that all the philosophers' opinions hereof are inferior unto theirs

IF Plato then affirm that a wise man is an imitator, a knower, and a lover of this God, whose participation makes a man blessed, why need we meddle with the rest, whereof none come so near us as he? Away therefore with this same fabulous theology, pleasing reprobate minds with the crimes of the gods: away with the civil, wherein the devils, working upon the willingness of the ignorant to impure acts, cause them to celebrate mortal errors for divine honours; in the beholding of which they make their servants the ushers of their vain villainies, both by the example of these dishonest sports alluring others to their worship, and making themselves also better sport with the guilt of the spectators of these impurities. Wherein also, if there be any honesty in the temples, it is polluted by attraction of turpitude from the stages, and if any filth be presented on the stages, it is graced with the coherence it has with that of the temples. And the explanations made by Varro who interpreted them as though they had reference to heaven, nature, and causes of production, failed wholly of his purpose, because the things themselves signified no such matters as he interpreted them by. And even though they did, yet the reasonable soul ought not to worship as God what is inferior to it in the order of nature; nor ought it to be subject to those things over which God has given it superiority. Away with those things also which Numa buried, having reference to these religious ordinances, and which being afterwards turned up by a plough, were by the senate buried. And of the same kind are the things (to temper our suspicion of Numa) which Alexander the Great wrote to his mother that he had learned of Leon, an Egyptian priest: where not only Picus, Faunus, Aeneas, Romulus, Hercules, Aesculapius, Bacchus, Castor and Pollux, and other mortal men, whom they had for their gods, but even the gods of the greater families, whom Tully (not naming them though) seems to touch at in his *Tusculan Questions*: [1] Jupiter, Juno, Saturn, Vulcan, Vesta, and many others which Varro would make nothing but elements and parts of the world, are all shown to have been but men. For the priest, fearing the revealing of these mysteries, warned Alexander that as soon as his mother had read them, he should burn them. So not only all this fabulous and civil theology shall give place to the Platonists (who held a true God the author of all things, the clearer of all doubts, and the giver of all goodness), but even the other philosophers also, whose gross bodily inventions held the world's beginning to be bodily. Let all these give place to those good god-conceiving

[1] *Tusc. Disp.* i. 13, 29.

men.   Let Thales depart with his water, Anaximenes with his air,
the Stoics with their fire, Epicurus with his atoms, his indivisible
and insensible bodies, and all others (that now are not for us to
recount) who placed nature's origin in bodies either simple or
compound, quick or dead.   For there were some, and the Epicureans were they, that held a possibility of producing the quick
out of the dead: others would produce out of the quick some things
quick and some dead; yet all bodily, as of a body produced.   But
the Stoics held the fire, one of this visible world's four elements, to
be wise, living, the creator of the world whole and part, yea even
God Himself.   Now these and others like them followed even the
bare surmises of their own fleshly opinions in these assertions.
For they had that in them which they saw not, and thought that
to be in them which they saw externally; nay, which they saw not,
but imagined only.   Now what is so imagined in the eye of the
mind, is no body, but a body's likeness.   But that wherewith our
mind sees this body's likeness, is neither body nor likeness; and
that which discerns the other, judging the deformity or beauty of
it, is more beauteous than that which it judges.   This is the nature
of man's mind and reasonable soul, which is no body; nor is the
body's likeness revolved in the mind a body either.   So then it is
neither fire, air, water, nor earth, which we call elements, of which
this visible world is composed.   Now if our soul be no body, how
can God that made it be a body?   So then let these give place to
the Platonists, and those also that shamed to say God was a body,
and yet would make Him of the same essence that our souls are,
being not moved by the soul's mutability, which it were vile to
ascribe unto God.   Aye, but (say they) the body it is that alters
the soul: of itself it is immutable.   So might they say that it is a
body that wounds the body: for of itself it is invulnerable.   That
which is immutable nothing external can change: but that which
any body alters is not unchangeable, because it is externally
alterable.

CHAPTER VI

How the Platonists conceived of the natural part of philosophy

WHEREFORE these philosophers whom fame (we see) has worthily
preferred before the rest, did well perceive that God was no bodily
thing: and therefore passed further than all bodies in this investigation.   They saw that no mutable thing was God, and
therefore went further than all mutable spirits and souls to seek for
Him.   Again they saw that all forms of mutable things, whereby
they are what they are (of what nature soever they be) have their
origin from none but Him that is true and unchangeable.   Consequently, neither the body of this universe, the figures, qualities,

motions, and elements, nor the bodies in them all from heaven to earth, either vegetative as trees, or sensitive also as beasts, or reasonable also as men, nor those that need no nutriment but subsist by themselves as the angels, can have being but from Him who has only simple being. For in Him to be and to live are not different things: as if He might have being without life: nor are to live and to understand different things, as if He could have life without intellect: nor to understand and to be blessed, as if He could have the one and not the other. But His life, understanding, and beatitude are all His being. From this invariable and simple essence of His they understood Him to be the uncreated Creator of all existence. For they considered that all things are either body, or life; that the life excels the body; that sensibility is but a species of the body; but understanding of the life: and therefore they preferred intellect before sense. Sensible things are those that are to be seen or touched. Intelligible things can only be understood by the mind. For there is no bodily sweetness, be it in the body as beauty, or in motion as a musical song, but the mind judges thereof: which it could not do if there were not in it a form more excellent than either in that quantity of body, or that sound of voices and keeping of tones and times. Yet if it were not mutable one could not judge better than another of these sensible species, nor one be wittier, cunninger, or more skilled than another, but he that began after should profit as much as he that learned before; and he that profited after should be unaltered from his ignorance before: but that which admits majority or minority is changeable doubtless. And therefore these learned men did well observe that the first form of things could not have existence in a mutable subject. And therefore beholding degrees of diversity in the forms of souls and bodies, and that the separation of all form from them directly destroyed them, they inferred a necessity of some unchangeable and consequently an all-excelling form, which they held the beginning of all things, uncreated, all-creating, exceeding right. Thus what they knew of God He did manifest unto them by teaching them the gradual contemplation of His parts invisible by His works visible: as also His eternity and divinity, who created all things both visible and temporal.[1] Thus much of their physical or natural philosophy.

✓ CHAPTER VII

The excellency of the Platonists above the rest in logic

Now as concerning the other part of their doctrine called logic, far be it from us to join them in comparison with those fellows that fetched the judgment of truth from the bodily senses, and held all

[1] Rom. i. 19, 20.

things to be swayed by their false and frivolous rules, as Epicurus held, yea, and even the Stoics. These men being passionately devoted to the art of disputation called logic, thought it was to be derived from the senses: affirming that from them the mind receives definable notions, ἐννοίας, and that thence the whole method of learning and teaching has propagation. Now here do I wonder how these men, affirming a wise man only to be beautiful, had any notion of this beauty from their sense: and how their carnal eyes could behold the fair form of wisdom. But those whom we do worthily prefer have distinguished the concepts of the mind from the forms received by the sense: giving them no more than their due, nor taking aught of their due from them. But the light of the mind giving power to conceive all, this they hold is God that created all.

CHAPTER VIII

That the Platonists are to be preferred in morality also

THERE remains the moral, in Greek, ἠθική, which inquires after the greatest good whereto all our actions have reference: and which is desired for itself only, for no other end but to make us blessed in attaining it only: and therefore we call it the end, as referring all the rest unto it, but desiring it only for itself. This bliss-affording good some would derive from the body, some from the mind, some from both: for seeing that a man consists but of soul and body, they believed that his chief good must have its origin from one of the two, and therein subsist as the final end, standing as the shot-mark of all their actions, which being once attained, their labours were crowned with perfection. And so they that added a third kind of good to these two, consisting of honour, riches, and such goods of fortune, otherwise called extrinsical, did not propose it as a final good, that is, to be desired in respect of itself, but referred it to another, being of itself good to the good and bad to the bad. So this good then that some derived from the body and some from the soul, and some from both, was all derived from the man's self. But they that derived it from the body had it from the worse side, and they that denied it from the soul had it from the better: while they that took it from both, expected this good from the whole man. So then, whether from a part or the whole, it is from man, nevertheless. These three differences made more than three several sects of philosophers: each man construing diversely both of the body's good, and the soul's good, and both their goods. But let all those stand by and give them place that say that he is not happy that enjoys a body, nor he that enjoys a mind, but he that enjoys God: not as the soul enjoys the body, or itself, nor as one friend enjoys another, but as the eye enjoys the light. If the rest can say anything for the other similes, or against this last, what it is, God willing, we shall in due season discover.

CHAPTER IX

Of that philosophy that comes nearest to Christianity

LET it suffice now to remember that Plato did determine that the end of all good was the attaining a virtuous life, which none could but he that knew and followed God: nor is any man happy by any other means. And therefore he affirms that to be a philosopher is to love God, whose nature is incorporeal; and consequently that wisdom's student, the philosopher, is then blessed when he enjoys God. For though the enjoying of each thing a man loves does not forthwith make him happy (for many by placing their love on hateful objects are wretched, and more wretched in enjoying them): yet is no man happy that enjoys not what he loves. For even those that love what they should not, think not themselves happy in loving, but in enjoying. But he that enjoys what he loves, and loves the true and greatest good, who but a wretch will deny him to be happy? This true and greatest good is God, says Plato; and therefore he will have a philosopher a lover of God, that, because philosophy aims at beatitude, the lover of God might be blessed by enjoying God. Wherefore whatever philosophers they were that held this of the high and true God, that He was the world's Creator, the light of understanding, and the good of all action; that He is the beginning of nature, the truth of doctrine, and the happiness of life; whether they be called Platonists (as fittest) or by the name of any other sect; whether we limit the number to those Ionian teachers who held as this Plato did, and understood him well; or whether we include also the Italians who held it from Pythagoras and his followers, or any others of the same doctrine, of what nation soever they were, and were counted philosophers, Atlantics, Libyans, Egyptians, Indians, Persians, Chaldees, Scythians, Gauls, Spaniards, or others that observed and taught this doctrine, them we prefer before all others, and confess their propinquity with our belief. For though a Christian, used only to the scriptures, may never have heard of the Platonists, nor knows whether Greece held two sects of philosophers, the Ionic and the Italian, yet is he not so ignorant of human affairs, but that he knows that the philosophers profess either the study of wisdom or wisdom itself. But let him beware of those that dispute of the elements of this world only, and reach not up to God that made the elements. The apostle gives us good warning of this. 'Beware,' says he, 'lest any deceive you by philosophy and vain deceit,'[1] according to the world's elements. But lest you

---

[1] Col. ii. 8.

should think that he held all philosophers to be such, he says elsewhere: 'For that which is known of God, is manifest in them, for God hath showed it unto them. For His invisible powers from the beginning of the world are manifested by His works, and so is His eternal virtue.'[1] And having spoken a great matter concerning God unto the Athenians which few of them understood, 'In Him we live, and move, and have our being':[2] he added 'as some also of your writers have said.' He knew how to beware of their errors. For he said that God had by His works laid open His invisible power to their understanding; there also he said that they did not worship Him aright, but gave the divine honours which were His peculiarly, unto other things than was lawful: 'because that when they knew God, they glorified Him not as God, neither were thankful: but became vain in their own imaginations. Oh, their foolish heart was full of darkness, for professing themselves wise, they proved fools, and turned the glory of the incorruptible God into the similitude of the image of a corruptible man, and of birds, and beasts, and serpents.'[3] In this place the Romans, Grecians, Egyptians, and all that gloried in their wisdom, are justly taxed. But they and we will argue this hereafter. As for those things wherein we and they consent, as concerning one God the Creator of this universe, who is not only incorporeal above all bodies, but also incorruptible above all spirits, our beginning, our light and our goodness, in these we prefer them before all others.

CHAPTER X

What the excellence of a religious Christian is in these philosophical arts

Now if a Christian for want of reading cannot use such of their words as fit disputations, because he never heard of them; or cannot call that part that treats of nature, either natural in Latin, or physical in Greek; nor that which inquires into the truth, rational or logical; nor that which concerns rectifying of manners and goodness of ends, moral or ethical: yet thence it follows not that he knows not that from the true God is both nature whereby He made us like His image, reason whereby we know Him, and grace whereby we are blessed in being united to Him. This then is the cause why we prefer these before the others. The others spent their wits in seeking out the causes of things, the means of learning, and order of life: these knowing God, found that in Him was both the cause of the whole creation, the light of all true learning, and the fount of all felicity. So that what Platonists or others soever held thus of God, they held as we do. But we choose rather to deal

[1] Rom. i. 19, 20.   [2] Acts xvii. 28.   [3] Rom. i. 21–3.

with the Platonists than others, because their works are most famous; for both the Greeks (whose language is very greatly esteemed of the nations) do preserve and extol them, and the Latins, moved by their excellence and glory, by learning them more willingly themselves, and by recording them in their tongues also, left them the more illustrious and plain to us and to all posterity.

CHAPTER XI

Whence Plato might have that knowledge that brought him so near the Christian doctrine

Now some of our Christians wonder at these assertions of Plato coming so near to our belief of God, so that some think that at his going to Egypt he heard the prophet Jeremiah, or came to read some of the prophet's books in his travels. These opinions I have elsewhere related. But by all true chronological computation, Plato was born one hundred years after Jeremiah prophesied. Plato lived eighty-one years, and from his death to the time that Ptolemy king of Egypt demanded the Hebrew prophecies, and had them translated by the seventy Jews that understood the Greek also, is reckoned almost sixty years. Hence Plato in his travels could never have seen Jeremiah, being dead, nor read the scriptures, being not as yet translated into the Greek, which he understood, unless (as he was of an indefatigable study) he had had them read by an interpreter, yet so as he might not translate them, or copy them (which Ptolemy as a friend might entreat, or as a king, command), but only carry away what he could in his memory. Some reason there is for this, because Genesis begins thus: 'In the beginning God created heaven and earth, and the earth was without form and void, and darkness was upon the deep, and the Spirit of God moved upon the waters.'[1] And Plato in his *Timaeus* says that God first joined the earth and the fire. Now it is certain that he means heaven by fire; so that here is a correspondence with the other: 'In the beginning God created heaven and earth.' Again he says that the two means conjoining these extremities are water and air; this some may think he had from the other, 'The Spirit of God moved upon the waters': not minding in what sense the scripture uses the word 'Spirit,' and because air is a spirit, therefore it may be gathered that He collected four elements from this place. And whereas he says a philosopher is a lover of God, there is nothing better squares with the holy scriptures: but that especially which makes me almost confess that Plato lacked not these books is that the angel that brought God's word to Moses, being asked what his name was that bade him go free the Israelites out of Egypt, answered his name was 'I am that I am: and thus shalt

[1] Gen. i. 1, 2.

thou say to the children of Israel, I am hath sent me to you': [1]
as if in comparison of that which truly is, being immutable, the
things that are mutable, are not—a truth which Plato held strongly,
and commended it highly.   And I make a doubt whether the like
is to be found in any one that ever wrote before Plato, except in
that book when it was first written: 'I am that I am, and thou shalt
tell them that I am sent me to you.'   But wheresoever he had it,
whether out of other books before him, or as the apostle says:
'Because that which is known of God is manifest unto them: for
God hath showed it them.   For the invisible things of Him, that
is His eternal power and godhead, are seen by the creation of the
world, being considered in His works'; [2] I rightly choose to deal
with the Platonists, in our intended question of natural theology;
namely, whether the service of one God or many suffice for the
felicity of the life to come.   For as touching the service of one or
many for the helps of this temporal life, I think I have said already
sufficient.

CHAPTER XII

*That the Platonists, for all their good opinion of the true God, yet
nevertheless held that worship was to be given to many*

THEREFORE have I chosen these before the rest, because their good
opinion of the true and only God made them more illustrious
than the rest, and so far preferred by posterity, that though Aristotle,
Plato's scholar, an excellent-witted man, Plato's inferior indeed,
but far above the rest, had instituted the Peripatetic sect, that taught
walking, and had many famous scholars of his sect in his master's
lifetime; and though after Plato's death, Speusippus, his sister's
son, and Xenocrates, his beloved scholar, succeeded in his
school, called the Academy, and their followers thereupon, Academics: yet the latter philosophers that liked to follow Plato would
not be called Peripatetics, nor Academics, but Platonists; of which
sort there were the famous Grecians, Plotinus, Iamblichus, and
Porphyry; while Apuleius, an African, was famous both for his
writings in the Greek and Latin tongues.   But all these, and their
followers, yea even Plato himself, held it fit to adore many gods.

CHAPTER XIII

Of Plato's affirmation that the gods were all good and lovers of virtue

WHEREFORE though in other points they and we do differ, yet to
overpass them in this great controversy now in hand, I ask them
what gods we must worship—the good, the bad, or both.   Nay,
herein we must take Plato's assertion, that holds all the gods to be

[1] Exod. iii. 14.   [2] Rom. i. 19, 20.

good, and no bad ones amongst them. So then this worship is
offered to the good ones, for then it is offered to the gods, since if
they be bad their godhead is gone. This being true (and what
else should we believe?), then down goes the opinion that affirms
a necessity of appeasing the bad gods by sacrifices, and invoking
the good. For there are no bad gods: and the good only (as they
say) must have the worship, without any other partakers. What
are they then that love stage plays, and to see their own crimes
thrust into their honours and religion? Their power proves them
something, but their tastes prove them wicked. Plato's opinion of
plays was shown in his judgment in favour of the expulsion of poets
as pernicious and baleful to an honest state. What gods are they
now that oppose Plato in defence of those plays? He cannot
endure that the gods should be slandered; they cannot endure
unless they be openly defamed. Nay, they added malicious cruelty
to their bestial desires, depriving T. Latinus of his son, and
striking him with a disease; and yet when they had done as they
pleased, then they freed him from his malady. But Plato very
wisely forbade all fear of their evil powers, and confirming himself
in his opinion, feared not to avow the expulsion of all these politic
absurdities from a firm state, and all those filthinesses that those
gods delighted in. And this Plato does Labeo make a semi-god:
even that Labeo that holds that sad, black, and bloody sacrifices
do fit the evil gods, and mirthful orgies the good. Why then dares
Plato, but a semi-god, boldly debar the gods themselves, the very
good ones, from those delights which he held obscene and unlawful? These gods, nevertheless, confute Labeo, for they showed
themselves cruel and barbarous against Latinus, not mirthful nor
gamesome. Let the Platonists, that hold all the gods to be good
and in virtue the fellows of the wise, and affirm it a sacrilege to
believe other of them, let them expound us this mystery. We
will, say they. Let us therefore listen with attention.

CHAPTER XIV

Of such as held three kinds of reasonable souls; in the gods, in airy spirits, and in men

ALL reasonable creatures (say they) are threefold: gods, men,
devils; the gods the highest, then the devils, lastly men; the first
having place in heaven, the second in the air, the third on the earth;
each with his change of place has difference in nature. The gods
are of more power than the spirits or men; and men are under the
spirits and gods, both by place of nature and worth of merit; the
spirits, in the midst, are under the gods and so their inferiors.
Above men in place, and therefore in power with the gods, they
are immortal; but like men they are passionate, and therefore

lovers of loose sports and poetical figments, and are subject to all
human desires, which the gods by no means can be. So Plato's
prohibition of poetry did not deprive the gods of their delights,
but only the airy spirits. Well, of this question divers, but
Apuleius, a Platonist of Madaura, chiefly in one whole work disputes, calling it *De Deo Socratis*, of Socrates' god, where he disputes
what kind of god this power that Socrates had attendant upon him
was. It was as his friend, and forbade him to proceed in any
action which he knew would not end prosperously. Now there he
plainly affirms that this was no god, but only an airy spirit, handling Plato's doctrine carefully concerning the height of the gods,
man's meanness, and the devils' middle interposition. But this
being thus, how durst Plato deprive not the gods (for them he
acquitted from all touch of human desires) but the airy spirits of
their stage pleasures by expelling of poets; unless by this act he
meant to warn man's soul, however enchained here in corruption,
to detest the impure and impious foulness of these devils, even for
honesty's sake? For if Plato's prohibition and proof be just, then
is their demand and desire most damnable. So either Apuleius
mistook the nature of Socrates' genius, or Plato contradicts himself,
now honouring those spirits and straight after abridging them their
pleasures, and expelling their delights from an honest state; or
else Socrates' spirit was not worth the approving, wherein Apuleius
offended in being not ashamed to style his book *De Deo Socratis*,
of his god, and yet proves by his own distinction of *dei et daemones*,
that he should have called it *De Daemone Socratis*, of his devil. But
this he preferred to profess in the body of his discourse than in his
title; for the name of a demon was by good doctrine brought into
such hate, that whosoever had read demon in the title ere he had
read the demons' commendations in the book, would have thought
Apuleius mad. And what found he praiseworthy in them, but
their subtle yet durable bodies, and elevation of place? When he
came to their conditions in general, he found no good, but spake
much evil of them: so that he that reads that book will never
marvel at their desiring plays, and that such gods as they should
be delighted with crimes, beastly shows, barbarous cruelty, and
whatever else is horrible or ridiculous: and that all this should
square with their tastes is no wonder.

CHAPTER XV

*That neither the airy spirits' bodies nor height of place make
them excel men*

WHEREFORE God forbid that a soul that fears God should think
those spirits to excel it because they have more perfect bodies.
So should beasts excel us also, many of which go beyond us in

quickness of sense, nimbleness, swiftness, strength, and long life. What man sees like the eagle or vulture, smells like the dog, is swifter than stags, hares, and birds? What man is strong as a lion or an elephant, or lives as long as the serpent, that with his skin puts off old age and becomes young again? But as we excel these in understanding, so do we the airy spirits in just living, or should do at least. For therefore has the high providence given them bodies in some sort excelling ours, that we might have the greater care to preserve and augment that wherein we excel them, rather than our bodies; and learn to contemn that bodily perfection, which we know they have, in respect of the goodness of life whereby we are before them, and shall obtain immortality of body also, not for the eternity of plagues to afflict, but which purity of soul shall effect. And as for their higher place, they having the air and we the earth, it were a ridiculous consequence to make them our betters in that: for so should birds be by the same reason. Aye, but birds being tired, or lacking meat, come down to earth to rest or to feed; so do not the spirits. Well, then, will you prefer them before us, and the spirits before them? If this be a mad position, as mad a consequence it is to make them excel us by place, whom we can, nay must excel by piety. For as the birds of the air are not preferred before us, but subjected to us for the equity of our reason; so the devils, being higher than we, are not our betters, because air is above earth; but we are their betters, because our faith far surmounts their despair. For Plato's reason dividing the elements into four, and parting movable fire and immovable earth by interposition of air and water, giving each an equal place above the other, proves that the worth of creatures depends not upon the placing of the elements. And Apuleius, making man an earthly creature, yet prefers him before the water creatures; whereas Plato puts the water above the earth, to show that the worth of creatures is to be discerned by another method than the posture of natural bodies. The meaner body may include the better soul, and the more perfect the worse.

CHAPTER XVI

What Apuleius the Platonist held concerning the qualities of those airy spirits

THIS same Platonist, speaking of their qualities, says 'that they are (as men) subject to passions of anger, delight, glory, inconstancy in their ceremonies, and fury upon neglect.' Besides, 'to them belong divinations, dreams, auguries, prophecies, and all magicians' miraculous works.' Briefly he defines them,[1] things 'created,

[1] *De Deo Socrat.* 12.

passive, reasonable, aerial, eternal.' In the three first they participate with us, in the fourth with none, in the fifth with the gods:
and two of the first the gods share with them also. For the gods
(says he) are creatures: and giving each element to his proper
inhabitants, he gives earth to men and the other creatures; water
to the fishes, etc.; air to these spirits, and ether to the gods. Now
in that the spirits are creatures, they have something in common
both with men and beasts, in reason with gods and men, in eternity
with gods only, in passion with men only, in airy essence with
none. So, that they are creatures is nothing, for so are beasts;
in that they are reasonable, so are we equally; in that they are
eternal, that is nothing without felicity, for temporal happiness
excels eternal misery. In that they are passive, what get they by
that? So are we, and were we not wretched we should not be so.
In that their bodies are airy, what of that, seeing a soul of any
nature is preferred before a body of what perfection soever? And
therefore the honour given by the soul is not due to the soul's
inferior. But if amongst these spirits' qualities he had reckoned
wisdom, virtue, and felicity, and had made them share these with
the gods, then had he spoken something worth noting; yet ought
we not to worship them as God for these ends, but rather we should
know Him of whom they had these good gifts. But as they are,
how far are they from being worthy of worship, being reasonable
to be wretched, passive to be wretched, eternal to be ever wretched!
Wherefore to leave all else and insist on this only which I said
those spirits shared with us, that is passion, if every element has
his creatures, fire and air immortals, earth and water mortals, why
are these spirits subject to perturbations (to that state which the
Greeks call πάθος, whence our word passion is derived: πάθος, and
passion, being a motion of the mind against reason)? Why are
these in these spirits that are not in beasts? For the appearance
of such in beasts is no perturbation, because it is not against reason,
which the beast lacks. And that it is a perturbation in men, their
foolishness or their wretchedness is cause. For we cannot have
that perfection of wisdom in this life that is promised us after our
acquittance from mortality. Now the gods they say cannot suffer
those perturbations, because their eternity is conjoined with
felicity: and this they affirm the reasonable soul, that is absolutely
pure, enjoys also. So then, if the gods be free from passion,
because they are creatures blessed, and not wretched: and the
beasts, because they are creatures neither capable of blessedness
nor wretchedness: it remains that these spirits are perturbed like
men, only because they are creatures not blessed but wretched.

CHAPTER XVII

Whether it becomes a man to worship those spirits from whose guilt he should be pure

WHAT fondness then, nay, what madness, subjects us unto that religion of devils, whereas by the truth of religion we should be saved from participation of their vices? For they are moved with wrath (as Apuleius for all his adoring and sparing them affirms): but true religion bids us not to yield to wrath, but rather resist it. They are won with gifts, we are forbidden to take bribes of any. They love honours, we are bidden to be unmoved by them. They are haters of some, and lovers of some, as their feelings transport them: truth teaches us to love all, even our very enemies.[1] Briefly, all the intemperance of mind, passions and perturbations, which the truth affirms of them, it forbids us. What cause is it then but thine own lamentable error, for thee to humble thyself to them in worship, whom thou seekest to oppose in uprightness of conversation, and to adore those thou hatest to imitate, whereas all religion teaches us to imitate those we adore?

CHAPTER XVIII

Of that religion that teaches that those spirits must be men's advocates to the good gods

IN vain therefore did Apuleius and all of his opinion honour them by placing them in the air, and because, God and man (as Plato says)[2] having no immediate commerce, these are the carriers of men's prayers to the gods, and their answers to men. For those men thought it unfit to join the gods with men; but held the spirits fit means for both sides, to take the prayers hence and bring answers thence, so that a chaste man, and one pure from magical superstition, might use them as his patrons, through whom the gods might be induced to hear him, though they love such things as, if he forbore to use them, would make him far more fit to be heard of good deities: for they love stage filth, which chastity loathes; they love all the villainies of witchcrafts, which innocence abhors. Thus chastity and innocence, if they would make any entreaty to God, must make their enemies their intercessors, or else go empty away. He may save his breath in defence of stage plays. Plato, his highly admired master, gives them too sore a blow; if any man be so shameless as to delight in obscenity himself, and think it accepted also of the gods.

---

[1] Matt. v. 44.   [2] *Symp.*, p. 203.

CHAPTER XIX

*Of the wickedness of magic art, depending on these wicked spirits'
ministry*

Now will I out of the light of public opinion bring overthrows to
the magic arts, whereof some wicked and some wretched do make
boast in the devils' name. Why, if they be the works of the gods,
are they so severely punished by the laws? Or have Christians
divulged these laws against them with any other intent than to
suppress a thing so generally pernicious unto all mankind? What
says that worthy poet?

> Testor, cara, deos, et te, germana, tuumque
> Dulce caput, magicas invitam accingier artes.[1]

> Sister, by heaven, and thee that hearest my vows;
> I would not use art magic, could I choose.

And that which he says elsewhere:

> Atque satas alio vidi traducere messes.[2]

> I saw the witch transport whole fields of corn.

In that these diabolical arts were reported to have power to remove
whole harvests of corn and fruits whither they pleased, was not this
(as Tully says) recorded in the twelve tables of Rome's ancient
laws, and a punishment proclaimed for all such as used it? Nay,
was not Apuleius himself brought before Christian judges for such
practices? If he had known them to be divine, he should have
vouched them at his accusation as congruous with the divine
powers, and have convicted the opposite laws of absurd impiety,
in condemning such admirable effects of the deities. For so might
he either have made the judges to be of his mind; or if they had
been refractory, and following their unjust laws put him to death,
then the spirits would have done his soul as good a turn as he had
deserved in dying fearlessly for the due avouching of their powerful
operations. Our martyrs, when Christianity was laid to their
charge, knowing it was the way to eternal glory, denied it not to
avoid a temporal torment, but confessed it constantly, bore all
tortures undauntedly, and dying free from care, stamped shame
upon the laws' foreheads that condemned it as unlawful. But this
Platonist wrote a large and eloquent oration now extant, wherein he
purges himself of all taint of using these arts, and sees no means to
prove his own innocence but by denying that which indeed no innocent can commit. But as for all these magic miracles, he rightly
condemns them as done by the works and operations of the devils:
wherefore let him look how he can justly give them divine honours,
as mediators between the gods and us, when he shows their works

---

[1] Virg. *Aen.* iv. 492–3.   [2] *Eclog.* viii. 99.

to be wicked, and such indeed as we must avoid if we will have our prayers come near to the true God. And then what are the prayers that he affirms they do bear unto the gods? Are they magical or lawful? If magical, the gods will receive no such prayers: if lawful, then use they no such ministers. But if a sinner (chiefly one that has sinned in magic) repent and pray, will they carry up his prayers, or obtain his pardon that were the causers of his guilt, and whom he accuses? Or do these devils (to obtain his pardon) first repent themselves for deceiving him, and receive a pardon themselves also afterward? Nay, none will say so: for they that hope to get pardon by repentance are far from being worthy of divine honours: for if they were desirous of them, and yet penitents also, their pride were to be detested in the first, though their humility were to be pitied in the latter.

CHAPTER XX

Whether it be credible that good gods had rather converse with those spirits than with men

BUT does a necessity bind these spirits in this place between the gods and men to carry and recarry messages and answers from the one to the other. If so, what is the necessity? Because no god has commerce immediately with man. Very good! Oh, that is a glorious holiness of God surely, that converses not with a penitent humble man, and yet will converse with a proud spirit! He has no commerce with a man that flies for succour to His deity, but with a spirit that counterfeits His deity He has. He meddles not with him that asks pardon, but with the spirit that imagines mischief He does. He deals not with a philosopher that expels stage plays out of an honest city, but He deals with a devil that forces stage plays from the priests and senators, as part of the religion of a city. He likes not the men's company that forbid slanders of the gods, but the devils that delight in them, theirs He likes. He converses not with the man that executes just laws upon magicians, but with the devils that teach magic and give it effect He converses. Nor is He joined with a man that flies the example of the devil, yet joins with the devil that hunts to deceive a man.

CHAPTER XXI

Whether the gods use the devils as their messengers, and are willing that they should deceive them, or ignorant that they do it

BUT there is forsooth a great necessity for this so vile an inconvenience, because the ethereal gods, unless these spirits of the air told them, otherwise could not know the affairs of earth: heaven (ye know) being far from earth, and air adjoining to both. Oh, rare wisdom! This is their opinion, that their good gods have a care of human businesses, else were they not worthy of worship, and yet the distance of place debars them from noticing how things pass, but that the spirits help them: so these are deemed necessary, and consequently worship-worthy, as the means that the gods have to know men's cases, and to send them help in time. If this then be so, the devils' contiguous body is better known to the gods than a man's good mind. Oh, lamentable necessity, nay, ridiculous detestable futility to save the gods from futility! If the gods by their freedom from the body's obstacles can behold our minds, what need they any spirit's help? And if the gods have corporeal means, as sight, speech, motion, and suchlike in bodies by which they receive the spirits' messages, then may the spirits lie and deceive them also. And so if the deities be not ignorant of the devils' deceits, no more are they barred the knowledge of our actions. But I would they would tell me whether the spirits told the gods that Plato disliked the slanders that the poets laid upon them, and yet concealed their approval of them; or concealed all, so that the gods never knew it: or revealed all, Plato's religious zeal, and their own vile affection. Or did they suppress Plato's opinion that would have such impious liberty abrogated as by poetic fables did injure the gods, and yet shamed not to lay open their own wickedness in desiring such plays as contained the gods' disgraces? Choose of these four which they will, and mark how vilely they thought of these good gods. If they choose the first, then it is granted that the gods might not converse with good Plato that restrained their shames, and yet conversed with those evil spirits that rejoiced at these injuries of the gods, and that the gods could not know a good man being afar but by these devils, though they could know these devils that were so near them. If they take the second, and say the spirits concealed both, that the gods should neither know Plato's religious law nor the devils' sacrilegious practice, what use can the gods have of these messengers for any knowledge, seeing they could not have knowledge of the good laws that honest men promulgated in their honour against the lust of those vile spirits? If they choose the third and make these spirits both to celebrate Plato's prohibition of the gods' injuries, and their own desire for their continuance; why were not this rather to insult them than to interpret to them? And so should the gods hear and judge of both these relations, that they neither should dismiss these spirits from their service, that opposed Plato's good zeal, nor forbear to send Plato rewards by them for his honest intent. For so are they placed in the chain of nature's elements, that they may have the company of those that injure them, but not of those that defend them. Both they may know, but the states of air and earth they cannot alter, nor change. Now if they choose

the fourth, it is worse than all. For who can endure that the devils
hould tell the gods how they are abused by players and poets, and
of the height of pleasure they themselves take in these shows, and
yet be silent of Plato's grave decree that abrogated all such obscenities? In this case the good gods would have intelligence of
the wickedness of the worst, their own messengers, and yet none
of the philosophers' goodnesses, that aimed all at their honour,
hereas the others professed their extreme disgrace.

CHAPTER XXII

The renouncing of the worship of those spirits against Apuleius

To avoid therefore all evil thoughts concerning the gods, all the
four are to be avoided. Nor must we all believe what Apuleius
would have us, and others with him, that the *daemones* are so
placed between the gods and men, that they bear up men's prayers,
and bring down the gods' help: but that they are spirits most
thirsty of mischief, wholly unjust, proud, envious, treacherous,
inhabiting the air indeed, as thrust out of the glorious heaven for
their unpardonable guilt, and condemned eternally to that prison.
Nor are they above man in merit because air is above earth, for
men do easily excel them, not in quality of body, but in the faith
and favour of the true God. Indeed they rule over many that are
not worthy of the participation of divine truth: such are their subjects, won to them by false miracles, and by illusions persuading
them that they are gods. But others that looked more closely into
them and their qualities, would not believe that they were gods,
but that they got this place in their opinion, namely to be held the
gods' messengers, and bringers of men's good fortunes. Yet those
that held them not gods, would not give them the honour of gods,
because they saw them evil, and held all gods to be good: yet durst
they not deny them all divine honours, for fear of offending the
people, whose inveterate superstition preserved them in so many
temples, altars, and sacrifices.

CHAPTER XXIII

*Hermes Trismegistus' opinion of idolatry, and how he might come to
know that the Egyptian superstitions were to be abrogated*

FOR Hermes the Egyptian, called Trismegistus, wrote contrary to
these. Apuleius indeed holds them no gods, but middle agents
between gods and men; and because they are so necessary, he con-
joins their adoration with the divine worship. But Trismegistus

says that the high God made some gods, and men made others.
These words, as I write them, might be understood of images,
because they are the works of men. But he calls visible and palpable
images the bodies of the gods, wherein are spirits (invited thereto)
that have power to hurt or please such as give them divine honours.
So then, to combine such an invisible spirit by art with a visible
image of some certain substance, which it must use as the soul
does the body, this is to make a god, says he, and this wonderful
power of making gods is in the hands of man. His words are
these: 'And whereas our discourse,' says he, 'concerns the affinity
between gods and men, mark, Asclepius, this power of man. Our
God the Lord and Father, is the Creator of the celestial gods; so is
man of the terrestrial, which are in the temples.'[1] And a little
after: 'So doth humanity remember its origin, and ever striveth
to imitate the Deity, making gods like his own image, as God the
Father hath done like His.' 'Do you mean statues?' replied
Asclepius. 'Statues,' quoth he. 'Do you not see them animate,
full of spirits and sense (trust your eyes), doing such wonders?
See you not statues that presage future events (far perhaps beyond
all prophetical inspiration to foretell), that cure diseases and cause
them, giving men mirth or sadness, as they deserve? Know you
not, Asclepius, that Egypt is heaven's image, or rather the place
whereinto all the celestial graces descend, the very temple of the
whole world? And since wisdom should foreknow all, I would
not have you ignorant herein. The time shall come that all the
zeal of Egypt shall be abrogated, and all the religious observances
held idle and vain.'[2] Then goes he forward, prophesying by all
likelihood of Christianity, whose true sanctity is the utter subversion of all fictions and superstitions, that the Saviour's true
grace might free us from those human gods, those handiworks of
man, and place us in God's service, man's Maker. But Hermes
presages these things as the devils' confederate, suppressing the
evidence of the Christian name, and yet foretelling with a sorrowful
intimation that from it should proceed the wreck of all their
idolatrous superstitions: for Hermes was one of those who (as the
apostle says), 'knowing God, glorified Him not as God, nor were
thankful, but became vain in their imaginations, and their foolish
heart was full of darkness. When they professed themselves wise,
they became fools, for they turned the glory of the incorruptible
God into the similitude of the image of a corruptible man, and
birds, and four-footed beasts, and serpents.'[3] For this Hermes
says much of God according to truth; but how blindness of heart
draws him to affirm this, I know not, that these gods should be
always subject whom man has made, and yet to bewail their
abrogations to come. As if man could be more miserable any
way, than in living a slave to his own handiwork: it being easier for

[1] *Asclep.* 23.   [2] *Asclep.* 24.   [3] Rom. i. 21–3.

him to put off all humanity in adoring these pieces he has made, than for them to put on deity by being made by him. For it comes oftener to pass that a man being set in honour and not in understanding is like to the beasts, than that his handiwork should be preferred before the work that God made like His own image, to wit, man's self. Worthily then does he fall from His grace that made him, that makes that his lord which he has made himself. Those vain, deceitful, pernicious sacrileges, Hermes, foreseeing that they should perish, deplores, but as impudently as he had known it foolishly. For the Spirit of God had not spoken to him as it did to the prophets, that spoke this with gladness: 'If a man make gods, behold they are no gods.' [1] And in another place: 'At that day,' says the Lord, 'I will take the names of their idols from the earth, and there shall be no remembrance thereof.' [2] And to the purpose of Egypt, hear Isaiah: 'The idols of Egypt shall be moved at His presence, and the heart of Egypt shall melt in the midst of her,' [3] and so forth. Such were they also that rejoiced for the fulfilling of that which they knew should come to pass: as Simeon, Anna, and Elizabeth, the first knowing Christ at His birth, the second at His conception: and Peter, that by God's inspiration said: 'Thou art that Christ the Son of the living God.' [4] But Hermes had his knowledge from those devils, that trembling in the flesh said to Christ: 'Why art thou come to torment us before the time?' [5] either because that came suddenly upon them which they expected not until afterwards, or that they called it their undoing to be known and so despised. And this was before the time, that is, the judgment wherein they and all men their sectaries are cast into eternal torments: as that Truth says, that neither deceives nor is deceived; not as he says that, following the puffs of philosophy, flies here and there, mixing truth and falsehood, grieving at the overthrow of that religion which afterwards he affirms is all error.

CHAPTER XXIV

How Hermes openly confessed his progenitors' error, and yet bewailed the destruction of it

FOR after much discourse, he comes again to speak of the gods men made. 'But of these sufficient,' says he: 'let us return again to man, and to reason, by which divine gift man has the name of reasonable. For we have yet spoken no wonderful thing of man. The wonder of all wonders is that man could find out the divine nature, and give it effect. Wherefore our fathers erring exceedingly in incredulity concerning the deities, and never penetrating

[1] Jer. xvi. 20. [2] Zech. xiii. 2. [3] Isa. xix. 1. [4] Matt. xvi. 16.
[5] Matt. viii. 29.

into the depth of divine religion, invented an art to make gods;
whereunto they joined a virtue out of some part of the world's
nature, like to the other: and conjoining these two, because they
could make no souls, they framed certain images whereunto they
called either angels or devils, and so by these mysteries gave these
idols power to hurt or help them.'[1] I know not whether the
devils being adjured would say as much as this man says. 'Our
fathers exceedingly erring,' says he, 'in incredulity concerning
the deities, and not penetrating into the depth of divine religion,
invented an art to make gods.' Was he content to say they but
erred in this invention? No, he adds 'exceedingly'; thus this exceeding error and incredulity of those that looked not into matters
divine gave life to this invention of making gods. And yet though
it were so, though this was but an invention of error, incredulity,
and irreligiousness, yet this wise man laments that future times
should abolish it. Mark now whether God's power compels him
to confess his progenitors' error, and the devils' to bewail the
future wreck of the said error. If it were their exceeding error,
incredulity, and negligence in manners divine that give first life
to this god-making invention, what wonder if this art be detestable,
and all that it did against the truth be cast out by the truth, this
truth correcting that error, this faith that incredulity, this conversion that neglect? If he conceal the cause, and yet confess
that rite to be their invention, we (if we have any wit) cannot but
gather that had they been in the right way, they would never have
*** to that folly, had they either thought worthily or meditated
*** ly of religion. Yet should we affirm that their great in-
*** ulous, contemptuous error in the cause of divinity was the
cause of this invention, we should nevertheless stand in need to
prepare ourselves to endure the impudence of the truth's obstinate
opponents. But since he that admires the power of this art above
all other things in man, and grieves that the time should come
wherein all those illusions should end with ruin, through the power
of legal authority; since he confesses the causes that give this art
its first origin, namely the exceeding error, incredulity, and negligence of his ancestors in matters divine: what should we do but
thank God for having overthrown these institutions by their just
contrary causes? That which error's multitude ordained has
truth's way abolished. Faith has subverted the work of incredulity, and conversion unto God's truth has suppressed the
neglect of the true God; not in Egypt only (where only the diabolical spirit bewails) but in all the world, which hears a new song
sung unto the Lord, as the holy scripture says: 'Sing unto the
Lord a new song: sing unto the Lord, all the earth.'[2] For the
title of this psalm is: 'When the house was built after the captivity.'
The city of God, the Lord's house is built, that is the Holy

---

[1] *Asclep.* 37.   [2] Ps. xcvi. 1.

Church all the earth over, after that captivity wherein the devils held those men slaves, who after by their faith in God became principal stones in the building. For man's making of these gods did not acquit him from being slave to these works of his, but by his willing worship he was drawn into their society, a society of subtle devils, not of stupid idols: for what are idols but as the Scripture says: 'They have eyes and see not,'[1] and all the other properties that may be said of a dead senseless image, how well soever carved? But the unclean spirits, therein by that truly black art, bound their souls that adored them in their society and most horrid captivity: therefore says the apostle: 'We know that an idol is nothing in the world: but the Gentiles offer to devils and not unto God: I will not have you to have society with the devils.'[2] So then after this captivity that bound men slaves to the devils, God's house began to be built through the earth: thence had the psalm the beginning: 'Sing unto the Lord a new song: sing unto the Lord, all the earth. Sing unto the Lord and praise His name, declare His salvation from day to day. Declare His glory amongst all nations, and His wonders amongst all people. For the Lord is great and much to be praised: He is to be feared above all gods. For all the gods of the people are idols, but the Lord made the heavens.'[3] He then that bewailed the abolishment of these idols in the time to come, and of the slavery wherein the devils held men captive, did it out of an evil spirit's inspiration, and from that did desire the continuance of that captivity, which being disannulled, the psalmist sung that God's house was built up through the earth. Hermes presaged it with tears; the prophet with joy; and because that spirit that the prophet spake by is ever victor, Hermes himself that bewailed their future ruin, and wished their eternity, is by a strange power compelled to confess their origin from error, incredulity, and contempt of God, not from prudence, faith, and devotion. And though he call them gods, yet in saying that men did make them (and such men as we should not imitate), what does he (despite his heart) but teach us that they are not to be worshipped of such men as are not like them that made them: namely, of those that be wise, faithful, and religious; showing also that those men that made them, bound themselves to adore such gods as were no gods at all? So true is that word of the prophet: 'If a man make gods, behold they are no gods.'[4] Now Hermes, in calling them gods that are made by such means, that is, devils bound in idols by an art, or rather by their own election, and affirming them the handiwork of men, gives them not so much as Apuleius the Platonist does (but we have shown already how grossly and absurdly), who makes them the messengers between the gods, that God made, and the men that He made also, to carry up prayers and bring down benefits: for it were folly to think that a god of

[1] Ps. cxv. 5.   [2] 1 Cor. viii. 4; x. 20.   [3] Ps. xcvi. 1-4.   [4] Jer. xvi. 20.

man's making could do more with the gods of God's making than
a man whom He made also could. For a devil being bound in a
statue by this damned art is made a god not to each man, but to
his binder such as he is. Is not this a sweet god now, whom none
but an erroneous, incredulous, irreligious man would go about to
make? Furthermore if the temple devils (being bound by art
forsooth in those idols by them that made them gods at such time
as they themselves were wanderers, unbelievers, and contemners
of God's true religion) are no messengers between the gods and
them; and if by reason of their damnable conditions, those men
that do so wander, believe so little, and despise religion so much,
be nevertheless their betters, as they must needs be, being their
godheads' makers; then remains but this: that which they do, they
do as devils only, either doing good for the more mischief, as most
deceitful, or doing open mischief. Yet neither of these can they
do without the high inscrutable providence of God. Nothing is
in their power as being the gods' friends, and messengers to and
from men: for such they are not. For the good divine powers,
whom we call the holy angels, and the reasonable creatures inhabiting heaven, whether they be thrones, dominations, principalities, or powers, can hold no friendship at all with these spirits:
from whom they differ as much in character as virtue differs from
vice, or malice from goodness.

CHAPTER XXV

Of such things as may be common to angels and men

WHEREFORE the devils are no means for man to receive the gods'
benefits by, or rather the benefits of good angels: but it is our good
wills, imitating theirs, making us live in one community with them
and in honour of that one God that they honour (though we see not
them with our earthly eyes) that are the means to their society: and
whereas our miserable frailty of will and infirmity of spirit effects
a difference between between them and us, therein we are far
short of them, in merit of life, not in habit of body. It is not our
earthly bodily habitation, but our unclean carnal affection, that
causes separation between them and us. But when we are purified,
we become as they; drawing near them nevertheless before, by our
faith, if we believe that (by their good favours also) He that blessed
them will make us also blessed.

CHAPTER XXVI

That all paganism was fully contained in dead men

BUT mark what Hermes, in his bewailing of the expulsion of these
idols out of Egypt, which had such erroneous, incredulous, and
irreligious institutors, says amongst the rest. 'Then,' says he, 'that

holy seat of temples shall become a sepulchre of dead bodies.'[1] As if men forsooth should not die unless these things were demolished, or being dead could be buried anywhere save in the earth? Naturally the more time that passes, the more carcasses shall still be buried and more graves made. But this (it seems) is his grief, that the memorials of our martyrs should have place in their temples: that the misunderstanding reader hereof might imagine that the pagans worshipped gods in the temples, and we dead men in their tombs. For men's blindness so carries them headlong against mountains, letting them not see till they be struck, that they do not consider that in all paganism there cannot be a god found but has been a man: but on will they persist, and honour them as eternally pure from all humanity. Let Varro pass, that said: 'All that died were held gods infernal,' proving it by the sacrifices done at all burials. There also he reckons the funeral plays as the greatest token of their divinity, plays being never presented but to the gods. Hermes himself (now mentioned) in his sorrowful prediction, saying: 'Then that holy seat of temples shall become a sepulchre of dead bodies,' plainly avers that the Egyptian gods were all dead men: for having said that his fathers in their exceeding error, incredulity, and neglect of religion, had found a means to make gods, hereunto (says he), they added a virtue out of some parts of the world's nature, and conjoining these two, because they could make no souls, they framed certain images, into which they called either angels or devils, and so by these mysteries gave those idols power to hurt or help them. Then he proceeds to examples. 'Thy grandfather, Asclepius,' saith he, 'the first inventor of physic, has a temple on Mount Libya, near the shore of crocodiles. There lies his worldly man, his body, but his residue or his whole (if the life be the whole man) has gone up to heaven, helping all sick persons now by his deity as he did before by his physic.'[2] Lo here he confesses a dead man worshipped for a god, there where his grave was: erring and making others err, in saying 'that he was ascended to heaven, and helpeth all sick persons by his deity.' Nay, he proceeds to another. 'My grandfather Hermes,' says he, 'lying in the town of his surname, doth he not assist and preserve all that implore his help?' This was Hermes, the elder Mercury, buried (they say) in Hermopolis, the town of his surname. Behold now, here are two men-gods already, Aesculapius and Mercury. For the first the opinion of both Greeks and Latins confirms it. But the second many think was never mortal: yet he says here that he was his grandfather, for this is one and that another, though both have one name. But this I do not argue. He and Aesculapius were both made gods of men, by this great testimony of his grandson Trismegistus, who proceeds and says: 'Isis, the wife of Osiris, doth much good (we see) being pleased, and being offended

much evil.' And then to show that these are of that kind of gods
that men make by this art, he gives us to understand that he
thinks those devils to be souls of dead men, which he says those
erring, incredulous, irreligious fellows called by art into statues:
because these could make no souls. And when he has spoken of
'Isis, being offended, much hurt,' he adds, 'for earthly and worldly
gods are soon offended, and moved to anger by reason they are
made by men, in both their natures': both their natures (saith he),
taking the devil for the soul, and the image for the body; whereupon
it came to pass (says he) that such and such creatures became holy
in Egypt, and their souls were adored in all the cities that consecrated them in their lives, so far that they have part of their worship
assigned them, and are called by their names. Where is now that
sad complaint that Egypt, the seat of temples, should become a
grave for carcasses? See, the false spirit that made Hermes speak
it, made him also confess that it was already filled with their carcasses whom they held as gods. But in his complaint he was but
the vent of the devils' woe, because future plagues were in store
for them at the martyrs' holy memorials; for in such places are
they often tormented and forced to confess themselves, and to
vacate the bodies possessed.

CHAPTER XXVII

Of the honour that Christians give to the martyrs

YET we erect no temples, altars, nor sacrifices to the martyrs, because not they, but their God, is our God. We honour their
memories, as God's saints, standing till death for the truth, that
the true religion might be propagated, and all idolatry demolished:
whereas if any others had believed right before them, yet fear forbade them confess it. And who has ever heard the priest at the
altar, that was built up in God's honour, and the martyrs' memories,
say over the body, I offer unto thee, Peter, or unto thee, Paul,
or Cyprian? He offers to God in the places of their memorials,
whom God had made men, and martyrs, and advanced into the
society of His angels in heaven, that we at that solemnity may both
give thanks to God for their victories, and be encouraged to endeavour the attainment of such crowns and glories as they have
already attained, still invoking Him at their memorials. Wherefore all the religious performances done there at the martyrs'
solemnities are ornaments of their memories, but no sacrifices to
the dead, as unto gods; and those that bring banquets thither,
which notwithstanding the better Christians do not (nor is this
custom observed in most places), yet, such as do so, setting them
down, praying over them, and so taking them away to eat, or

bestow on those that need—all this they do only with a desire that these meats might be sanctified by the martyrs, in the God of martyrs' name. But he that knows the only sacrifices that the Christians offer to God, knows also that these are no sacrifices to the martyrs. Wherefore we neither worship our martyrs with God's honours nor men's crimes, neither offer them sacrifices nor turn their disgraces into any religion of theirs. As for Isis, Osiris' wife and the Egyptian goddess, and her parents, that have been recorded to have been all mortal, to whom she sacrificing found three grains of barley, and showed it unto her husband and Hermes, her counsellor, and so they will have her to be Ceres also—what gross absurdities are hereof recorded, not by poets, but their own priests (as Leon showed to Alexander and he to his mother Olympia), let them read that will, and remember that have read; and then but consider, unto what dead persons and dead persons' works their divinest honours were exhibited. God forbid they should in the least respect compare them with our martyrs, whom nevertheless we account no gods. We make no priests to sacrifice unto them; it is unlawful, indecent, and God's proper due: neither do we please them with their own crimes, or obscene spectacles; whereas they celebrate both the guilt that their gods incurred who were men, and the feigned pleasures of such of them as were harmful devils. If Socrates had had a god, he could not have been of this sort. But such perhaps as loved to excel in this damnable art of making gods, thrust such a one upon him, being an innocent honest man, and unskilful in this their pernicious practice. What need we say more? None that has his wits about him will now hold that these spirits are to be adored for the attainment of eternal bliss in the life to come. Perhaps they will say that all the gods are good, but, of these spirits some are good and some bad; and that by those that are good we may come to eternity, and therefore ought to adore them: well, to examine this question the next book shall serve the turn.

THE NINTH BOOK OF THE CITY OF GOD

CHAPTER I

The scope of the aforesaid disputation, and what is remaining to treat of

IN these controversies of the gods, some have held deities of both natures, good and evil: others (of better minds) did the gods that honour to hold them all good. But those that held the first, held the airy spirits to be gods also, and called them gods, as they called the gods spirits, but not so usually. Indeed they confess that Jove, the prince of all the rest, was by Homer called a *daemon*. But such as affirmed all the gods were good ones, and far better than the best men, are justly moved by the acts of the airy spirits to hold firmly that the gods could do no such matters, and therefore of force there must be a difference between them and these spirits: and that whatever unpleasant desire or bad act they see caused, wherein these spirits do show their secret power, that they hold is the devils' work, and not the gods'. But yet because they place these spirits as mediators between the gods and men (as if God and man had no other means of commerce), to carry and recarry prayers and benefits from the one to the other, this being the opinion of the most excellent philosophers the Platonists, with whom I chose to discuss this question, whether the adoration of many gods be helpful to eternal felicity; in the last book we disputed how the devils, delighting in that which all wise and honest men abhor, as in the foul, enormous, irreligious fictions of the gods' crimes (not men's), and in the damnable practice of magic can be so much nearer to the gods that men must make them the means to attain their favours: and we found it utterly impossible. So now this book (as I promised in the end of the other) must not concern the difference of the gods betwixt themselves (if they make any such), nor the difference of the gods and spirits (the one being far distant from men, as they say, and the other in the midst between the gods and men), but of the difference of these spirits amongst themselves. This is the present question.

CHAPTER II

Whether amongst the spirits of the air that are under the gods, there be any good ones, that can further a man in the attainment of true blessedness

FOR many are wont to say there are some good devils and some bad: but whether this opinion be Plato's or whosoever, it is not to be omitted, because no man should be deluded in honouring those spirits as if they were good; seeing that they, while he thinks they should by their place be a means of reconciliation betwixt him and the gods, and desires their furtherance so as to be with them after death, do inveigle him and draw him in with deceit, quite away from the true God, with whom only and in whom only, and from whom only, every reasonable soul must expect and enjoy beatitude.

CHAPTER III

What qualities Apuleius ascribes to the devils, to whom he gives reason but no virtue

How is this difference of good and evil then extant, whereas Apuleius the Platonist, disputing so much hereof, and attributing so much to those airy powers, yet never speaks a word of their virtues, which he would have done if they had had any? He shows not the cause why they are happy, but the signs of their misery he expatiates upon: confessing that though they have reason, they lack virtue, who not only give way to unreasonable passions, but (as fools are wont to be) are often perturbed with tempestuous and unquiet emotions. His words are these: 'Of these *daemones*, the poets (not much amiss) do feign some to be haters, and some lovers of some particular men: preferring some, and degrading others; so that pity, anger, joy, and all human feelings are easily accidental unto them; and so is their mind exposed to the dominion of all perturbations, which the gods (whose minds are quiet, and retired) are not.' [1] Here you hear plainly that the devils' souls as well as mortals' are subject to every disturbance of passion, and thereby not to be compared unto wise men, who can curb and suppress those exorbitant feelings, however natural unto them by reason of their humanity; giving then no predominance to work any unreasonable effect opposite to justice. But they are more like (not to say worse) unto fools and wicked persons, not in bodies, but qualities; being older in guilt and incurable by punishment, still floating in the sea of perturbation, having no hold at all of verity or virtue, which are the means to repress all outrageous emotions.

CHAPTER IV

The opinions of the Stoics and Peripatetics concerning perturbations of the mind

CONCERNING motions of the mind which the Greeks call $\pi\acute{a}\theta\eta$, and some of us (with Tully), perturbations, others affects, or affections, and some more expressly from the Greek, passions, there be two

[1] *De Deo Socrat.* 11.

opinions of the philosophers. Some say they may befall a wise man, yet so as they are still awed by reason and by the rule of the mind, and bound to what conditions discretion imposes. The holders of this are Platonists, or Aristotelians, for Aristotle the first Peripatetic was Plato's scholar. But others (as the Stoics) exempt a wise man from any touch of those passions. And those Tully in his books *De Finibus* proves to be rather materially than formally opposite unto the Platonists or Peripatetics: because the Stoics will not admit the external helps of the body, or estate, to the name of 'goods,' reserving that only for virtue, as the art of living, fixed in the mind. But the others, following the common fashion, call them goods, though many are of small value in respect of virtue. So then howsoever they differ in their name, they concur in their esteem, nor do the Stoics show anything in this controversy but novelty of phrase. And so I hold directly, that in this question, whether a wise man may have passions of mind or not, their controversy is rather verbal than real; for I am persuaded that the Stoics are just of the Platonists' and Peripatetics' mind herein though their words pretend a difference. This one proof alone will show to avoid the tediousness of a longer discourse. A. Gellius, an eloquent and excellent scholar, writes in his *Noctes Atticae* that he was at sea in the company of a famous Stoic. This philosopher (as Gellius tells at large, but I in brief) seeing the ship in great peril by reason of a dangerous and dreadful tempest, was pale for very fear: which some that were by (being even in the jaws of death curious to observe whether the philosopher were perturbed or not) did perceive. The storm ending, and fear letting men's tongues loose, a rich glutton of Asia fell a scoffing the Stoic for being so terribly afraid of that onset which he himself had passed without any passions at all: but he replied as Aristippus the Socratist did, upon the like case, 'that the other having but the soul of a base knave needed not care for it, but he was careful for the soul of Aristippus.' This answer packed away the rich man's chaff, and then Gellius asked the philosopher (not desiring to offend, but to learn) what was the cause of his fear. He, desiring to satisfy a man so desirous to know, pulls out of his wallet the book of Epictetus, a Stoic, containing the axioms of Zeno and Chrysippus, Stoicism's founders: wherein Gellius says he showed him this position: 'That the mind's apprehensions (they call them fantasies) arising from fearful and terrifying objects, can neither be hindered from befalling a wise man, nor from moving his mind when they do befall: that he shall fear or be sad a little by these passions' too hasty intrusion upon his reason; yet not so far that they leave an acceptance or consent of the mind unto their effect behind them: for this consent they hold lies in their freedom, and is the difference between the fool and the wise: the fool consents to his passions; the wise man, though he suffer them, yet keeps his election and his reprobation of them all firm and free.' Thus much from A. Gellius, no better, but briefer than his own account of that which himself read in Epictetus, about the positive doctrine of the Stoics. And this being true leaves small difference between them and other philosophers in this point of feelings. For both do acquit man's reason from being overruled by passions. And perhaps therefore the Stoics deny that a wise man is subject unto them, because they alter him not nor hurt his wisdom. But they befall him (not moving his wisdom) in respect of the advantages or disadvantages of this life, which notwithstanding he will not call goods or evils. For if the philosopher had not esteemed that which he doubted not he would lose by that shipwreck, namely his life and bodily safety, he would never have been pale on that account: yet might his mind stand fixed for all that external pallor, and he still hold firm, that life and bodily safety which there he feared to lose were not of those goods that make their possessors good, as virtue does. But in that they say they are not to be called goods at all, but only commodities, in this their mind is more upon the word than the matter. For what care is there of their name, when their loss leaves both Stoic and Peripatetic alike affected; proving thereby their equal esteem of them, call them what they will? If the danger of losing these goods or commodities should draw either of them to mischief, they both agree in this rather to abjure the use of bodily benefits than to transgress the rules of justice. Thus is the mind still fixed, holding steadfastly that no passion (though it insult the soul's weaker parts) can domineer over reason, but reason over them, exercising virtue's sovereignty over them by opposition, nor by consent. For such a one does Virgil say Aeneas was:

> Mens immota manet, lacrimae volvuntur inanes.[1]

> His mind stood fixed, yet fruitless tears must out.

CHAPTER V

That the Christians' passions are causes of the practice of virtue, not inducers unto vice

HERE is no need to expound fuller what the Christian scripture teaches on this point of feelings. It subjects the whole mind to God's governance and assistance, and all the passions unto it, in such manner that they are all made to serve the increase of justice. Finally our doctrine inquires not so much whether one be angry, but wherefore; why he is sad, not whether he be sad; and so of fear. For anger with an offender to reform him; pity upon one

[1] *Aen.* iv. 449.

afflicted to succour him; fear for one in danger to deliver him—these no man, not mad, can reprehend. The Stoics indeed are wont to reprehend pity. But that Stoic might more honestly have pitied another man's danger than have feared his own. But with far more humanity and piety said Tully in Caesar's praise: 'Of all thy virtues is none more admired, nor applauded, than thy mercy.' [1]   What is mercy but a compassion in our own heart of another's misfortunes, urging us as far as our power stretches to relieve him? This feeling serves reason, when our pity offends not justice, either in relieving the poor or forgiving the penitent. This that eloquent Cicero hesitated not to call a virtue, which the Stoics reckon with the vices: yet does Epictetus out of the doctrines of Zeno and Chrysippus, the first patrons of this sect, allow these passions unto a man, whom none the less they must needs keep from all vice; and consequently these passions that befall a wise man, so as they do not offer any prejudice to his reason or virtue, are no vices; and the Stoics, Platonists, and Peripatetics do all agree in one. But (as Tully says) [2] the Grecians (of old) affect verbosity of contention rather than truth. But now it is a further question whether it appertains unto the infirmity of this present life to suffer these feelings in all good offices whatsoever. For the holy angels, though they punish such as God's eternal providence appoints with anger, though they help those that they love out of danger without any fear, and succour the wretched without feeling any compassion, are notwithstanding said (after our phrase of speaking) to be partakers of those passions, because of the similitude of their works, not in any way because of the infirmity of feelings. And so God in the scripture is said to be angry; yet far is He from feeling passion; the effect of His revenge is the cause of this phrase, not the turbulence of His passion.

CHAPTER VI

What passion the spirits that Apuleius makes mediators between the gods and men are subject unto, by his own confession

BUT to defer the question of the holy angels awhile, let us see how the Platonists teach [3] of their mediating spirits, in this matter of passion. If those *daemones* ruled over all their feelings with freedom and reason, then Apuleius would not have said that they are tossed in the same tempestuous cogitations that men's hearts do float in. So then their mind, their reasonable part, which, if it had any virtue seated in it, should be the dominator over these turbulent desires of the inferior parts—this very mind floats (say the Platonists) in this sea of perturbation. So then the devils'

[1] *Pro Ligar.* xii. 37.   [2] *De Oratore,* i. 11, 47.   [3] *De Deo Socrat.* 11.

minds lie open to the passions of lust, fear, wrath, and the rest. What part then have they free, wise, and unaffected, whereby to please the gods and converse with good men, when their whole mind is so subjugated unto passions and their vices, that their whole reason is eternally employed upon deceit and illusion, as their desire to injure all creatures is eternal?

CHAPTER VII

That the Platonists do but seek contentions in saying the poets defame the gods, whereas their imputations pertain to the devils, and not to the gods

IF any say the poets' tolerable fictions, that some gods were lovers or haters of some men, were not spoken universally but restrictively, respecting the evil spirits only who Apuleius says 'do float in a sea of turbulent thoughts'—how can this stand, when in his placing of them in the midst between the gods and us, he says not 'some,' namely the evil, but 'all,' because all have airy bodies? For this, he says, is a fiction of the poets that make gods of those spirits, and call them so, making them friends to such or such men, as their own loose feelings do put in their heads to poetize: whereas indeed the gods are far from these in place, blessedness, and quality. This is the fiction then, to call them gods that are not so: and to set them at odds or at amity with such or such particular men, under the titles of deities. But this fiction (says he) was not much: for though the spirits be called gods which they are not, yet as spirits they are described as they are. And thence (says he) is Homer's tale of Minerva, that stayed Achilles from striking in the midst of the Greek host. That this was Minerva he holds to be false, because she (in his opinion) was a goddess highly placed amongst the greatest deities, far from conversation with mortals. Now if it were some spirit that favoured the Greeks against Troy, as Troy had divers spirits against them, one of whom he calls Venus, and another Mars, who indeed are higher gods than to meddle with such trifles, and if those spirits contended each for his own side, then this fiction is not far wide, says he. For it was spoken of them whom he himself has testified subject to passions, as mortal men are; so that they might use their loves and hates not according to justice, but even as the people do in huntings and races, each one doing the best for his own party. For the philosopher's care it seems was this, to prevent the imputation of such acts upon the gods (whose names the poets used) and to lay them upon the spirits, to whom of right they belonged.

CHAPTER VIII

Apuleius' definition of the gods of heaven, spirits of air, and men of earth

WHAT of his definition of spirits? It is universal and therefore worth inspection. They are (says he) [1] creatures, passive, reasonable, aerial, and eternal. In all of these five qualities there is nothing that those spirits have in common with good men, but they have it with bad also. For making a large description of men in their place, being the last, as the gods are the first, to pass from commemoration of both their extremes unto that which was the mean between them, viz. these devils, thus he says: 'Men, joying in reason, perfect in speech, mortal in body, immortal in soul, passionate and inconstant in mind, brutish and frail in body, of discrepant conditions, and similar errors, of impudent boldness, of bold hope, of indurate labour, and uncertain fortune, particularly mortal, generally eternal, propagating one another, short of life, slow of wisdom, sudden of death, and discontented in life, these dwell on earth.' [2] In these general characteristics (common to many) he added one that he knew was false in few, 'slow of wisdom': which had he omitted, he had neglected to perfect his description. For in his description of the gods, he says that that beatitude, which men do seek by wisdom, excels in them; so had he thought of any good devils, their definition should have mentioned it, either by showing them to participate some of the gods' beatitude, or of man's wisdom. But he has no separation between them and wretches. And though he refrained from exposing their malevolent natures, not so much for fear of them, as of their servants that should read his expositions; yet to the wise he leaves his opinion open enough, and what theirs should be, both in his separation of the gods from all tempest of feelings, and therein from the spirits, in all but their eternity; and in his intimation that their minds were like men's, not the gods', and that not in wisdom, which men may partake with the gods, but in being prone to passions, which rule both in the wicked and the witless, but are ruled over by the wise man, yet so as he had rather be without them than conquer them. For if he seek to make the devils to share with the gods in eternity of mind only, not of body, then should he not exclude man, whose soul he held eternal as well as the other Platonists: and therefore he says that 'man is a creature mortal in body, and immortal in soul.'

CHAPTER IX

Whether the airy spirits can procure a man the gods' friendships

WHEREFORE, if men by reason of their mortal bodies have not that participation of eternity with the gods that these spirits by reason

[1] *De Deo Socrat.* 12.   [2] *De Deo Socrat.* 4.

of their immortal bodies have: what mediators can they be between the gods and men that in their best part, their soul, are worse than men, and better in the worst part of a creature, the body? For, all creatures consisting of body and soul have the soul for the better part, be it never so weak and vicious, and the body never so firm and perfect: because it is of a more excelling nature; nor can the corruption of vice depose it to the baseness of the body: but like base gold, that is dearer than the best silver, so far does it exceed the body's worth. So then those mediators, interposed between heaven and earth, have eternity of body with the gods and corruption of soul with the mortals, as though religion, that must make god and man to meet, were rather corporal than spiritual! But what guilt or sentence has hung up those juggling interceders by the heels, and the head downward, that their lower parts, their bodies, participate with the higher powers, and their higher, their souls, with the lower; holding correspondence with the gods in their servile part, and with mortals in their principal? For the body (as Sallust says) [1] is the soul's slave; at least should be in the true use: and he proceeds: the one we have common with beasts, the other with gods; speaking of man whose body is as mortal as a beast's. Now those whom the philosophers have put between the gods and us may say thus also: 'We have body and soul, in common with gods and men': but then (as I said) they are bound with their heels upward, having their slavish body common with the gods, and their predominant soul common with wretched men; their worst part aloft and their best underfoot. Wherefore if any one think them eternal with the gods, because they never die the death with creatures, let us not understand their bodies to be the eternal palace wherein they are blessed, but the eternal prison wherein they are damned: and so he thinks as he should.

CHAPTER X

Plotinus' opinion that men are less wretched in their mortality than the devils are in their eternity

It is said that Plotinus, that lived but lately, understood Plato the best of any. He, speaking of men's souls, says thus: 'The Father out of His mercy bound them but for a season,' [2] so that in that men's bonds (their bodies) are mortal, he imputes it to God the Father's mercy, thereby freeing us from the eternal tediousness of this life. Now the devils' wickedness is held unworthy of this favour whose passive souls have eternal prisons, not temporal as men's are, for they were happier than men, had they mortal bodies with us, and blessed souls with the gods. And men's equals were

---

[1] *Catil.* i. 1.   [2] *Ennead.* iv. 3, 12.

they if they had but mortal bodies to their wretched souls, and
then could achieve for themselves rest after death by faith and
piety. But as they are, they are not only more unhappy than man
in the wretchedness of their souls, but far more in eternity of
bondage in their bodies. He would not have men to understand
that they could ever come to be gods by any grace or wisdom,
seeing that he calls them eternal devils.

CHAPTER XI

Of the Platonists that held men's souls to become demons after death

APULEIUS says also that men's souls are demons, and become *lares*
if their merits be good; if evil, *lemures*, goblins; if indifferent,
manes. But how pernicious this opinion is to all goodness, who
sees not? For be men never so mischievous, if they hope to
become *lemures* or *manes*, the more desirous are they of hurt, and
the worse they turn into, being persuaded that some sacrifices will
invoke them to do mischief when they are dead, and become such:
for these *lares* (said he) are evil demons that have been men on
earth. But here is another question. Let it pass. He says
further, the Greeks call such as they hold blessed εὐδαίμονες, good
demons: herein confirming his position that men's souls become
demons after death.

CHAPTER XII

*Of the three contraries whereby the Platonists distinguish the devils'
natures from the men's*

BUT now let us turn to those creatures whom he places properly
between the gods and men, being reasonable, passive, aerial, and
immortal. Having placed the gods the highest, and the men the
lowest, here (says he) [1] are two of your creatures, the gods and
men, much differing in height of place, immortality, and perfection;
their habitations being immeasurably distant, and the life there
eternal, and perfection here frail and faltering: their wits advanced
to beatitude, ours dejected unto misery. Here now are three
contraries between nature's two uttermost parts, the highest and
the lowest: for the three praises of the gods' estate he compares
with the contraries of man's. Theirs are height of place, eternity
of life, perfection of nature. All these are thus opposed by him
to humanity: the first, height of place immeasurably distant from
us: the second, eternity of life, compared with our frail and faltering
state: the third, perfection of nature and wit, counterpoised by our

[1] *De Deo Socrat.* 4.

wit and nature, that are dejected unto misery. Thus the gods'
three, height, eternity, beatitude, are contrary to our three, baseness, mortality, and misery. Now the devils being midway
between them and us, their place is known, for that must needs be
the mid distance between the highest and the lowest. But the
other two must be better looked into, whether the devils are either
quite excluded from them, or participate as much of them as their
middle position requires. Excluded from them they cannot be,
for we cannot say that they are neither happy nor wretched, as
we may say that the mid place is neither the highest nor the lowest,
or as we might say beasts and unreasonable creatures are neither.
But such as have reason must be the one or the other. Nor can
we say they are neither mortal nor eternal, for all things alive are
one or the other. But he has said they are eternal. It remains,
then, that they have one part from the highest, and another from
the lowest, so being the mean themselves. For if they take both
from either, their mediocrity is overthrown, and they rely wholly
upon the lower part or the higher. Seeing, therefore, they cannot
lack these two qualities abovesaid, their mediation arises from their
partaking one from either. Now eternity from the lowest they
cannot have, for there it is not; so from the highest they must have
that. So then is there nothing to participate for the sake of their
middle position between them and mortals but misery.

CHAPTER XIII

*How the devils, if they be neither blessed with the gods nor wretched
with men, may be in the mean betwixt both without participation
of either*

So then, according to the Platonists, the gods are in eternal blessedness, or blessed eternity, and men are in mortal misery or miserable
mortality: and the spirits of the air between both, in miserable
eternity, or eternal misery. For in his five attributes given them
in their definition, is none that shows (as he promised) that they
are mediate: for with us they share their reason, their being
creatures, and their being passive; with the gods they share only
eternity; their airy nature they share with neither. How are they
mediate then, having but one from the higher, and three from the
lower? Who sees not how they are thrust from the mediate to
the lower side? But in this perhaps they may be found to be in
the midst—they have one thing proper to themselves only, their
airy bodies, as the gods have their celestial, and man his terrestrial;
and two things they have common to both, their being creatures
and their gift of reason: for he, speaking of the gods and men, said:
'Here have you two creatures.' Nor do they affirm but that the

gods have reason. Two then remain, their passiveness and their eternity; one common with the lower and the other with the higher, so being proportioned in the mean place that they decline to neither side. Thus, then, are they eternally miserable or miserably eternal. For in calling them passive he would have called them miserable, but for offending them that served them. Besides, because the world is not ruled by rash chance but by God's providence, these spirits should never have been eternally miserable, were they not extremely malicious. Wherefore if the *eudae-mones* be blessed, then it is not they that are in this mediety between gods and men that are *eudaemones*. Where is their place, then, admitting their ministry between gods and men? If they be good and eternal, then they are blessed. If blessed, then not in the midst, but nearer to the gods and further from men. Frustrate then is all their labour that seek to prove the mediety of those spirits being good, immortal, and blessed, between the gods immortal and blessed, and men mortal and wretched. For if they had beatitude and immortality, both attributes of the gods, and neither proper unto man, they must needs hold nearer correspondence with gods than with men. And if they were intermediate, their two attributes should communicate with one upon either side, not with two upon one side: as a man is in the midst between a beast and an angel; a beast being unreasonable and mortal, an angel reasonable and immortal; a man mortal and reasonable, holding the first with a beast, the second with an angel, and so stands midway; under angels, above beasts. Even so in seeking a mediety between immortality blessed and mortality wretched, we must either find mortality blessed or immortality wretched.

CHAPTER XIV

Whether mortal men may attain true happiness

IT is a great question whether a man may be both mortal and happy. Some, considering their estate with humility, affirmed that in this life man could not be happy; others extolled themselves and avouched that a wise man was happy. Which if it be so, why are not wise men appointed mediators between the immortally happy and the mortally wretched? Hold they their beatitude of the first, and their mortality of the latter? Truly if they be blessed, they envy no man. For what is more wretched than envy? And therefore they shall do their best in giving wretched mortals good counsel to beatitude, that they may become immortal after death and be joined in fellowship with the eternal blessed angels.

CHAPTER XV

Of the mediator of God and man, the man Christ Jesus

BUT if that be true (which is far more probable) that all men of necessity must be miserable whilst they are mortal, then must a mean be found which is God as well as man, who by the mediation of his blessed mortality may help us out of this mortal misery unto that immortal happiness: and this mean must be born mortal, but not continue so. He became mortal not by any weakening of His deity, but by taking on Him this our frail flesh. He remained not mortal, because He raised Himself up from death: for the fruit of His mediation is to free those whom He is mediator for from the eternal death of the flesh. So then it was necessary for the mediator between God and us to have a temporal mortality and an eternal beatitude; to have correspondence with mortals by the first, and to transfer them to eternity by the second. Wherefore the good angels cannot have this place, being immortal and blessed. The evil may, as having their immortality and our misery. And to these is the good mediator opposed being mortal for a while, and blessed for ever, against their immortal misery. And so these proud immortals and hurtful wretches, lest by the boast of their immortality they should draw men to misery, has He by His humble death and bountiful beatitude prevented from swaying all such hearts as He has pleased to cleanse and illuminate by faith in Him. What medium then shall a wretched mortal, far separate from the blessed immortals, choose to attain their societies? The devils' immortality is miserable: but Christ's mortality has nothing undelectable. There we had need beware of eternal wretchedness: here we need not fear the death which cannot be eternal, and we cannot but love the happiness which is eternal. For the mean that is immortally wretched aims entirely at keeping us from immortal beatitude, by persisting in the contrary misery: but the mean that is mortal and blessed shares our mortality to make us immortal (as He showed in His resurrection), and from being wretches to make us blessed, a state which He never lacked. And so there is an evil mean that separates friends, and a good that reconciles them. And of the first sort are many, because the blessedness that the other multitude attains comes all from participating of one God; whereof the miserable multitude of evil angels being deprived (which rather is opposite to hinder, than interposes to help) does all that in it lies to withdraw us from that one way alone that leads to this blessed good, namely the Word of God, not made, but the Maker of all. Yet is He no mediator as He is the Word (for so is He most blessed, and immortal, far from us miserable men) but as He is man; therein making it plain that to the attainment of this blessed and beatific good, we must use no other mediators whereby to work; God Himself, blessed and blessing all, having graced our humanity with participation of His deity. For when He frees us from misery and mortality, He does not make us happy by participation of blessed angels but of that Trinity, in whose participation the angels themselves are blessed: and therefore when He was below the angels [1] in form of a servant,[2] then was He also above them in form of a god: being both the way of life below, and life itself above.

CHAPTER XVI

Whether it be probable that the Platonists say, that the gods, avoiding earthly contagion, have no commerce with men, but by the means of the airy spirits

FOR it is false that this Platonist says Plato said: 'God hath no commerce with man,' [3] and makes this absolute separation the most perfect note of their glory and height. So then the devils are left to deal with and to be infected by man's conversation, and therefore they cannot cleanse those that infect them, so that both become unclean—the devils by conversing with men, and men by adoration of the devils. Or if the devils can converse with men, and not be infected, then are they better than the gods: for they could not avoid this inconvenience: for he makes the gods so peculiar as to be far above the reach of man's corruption. But God the Creator (whom we call the true God), he makes such a one (out of Plato) as words cannot describe at all, nay, and as the wisest men in their greatest height of abstractive speculation can have but now and then a sudden and momentary glimpse of the understanding of Him. Well then, if this high God afford His ineffable presence unto wise men sometimes in their abstractive speculation (though after a sudden fashion), and yet is not contaminated thereby, why then are the gods placed so far off, for fear of this contamination? As though the sight of those ethereal bodies that light the earth were not sufficient to refute such a notion! And if our sight of the stars (whom he makes visible gods) do not contaminate them, then no more does it contaminate the spirits, though seen nearer at hand. Or is man's speech more infectious than his sight, and therefore the gods (to keep themselves pure) receive all their requests at the delivery of the devils? What shall I say of the other senses? Man's smelling would not infect the gods if they were below, or when they are below as devils, for the smell of a living man is not infectious at all, if the steam of so many dead carcasses in sacrifices infect not. Their taste is not so strong a craving that they should be driven to come and ask their meat of

[1] Heb. ii. 7, 9.   [2] Phil. ii. 7.   [3] Apuleius, *De Deo Socrat.* 4.

men: and as for their touch, it is in their own choice. For though handling be peculiar to that sense indeed, yet may they handle their business with men, to see them and hear them, without any necessity of touching; for men would dare no further than to desire to see and hear them: and if they should, what man can touch a god or a spirit against their wills, when we see one cannot touch a sparrow, unless he have first taken her? So then in sight, hearing, and speech, the gods might have corporal contact with man. Now if the devils have thus much without infection, and the gods cannot, why then the gods are subject to contamination, and not the devils! But if they be infected also, then what good can they do a man unto eternity, whom, being themselves infected, they cannot make clean, nor fit to be adjoined with the gods, between whom and men they are mediators? And if they cannot do this, what use has man of their mediation? Unless it be that after death they live together corrupted, and never come near the gods, nor enjoy any beatitude, either of them: or unless some will make the spirits like to sponges, fetching all the filth from others, and retaining it in themselves: which if it be so, the gods converse with spirits that are more unclean than the man whose conversation they avoid for uncleanness' sake. Or can the gods cleanse the devils from their infection, uninfected, and cannot do so with men? Who believes this that believes not the devils' illusions? Again, if the looks of man infect, then those visible gods, the world's bright eyes, and the other stars, are liable to this infection, and the devils that are not seen but when they wish are in better state than they. But if it is the sight of man (not their being seen by man) which infects, then let them deny that they do see man, when we see their beams stretched to the very earth. Their beams in that case look uninfected through all infection, and yet they themselves cannot converse purely with men only, though man stand in never so much necessity of their help. We see the sun's and moon's beams reflected upon the earth without contamination of the light. But I wonder that so many learned men, preferring things intelligible evermore before sensible, would mention any corporal matter in the doctrine of beatitude. Where is that saying of Plotinus: 'Let us fly to our bright country; there is the father, and there is all'? What flight is that? To become like to God. If then the liker a man is to God the nearer he is also, why then the more unlike, the farther off: and man's soul, the more it looks after things mutable and temporal, the more unlike is it to that essence that is immutable and eternal.

CHAPTER XVII

*That unto that beatitude, that consists in participation of the greatest
good, we must have only such a mediator as Christ, not such as
the devil*

To avoid this inconvenience, seeing that mortal impurity cannot
attain to the height of the celestial purity, we must have a mediator,
not one bodily mortal as the gods are, and mentally miserable as
men are, for such a one will rather grudge than further our cure;
but one adapted unto our body by nature, and of an immortal
righteousness of spirit, whereby (not for distance of place but
excellence of similitude) even while on earth he remained above.
Such a one must give us his truly divine help in our cure from
corruption and captivity. Far be it from this incorruptible God
to fear the corruption of that man which He put on, or of those men
with whom as man He conversed. For these two facts about His
incarnation are of no small value, that neither true divinity could
be contaminated by the flesh, nor that the devils are our betters in
having no flesh. This, as the scripture proclaims,[1] is the Mediator
between God and man, the man Christ Jesus, of whose divinity,
equal with the Father, and of whose humanity, like unto ours, this
is now no fit place to dispute.

CHAPTER XVIII

*That the devils, under colour of their intercession, seek but to
draw us from God*

BUT those false and deceitful mediators, the devils, wretched in
uncleanness of spirit, yet working strange effects by their aerial
bodies, seek to draw us from profit of soul, showing us no way to
God, but striving to conceal that wholly from us. For in the
corporal way, which is most false and erroneous, a way that
righteousness walks not (for our ascent to God must be by this
spiritual likeness, not by corporal elevation), but (as I said), in
this corporal way that the devils' servants dream lies through the
elements, the devils are placed in the midst between the celestial
gods and the earthly men; and the gods have this pre-eminence
that the distance of place keeps them from contagion of man: so
that rather they believe that the devils are infected by man, than
he cleansed by them, for so would he infect the gods (think they)
but for the far distance that keeps them clean. Now who is he so
wretched as to think any way to perfection there where the men
do infect, the spirits are infected, and the gods subject to infection?

[1] 1 Tim. ii. 5.

Who will not rather select that way where the polluted spirits are abandoned, and men are purged from infection by that unchangeable God, and so made fit persons for the fellowship of the angels ever unpolluted?

CHAPTER XIX

That the word demon is not used now of any idolater in a good sense

BUT to avoid controversy concerning words, because some of these demon-servers, and Labeo for one, say that whom they call demons, others call angels: now must I say somewhat of the good angels, whom indeed they deny not, but had rather call them demons than angels. But we (as scripture, and consequently Christianity, instructs us) acknowledge angels both good and evil, but no good demons. But wheresoever in our scripture demon or a cognate word is read, it signifies an evil and unclean spirit: and is now so universally used in that sense, that even the pagans themselves that hold a multitude of gods and demons to be adored, yet be they never such scholars, dare not say to their slave as in his praise: 'Thou hast a demon.' Whosoever does say so knows that he is held rather to curse than commend. Seeing therefore that all ears do so dislike this word and that almost none but takes it in ill part, why should we be compelled to express our assertion further, seeing that the use of the word angel will quite abolish the offence that the use of the word demon causes?

CHAPTER XX

Of the quality of the devils' knowledge, whereof they are so proud

YET the original of this name (if we look into divinity), affords somewhat worth observation, for they were called in Greek, δαίμονες, for their knowledge. Now the apostle, speaking in the Holy Spirit, says: 'Knowledge puffs up, but charity edifies': [1] that is, knowledge is then good when it links with charity; otherwise it puffs up, that is, fills one with vainglory. So then in the devils is this knowledge without charity, and thence are they puffed so big and so proud, that the religious honours which they well know to be God's due they have ever arrogated to themselves, and as far as they can, do so still. Now what power the humility of Christ, that came in form of a servant, has against this devils' pride, by which the human race was domineered as it deserved to be, men's wretched minds being devilishly as yet puffed up can by no means because of their unclean pride comprehend or conceive.

[1] 1 Cor. viii. 1.

CHAPTER XXI

In what manner the Lord would make Himself known to the devils

FOR the devils had this knowledge, so that they could say to the
Lord in the flesh: 'What have we to do with Thee, O Jesus of
Nazareth? Art Thou come to destroy us before our time?'[1]
Here is a plain knowledge without charity: they fear to be plagued
by Him, but loved not the justice in Him. Their knowledge was
bounded by His will, and His will by what was needful. But they
knew Him not as the angels knew Him, that participate of His
deity in all eternity, but unto their terror, out of whose clutches
He freed those that He had predestined to His kingdom of true
eternal glory, and eternal glorious truth. The devils therefore
knew Him not as the life eternal, the unchangeable light, illuminating all the godly who receive that light to the purification of
their hearts by faith; but they knew Him by some temporal effects
of His presence, and secret signs of His virtue, which the devils'
angelical senses might more easily observe than man's natural
infirmity: which signs when He suppressed, the prince of devils
made question of His deity, and tempted Him for the trial of His
deity, trying how far He would suffer Himself to be tempted, in
adapting His humanity unto our imitation. But after His temptation when the good and glorious angels (whom the devils extremely
feared) came and ministered unto Him,[2] then the devils got more
and more knowledge of Him, and not one of them durst resist His
command, though He seemed infirm and contemptible in the flesh.

CHAPTER XXII

The difference of the holy angels' knowledge and the devils'

UNTO the good angels, the knowledge of all temporal things (that
puffs up the devils) is vile; not that they lack it, but because they
wholly respect the love of that God that sanctifies them, in comparison of which ineffable and unchangeable glory, with the love
of which they are inflamed, they contemn all that is under it, that
is not it, yea and even themselves, that all their good may be
employed in enjoying that good alone. And so came they to a
more sure knowledge of the world, viewing in God the principal
causes of the world's creation, which causes do confirm this,
frustrate that, and dispose of all. Now the devils are far from
beholding those eternal and fundamental causes in the wisdom of
God. They can only extract a notion from certain secret signs,
of which man is ignorant, by reason of their greater experience, and

¹ Mark i. 24.   ² Matt. iv. 11.

therefore may oftener presage events. But they are often deceived, yet the angels never. For it is one thing to presage changes and events from changeable and casual grounds, and to confound them by as changeable a will (as the devils are permitted to do), and another thing to foresee the changes of times, and the will of God in His eternal unalterable decrees most certain and most powerful by the participation of His divine Spirit, as the angels are vouchsafed by due gradation to do. So are they eternal and blessed. He is their God that made them; for His participation and contemplation they do continually enjoy.

CHAPTER XXIII

That the pagan idols are falsely called gods, yet the scripture allows it to saints and angels

Now if the Platonists had rather call these gods than the demons, and reckon them among those gods whom the supreme God created (as their master Plato writes),[1] let them do so. We will have no verbal controversy with them. If they call them immortal, and yet God's creatures, made immortal by adherence with Him and not by themselves, they hold with us, call them what they will. And the best Platonists (if not all) have left records that thus they believed: for whereas they call such an immortal creature a god, we contend not with him, our scriptures saying: 'The God of gods, even the Lord hath spoken':[2] again: 'Praise ye the God of gods':[3] again: 'A great King above all gods':[4] And in that it is written: 'He is to be feared above all gods': the sequel explains it: 'For all the gods of the people are idols: but the Lord made the heavens.'[5] He calls Him over all gods, to wit, of the peoples, those that the nations called their gods being idols; therefore He is to be feared above them all, and in this fear they cried: 'Art Thou come to destroy us before our time?'[6] But whereas it is written, 'the God of gods,' this is not to be understood, the God of idols or devils: and God forbid we should say, 'a great King above all gods,' in reference to His kingdom over devils: but the scripture calls the men of God's family gods: 'I have said you are gods, and all children of the Most High.'[7] Of these must the 'God of gods' be understood, and over these gods is the King, 'the great King above all gods.' But now one question. If men being of God's family, whom He speaks unto by men or angels, be called gods, how much more are they to be so called that are immortal, and enjoy that beatitude which men by God's service do aim at? We answer that the scripture rather calls men by the name of gods than those immortal blessed creatures whose likeness was promised to man

---

[1] *Tim.*, p. 41A.   [2] Ps. l. 1.   [3] Ps. cxxxvi. 2.   [4] Ps. xcv. 3.
[5] Ps. xcvi. 4, 5.   [6] Mark i. 24.   [7] Ps. lxxxii. 6.

after death, that our unfaithful infirmity should not be seduced by reason of their supereminence to make gods of them: which inconvenience in man is soon avoided. And the men of God's family are the rather called gods, to assure them that He is their God that is the God of gods: for though the blessed angels be called gods, yet they are not called the gods of gods, that is, of those servants of God of whom it is said: 'You are gods, and all children of the Most High.' Hereupon the apostle says: 'Though there be that are called gods, whether in heaven or in earth, as there be many gods, and many lords: yet unto us there is but one God, which is the Father, of whom are all things and we in Him; and one Lord Jesus Christ, by whom are all things and we by Him.'[1] No matter for the name then, the matter being thus past all scruple. But whereas we say that from those immortal choirs angels are sent with God's command unto men, this they dislike as believing that this business belongs not to those blessed creatures whom they call gods, but unto the demons, whom they dare not affirm blessed but only immortal: or so immortal and blessed as good demons are, but not as those high gods whom they place so high or so far from man's infection. But (though this seem a verbal controversy) the name of a demon is so detestable, that we may by no means attribute it unto our blessed angels. Thus then let us end this book. Know all, that those blessed immortals (however called) that are mere creatures, are no means to bring miserable man to beatitude, being from them doubly different. Secondly, those that partake immortality with them, and misery (for reward of their malice) with us, can rather envy us this happiness, than obtain it for us. Therefore the friends of those demons can bring no proof why we should honour them as gods, and not rather avoid them as deceivers. As for those who they say are good, immortal, and blessed, calling them gods and allotting them sacrifices for the attainment of beatitude eternal, in the next book (by God's help) we will prove that their desire was to give this honour not to them, but unto that one God, through whose power they were created, and in whose participation they are blessed.

[1] 1 Cor. viii. 5, 6.

THE TENTH BOOK OF THE CITY OF GOD

CHAPTER I

That the Platonists themselves held that one God alone was the giver of all beatitude unto men and angels: but the controversy is, whether they that they hold are to be worshipped for this end would have sacrifices offered to themselves, or resign all unto God

IT is perspicuous to the knowledge of all such as have use of reason, that man desires to be happy. But the great controversies arise upon the inquisition whence or how mortal infirmity should attain beatitude: on which the philosophers have bestowed all their time and study, which to relate were here too tedious, and too fruitless. He that has read our eighth book, wherein we selected with what philosophers to handle this question of beatitude, whether it were to be attained by serving one God the Maker of the rest, or the others also, need not look for any repetitions here, being able there to repair his memory if it fail him. We choose the Platonists, being worthily held the most worthy philosophers, because as they could conceive that the reasonable immortal soul of man could never be blessed but in participation of the light of God the world's Creator; so could they affirm that beatitude (the aim of all humanity) was unattainable without a firm adherence in pure love, unto the unchangeable One, that is, God. But because they also gave way to pagan errors (becoming vain, as Paul says, in their own imaginations)[1] and believed (or would be thought to believe) that man was bound to honour many gods, and some of them extending this honour even to devils, whom we have impartially confuted; it rests now to examine by God's grace how these immortal and blessed creatures in heaven (be they thrones, dominations, principalities, or powers) whom they call gods, and some of them good demons, or angels, as we do, may be thought to desire our preservation of truth in religion and piety: that is (to be more plain) whether their wills be, that we should offer prayer and sacrifice, or consecrate ours or ourselves unto them, or only to God, who is both their God and ours. The peculiar worship of the divinity or (to speak more expressly) the deity, because I have no one fit Latin word to express it, when I need, I will call by the Greek λατρεία, which our brethren (in every translation of scripture) do translate 'service.' But that service wherein we serve men, intimated by the apostle in these words: 'Servants, be obedient to your masters,'[2] that is

[1] Rom. i. 21.   [2] Eph. vi. 5; Col. iii. 22.

expressed by another Greek word.   But λατρεία, as our evangelists
do use it either wholly or most frequently, signifies the honour due
unto God.   If we therefore translate it *cultus*, from *colo*, to worship
or to till, we associate it with more than God, for we worship
[*colimus*] all men of honourable memory or presence; besides *colo*,
in general use, is proper to things under us, as well as those whom
we reverence or adore; for hence comes the word *colonus*, for an
husbandman, or an inhabitant.   And the gods are called *caelicolae*,
from *caelum*, heaven, and *colo*, to inhabit, not to adore, or worship,
nor yet as husbandmen, that have their name from the tillage of the
soil they possess, but as that rare Latinist says: *Urbs antiqua fuit,
Tyrii tenuere coloni*,[1] *coloni* being here the inhabitants, not the
husbandmen.   And hereupon the towns that have been planted
and peopled by other greater cities (as one hive of bees produces
divers) are called colonies.   So then we cannot use *colo* with
reference to God without a restraint of the usual signification,
seeing it is used with so many senses: therefore no one Latin word
that I know is sufficient to express the worship due unto God.   For
though religion signify nothing so distinctly as the worship of God,
and thereupon we so translate the Greek θρησκεία; yet because in
the use of it in Latin, both by learned and ignorant, it is referred
unto lineages, affinities, and all kindreds, therefore it will not serve
to avoid ambiguity in this theme: nor can we truly say, religion is
nothing else but God's worship; the word seeming to be taken
originally from human duty and observance.   So piety also is taken
properly for the worship of God, where the Greeks use εὐσέβεια:
yet is it attributed also unto the duty towards our parents; and
ordinarily used for the works of mercy, I think because God commands it so strictly, putting it in His sight for, and before, sacrifices.
Whence came a custom to call God pious.   Yet the Greeks never
call Him εὐσεβής, though they use εὐσέβεια for mercy or piety
often.   But in some places (for more distinction) they choose
rather to say θεοσέβεια, God's worship, than εὐσέβεια, plainly worship, or good worship.   But we have no one fit word for to express
either of these.   The Greek λατρεία we translate 'service,' but
with a limiting of it to God alone: their θρησκεία we translate 'religion,' but still with a peculiar reference to God: their θεοσέβεια
we have no one word for, but we may call it God's worship; which
we say is due only to Him that is the true God, and makes His
servants gods.   Wherefore if there be any blessed immortals in
heaven, that neither love us, nor would have us blessed, them we
must not serve: but if they both love us and wish us happiness,
then truly they wish it us from the fount whence they have it.   Or
shall theirs come from one stock, and ours from another?

[1] Virg. *Aen*. i. 12.

CHAPTER II

The opinion of Plotinus the Platonist concerning the supernal illumination

BUT we and those great philosophers have no conflict about this question; for they well saw, and many of them plainly wrote, that both their beatitude and ours had its origin from the participation of an intellectual light, which they counted God, and different from themselves. This gave them all their light, and by the fruition of this they were perfect and blessed. In many places does Plotinus explain Plato thus—that that which we call the soul of this universe has the beatitude from one fount with us, namely, a light which it is not, but which made it: and from whose intellectual illustration it has all the intelligible splendour. This he argues in a simile drawn from the visible celestial bodies compared with these two invisible things, putting the sun for one, and the moon for another; for the light of the moon is held to proceed from the reflection of the sun. So (says the great Platonist) the reasonable or intellectual soul, of whose nature all the blessed immortals are that are contained in heaven, has no essence above it, but only God's that created both it and all the world; nor have those supernal creatures their beatitude or understanding of the truth from any other origin than ours has: herein truly agreeing with the scripture, where it is written: 'There was a man sent from God whose name was John. The same came for a witness to bear witness of the Light, that all men through him might believe. He was not the Light, but came to bear witness of the Light. That was the true Light which lighteth every man that cometh into the world': [1] which difference shows, that that reasonable soul which was in John could not be its own light, but shone by participation of another, the true Light. This John the evangelist confessed in his testimony, where he said: 'Of His fullness have all we received.' [2]

CHAPTER III

Of the true worship of God, wherein the Platonists failed in worshipping good or evil angels, though they knew the world's Creator

THIS being thus, what Platonist or other philosopher soever who had known God, and glorified Him as God, and been thankful, and not become vain in his conceits, nor been an author of the people's error, nor winked at them for fear they would have confessed—

---

[1] John i. 6–9.   [2] John i. 16.

what Platonist would not hold that both the blessed immortals and
we wretched mortals are bound to the adoration of one sole God
of gods, both their God and ours?

CHAPTER IV

That sacrifice is due only to the true God

To Him we owe that Greek λατρεία or service, both in ourselves and
sacrifices, for we are all His temple, and each one His temple,
He vouchsafing to inhabit us all in some and each in particular,
being no more in all than in one: for He is neither multiplied nor
diminished. Our hearts elevated to Him are His altars. His only
Son is the Priest by whom we please Him. We offer Him bloody
sacrifices when we shed our blood for His truth, and incense when
we burn in zeal to Him. The gifts He giveth us, we do in vows
return Him. His benefits we consecrate unto Him in set solemnities, lest the length of time should bring them into ungrateful
oblivion. We offer Him the sacrifices of humility and praises on
the altar of our heart in the fire of fervent love; for by the sight of
Him (as we may see Him), and by being joined with Him, are
we purged from our guilty and filthy longing and consecrated in
His name. He is our blessed founder, and our desires' accom-
plishment. Him we elect or rather re-elect, for by our neglect we
lost Him. Him, therefore, we re-elect (whence religion is derived),
and to Him we do hasten with the wings of love to attain rest in
Him: being blessed by attainment of that final perfection. For our
good (whose end the philosophers jangled about) is nothing but
to adhere unto Him, and by His intellectual and incorporeal embrace our soul grows great with all virtue and true perfection. This
good are we taught to love with all our heart, with all our soul, and
all our strength. To this good we ought to be led by those that
love us, and to lead those we love. So are the two commandments
fulfilled, wherein consist all the law and the prophets: 'Thou shalt
love the Lord thy God with all thine heart, with all thy soul, and
with all thy mind; and thou shalt love thy neighbour as thyself.' [1]
For to teach a man how to love himself was this end appointed,
whereunto he refers all his works for beatitude; for he that loves
himself desires but to be blessed: and the end of this is adherence to
God. So then the command of loving his neighbour, being given
to him that knows how to love himself, what does it command but
to commend the love of God unto him? This is God's true worship, true piety, true religion, and due service to God only. Where-

[1] Matt. xxii. 37, 39.

fore every immortal power soever (virtuous or otherwise) that loves us as itself, desires we should but be His servants for beatitude, whence it has beatitude by serving Him. If it worship not God, it is wretched, as lacking God: if it do, then will not it be worshipped for God. It rather holds, and loves to hold as the holy scripture writes: 'He that sacrifices to any gods but the one God, shall be rooted out' ; [1] for to be silent in other points of religion, there is none dare say that a sacrifice is due but unto God alone. But much is taken from divine worship and thrust into human honours, either by excessive humility or pestilent flattery: yet still with a reserved notice that they are men held worthy indeed of reverence and honour, or at most of adoration. But who ever sacrificed but to him whom he knew, or thought, or feigned to be a God? And how ancient a part of God's worship a sacrifice is, Cain and Abel do show full proof; God Almighty rejecting the elder brother's sacrifice, and accepting the younger's.

CHAPTER V

Of the sacrifices which God requires not, save as significations of what He does require

BUT who is so fond to think that God needs anything that is offered in sacrifice? The scripture condemns them that think so, in different places; one text of the psalmist will suffice in brief for all: 'I said unto the Lord, Thou art my God, because Thou needest none of my goods.' [2]   Believe therefore that God had no need of man's cattle, nor any earthly good of his, no not his justice: but all the worship that he gives God, is for his own profit, not God's. One cannot say he does the fountain good by drinking of it, or the light by seeing by it. Nor had the patriarchs' ancient sacrifices (which now God's people read of, but use not) any other intent, but to signify what should be done of us in adherence to God and charity to our neighbour to promote in him the same end. So then an external offering is a visible sacrament of an invisible sacrifice, that is, a holy sign. And thereupon the penitent man in the prophet (or rather the penitent prophet), desiring God to pardon his sins, 'Thou desirest no sacrifice though I would give it,' says he, 'but Thou delightest not in burnt-offering. The sacrifices of God are a contrite spirit: a broken and humbled heart, O God, Thou wilt not despise.' [3]   Behold, here he says, God will have sacrifices, and God will have no sacrifices. He will have no slaughtered beast, but He will have a contrite heart. So in that

[1] Exod. xxii. 20.   [2] Ps. xvi. 2.   [3] Ps. li. 16, 17.

which He denied was implied that which He desired. The prophet then saying He will not have such, why do fools think He will, as delighting in them? If He would not have had such sacrifices as He desired (whereof a contrite heart is one) to have been signified in those others (wherein they thought He delighted), He would not have given any command concerning them in Leviticus. But there are set times appointed for their changes, lest men should think He took pleasure in them, or accepted them of us otherwise than as signs of the others. Therefore, says another psalm: 'If I be hungry I will not tell thee, for all the world is mine, and all that therein is: will I eat the flesh of bulls or drink the blood of goats?'[1] as if He should say, If I would, I would not beg them of thee, having them in My power. But then adds He their signification: 'Offer praise to God, and pay thy vows to the Most High; and call upon Me in the day of trouble, and I will deliver thee, and thou shalt glorify Me.'[2] And in another prophet: 'Wherewith shall I come before the Lord and bow myself before the high God? Shall I come before Him with burnt offerings, and with calves of a year old? Will the Lord be pleased with thousands of rams, or with ten thousand rivers of oil? Shall I give my first-born for my transgression, even the fruit of my body for the sin of my soul? He has shown thee, O man, what is good, and what the Lord requires of thee save to do justice and to love mercy, and to humble thyself to walk with thy God.'[3]

In these words are the two sacrifices kept distinct; and it is shown that God does not require those sacrifices, in which are signified the other sacrifices which He does require. As the Epistle entitled to the Hebrews says: 'To do good and to distribute forget not; for with such sacrifices God is pleased':[4] and as it is elsewhere: 'I will have mercy and not sacrifice.'[5] This shows that the external sacrifice is but a type of the better, and that which men call a sacrifice is the sign of the true one. And mercy is a true sacrifice, whereupon it is said as before: 'With such sacrifices God is pleased.' Wherefore the precepts concerning sacrifices in the tabernacle and the temple all have reference to the love of God and our neighbour. For in these two, as is said,[6] is contained all the law and the prophets.

CHAPTER VI

Of the true and perfect sacrifice

EVERY work therefore tending to effect our beatitude by an holy conjunction with God is a true sacrifice. Compassion shown

---

[1] Ps. l. 12, 13.   [2] Ps. l. 14, 15.   [3] Mic. vi. 6-8.   [4] Heb. xiii. 16.
[5] Hos. vi. 6.   [6] Matt. xxii. 40.

upon a man, and not for God's sake, is no sacrifice. For a sacrifice (though offered by a man) is a divine thing, and so the ancient Latinists term it: whereupon a man, consecrated wholly to God's name, to live to Him and die to the world, is a sacrifice. For this is mercy shown upon himself. And so is it written: 'Pity thine own soul, and please God.'[1] And when we chastise our body by abstinence, if we do it as we should, not making our members instruments of iniquity but of God's justice, it is a sacrifice, where-unto the apostle exhorts us, saying: 'I beseech you therefore, brethren, by the mercies of God, that you give up your bodies, a living sacrifice, holy and acceptable unto God, which is your reasonable serving of God.'[2] If therefore the body being but servant and instrument unto the soul, being rightly used in God's service, be a sacrifice, how much more is the soul one when it relies upon God, and being inflamed with His love loses all form of temporal concupiscence, and is framed according to His most excellent figure, pleasing Him by participating of His beauty? This the apostle adjoins in these words: 'And fashion not your-selves like this world, but be ye changed in newness of heart, that ye may prove what is the good will of God, and what is good, acceptable, and perfect.'[3] Wherefore seeing the works of mercy being referred unto God (be they done to ourselves or our neigh-bours) are true sacrifices, and that their end is nothing but to free us from misery and make us happy by that God (and none other) of whom it is said: 'It is good for me to adhere unto the Lord,'[4] truly it follows that all the whole and holy society of the redeemed and sanctified city be offered unto God by that great Priest who gave up His life in so mean a form for us to make us members of so great a head. This form He offered, and herein was He offered; in this is He our priest, our mediator, and our sacrifice. Now therefore the apostle, having exhorted us to give up our bodies a living sacrifice, pure and acceptable, to God, namely our reasonable serving of God, and not to fashion ourselves like this world, but be changed in newness of heart, that we might prove what is the will of God, and what is good, acceptable, and perfect, all which sacrifice we are: 'For I say,' quoth he, 'through the grace that is given to me, to every one among you, that no man presume to understand more than is meet to understand; but that he understand according to sobriety, as God hath dealt to every man the measure of faith. For as we have many members in one body, and all members have not one office: so we being many are one body in Christ, and every one one another's members, having divers gifts according to the grace that is given us,' etc.[5] This is the Christian's sacrifice. We are one body with Christ, as the Church celebrates in the

---

[1] Ecclus. xxx. 24.   [2] Rom. xii. 1.   [3] Rom. xii. 2.
[4] Ps. lxxiii. 28.   [5] Rom. xii. 3–6.

sacrament of the altar, so well known to the faithful, wherein is shown that in that oblation the Church is offered.

CHAPTER VII

That the good angels do so love us that they desire we should worship God only and not them

WORTHILY are those blessed immortals placed in those celestial habitations, rejoicing in the participation of their Creator, being firm, certain, and holy by His eternity, truth, and bounty: because they love us mortal wretches with a zealous pity, and desire to have us immortally blessed also, and will not have us sacrifice to them, but to Him to whom they know both us and themselves to be sacrifices. For with them we are one city of God whereof the psalm speaks: 'Glorious things are spoken of thee, thou city of God': [1] part whereof is a pilgrim still with us, and part with them assisting us. From that eternal city where God's unchangeable will is all their law: and from that supernal court (for there are we cared for) by the ministry of the holy angels was that holy scripture brought down unto us, that says: 'He that sacrifices to any but God alone, shall be rooted out.' [2] This scripture, this precept is confirmed unto us by so many miracles, that it is plain enough to whom the blessed immortals, so loving us, and wishing us to be as themselves, would have us to offer sacrifice.

CHAPTER VIII

Of the miracles whereby God has confirmed His promises in the minds of the faithful by the ministry of His holy angels

I SHOULD seem tedious in enumerating the miracles of too abstruse antiquity; with which miraculous tokens God assured His promises to Abraham, 'that in his seed should all the earth be blessed,' [3] made many thousand years ago. Is it not miraculous for Abraham's barren wife to bear a son, she being of age both past childbirth and conception; [4] that in the same Abraham's sacrifices, the fire came down from heaven between them as they lay divided; [5] that

[1] Ps. lxxxvii. 3.   [2] Exod. xxii. 20.   [3] Gen. xxii. 18.
[4] Gen. xviii. 9–14; xxi. 1–3.   [5] Gen. xv. 17.

the angels, whom he entertained in men's shapes, foretold him
the destruction of Sodom; and from them had God's promise for
a son; [1] and by the same angels was certified of the miraculous
delivery of his brother Lot, a little before the burning of Sodom; [2]
whose wife being turned into a statue of salt for looking back,[3] is
a great mystery, that none being on the road to freedom should cast
his eyes behind him? And what stupendous miracles did Moses
effect in Egypt by God's power for the freedom of God's people!
There the magicians of Pharaoh (the king of Egypt that held God's
people in thrall) were suffered to work some wonder, to be defeated
all the more strikingly; for they wrought by charms and enchant-
ments (the delights of the devils); but Moses had the power of the
God of heaven and earth (to whom the good angels do serve), and
therefore must needs be victor. And the magicians failing in the
third plague, strangely and mystically did Moses effect the other
seven following; and then the hard-hearted Egyptians and Pharaoh
yielded God's people their passage. And by and by when he
repented and pursued them, the people of God passed through
the waters (standing for them as ramparts) and the Egyptians
lost all their lives in the depth, the waters then returning. Why
should I rehearse the ordinary miracles that God showed them in
the desert—the sweetening of the bitter waters by casting wood
therein, the manna from heaven, that rotted when one gathered
more than a set measure, yet gathering two measures the day before
the sabbath (on which they might gather none) it never putrefied
at all; how their desire to eat flesh was satisfied with fowls that fell
in the tents, sufficient (O miracle) for all the people, even till they
loathed them; how the holding up of Moses' hands in form of a
cross, and his prayer, caused that not a Hebrew fell in the fight:
and how the seditious, separating themselves from the society
ordained by God, were by the earth swallowed up alive, to invisible pains, for a visible example: how the rock burst forth into
streams, being struck with Moses' rod, and the serpents' deadly
bitings, being sent amongst them for a just plague, were cured by
beholding a brazen serpent set up upon a pole, herein being both a
present help for the hurt, and a type of the future destruction of
death by death in the passion of Christ crucified; the brazen
serpent, being for this memory reserved, and afterwards by the
seduced people adored as an idol, Hezekiah, a religious king, to
his great praise brake in pieces.[4]

[1] Gen. xviii. 10.   [2] Gen. xix. 15–17.   [3] Gen. xix. 26.
                    [4] 2 Kings xviii. 4.

CHAPTER IX

Of unlawful arts concerning the devils' worship, whereof Porphyry approves some, and disallows others

THESE, and multitudes more, were done to commend the worship of one God unto us, and to prohibit all other. And they were done by pure faith and confident piety, not by charms and conjurations, tricks of damned curiosity, by magic, or (which is in name worse) by *goetia* or (to call it more honourable) theurgy, which those who seek to distinguish (which none can) say that the damnable practices of all such as we call witches belong to *goetia*, but the effects of theurgy they hold laudable. But indeed they are both damnable, and bound to the rites of false filthy devils, instead of angels. Porphyry indeed promises a certain purging of the soul to be done by theurgy, but he falters and is ashamed of his text. He denies utterly that one may have any recourse to God by this art. Thus floats he between the surges of sacrilegious curiosity and honest philosophy; for, now he condemns it as doubtful, perilous, prohibited, and gives us warning of it; and by and by, giving way to the praisers of it, he says it is useful in purging the soul, not in the intellectual part, that apprehends the truth of intelligibilities abstracted from all bodily forms, but the spiritual, that apprehends all from corporal objects. This he says may be prepared by certain theurgic consecrations called *teletae*, to receive a spirit or angel, by which it may see the gods. Yet confesses he that these theurgic *teletae* profit not the intellectual part a jot, to see the one God and receive apprehensions of truth. Consequently, we see what sweet apparitions of the gods these *teletae* can cause, when there can be no truth discerned in these visions. Finally he says the reasonable soul (or, as he likes better to say, the intellectual) may mount aloft, though the spiritual part have no theurgic preparation: and if the spiritual do attain such preparation, yet it is thereby not made capable of eternity. For though he distinguish angels and demons, placing these in the air, and those in the sky, and give us counsel to get the amity of a demon whereby to mount from the earth after death, professing no other means for one to attain the society of the angels, yet does he (in manner, openly) profess that a demon's company is dangerous: saying that the soul being plagued for it after death, abhors to adore the demons that deceive it. Nor can he deny that this theurgy (which he commends as the league between the gods and angels) deals with those devilish powers, which either envy the soul's purgation, or else are servile to them that envy it. A Chaldaean (says he), a good man, complained that all his endeavour to purge his soul was frustrate, because a great artist in these matters, envying him this goodness, adjured the powers he was to deal with by holy invocations, and bound them from granting him any of his requests. So he bound them (says he), and this other could not loose them. Here now is a plain proof that theurgy is an art effecting evil as well as good both with the gods and men: and that the gods are wrought upon by the same passions and perturbations that Apuleius lays upon the devils and men alike: who notwithstanding (following Plato in that), acquits the gods from all such matters by their height of place, being celestial.

CHAPTER X

Of theurgy that falsely promises to cleanse the mind by the invocation of devils

BEHOLD now this other (and they say more learned) Platonist Porphyry, with his own theurgy makes all the gods subject to passion and perturbation. For they may by his doctrine be so terrified from purging souls by those that envy their purgation, that he that means evil may chain them for ever from benefiting him that desires this good (and that by the same theurgic art) so that the other can never free them from this fear and attain their helps, though he use the same art. Who sees not that this is the devils' clear deceit save he that is their hapless slave, and quite barred from the grace of the Redeemer? If the good gods had any hand herein, surely the good desire of a man that would purge his soul should vanquish him that would hinder it. Or if the gods were just and would not allow him it for some guilt of his, yet it should be their own choice, not their being terrified by that envious party, nor (as he says) the fear of greater powers that should cause this denial. And it is strange that that good Chaldean that sought to be thus purged by theurgy could not find some higher god, that could either terrify the others worse, and so force them to further him, or take away their terror, and so set them free to benefit him: if we are to suppose that this good theurgic lacked the rites wherewith to purge these gods from fear first ere they came to purge his soul. For why should he call a greater god to terrify them, and not to purge them? Or is there a god that hears the malicious, and so frights the lesser gods from doing good, and none to hear the well-minded, and to set them at liberty to do good again? O goodly theurgy! O rare purgation of the mind, where impure envy does more than pure devotion! No, no, avoid these damnable trapfalls of the devil; fly to the healthful and firm truth. For whereas the workers of these sacrilegious expiations do behold (as he says) some admirable shapes of angels, or gods, as if their spirits were purged: why if they do, note the apostle's reason: 'For Satan transformeth himself into an angel of light.' [1]

These are his apparitions, seeking to chain men's poor deluded souls in fallacies and lying ceremonies, wresting them from the true and only purging and perfecting doctrine of God: and as it is said of Proteus, he turns himself to all shapes,[2] pursuing us as an enemy, fawning on us as a friend, and subverting us in both shapes.

CHAPTER XI

Of Porphyry's epistle to Anebos of Egypt desiring of him instruction in the several kinds of demons

TRULY Porphyry showed more wit in his epistle to Anebos of Egypt, where between learning and instructing he both unmasks and subverts all these sacrileges. Therein he reproves all the demons, that because of their foolishness do draw (as he says) the humid vapours up unto them, and therefore are not in the sky but in the air, under the moon, and in the moon's body. Yet dares he not ascribe all the vanities that stuck in his mind to all the devils: for some of them he (as others do) calls good, whereas before he had called them all fools. And much is his wonder why the gods should love sacrifices, and be compelled to grant men's suits. And if the gods and demons be distinguished as incorporeal and corporal, why should the sun, moon, and other stars visible in heaven (whom he avouches to be bodies) be called gods? And if they be gods, how can some be good and some evil? Or, being bodies, how can they be joined with the gods that have no bodies? Furthermore, he makes doubts whether the soul of a diviner, or a worker of strange things, or an external spirit, cause the effect.

But he conjectured on the spirits' side the rather of the two, because they may be bound, or loosed, by herbs and stones in this or that strange operation. And some, therefore, he says, do hold a kind of spirits, that properly hear us, of a subtle nature and a changeable form, counterfeiting gods, demons, and dead souls; and those are agents in all good or bad effects. But they never further man in good actions, as not knowing them, but they do entangle and hinder the progress of virtue by all means. They

---

[1] 2 Cor. xi. 14.   [2] Virg. *Georg.* iv. 411.

are rash and proud lovers of fumigations, and taken easily by
flattery. Such are the characteristics of those spirits that come
externally into the soul and delude man's senses sleeping and
waking: yet all this he does not affirm, but conjectures or doubts, or
says that others affirm; for it was hard forsooth for so great a philosopher to know all the devils' vileness fully, and to accuse it freely,
of which no Christian, however ignorant,[1] doubts the existence,
but which he freely detests. Perhaps he was afraid to offend
Anebos, to whom he wrote, as a great priest of such sacrifices, and
the other admirers of those things as appurtenances of the divine
honours. Yet makes he, as it were, an inquisition into those things
which, being well pondered, will prove attributes to none but
malignant spirits. He asks why, the best gods being invoked, the
worst are commanded to fulfil men's pleasures; why they will not
hear the prayers of one that is stained with harlotry, whereas they
have such incestuous contracts amongst themselves, as examples
to others; why they forbid their priests the use of living creatures
lest they should be polluted by their smells, whereas they are invoked and invited with continual suffumigations and smells of
sacrifices; why the soothsayer is forbidden to touch the carcass,
whereas their religion depends wholly upon carcasses; and why
the charmer threatens not the gods, or demons, or dead men's souls,
but the sun or the moon, or such celestial bodies, to fetch the truth
out by this so false a terror. He will threaten to knock down the
sky, and such impossibilities, so that the gods being, like foolish
babes, afraid of this ridiculous terror, may do as they are charged.
He says further that one Charemon, one of the sacred (or rather
sacrilegious) priests, has written that the Egyptian mystery of Isis,
or her husband Osiris, is most powerful in compelling the gods to
do men's pleasures, when the invoker threatens to reveal it, or to
cast abroad the members of Osiris, if they do not dispatch his
bidding quickly. That these idle fond threats of man, yea unto
the gods and heavenly bodies, the sun, the moon, etc., should have
that violent effect to force them to perform what men desire, Porphyry justly wonders at; nay rather, under colour of one admiring
and inquiring, he shows these to be the actions of those spirits
whom he describes, under shadow of relating others' opinions, to
be such deceitful counterfeiters of the other gods, though they are
devils themselves without dissembling. As for the herbs, stones,
creatures, sounds, words, characters, and constellations used in
drawing the powers of those effects, all these he ascribes to the
devils' delight in deluding and abusing the souls that serve and
observe them.

So that Porphyry either in a true doubt describes such of those
acts as can have no reference to those powers by which we must

[1] Lat. *anicula Christiana.*—ED.

aim at eternity, but which prove themselves to be peculiar to the
false devils'; or else he desires by his humility in inquiring, not by
his contentious opposing, to draw this Anebos (that was a great priest
in those ceremonies, and thought he knew much) unto a due speculation of these things, and to detect their detestable absurdity unto
him.   Finally in the end of his epistle he desires to be informed
what doctrine of beatitude the Egyptians held.   But yet he affirms
that such as converse with the gods and trouble the deity about the
discovery of thieves, buying of lands, marriages, bargains, or such
like, seem all in a wrong way to wisdom.   And the gods they use
herein, though they tell them true in other matters, yet in teaching
them nothing concerning beatitude, are neither gods nor good
demons, but either false ones, or all is but a figment of man.   But
because these arts effect many things beyond all human capacity,
what remains but firmly to believe, and credibly to affirm, that
such wonders (in word or deeds) as have no reference to the con-
firmation of their worship of that one God (to whom to adhere,
as the Platonists affirm, is the only beatitude) are only seducements
of the deceitful fiends, to hinder man's progress to virtue, and
solely to be avoided and discovered by true zeal and piety?

CHAPTER XII

Of the miracles that God works by His angels' ministry

BUT all miracles (done by angels or whatever divine power), confirming the true adoration of one God unto us (in whom only we
are blessed), we believe truly are done by God's power working in
these immortals that love us in true piety.   Hear not those that
deny that the invisible God works visible miracles.   Is not the
world a miracle, yet visible, and of His making?   Nay, all the
miracles done in this world are less than the world itself, the heaven
and earth and all therein; yet God made them all, and after a
manner that man cannot conceive nor comprehend.   For though
these visible miracles of nature be now no more admired, yet
ponder them wisely, and they are more admirable than the strangest:
for man is a greater miracle than all that he can work.   Wherefore
God that made heaven and earth (both miracles) scorns not as yet
to work miracles in heaven and earth, to draw men's souls that
yet desire visibilities, unto the worship of His invisible essence.
But where and when He will do this, His unchangeable will only
can declare: at whose disposing all time past has been, and all to
come is.   He moves all things in time, but time moves not Him,
nor knows future effects otherwise than present.   Nor hears He

our prayers otherwise than He foresees them ere we pray: for when His angels hear them, He hears in them, as in His true temples not made with hands, and so does He hold all things effected temporally in His saints, by His eternal disposition.

CHAPTER XIII

How the invisible God has often made Himself visible, not as He is really but as we could be able to comprehend His sight

NOR hurts it His invisibility to have appeared visibly oftentimes unto the patriarchs. For as the impression of a sound of a sentence in the intellect is not the same that the sound was: so the shape wherein they conceived God's invisible nature was not the same that He is: yet was He seen in that shape, as the sentence was conceived in that sound, for they knew that no bodily form could contain God. He talked with Moses, yet Moses entreated Him: 'If I have found favour in Thy sight, show me Thy face, that I may know Thee.' [1] And seeing it behoved the law of God to be given from the mouths of angels with terror, not to a few of the wisest, but to a whole nation, great things were done in the mount before the said people, the law being given through one, and all the rest beholding the admirable and strange things that were done. For the Israelites had not that confidence in Moses that the Lacedaemonians had in Lycurgus, to believe that he had his laws from Jove or Apollo. For when that law was given the people that enjoins the worship of one God, in the view of the same people were strange proofs shown (as many as God's providence thought fit) to prove that that was the Creator whom they His creatures ought to serve in that law.

CHAPTER XIV

How but one God is to be worshipped for all things, temporal and eternal: all being in the power of His providence

BUT the true religion of all mankind (referred to the people of God) as well as of one, has had increase, and received more and more perfection, by the succession and continuance of time, drawing from temporalities to eternity, and from things visible to the

---

[1] Exod. xxxiii. 13.

invisible: so that even then when the promise of visible rewards
was given, the worship of one God alone was taught, lest mankind
should be drawn to any false worship for those temporal blessings:
for he is mad that denies that all that men or angels can do unto
man is in the hand of the one Almighty.   Plotinus the Platonist disputes of providence,[1] proving it to be derived from the high ineffable and beauteous God and to reach unto the meanest creature
on earth, by the beauty of the flowers and leaves: all of which
things, so transitory and momentary, could not have their peculiar,
richly assorted beauties, but from that intellectual and immutable
beauty forming them all.   This our Saviour showed, saying:
'Learn how the lilies of the field do grow: they labour not, neither
spin, yet say I unto you that even Solomon in all his glory was not
arrayed like one of these: wherefore if God so clothe the grass of
the field which is to-day and to-morrow is cast into the oven, shall
not He do much more unto you, O you of little faith?'[2]   Wherefore if the mind of man be weak, and clogged with earthly desires,
and longings for those things that are so frail and contemptible
in comparison with the blessings celestial (though necessaries for
this present life), yet does it well to desire them at the hands of one
God alone, and not to depart from His service to obtain them elsewhere, though they may soonest attain His love by neglect of such
trifles, and with that love obtain all necessaries both for this life
and the other.

CHAPTER XV

Of the holy angels that minister to God's providence

IT pleased the divine providence therefore so to dispose of the
times, that as I said, and we read in Acts,[3] the law should be
given by the angels' mouths concerning the worship of the true
God, wherein God's person (not in His proper substance, which
corruptible eyes can never see, but by certain indications of a
creature for the Creator) would appear, and speak syllabically in a
man's voice, unto us: even He that in His own nature speaks not
corporally but spiritually, not sensibly but intelligibly, not temporally, but (as I may say) eternally, neither beginning speech,
nor ending: whom His blessed and immortal messengers and
ministers heard not with ears, but more purely with intellects;
and hearing His commands after an ineffable manner, they in-

---

[1] *Ennead* iii. 2, 13.   [2] Matt. vi. 28–30.   [3] Acts vii. 53.

stantly and easily frame them to be delivered us in a visible and sensible manner. This law was given (as I say) in a division of time, first having all earthly promises that were types of the goods eternal, which many celebrated in visible sacred rites, but few understood. But there the true religious worship of one God alone is directly and plainly taught and testified, not by one of a crowd of gods, but by Him that made heaven and earth, and every soul and spirit that is not Himself: for He makes them that are made; and they have need of his help that made them in all their existence.

CHAPTER XVI

Whether in this question of beatitude we must trust those angels that refuse the divine worship, and ascribe it all to one God, or those that require it to themselves

WHAT angels shall we trust then in this business of eternal bliss? Those that require mortal men to offer them sacrifice and honours, or those that say it is all due unto God the Creator, and teach us most piously to give it Him above all, as one in the contemplation of whom alone we may attain this happiness? For the sight of God is a sight of such beauty, and worthy of such love, that Plotinus did not doubt to call him that lacked this unhappy, had he never such store of goods besides. Seeing then that some angels resign all this religious worship to Him, and some would have it themselves; the first refusing all part of it, and the second not hesitating to rob Him of part of it: let the Platonists, theurgics (or rather periurgics, for so may all those arts be fitly termed), or any other philosophers, answer which we should follow. Nay, let all men answer that have any use of natural reason, and say whether we shall sacrifice to these gods or angels that exact it, or to Him only to whom they bid us, that forbid it both to themselves and the others. If neither of them did any miracles, but the one side demanded sacrifice, and the others said: 'No. God must have all,' then ought piety to discern between the pride of the one and the virtue of the other. Nay, I will say more. If these that do claim sacrifice should work upon men's hearts with wonders, and those that forbid it and stand all for God should not have power at all to work the like, yet their part should gain more by reason, than the others' by sense. But seeing that God, to confirm His truth, has by their ministry that debase themselves for His honour wrought more great, clear, and certain miracles than the others,

lest they should draw weak hearts unto their false devotion by in-
veigling their senses with amazements; who is so grossly stupid
as not to choose to follow the truth, seeing it confirmed with more
miraculous proofs? For the recorded miracles of the pagan gods
(I speak not of such as time and nature's secret causes by God's
providence have produced beyond custom, as monstrous births,
sights in the air and earth, fearful only, or hurtful also, all which
the devils' subtlety persuaded the world they both procured and
cured), I mean such miracles as were their evident acts, as the removal of the gods that Aeneas brought from Troy from place to
place of their own accord; Tarquin's cutting of a whetstone; the
Epidaurian serpents accompanying Aesculapius in his transporta-
tion to Rome; the drawing on of the ship that brought Berecynthia's
statue from Phrygia (being otherwise not to be moved by so huge
strength of men and beasts) by one woman with her girdle, in
testimony of her chastity; and the carrying of water from Tiber
in a sieve by a vestal, thereby acquitting herself from an accusation
of adultery—neither these, nor such as these, are comparable to
those done in the presence of the people of God, either for rarity or
greatness. How much less then the strange effects of those arts
which the pagans themselves did legally prohibit, namely, of
magic and theurgy, many whereof are mere *deceptiones visus*, and
flat falsehoods indeed, as the fetching down of the moon, till (says
Lucan)[1] she spume upon such herbs as they desire! Now though
some in their art seem to come near to some of the saints' wondrous deeds, yet whoso considereth the end for which they are
wrought discerneth the latter ones far to excel the first. For
as for the multitude of their gods, the more sacrifices they desire,
the fewer they deserve. But our sacrifices do but prove unto us
one God, that needs no such, as He has shown both by His holy
writ and the whole abolishment of these ceremonies afterwards.
If therefore these angels require sacrifice, then are those their
betters that require none, but refer all to God: for herein they show
their true love to us, that they desire not our subjection to them
by sacrifice, but unto Him in contemplation of whom is their
felicity, and desire to see us joined to Him from whom they never
are separate. But suppose the other angels that seek sacrifices for
many and not for one only, would not have them for themselves,
but for the gods they are under; yet for all this are the others to be
preferred before them, as being under God alone, to whom only
they refer all religion, and to none other; while the others in no way
dare to forbid this God all worship, to whom the former ascribe
all. But if they be neither good angels nor gods (as their proud
falseness proves), but wicked devils, desiring to share divine honours
with that one glorious God, what greater aid can we have against

[1] *Phars.* vi. 506.

them than to serve that one God, whom those good angels serve, that charge us to sacrifice not to them but unto Him, to whom ourselves ought to be a sacrifice.

CHAPTER XVII

Of the ark of the testament and the miracles wrought to confirm this law and promise

THE law of God, given by the angels, commanding the worship of one God, and forbidding all other, was put up in an ark called the ark of the testament: whereby is meant not that God (to whose honour all this was done) was included in that place or any other, because He gave them certain answers from the place of the ark, and showed miracles also from thence; but that the testament of His will was there—the law (that was written upon tables of stone and put in the ark) being there; which being in their travel carried in a tabernacle, gave it also the name of the tabernacle of the testament, which the priests with due reverence did bear. And their sign was a pillar of a cloud in the day, which shone in the night like fire: and when it removed, the tents removed, and where it stayed, they rested.[1]   Moreover, the law had many more great testimonies given for it, besides what I have said, and besides those that were uttered out of the place where the ark stood: for when they and the ark were to pass Jordan into the land of promise, 'The waters cleft, and left them a dry way.' [2]   Moreover having borne it seven times about the first city that was their foe, and (as the land was then) slave to paganism, 'The walls fell flat down without ruin or battery.' [3]   And when they had gotten the land of promise, and the ark (for their sins) was taken from them, and placed by the victor idolater in their chief god's temple and locked fast in, coming again the next day, they found their idol thrown down and broken all to pieces: and being terrified by these prodigies (besides a more shameful scourge) they restored the ark to those they took it from.   And how?   They set it upon a carriage yoking kine in it (or heifers) whose calves they took from them, and so (in trial of the divine power) turned them loose to go whither they would.   They without guide came straight to the Hebrews, never turning again for the bleating of their calves, and so brought home this great mystery to those that honoured it.[4]   These and such like are nothing to God, but much to the terror and instruction of man.

[1] Exod. xiii. 21; xl. 36-8; Num. ix. 15, 16.
[2] Joshua iii. 16, 17.   [3] Joshua vi. 12-20.   [4] 1 Sam. v, vi.

For if the philosophers (chiefly the Platonists) that held the providence of God to extend to everything great and small, by the
proof drawn from the several forms and beauties of herbs and
flowers as well as living creatures, were held to be more wisely
persuaded than the rest: how much more do these things testify
the deity, coming to pass at the hour when this religion was
taught, which commands the adoration of one God, the only loving
and beloved God, blessing all, limiting these sacrifices in a certain
time, and then changing them into better by a better priest; and
testifying hereby that He desires not these but what they signify,
not to have any honour from them either, but that we by the fire
of His love might be inflamed to adore Him, and adhere unto
Him, which is all for our own good, and adds nothing to His!

CHAPTER XVIII

*Against such as refuse to believe the scriptures concerning those
miracles shown to God's people*

WILL any one say there were no such miracles, but that all is lies?
He that says so and takes away the authority of scripture herein,
may as well say that the gods respect not men.   For they had no
means but miracles to attain men's worship, wherein their pagan
stories show how far they had power to prove themselves always
rather wonderful than useful.   But in this our work (whereof this is
the tenth book) we deal not against atheists, nor such as exclude the
gods from dealing in man's affairs, but with such as prefer their
gods before our God, the founder of this glorious city; knowing that
He is the Creator invisible and immutable of this visible and changeable world, and the giver of beatitude, from none of His creatures,
but from Himself entirely.   For His true prophet says: 'It is good
for me to adhere unto the Lord.'[1]   The philosophers contend
about the final good to which all the pains man takes has relation.
But he said not, 'It is good for me to be wealthy, honourable or
invested a king': or (as some of the philosophers shamed not to say)
'It is good for me to have fullness of bodily pleasure': or (as the
better sort said) 'It is good for me to have virtue of mind': but he
said: 'It is good for me to adhere unto God.'   This had He taught
him, unto whom alone both the angels and the testimony of the
law do teach all sacrifice to be due: so that the prophet became a
sacrifice unto Him, being inflamed with His intellectual fire, and
holding a fruition of His ineffable goodness in a holy desire to be
united to Him.   Now if these men of many gods in the discourse

[1] Ps. lxxiii. 28.

of their miracles give credence to their histories and books of magic, or (to speak to please them) theurgical books, why should not the scripture be believed in these other, which are as far beyond the rest as He is above the others, to whom only these our books teach all religious honour to belong?

CHAPTER XIX

The reason for that visible sacrifice that the true religion commands us to offer unto one God

BUT as for those that think visible sacrifices pertain to others, and invisible to Him, as only invisible, as greater to the greater, and better to the better (viz. the duties of a pure heart and a holy will), verily these men conceive not that the others are symbols of these, as the sounds of words are significations of things. Wherefore as in our praises and prayers to Him, we speak vocal words, but offer the contents of our hearts, even so we in our sacrifice know that we must offer thus visibly to none but Him to whom our hearts must be an invisible sacrifice. For then the angels and predominate powers do rejoice with us and further us with all their power and ability. But if we offer unto them, they are not willing to take it; and when they are personally sent down to men, they expressly forbid it. And this the scriptures testify. Some held that the angels were either to have adoration, or (that which we owe only to God) sacrifice: but they were forbidden, and taught that all was God's alone and lawfully given Him.[1] And those angels the saints did follow. Paul and Barnabas being in Lycaonia the people (for a miraculous cure) held them gods, and would have sacrificed unto them, but they humbly and piously denied it, and preached unto them that God in whom they believed.[2] But the wicked spirits do desire it just because they know it to be God's due alone. For (as Porphyry and others think) it is the divine honours not the smells of the offerings that they delight in. For those smells they have in plenty, and may procure themselves more if they list. So then these arrogant spirits desire not the smoke ascending from a body, but the honours given them from the soul, which they may deceive and domineer over, stopping man's way to God, and keeping him from becoming God's sacrifice, by offering unto other than God.

---

[1] Judges xiii. 15, 16; Rev. xxii. 8, 9.   [2] Acts xiv. 8-18.

CHAPTER XX

Of the only and true sacrifice, which the mediator between God and man became

WHEREFORE the true mediator, being in the form of a servant, made mediator between God and man, the man Christ Jesus, receiving sacrifices with His Father as God, yet in a servant's form chose rather to be one than to take any, lest some hereby should gather that one might sacrifice unto creatures. By this is He the Priest, offering and offerer. The true sacrament whereof is the Church's daily sacrifice: which, being the body of Him the Head, learns to offer itself by Him. The ancient sacrifices of the saints were all divers types of this also, this being figured in many and divers ways as one thing is told in many words, that it might be commended without tediousness. And to this great and true sacrifice all false ones gave place.

CHAPTER XXI

Of the power given to the devils to the greater glorifying of the saints, that have suffered martyrdom and conquered the airy spirits not by appeasing them but adhering to God

THE devils had a certain temporary power allowed them, whereby to excite such as they possessed against God's city, and both to accept sacrifices of the willing offerers, and to require them of the unwilling, yea even to extort them by violent plagues. Nor was this at all prejudicial, but very commodious for the Church, that the number of martyrs might be fulfilled, whom the city of God holds so much the dearer, because they spent their blood for it against the power of impiety. These now (if the Church admitted the word's use) we might worthily call our heroes. For this name came from ῞Ηρα, Juno, and therefore one of her sons (I know not which) was called Heros, the mystery being that Juno was queen of the air, where the heroes (the well-deserving souls) dwell with the demons. But ours (if we might use the word) should be called so for a contrary reason, namely, not for dwelling with the demons in the air, but for conquering those demons, those aerial powers, and in them, all that is called Juno; whom it was not for nothing that the poets made so envious, and so opposite to good men deified for their virtue. But unhappily Virgil gives way to her making her first to say: 'I am conquered by Aeneas,' [1] and then to bring in Helenus warning Aeneas, as his ghostly father, in these words:

> Junoni cane vota libens, dominamque potentem,
> Supplicibus supera donis . . . [2]

> Purchased great Juno's wrath with willing prayers
> And conquered her with humble gifts . . .

And therefore Porphyry (though not of himself) holds that a good god or genius never comes to a man till the bad be appeased: as if the bad were of more power than the other, seeing that the bad can hinder the good from working, and must be entreated to give them place, whereas the good can do no good unless the others will, and the others can do mischief despite the good. This is not the way of true religion. Our martyrs do not conquer Juno, that is, the airy powers that envy their virtues, in this fashion: our heroes (if I may say so) conquer Hera not by humble gifts but by divine virtues. Surely Scipio deserved the name of Africanus rather for conquering Africa than for begging or buying his honour of his foes.

CHAPTER XXII

From whence the saints have their power against the devils and their pure purgation of heart

GODLY men do expel the aerial powers, ejecting them from their possession by exorcisms, not by pacification: and they break their temptations by prayer not unto them but unto God against them. For the devils neither conquer nor chain any man but by the fellowship of sin. And so His name that took on Him humanity, and lived without sin, confounds them utterly. He is the priest and sacrifice of the remission of sins. He is the mediator between God and men, even the man Christ Jesus by whom we are purged of sin and reconciled unto God; for nothing severs man from God but sin, which not our merits but God's mercy wipes off us. It is His pardon, not our power, for all the power that is called ours is ours by His bounteous goodness; for we should think too well of our flesh, unless we lived under a pardon all the while we are in the flesh. Therefore have we our grace by a mediator, that being polluted by the flesh, we might be purged by the like flesh. This

[1] Virg. *Aen.* vii. 310.   [2] *Aen.* iii. 438-9.

grace of God wherein His great mercy is shown us, doth rule us
by faith in this life, and, after this life is ended, it will transport us
by that unchangeable truth unto most absolute perfection.

CHAPTER XXIII

Of the Platonists' principles in their purgation of the soul

PORPHYRY says that the oracles said that neither the sun's nor
moon's *teletae* could purge us, and consequently the *teletae* of no
gods can. For if the sun's and moon's (the chief gods) cannot,
whose is more powerful? But the oracles answered (quoth he)
that the 'beginnings'[1] may: lest one should think that upon the
denial of his power to the sun and moon some other god of the
multitude might do it. But what 'beginnings' he has as a Platonist we know. For he speaks of God the Father and God the
Son, called in Greek the Father's intellect: but of the Spirit not a
word, at least not a plain one, though what he means by a mean
between the two I cannot tell. For if he follow Plotinus in his
discourse of the three prime essences, and would have this third
the soul's nature, he should not have put it as the mean between the
Father and the Son. For Plotinus puts it after the Father's intellect; but Porphyry, in calling it the mean, interposes it between
them. And this he says as well as he could or would: but we call
it neither the Father's spirit alone, nor the Son's, but both. The
philosophers speak freely, never fearing to offend religious ears in
those incomprehensible mysteries; but we must regulate our words,
that we produce no impious error by our freedom of speech concerning these matters. Wherefore when we speak of God, we
neither talk of two principles, nor three, any more than we say there
are two Gods or three, though when we speak of the Father, the
Son, or the Holy Ghost, we say that each of these is God. Nor say
we with the Sabellian heretics, that He that is the Father is the
Son, and He that is the Holy Ghost is the Father and the Son, but
the Father is the Son's Father, and the Son the Father's Son, and
the Holy Spirit both the Father's and the Son's, but neither Father
nor Son. True then it is that man is purged by none but the
'beginning,' but this 'beginning' is by them too variably taken.

---

[1] *Principia,* ἀρχαί.

CHAPTER XXIV

*Of the true and only 'beginning' that purges and renews man's whole
nature*

BUT Porphyry, being slave to the malicious powers (of whom he
was ashamed, yet durst not accuse them), would not conceive that
Christ was the beginning, by whose incarnation we are purged,
but contemned Him in that flesh which He assumed to be a sacrifice
for our purgation, not apprehending the great mystery, because of
his devil-inspired pride, which Christ the good mediator by His
own humility subverted, showing Himself to mortals in that mortal
state which the false mediators lacked, and therefore insulted the
more men's wretched souls, falsely promising them succours from
their immortality. But our good and true mediator made it
apparent that it was not the fleshly substance but sin that is evil.
The flesh and soul of man may be both assumed, kept, and put off
without guilt, and be bettered at the resurrection. Nor is death,
though it be the punishment of sin (yet paid by Christ for our sins),
to be avoided by sin, but rather, if occasion serve, to be endured
for justice. For Christ's dying, and that not for His own sin, was
of force to procure the pardon of all other sins. That He was
the beginning this Platonist did not understand, else would he
have confessed His power in purgation. For neither the flesh nor
the soul was the beginning, but the Word, all-creating. Nor can
the flesh purge us by itself, but by that Word that assumed it,
when 'the Word became flesh and dwelt in us.' [1] For He, speaking
of the mystical eating of His flesh (and some, that understood it
not, being offended at it, and departing, saying: 'This is a hard
saying, who can hear it?' [2]) answered to those that stayed with
Him: 'It is the spirit that quickeneth, the flesh profiteth nothing.' [3]
Therefore the 'beginning,' having assumed flesh and soul, cleanses
both in the believer. And so when the Jews asked Him who He
was, He answered them that He was the beginning,[4] which our
flesh and blood, being encumbered with sinful corruption, can
never conceive, unless He, by what we were and were not, do
purify us. We were men, but just we were not. But in His incarnation was our nature; and that just, not sinful. This is the
mediation that helps up those that are fallen and down. This is
the seed that the angels sowed, by dictating the law wherein the
true worship of one God was taught, and this our mediator truly
promised.

---

[1] John i. 14.   [2] John vi. 60.   [3] John vi. 63.
          [4] John viii. 25.

CHAPTER XXV

*That all the saints in the old law, and other ages before it, were justified
only by the mystery and faith of Christ*

BY the faith of this mystery (together with godly life) might the
ancient saints of God also be justified, not only before the law was
given the Hebrews (for they lacked not God's instructions nor the
angels'), but also in the very times of the law, though they seemed
to have carnal promises in the types of spiritual things, it being
therefore called the Old Testament. For there were prophets
then that taught the promise as well as the angels; and one of them
was he whose sacred opinion of man's good I related before: 'It is
good for me to adhere unto God.' [1] In which psalm the two testa-
ments are distinguished. For first, he (seeing those earthly promises abound so to the ungodly) says his feet slipped, and that he
was almost down, as if he had served God in vain, seeing that
felicity that he hoped of God was bestowed upon the impious: and
that he laboured sore to know the reason of this, and was much
troubled until he entered into the sanctuary of God, and there
beheld their end whom he in error thought happy. But then as
he says, he saw them cast down in their exaltation, and destroyed
for their iniquity, and that all their pomp of temporal felicity was
become as a dream, leaving a man when he is awake frustrate of the
feigned joys he dreamed of. And because they showed themselves
great here upon earth, 'Lord,' says he, 'in Thy city Thou shalt make
their image be held as nothing.' But how good it was for him to
seek those temporalities at none but God's hands he shows, saying:
'I was as a beast before Thee, yet was I always with Thee; as a
beast not understanding.' For I should have desired such goods
as the wicked could not share with me: but seeing them abound
with goods, I thought I had served Thee to no end, whereas they
that hated Thee enjoyed such felicity. 'Yet was I always with
Thee.' I sought no other gods to beg these things of. And then
it follows: 'Thou hast holden me by my right hand, Thou hast
guided me by Thy will, and hast assumed me into glory.' As if all
that which he saw the wicked enjoy were belonging to the left hand,
though seeing it he had almost fallen. 'What have I in heaven but
Thee?' says he, 'and what have I upon earth but Thee?' Then
he doth check himself justly, for having so great a good in heaven
(as afterwards he understood), and yet begging so transitory, frail,
and earthy a thing of God here below: 'Mine heart faileth, and
my flesh, but God is the God of mine heart.' [2] A good failing, to
leave the lower and elect the loftier. And so in another psalm he

[1] Ps. lxxiii. 28.   [2] Ps. lxxiii. 20-6.

says: 'My soul longeth and fainteth for the courts of the Lord.' [1]
And in another: 'My heart fainteth for Thy saving health.' [2]
But having said both heart and flesh faint, he rejoined not, 'the
God of mine heart and flesh,' but, 'the God of my heart': for it is
by the heart that the flesh is cleansed, as the Lord says: 'Cleanse
that which is within, and then that which is without shall be clean.' [3]
Then he calls God his portion, not anything of God's but himself:
'God is the God of my heart, and my portion for ever'; because
amongst men's manifold choices, he chose Him only. 'For, behold,' says he, 'they that withdraw themselves from Thee shall
perish: Thou destroyest all them that go a-whoring from Thee'; [4]
that is, that make themselves prostitute unto many gods. And then
follows that which is the cause I have spoken all this of the psalm:
'As for me, it is good for me to adhere unto God,' not to withdraw
myself, nor to go a-whoring. And then is our adherence to God
perfect, when all is freed that should be freed. But as we are now,
we can only say what follows: 'I put my trust in the Lord God.'
'For hope that is seen is no hope; how can a man hope for that
which he seeth?' [5] says the apostle. 'But when we see not our
hope, then we expect with patience': wherein let us do that which
follows, each one according to his talent becoming an angel, a messenger of God, to declare His will and praise His gracious glory.
'That I may declare all Thy works,' says he, 'in the gates of the
daughter of Sion.' This is that glorious city of God, knowing and
honouring Him alone. This the angels declared, inviting us to inhabit it, and become fellow citizens in it. They like not that we
should worship them as our elected gods, but, with them, Him that
is God to us both; nor to sacrifice to them, but, with them, be a
sacrifice to Him. Doubtless then (if malice give men leave to see
the doubt cleared), all the blessed immortals that envy us not (and
if they did, they were not blessed), but rather love us, to have us
partners in their happiness, are far more favourable and beneficial
to us, when we join with them in sacrificing ourselves to the
adoration of the Father, the Son, and the Holy Spirit.

CHAPTER XXVI

*Of Porphyry's wavering between confession of the true God and
adoration of the devils*

METHINKS Porphyry (I know not how) is ashamed of his theurgical
acquaintance. He had some knowledge of good, but he durst not
defend the worship of one God against the adoration of many. He

[1] Ps. lxxxiv. 2.   [2] Ps. cxix. 81.   [3] Matt. xxiii. 26.
          [4] Ps. lxxiii. 27.   [5] Rom. viii. 24, 25.

said there were some angels that came down and taught theurgic practisers things to come: and others that declared the will of the Father upon earth, and His altitude and immensity. Now whether would he have us subject to those angels that declare the will of the Father upon earth, or unto Him whose will they declare? It is plain, he bids us rather imitate them than invoke them. So then we need not fear to give no sacrifices to these blessed immortals, but refer them all freely unto God. For without doubt that which they know to be due to that God only in whose participation they are blessed, they will never ascribe to themselves either by figures or significations. This is arrogance proper to the proud and miserable devils, from which the zeal of God's servants and such as are blessed by allegiance to Him ought to be far separate. To this blessed allegiance it behoves the angels to favour our attainment, not arrogating our subjection to them, but declaring unto us God, to whom we are united with them in allegiance. Why fearest thou now, philosopher, to censure these adverse powers, enemies both to the true God and true virtue? Thou saidst but now that the true angels, that reveal God's will, do differ from them that descend unto men that use theurgical conjurations. Why dost thou honour them so much as to say they teach divine things? How can that be, if they teach not the will of the Father? These now are they whom the malicious theurgic prevented from purging the soul of the good man; whom he could not loose, for all that they desired to be let loose and to do him some good. Doubtest thou yet that these are wicked devils? Or dost thou but dissemble for fear of offending the theurgics, whose curiosity inveigled thee so that they made thee believe they did thee a great pleasure in teaching thee this damnable cunning? Darest thou elevate that malicious plague (no power) that is a slave, and not a master of the envious, above the air into heaven, and by placing them among the starry gods do the stars themselves such foul disgrace?

CHAPTER XXVII

Of Porphyry exceeding Apuleius in impiety

How much more tolerable was the error of Apuleius, thy fellow sectary, who confessed (yet under constraint, for all his honouring them) that the devils under the moon only were subject to perturbation; thereby quitting the gods ethereal, both visible as the sun, moon, etc., and invisible also from these passions by all the arguments he could devise. Plato taught thee not this thine impiety, but thy Chaldee masters, to thrust up mortal vices amongst the ethereal powers, that the gods might instruct your theurgics in divinity; in which notwithstanding thou in thine intellectual life makest thyself excel. And so though thou dost regard theurgic art as not necessary for thee, but only for others that will be no philosophers; yet thou teachest it to repay thy masters, by seducing those to it that are no philosophers, and yet holding it of no use for a philosopher as thou thyself art. As a result all that fancy not the study of philosophy (which being hard to attain is professed by few) may by thine authority inquire out theurgics, and of them attain not an intellectual but a spiritual purification. And because the multitude of those do far exceed the philosophers, therefore more are drawn to thy unlawful magical masters than to Plato's schools; for this the unclean devils (those counterfeit ethereal gods whose messenger thou art become) promised thee that such as were purged by theurgy should never return to the Father, but inhabit above the air amongst the ethereal gods. But those whom Christ came to free from those devilish powers endure not this doctrine. For in Him have they most merciful purification of body, soul, and spirit. For therefore put He on man's nature entire without sin, to cleanse the whole man from sin. I wish thou hadst but known Him, and laid the cure of thyself upon Him rather than upon thine own frail weak virtue, or thy pernicious curiosity. For He whom your own oracles (as thou writest) acknowledged for holy and immortal, would never have deceived thee. Of whom also that famous poet says (poetically indeed) as referring to another person, but with a true reference to Him:

> Te duce si qua manent sceleris vestigia nostri
> Irrita perpetua solvent formidine terras,[1]

> Thy conduct all sin's marks from men shall clear,
> And quit the world of their eternal fear,

speaking of those traces of sin (if not sins) which by reason of our infirmity may have residence in those advanced in righteousness, and are cured by none but Christ, of whom the verse speaks. For Virgil spoke it not of himself, as he shows in the fourth verse of his eclogue, where he says:

> Ultima Cumaei venit jam carminis aetas,

> Time and Sibylla's verse are now new met,

plainly showing he had it from the Cumaean Sibyl. But those theurgics (or rather fiends in the shapes of gods) do rather putrefy than purify men's hearts by their false apparitions and deceitful illusion in change of forms. For how should they cleanse another,

[1] Virg. *Eclog*. iv. 13, 14.

being unclean themselves? Otherwise could they not be bound
by the charms of the envious, either to fear to infect, or to grudge
to bestow the empty good they seemingly were about to do. But
it suffices that thou confessest that neither the soul's intellectual
part is made pure, nor the spiritual (which is under the other part)
eternal, by theurgic art. But Christ promises this eternity, and
therefore (to thine own great wonder and deep grief) the world
flocks to Him. What avails it, that thou canst not deny that the
theurgics do often err and draw others into the same blindness,
and that it is a most plain error to become suppliant to those
angelical powers, and that then (as though thou hadst not spent
thy labour in vain in the former assertion) thou sendest such as
live not intellectually to the theurgics to be purged in the mind's
spiritual part?

CHAPTER XXVIII

*What persuasions blinded Porphyry from knowing Christ to be the true
wisdom*

THUS drawest thou men into most certain error, and art not ashamed
of it, being a professor of virtue and wisdom, which if thou truly re-
spectedest, thou wouldst have known Christ to be the virtue and wisdom of God the Father, and not have left His saving humility for the
pride of vain knowledge. Yet thou confessest that the virtue of
continence only, without theurgy, and with those *teletae* (thy fruitless studies) is sufficient to purge the soul spiritually. And once
thou saidst that the *teletae* elevate not the soul after death as they do
now, nor benefit the spiritual part of the soul after this life: and this
thou tossest and turnest, only, I think, to show thyself skilful in
those matters, and to please curious ears, or to make others curious.
But thou dost well to say this art is dangerous both for the laws
against it and for the performance of it. I would to God that
wretched men would hear thee in this, and leave the gulf, or never
come near it, for fear of being swallowed up therein. Ignorance
(thou sayest) and many vices annexed thereunto, are not purged
away by any *teletae* but only by the πατρικὸς νοῦς, the *mens,*
that knoweth His will. But that this is Christ thou believest not,
contemning Him for assuming flesh of a woman, for being crucified
like a felon, because thou thinkest it was fit that the eternal wisdom
should contemn those base things, and be embodied in a more
elevated substance. Aye, but He fulfils that word of the prophet:
'I will destroy the wisdom of the wise, and cast away the under-

standing of the prudent.'[1]   He does not destroy His wisdom in
such as He has given it unto, but that which others ascribe to
themselves, who have none of His.   And therefore the apostle
follows the prophetical testimony, thus: 'Where is the wise?
Where is the scribe?   Where is the disputer of the world?   Hath
not God made the wisdom of this world foolishness?   For seeing
the world by wisdom knew not God in the wisdom of God, it
pleased God by the foolishness of preaching to save them that
believe.   For the Jews require a sign, and the Grecians seek after
wisdom: but we preach Christ crucified, a stumbling-block unto
the Jews, and foolishness unto the Grecians.   But unto them
that are called, both Jews and Grecians, we preach Christ, the
power and wisdom of God: for the foolishness of God is wiser
than men, and the weakness of God is stronger than men.'[2]   This
now the wise and strong in their own conceit do account as foolish
and weak.   But this is the grace that cures the weak, and such as
boast not proudly of their false happiness, but humbly confess
their true misery.

CHAPTER XXIX

*Of the incarnation of our Lord Jesus Christ, which the impious
Platonists shame to acknowledge*

THOU teachest the Father and His Son, calling Him His intellect,
and One between them, by which we think thou meanest the Holy
Spirit, calling them after your manner three Gods.   Wherein
though your words be extravagant, yet you have a little glimpse of
what we must all rely upon.   But the incarnation of the unchangeable Son, that saves us all, and brings us all to that Other whom we
believe and rely upon, that you shame to confess.   You see your
true country (though a long, long way off) and yet you will not
see which way to get thither.   Thou confessest that the grace to
understand the deity is given to a very few.   Thou sayest not, few
like it, or few desire it; but, it is given to a few: fully confessing the
cause of it to lie in God's bounty, and not in man's sufficiency.
Now thou playest the true Platonist and speakest plainer, saying
that no man in this life can come to perfection of wisdom, yet
that God's grace and providence doth fulfil all that the understanding lacks, in the life to come.   Oh, hadst thou known God's
grace resident in Jesus Christ our Lord!   Oh, that thou couldest
have discerned His assuming of body and soul to be the greatest

[1] Isa. xxix. 14; 1 Cor. i. 19.   [2] 1 Cor. i. 20–5.

example of grace that ever was! But in vain do I speak to the dead. But as for those that esteem thee for that wisdom or curiosity in arts unlawful for thee to learn, perhaps this shall not be in vain. God's grace could never be more gracefully extolled than when the eternal Son of God came to put on man, and made man the means to bestow His love to all men; whereby all men might come to Him, who was so far above all men, being compared to them, immortal to mortal, unchangeable to changeable, just to unjust, and blessed to wretched. And because He has given us a natural desire to be eternally blessed, He remaining blessed, and putting on our nature to give us what we desired, taught us by suffering to contemn what we feared. But humility, humility a burden unfamiliar to your stiff necks, must be the means to bring you to credence of this truth. For can it seem incredible to you (that know such things, and ought to enjoin yourselves to believe it), can it seem incredible to you that God should assume man's nature and body? You give so much to the intellectual part of the soul (being but human) that you make it consubstantial with the Father's intellect, which you confess is His Son. How then is it incredible for that Son to assume one intellectual soul to save many of the rest by? Now nature teaches us the union of the body and the soul to the making of a full man. And this, if it were not ordinary, were more incredible than the other. For we may the more easily believe that a spirit may unite with a spirit (being both incorporeal, though the one human, and the other divine) than a corporal body with an incorporeal spirit. But are you offended at the strange childbirth of a virgin? This ought not to procure offence, but rather pious admiration, that He was so wonderfully born. Or dislike you that He changed His body after death and resurrection into a better, and so carried it up into heaven, being made incorruptible and immortal? This perhaps you will not believe, because Porphyry says so often in his work *De Regrussu Animae* (whence I have cited much), that the soul must leave the body entirely, ere it can be joined with God. But that opinion of his ought to be retracted, seeing that both he and you do hold such incredible things of the world's soul animating the huge mass of the bodily universe. For Plato teaches you to call the world a creature, a blessed one, and you would have it an eternal one. Well then, how shall it be eternally happy, and yet never put off the body, if your former rule be true? Besides, the sun, moon, and stars, you all say, are creatures, which all men both see and say also. But your skill (you think) goes further: it calls them blessed creatures, and eternal with their bodies. Why do you then forget or dissemble this, when you are invited to Christianity, which you otherwise teach and profess so openly? Why will you not leave your contradictory opinions for Chris-

tianity, if it be not because Christ came humbly, and you are all
pride? Of what quality the saints' bodies shall be after resurrection may well be a question amongst our greatest Christian doctors,
but we all hold they shall be eternal, and such as Christ showed in
His resurrection. But howsoever, seeing it is taught that they are
incorruptible, immortal, and no impediment to the soul's contemplation of God, and you yourselves say that they are celestial
bodies immortally blessed with their souls; why should you think
that we cannot be happy without leaving our bodies (to put forth a
reason for avoiding Christianity) but only as I said, because Christ
was humble, and you are proud? Are you ashamed to be corrected in your faults? A true character of a proud man. You
that were Plato's learned scholars, shame to become Christ's, who
by His spirit taught a fisher wisdom to say: 'In the beginning was
the Word, and the Word was with God, and God was the Word.
The same was in the beginning with God: all things were made by
it, and without it was made nothing that was made. In it was
life, and the life was the light of men. And the light shineth in the
darkness, and the darkness comprehended it not.' [1] Which beginning of Saint John's gospel a certain Platonist (as old holy
Simplicianus, afterwards Bishop of Milan, told me) said was fit to
be written in letters of gold, and set up to be read in the highest
places of all churches. But those proud fellows scorn to have God
their master, because 'the Word became flesh, and dwelt in us.'
So then it is not enough for these wretched to be sick and weak, but
they must exalt themselves in their sickest weakness, and shame
to take the only medicine that must cure them. Nor do they this
to rise, but to take a more wretched fall.

CHAPTER XXX

What opinions of Plato Porphyry confuted and corrected

IF it be unfit to correct aught after Plato, why does Porphyry correct
such, and so many of his doctrines? Sure it is that Plato held a
transmigration of men's souls into beasts: yet though Plato the
learned held thus, Porphyry his scholar justly refuted him, holding
that men's souls returned no more to the bodies they once left,
but into other human bodies. He was ashamed to believe the
other, lest a mother, living in a mule, should carry her son; but
never shamed to believe that the mother living in some other maid
might become her son's wife. But how far better were it to believe

[1] John i. 1–5.

the sanctified and true angels, the holy inspired prophets, Him that
was foretold as the coming Christ, and the blessed apostles, that
spread the gospel through the world? How far more honestly
might we believe that the souls return but once into their own
bodies, rather than so often into others? But as I said, Porphyry
improved upon this opinion much in subverting those bestial
transmigrations, and restraining them only to human bodies. He
says also that God gave the world a soul, that it, learning the badness of the corporal substance by inhabiting it, might return to the
Father, and desire no more to be joined to such contagion. Wherein though he err somewhat) for the soul is rather given to the body
to do good by, nor should it learn any evil but that it does evil), yet
herein he exceeds and corrects all the Platonists, in holding that
the soul being once purified and placed with the Father shall nevermore suffer worldly inconvenience. Herein he overthrows one
great Platonism, viz. that the dead are continually made of the
living and the living of the dead: proving that Platonical position
of Virgil false, where he says that the souls being purified and sent
unto the Elysian fields (under which fabulous name they figured
the joys of the blessed) were brought to drink of the river Lethe,
that is, to forget things past:

> Scilicet immemores supera ut convexa revisant,
> Rursus et incipiant in corpora velle reverti.[1]

> The thought of heaven is quite out of the brain.
> Now 'gins the wish to live on earth again.

Porphyry justly disliked this, because it were foolish to believe
that men, being in that life which the assurance of eternity alone
makes most happy, should desire to see the corruption of mortality,
as if the end of purification were to return to new pollution; for if
their perfect purification require a forgetfulness of all evils, and
that forgetfulness produce a desire in them to be embodied again,
and consequently to be again corrupted, truly the height of happiness shall be the cause of the greatest unhappiness, the perfection
of wisdom the cause of foolishness, and the fullness of purity
mother to impurity. Nor can the soul ever be blessed, being still
deceived in the blessedness. To be blessed it must be secure; yet
to be secure it must believe it shall be ever blessed, and that falsely,
because it will sometimes be wretched! And so if this joy must
needs arise from a false cause, how can it be truly joyful? This
Porphyry saw well, and therefore held that the souls once fully
purified returned immediately to the Father, lest they should be
any more polluted with the contagion of earthly and corruptible
desires.

---

[1] *Aen.* vi. 750–1.

CHAPTER XXXI

Against the Platonists holding the soul co-eternal with God

BUT altogether erroneous was that opinion of some Platonists regarding the continual and necessary revolution of souls from this or that, and to it again: which, if it were true, what would it profit us to know it, unless the Platonists will prefer themselves before us, because we know not, in this life, something which they themselves at their purest and wisest, in another and better life, are destined not to know (their supposed future happiness being based on a false belief)? If it be absurd and foolish to affirm this, then is Porphyry to be preferred before all those transporters of souls from misery to bliss, and back again: and if this be true, then here is a Platonist who disagrees with Plato for the better, and sees that which he saw not, not refusing to correct so great a master, but preferring truth before man. Why, then, do we not rather believe divinity in things above our capacity, which teaches us that the soul is not co-eternal with God, but created by God? The Platonists deny this, for this seemingly sufficient reason, that that which has not been for ever cannot be for ever. Aye, but Plato says plainly that both the world and the gods, made by that great God in the world, had a beginning, but shall have no end, but by the will of the Creator shall endure for ever. But they have a meaning for this. They say this beginning concerned not time but succession. For even as the foot (say they), if it had stood eternally in the dust, the footstep should have been eternal also, yet no man can doubt that some foot made this step; nor should the one be before the other, though one were made by the other: so the world and the gods therein have been ever co-eternal with the Creator's eternity, though by Him created. Well then, if the soul be and has been eternal, has the soul's misery been so also? Truly if there be something in the soul that had a temporal beginning, why might not the soul itself have a beginning also? And then the beatitude, being firmer by trial of evil, and destined to endure for ever, without question had a beginning, though it shall never have an end. So then the position that nothing can be endless that had a temporal beginning is quite overthrown. For the blessedness of the soul has a beginning, but it shall never have an end. Let our weakness therefore yield unto the divine authority, and let us trust those holy immortals in matter of religion, who desire no worship to themselves, knowing that all belongs to their and our God, and who do not command us to sacrifice but unto Him to whom (as I said often, and must say still) they and we both are a sacrifice to be offered by that Priest that took our manhood, and in that manhood, this priesthood upon Him, and sacrificed Himself even to the death for us.

CHAPTER XXXII

Of the universal way of the soul's freedom, which Porphyry sought amiss, and therefore found not: and that only Christ has declared it

THIS is the religion that contains the universal way of the soul's freedom: for nowhere else is it found but herein. This is the king's highway that leads to the eternal dangerless kingdom, to no temporal or transitory one. And whereas Porphyry says in the end of his first book *De Regressu Animae,* that there is no one sect yet, either truly philosophical, Indian, or Chaldaean, that teaches this universal way, and that he has not had so much as any historical reading of it; yet he confesses that such a one there is, but what it is he knows not. So insufficient was all that he had learnt to direct him to the soul's true freedom and all that himself held, or others thought him to hold: for he observed the lack of an authority fit for him to follow. But whereas he says that no sect of the true philosophy ever had notice of the universal way of the soul's freedom, he shows plainly that either his own philosophy was not true, or else that it lacked the knowledge of this way; and if so, then how could it be true? For what universal way of freeing the souls is there but that which frees all souls, and consequently without which none is freed? But whereas he adds Indian or Chaldaean, he gives a clear testimony that neither of their doctrines contained this way of the soul's freedom: yet could not he conceal, but is still telling us, that from the Chaldaeans he received the divine oracles. What universal way then does he mean, that is neither received in philosophy nor in those pagan doctrines that were considered important in matters of divinity (because they showed a powerful curiosity in the knowledge and worship of angels), and which he never had so much as read of?

What is that universal way, not peculiar to any particular nation but common to all the world and given to it by the power of God? Yet this clever philosopher knew that some such way there was. For he believes not that God's providence would leave mankind without means of the soul's freedom. He says not, there is no such, but that so great and good a help is not yet known to us, nor unto him. No marvel: for Porphyry was yet all for the world, when that universal way of the soul's freedom, Christianity, was suffered to be opposed by the devils and their servants' earthly powers, to make up the holy number of martyrs, that is, witnesses of the truth, who might show that all corporal tortures were to be endured for advancement of the truth of piety. This Porphyry saw, and thinking persecution would soon extinguish this way, therefore held not this the universal, not conceiving that that which he stuck at, and feared to endure in his choice, belonged to its greater commendation and confirmation. This therefore is that universal way of the soul's freedom, that is granted unto all nations out of God's mercy, the knowledge whereof comes and is to come unto all men. We may not, nor any hereafter, say, Why comes it so soon? or, Why so late? for His wisdom that does send it is unsearchable unto man. Which he well perceived when he said it was not yet received, or known unto him. He denied not the truth thereof, because he as yet had it not. This I say is the way that will free all believers, wherein Abraham trusting, received that divine promise: 'In thy seed shall all the nations be blessed.'[1] Abraham was a Chaldaean, but to receive this promise, and so that the seed which was 'disposed by angels in the mediator's hand' might be propagated from him and a universal way of the soul's freedom for all nations be found, he was commanded to leave his own land and kindred, and his father's house. And then was he first freed from the Chaldaean superstitions, and served the true God, to whose promise he firmly trusted. This is the way recorded in the prophet: 'God be merciful unto us, and bless us: and show us the light of His countenance and be merciful unto us. That Thy way may be known upon earth, Thy saving health among all nations.'[2] And long after, Christ being incarnate of Abraham's seed says of Himself: 'I am the way, the truth, and the life.'[3] This is the universal way, mentioned so long before by the prophets. 'It shall be in the last days, that the mountain of the house of the Lord shall be prepared in the top of the mountains, and shall be exalted above the hills; and all nations shall fly unto it. And many people shall go and say, Come, let us go up to the mountain of the Lord, to the house of the God of Jacob, and He will teach us His way, and we will walk therein. For the law shall go forth of Sion, and the word of the Lord from Jerusalem.'[4] This way therefore is not peculiar to some one nation, but common to all. Nor did the law and word of God stay in Jerusalem, or Sion, but came from thence to overspread all the world. Thereupon the mediator being risen from death said unto His amazed disciples: 'All things must be fulfilled which are written of Me in the law, the prophets, and the psalms.' Then opened He their understanding, that they might understand the scriptures, saying: 'Thus it behoved Christ to suffer and to rise again from the dead the third day: and that repentance and remission of sins should be preached in His name amongst all nations, beginning at Jerusalem.'[5] This then is the universal way of the soul's freedom, which the saints and prophets (being at first but a few, as God gave grace, and those all Hebrews, for that estate was in a manner consecrated) did both adumbrate in their temple sacrifice and priesthood,

[1] Gen. xxii. 18.   [2] Ps. lxvii. 1, 2.   [3] John xiv. 6.
[4] Isa. ii. 2, 3.   [5] Luke xxiv. 44–7.

and foretold also in their prophecy, often mystically, and some-times plainly. And the mediator Himself and His apostles, re-vealing the grace of the New Testament, made plain all that had been more obscurely signified in previous times, as it pleased God; the miracles which I spoke of before evermore giving con-firmation to them. For they had not only angelical visions, and saw the ministers of heaven; but even these simple men, relying wholly upon God's word, cast out devils, cured diseases, com-manded wild beasts, waters, birds, trees, elements, and stars, and raised the dead. I do except the miracles peculiar to our Saviour, chiefly in His birth and resurrection; showing in the first the mystery of maternal virginity, and in the other the example of our renovation. This way cleanses every soul, and prepares a mortal man in every part of him for immortality. For lest that which Por-phyry calls the intellectual should have one purgation, and the spiritual another, and the body another, therefore did our true and powerful Saviour take all upon Him. Besides this way (which has never failed mankind, either in prophecies or in their performances), no man has ever had freedom, or ever has or ever shall have. And whereas Porphyry says he never had any historical notice of this way, what history can be more famous than this that looks from such a towering authority down upon all the world? Or what more faithful, since it so relates things past, as it prophesies things to come; a great part whereof we see already performed, which gives us assured hope of the fulfilling of the rest? Neither Porphyry, nor any Platonist in the world can contemn the predictions of this way (albeit they concern but temporal affairs), as they do all other prophecies and divinations of what sort soever. For these they say are neither spoken by worthy men, nor to any worthy purpose: true, for they are either drawn from inferior causes, as physic can predict much concerning health upon such or such signs; or else the unclean spirits foretell the arts that they have already disposed of, confirming the minds of the guilty and wicked with deeds fitting their words, or words fitting their deeds, to get themselves a domination in man's infirmity. But the holy men of this univer-sal way of ours never respect the prophesying of those things, justly accounting them trifles: yet do they both know them and often foretell them to confirm the faith in things beyond sense and hard to verify by experience. But they were other and greater matters which they (as God inspired them) did prophesy: namely, the incarnation of Christ, and all things thereto belonging and fulfilled in His name, repentance and conversion of the will unto God, remission of sins, the grace of justice, faith, and increase of believers throughout all the world, destruction of idolatry, tempta-tion for trial, cleansing of the persevering, freedom from evil, the day of judgment, resurrection, damnation of the wicked, and glorification of the city of God in an eternal kingdom. These are the prophecies of them of this way. Many are fulfilled, and the rest assuredly are to come. This strait way, leading to the knowledge of God and fellowship with Him, lies plain in the holy scriptures, upon whose truth it is grounded. They that believe not, and therefore know not, may oppose this, but can never overthrow it. And therefore in these ten books I have spoken, by the good assistance of God, sufficient in sound judgments (though some expected more) against the impious contradictors that prefer their gods before the Founder of the holy city whereof we are to dispute. The first five of the ten opposed them that adored their gods for temporal respects: the five latter were against those that adored them for the life to come. It remains now, according as we promised in the first book, to proceed in our discourse of the two cities that are confused together in this world and distinct in the other; whose origin, progress, and consummation I will now unfold, evermore invoking the assistance of the Almighty.

THE ELEVENTH BOOK OF
THE CITY OF GOD

CHAPTER I

Of that part of the work wherein the demonstration of the beginnings and ends of the two cities, the heavenly and the earthly, are declared

WE give the name of the city of God unto that society whereof that scripture bears witness, which has gained the most exalted authority and pre-eminence over all other works whatsoever, by the disposing of the divine providence, not the chance decisions of men's judgments. For there it is said: 'Glorious things are spoken of thee, thou city of God':[1] and in another place: 'Great is the Lord, and greatly to be praised in the city of our God, even upon His holy mountain, increasing the joy of all the earth.'[2] And by and by in the same psalm: 'As we have heard, so have we seen in the city of the Lord of Hosts, in the city of our God: God has established it for ever.' And in another: 'The rivers' streams shall make glad the city of God, the most High has sanctified His tabernacle, God is in the midst of it unmoved.'[3] These testimonies, and thousands more, teach us that there is a city of God, whereof His inspired love makes us desire to be members. The earthly citizens prefer their gods before this heavenly city's holy Founder, knowing not that He is the God of gods, not of those false, wicked, and proud ones (which lacking His light so universal and unchangeable, and being thereby reduced to a state of extreme need, each one follows his own state, as it were, and begs divine honours of his deluded servants), but of the godly and holy ones, who select their own submission to Him, rather than the world's to them, and love rather to worship Him their God, than to be worshipped for gods themselves. The foes of this holy city, our former ten books (by the help of our Lord and King) I hope have fully answered. And now, knowing what is next expected of me, as my promise—viz. to dispute (as far as my poor talent allows) of the origin, progress, and consummation of the two cities that in this world lie confusedly together, by the assistance of the same God and King of ours, I set pen to paper, intending first to show the beginning of these two, arising from the difference between the angelical powers.

[1] Ps. lxxxvii. 3. [2] Ps. xlviii. 1, 2, 8. [3] Ps. xlvi. 4, 5.

CHAPTER II

Of the knowledge of God, which none can attain but through the mediator between God and man, the man Christ Jesus

IT is a great and admirable thing for one to transcend all creatures, corporal or incorporeal, frail and mutable, in his speculation; and to attain to the Deity itself, and learn of that, that it made all things that are not of the divine essence.   For so does God teach a man, speaking not by any corporal creature unto him, nor reverberating the air between the ear and the speaker, nor by any spiritual creature, or apparition, as in dreams or otherwise.   For so He does speak as unto bodily ears, and as by a body, and with an interval of air and distance.   For visions are very like bodies.   But He speaks by the truth, if the ears of the mind be ready, and not the body. For He speaks unto the best part of the whole man, and that wherein God alone does excel him; and if you understand a man in the best fashion, you cannot then but say he is made after God's image, being nearer to God by that part alone wherein he excels his other parts, which he has in common with beasts.   But yet the mind itself, wherein reason and understanding are natural inherents, is weakened and darkened by the mist of inveterate error, and disenabled to enjoy by inherence, nay, even to endure that immutable light, until it be gradually purified, cured, and made fit for such an happiness.   Therefore it must first be purged, and instructed by faith, to set it the surer; wherein Truth itself, God's Son, and God, taking on our manhood without wasting of godhead, ordained that faith to be a pass for man to God, by His means that was both God and man; for by His manhood is He mediator, and by man He is our way.   For if the way lie between him that goes and the place to which he goes, there is hope to attain it.   But if one have no way, nor know which way to go, what boots it to know whither to go?   And the only sure, plain, infallible highway is this mediator, God and man: God, our journey's end, and man, our way unto it.

CHAPTER III

Of the authority of the canonical scriptures made by the Spirit of God

THIS God, having spoken what He held convenient, first by His prophets, then by Himself, and afterwards by His apostles, made that scripture also, which we call canonical, of most eminent

authority, on which we rely in things that befall our understanding, and yet cannot be attained by ourselves.   For if things
sensible either to our exterior or interior sense (we call them things
present)[1] may be known in our own judgments, because we see
them before our eyes, and have them as infallible objects of our
sense : then truly in things that are remote from our senses, because
our own judgments do fail us, we must seek out other authorities,
to whom such things (we think) have been more apparent, and
them we are to trust.   Wherefore, as in things visible, having not
seen them ourselves, we trust those that have (and so in all other
objects of the senses) : even so in things mental and intelligible
which are perceived by man by what is rightly called a sense or
perception,[2] that is, in things invisible to our interior sense, we
must needs trust them, who have learned them of that incorporeal
light, or behold them continually before them.

CHAPTER IV

*That the state of the world is neither eternal, nor ordained by any new
thought of God's, as if He meant that after, which He meant not
before*

OF things visible, the world is the greatest : of invisible, God.   But
the first we see, the second we but believe.   That God made the
world, whom shall we believe with more safety than Himself?
Where have we heard Him?   Never better than in the holy
scriptures, where the prophet says : ' In the beginning God created
heaven and earth.'[3]   Was the prophet there when He made it?
No.   But God's wisdom, whereby He made it, was there; and
that does infuse itself into holy souls, making prophets and saints,
declaring His works unto them inwardly, without any noise.
And the holy angels that eternally behold the face of the Father,[4]
they come down when they are appointed, and declare His will
unto them, of whom he was one that wrote : ' In the beginning God
created heaven and earth,' and who was so fit a witness to believe
God by, that by the same spirit that revealed this unto him, did
he prophesy the coming of our faith.   But what made God create
heaven and earth, then, and not sooner?   They that say this to
impart an eternity to the world, being not by God created, are
damnably and impiously deceived and infected.   For (to except
all prophecy) the very order, disposition, beauty, and variety of the

---

[1] St. Augustine derives 'present' from *prae sensibus*.—ED.
[2] St Augustine derives *sententia* from *sensus*.—ED.
[3] Gen. i. 1.   [4] Matt. xviii. 10.

world and all therein proclaims itself to have been made in no other possible way except by God, that ineffable, invisible Great One, ineffably and invisibly beauteous. But they that say God made the world, and yet allow it no temporal, but only a formal origin, being made after a manner almost incomprehensible, seem to say something to defend God from that hazardous rashness, to take a thing into His head that was not therein before, viz. to make the world, and to be subject to change of will, He being wholly and for ever unchangeable. But I see not how their reason can stand in other respects, chiefly in that of the soul, which if they make it co-eternal with God, they can never show how that misery befalls it anew that was never accidental to it before. If they say that the happiness and misery have been co-eternal, then must they be so still, and then follows this absurdity, that the soul being called happy, shall not be happy in this, that it foresees the misery to come. If it do neither foresee its bliss nor its woe, then is it happy through a false understanding; and that were a most foolish assertion. But if they hold that the misery and the bliss have succeeded each other from all eternity, but that afterwards the soul, being once blessed, returns no more to misery, yet does not this save them from being convicted that the soul was never truly happy before, but then begins to enjoy a new and uncertain happiness: and so they confess that this so strange and unexpected a thing befalls the soul then, that never befell it before. And if they deny that God eternally foreknew the cause of these new changes they deny Him also to be the author of that happiness (which were wicked to do). And then if they should say that He had newly resolved that the soul should become eternally blessed, how far are they from acquitting Him of that mutability which they disallow. But if they acknowledge that it had a true temporal beginning, but shall never have temporal end, and having once tried misery, and gotten clear of it, shall never be miserable more, this they may boldly affirm without prejudice to God's immutability of will. And so they may believe that the world had a temporal origin, and yet that God did not alter His eternal resolution in creating it.

CHAPTER V

That we ought not to seek to comprehend the infinite spaces of time or place, ere the world was made

AND then let us see what we must say to those that make God the world's maker and yet examine the time of it: and what they will say to us, when we examine them of the place of it. They ask why it was made then, and no sooner; so we may ask why was it made in this place and in no other.   For if they imagine infinite spaces of time before the world, wherein they cannot think that God did nothing, so likewise may they suppose infinite spaces of place besides the world, wherein if they do not make the Deity to rest and not operate, they must fall to Epicurus' dream of innumerable worlds, with this difference alone: he makes all his worlds of the casual coming together of atoms, and so by their parting dissolves them; but they must make all their worlds God's handiwork, if they will not let Him rest in all the interminable space beyond the world, and will allow none of all these worlds (any more than this of ours) to be subject to dissolution.   For we now dispute with those that do, as we do, make God the incorporeal Creator of all things that are not of His own essence.   As for those that stand for many gods, they are unworthy to be made disputants in this question of religion. The other philosophers have quite outstripped all the rest in fame and credit because, though they were far from the truth, yet were they nearer than the rest.   Will these then affirm that the divine essence, which they neither confine, limit, nor extend, but which they hold, as one should indeed hold in thinking about God, is everywhere present wholly though not in bodily form—will they affirm that this was employed only in this world, a tiny spot in comparison with the rest?   I do not think they will talk so idly. If they set God to work only in this one determinate (though greatly dilated) world: that reason that they gave why God should not work in all those infinite places beyond the world let them also give why God worked not in all the infinite times before the world.   But as it is not consequent that God followed chance rather than reason in placing the world's frame where it now stands, and in no other place, though this place had no merit to give it preference over the infinite others (yet no man's reason can comprehend why the divine will placed it so): even so no more is it consequent that we should think that it was any chance made God create this world then, rather than at any other time, whereas all times before had their equal course, and none was a more fitting time for the creation than another.   But if they say men are foolish to think there is any place besides that wherein the world is: so are they (say we) to imagine any time for God to be idle in, since there was no time before the world's creation.

CHAPTER VI

That the world and time had both one beginning, nor was the one before the other

FOR if eternity and time be rightly distinguished, time never to be extant without motion, and eternity to admit no change, who would not see that time could not have being before some movable thing were created; whose motion and successive alteration (necessarily following one part another) the time might run by? Seeing therefore that God, whose eternity alters not, created the world and time, how can He be said to have created the world in time, unless you will say there was something created before the world, whose course time did follow? And if the holy and most true scriptures say that 'In the beginning God created heaven and earth,' to wit, that there was nothing before then, because this was the beginning, which the other should have been if aught had been made before, then verily the world was made with time, and not in time, for that which is made in time, is made both before some time, and after some. Before, it is time past; after, it is time to come: but no time passed before the world, because no creature was made by whose course it might pass. But it was made with time if motion be time's condition, as that order of the first six or seven days seems to show, wherein were counted morning and evening until the Lord fulfilled all the work upon the sixth day, and commended the seventh to us in the mystery of sanctification. Of what fashion those days were, it is either exceeding hard or altogether impossible to think, much more to speak.

CHAPTER VII

Of the first six days that had morning and evening ere the sun was made

As for ordinary days, we see they have neither morning nor evening but as the sun rises and sets. But the first three days of all had no sun, for that was made the fourth day. And first, God made the light, and severed it from the darkness, calling it day, and darkness night: but what that light was, and how it ran a course to make morning and night, is out of our sense to judge, nor can we understand it, which nevertheless we must not question but believe; for the light was either a bodily thing placed in the world's highest parts far from our eye, or there where the sun was afterwards made;

or else the name of light signified that holy city, with the angels and spirits, whereof the apostle says: 'Jerusalem which is above is our eternal mother in heaven.' [1]   And in another place he says: 'Ye are all the children of light, and the sons of the day: we are not sons of night and darkness.' [2]   Yet has this day the morn and evening, because the knowledge of the creature, compared to the Creator's, is but a very twilight.   And day breaks with man when he draws near the love and praise of the Creator.   Nor is the creature ever benighted, but when the love of the Creator forsakes him.   The scripture, reciting in order those days, never mentions the night: nor says, 'night was,' but, 'the evening and the morning were the first day,' [3] so of the second, and so on.   For the creature's knowledge, of itself, is as it were far more discoloured, than when it joins with the Creator's, as in the art that framed it.   Therefore, even is more congruently spoken than night, yet when all is referred to the love and praise of the Creator, night becomes morning: and when it comes to the knowledge of itself it is one full day.   When it comes to the firmament that separates the waters above and below, it is the second day.   When unto the knowledge of the earth, and all things that have root thereon, it is the third day. When unto the knowledge of the two lights, the greater and the less, the fourth.   When it knows all water-creatures, fowls, and fishes, it is the fifth; and when it knows all earthly creatures, and man himself, it is the sixth day.

CHAPTER VIII

What we must think of God's resting the seventh day after His six days' work

BUT whereas God rested the seventh day from all His works, and sanctified it, this is not to be childishly understood, as if God had expended toil; He but spake the word, and by that intelligible and eternal word (not vocal nor temporal) were all things created.   But God's rest signifies theirs that rest in God, as the gladness of the house signifies those that are glad in the house, though something else (and not the house) be the cause thereof.   How much more then if the beauty of the house make the inhabitants glad, so that we may not only call it glad, using the container for the contained, as, the whole theatre applauded, when it was the men: the whole meadows bellowed, for the oxen; but also using the efficient for the effect, as a merry epistle—that is, making the readers merry.

[1] Gal. iv. 26.   [2] 1 Thess. v. 5.   [3] Gen. i. 5.

Therefore the scripture, affirming that God rested, means the rest of all things in God, whom He by Himself makes to rest: for this the prophet has promised to all such as he speaks unto, and for whom he wrote, that after their good works which God does in them or by them (if they first have apprehended Him in this life by faith) they shall in Him have rest eternal. This was prefigured in the sanctification of the sabbath by God's command in the old law, whereof more at large in due season.

CHAPTER IX

What is to be thought of the qualities of angels, according to scripture

Now having resolved to relate this holy city's origin, and first of the angels, who make a great part thereof, so much the happier in that they never were pilgrims, let us see what testimonials of holy writ concern this point. The scriptures, speaking of the world's creation, speak not plainly of the angels, when or in what order they were created, but that they were created, the word heaven includes. 'In the beginning God created heaven and earth,' or rather in the word light, whereof I speak now, are there signified. That they were omitted I cannot think, holy writ saying that God rested in the seventh day from all His works, and the same book beginning with: 'In the beginning God created heaven and earth': to show that nothing was made ere then. Beginning therefore with heaven and earth, and earth, the first thing created, being, as the scripture plainly says, without form and void, light being yet unmade, and darkness being upon the deep (that is, upon a certain confusion of earth and waters; for where light is not, darkness must needs be); then the creation proceeding, and all being accomplished in six days, how should the angels be omitted, as though they were none of God's works, from which He rested the seventh day? This, though it be not omitted, yet here is it not plain; but elsewhere it is most evident. The three children sang in their hymn: 'O all ye works of the Lord, bless ye the Lord,' [1] amongst which they reckon the angels. And the psalmist says: 'Oh, praise God in the heavens, praise Him in the heights: praise Him all ye His angels, praise Him all His hosts; praise Him sun and moon, praise Him stars and light. Praise Him ye heavens of heavens, and the waters that be above the heavens, praise the name of the Lord, for He spake the word and they were made: He commanded and they were created': [2] here divinity calls the angels God's creatures

[1] Dan. iii. 57 (LXX).   [2] Ps. cxlviii. 1–5.

most plainly: inserting them with the rest, and saying of all: 'He spake the word and they were made.' Who dares think that the angels were made after the six days? If any one be so foolish, hearken, this place of scripture confounds him utterly: 'When the stars were made, all mine angels praised Me with a loud voice.' [1] Therefore they were made before the stars, and the stars were made the fourth day. That they were made the third day, may we say so? God forbid. That day's work is fully known, the earth was parted from the waters, and two elements took forms distinct, and earth produced all her plants. In the second day then? Neither. Then was the firmament made between the waters above and below, and was called heaven, in which firmament the stars were created the fourth day. Wherefore if the angels belong unto God's six days' work, they are that light called day; to commend whose unity, it was called one day, not the first day; nor differs the second or third from this, all are but this one, doubled unto six or seven, six of God's works, the seventh of His rest. For when God said: 'Let there be light, and there was light'; if we understand the angels' creation aright herein, they are made partakers of that eternal Light, the unchangeable Wisdom of God, all-creating, namely, the only begotten Son of God, with whose light they in their creation were illuminate, and made light, and called day in the participation of the unchangeable light and day, that Word of God by which they and all things else were created. For 'the true Light that lighteneth every man that cometh into this world,' [2] this also lighteneth every pure angel, making it light, not in itself but in God, from whom if an angel fall, it becomes impure, as all the unclean spirits are, being no more a light in God, but a darkness in itself, deprived of all participation of the eternal light: for evil has no nature; but the loss of good, *that* is evil.

CHAPTER X

Of the uncompounded, unchangeable Trinity, the Father, the Son, and the Holy Spirit, one God in substance and quality, ever one and the same

GOOD therefore (which is God) is alone simple, and consequently unchangeable. This good created all things, but not simple, and therefore changeable. I say created, that is, made not begot, For that which the simple good begot, is as simple as it is, and is the same as that which begot it. These two we call Father and

------

[1] Job xxxviii. 7.   [2] John i. 9.

Son, both of which with their Spirit are one God: that Spirit, being the Father's and the Son's, is properly called in scriptures, 'the Holy Spirit.' It is neither Father nor Son, but *personally* distinct from both, being not another *thing*: for it is a simple and unchangeable good with them, and co-eternal. And this Trinity is one God: not simple because a Trinity (for we call not the nature of that good simple, because the Father is alone therein, or the Son, or Holy Ghost alone, for that name of the Trinity is not concerned only with personal subsistence, as the Sabellians held); but it is called simple, because it is *one* in essence and the same *one* in quality (excepting their personal relation: for therein the Father has a Son, yet is no Son, and the Son a Father, yet is no Father). But as regards each of itself, the quality and essence are both one therein, as each lives, that is, has life, and is life itself. This is the reason of the nature's simplicity, wherein nothing adheres that can be lost. Nor is the container one and the thing contained another—as vessels and liquors, bodies and colours, air and heat, or the soul and wisdom are: for those are not co-essential with their qualities; the vessel is not the liquor, nor the body the colour, nor air heat, nor the soul wisdom; therefore may they all lose these adjuncts and assume others; the vessel may be empty, the body discoloured, the air cold, the soul foolish. But the body being once incorruptible (as the saints shall have it in the resurrection), that incorruption it shall never lose, yet is not that incorruption of one essence with the bodily substance. For it is alike in all parts of the body; all are incorruptible. But the body is greater in whole than in part, and the parts are some larger, some lesser, yet neither enlarging nor lessening the incorruptibility. So then the body being not entire in itself, and incorruptibility being entire in itself, do differ: for all parts of the body have inequality in themselves, but none in incorruptibility. The finger is less than the hand, but neither more nor less corruptible than the hand: being unequal to themselves, their incorruptibility is equal. And therefore though incorruptibility be the body's inseparable inherent, yet the substance making the body, and the quality making it incorruptible, are absolutely different. And so it is in the adjunct aforesaid of the soul, though the soul be always wise (as it shall be when it is delivered from misery to eternity), though it be from thence evermore wise, yet it is by participation of the divine wisdom, of whose substance the soul is not. For though the air be ever light, it follows not that the light and the air should be all one. (I say not this as though the air were a soul, as some that could not conceive an incorporeal nature did imagine. But there is a great similitude in this disparity: so that one may fitly say, as the corporal air is lightened by the corporal light, so is the incorporeal soul by the incorporeal light of God's wisdom, and as the air, being deprived of that light, becomes dark, corporal darkness being nothing but air deprived of light, so does the soul grow darkened, by want of the light of wisdom.) According to this, then, are they called simple things, that are truly and principally divine, because their essence and their quality are indistinct; nor do they partake of any deity, substance, wisdom, or beatitude, but are all these entirely themselves. The scripture indeed calls the Holy Ghost the manifold spirit of wisdom, because the powers of it are many, but all one with the essence, and all included in one, for the wisdom thereof is not manifold, but one; and therein are infinite and immeasurable treasuries of things intelligible, wherein are all the immutable and inscrutable causes of all things, both visible and mutable, which are thereby created: for God did nothing unwittingly. (It were disgrace to say so of any human artificer.) But if He made all knowingly, then made He but what He knew. This now produces a wonder, but yet a truth in our minds; that the world could not be known unto us, but that it is now extant; but it could not have been at all but that God knew it.

CHAPTER XI

Whether the spirits that fell did ever partake with the angels in their bliss at their beginning

WHICH being so, the angels were never darkness at all, but as soon as ever they were made they were made light: yet not created only to live, and be as they willed, but to live happily and wisely in their illumination, from which some of them turning away were so far from attaining that excellence of blessed wisdom which is eternal, with full security of the eternity, that they fell to a life of bare foolish reason only, which they cannot leave although they would. How they were partakers of that wisdom, before their fall, who can define? How can we say they were equally partakers with those that are really blessed by the assurance of their eternity, when if they had been therein equal, they had still continued in the same eternity by the same assurance? For life indeed must have an end, last it never so long, but this cannot be said of eternity; for it is life, because of living; but it is eternity because never ending: wherefore though all eternity be not blessed (for hell fire is eternal), yet if there be no true beatitude without eternity, their beatitude was not true, as having end, and therefore not being eternal, whether they knew it or knew it not: fear keeping their knowledge, and error their ignorance from being blessed. But if their ignorance was founded not on complete uncertainty, but on either side wavered between the end or the eternity of their beatitude; this protraction proves them not partakers of the blessed angels' happiness. We tie not this word, beatitude, unto such strictness, as to hold it peculiar to God only: yet is He so blessed as none can be more. In comparison of which (be the angels as blessed of themselves as they can), what is all the beatitude of anything, or what can it be?

CHAPTER XII

The happiness of the just that as yet have not the reward of the divine promise, compared with the first man in paradise, before sin's origin

NEITHER do we call them blessed alone amongst all reasonable intellectual creatures; for who dares deny that the first man in paradise was blessed before his sin, though he knew not whether he should continue to be so or not? He had been so eternally, had he not sinned: for we call them happy whom we see live well in this life, in hope of the immortality to come, without terror of conscience, and with true attainment of pardon for the crimes of our natural imperfection. These, though they be assured of reward for their perseverance, yet they are not sure to persevere. For what man knows that he shall continue to the end in action and increase of justice, unless he have it by revelation from Him, that by His secret providence instructs few (yet fails none) herein? But as for present delight, our first father in paradise was more blessed than any just man of the world: but as for his hope, every man in the miseries of his body is more blessed, as one to whom Truth (not opinion) has said that he shall be rid of all molestation, and partake with the angels in that great God, whereas the man that lived in paradise, in all that felicity, was uncertain of his fall or continuance therein.

CHAPTER XIII

Whether the angels were created in such a state of happiness that neither those that fell knew they should fall, nor those that persevered foreknew they should persevere

WHEREFORE now it is plain, that beatitude requires both these things conjoined (such beatitude I mean, as the intellectual nature does fitly desire): that is, to enjoy God, the unchangeable good,

without any molestation, and to remain in Him for ever without
delay of doubt, or deceit of error.   This we faithfully believe the
holy angels have: but consequently that the angels that offended,
and thereby lost that light, had not it, even before their fall.   Some
beatitude they had, but not that of foreknowing—this we must
think, if they were created any while before they sinned.   But if it
seem hard to believe some angels to be created without foreknowledge of their perseverance, or fall, and other some to have true
prescience of their beatitude, rather than that all had knowledge
alike in their creation, and continued so, until these that now are
evil, left that light of goodness—then verily it is harder to think that
the holy angels now are in themselves uncertain of that beatitude,
whereof the scriptures afford them so much certainty, and us also
that read them.   What Catholic Christian but knows that no angel
that now is shall ever become a devil, nor any devil an angel, from
henceforth?   The truth of the gospel tells the faithful that they
shall be like the angels, and that they shall go to life eternal.   But
if we be sure never to fall from bliss, and they be not sure, we are
above them, not like them: but the truth affirming (and never
erring) that we shall be their like and equals, then are they sure
of their blessed eternity: whereof those other being uncertain (for
it had been eternal had they been certain of it), it remains that they
were not the others' equals, or if they were, these that stood firm
had not this certainty of knowledge until afterwards.   Unless we
will say that what Christ says of the devil: 'He hath been a murderer from the beginning, and abode not in the truth,' [1] is not only
to be understood from the beginning of mankind, that is, since
man was made, whom he might kill by deceiving; but even from
the beginning of his own creation: and therefore because of his
aversion from his Creator, and proud opposition (herein both
erring and seducing), was debarred ever since his creation from
happiness, because he could not delude the power of the Almighty.
And he that would not in piety hold with the truth, in his pride
counterfeits the truth, as the apostle John's saying, 'The devil
sinneth from the beginning,' [2] may be understood also: that is,
ever since his creation he rejected righteousness, which none can
have but a will subject unto God.   Whosoever holds thus, is not
of the heretics' opinion, called the Manichees, nor of that of any
similar pests that hold that the devil had a wicked nature given
him in the beginning.   They do so dote that they conceive not
what Christ said: 'He abode not in the truth,' but think He said:
'He was made enemy to the truth': but Christ did intimate his
fall from the truth, wherein if he had remained, he had participated
it with the holy angels, and been eternally blessed with them.

---

[1] John viii. 44.   [2] 1 John iii. 8.

CHAPTER XIV

How this is meant of the devil: 'He abode not in the truth, because there is no truth in him' [1]

BUT Christ set down the reason, as if we had asked why he stayed not in the truth? Because 'there is no truth in him.' Had he stood in it, truth had been in him. The phrase is improper: it says: 'He abode not in the truth, because there is no truth in him,' whereas it should reverse it, and say, 'there is no truth in him because he abode not therein.' But the psalmist uses it so also: 'I have cried, because Thou hast heard me, O God': [2] whereas properly it is: 'Thou hast heard me, O God, because I have cried.' But he, having said: 'I have cried': as if he had been asked the reason, adjoined the cause of his cry in the effect of God's hearing: as if he said: 'I show that I cried, because Thou hast heard me, O God.'

CHAPTER XV

The meaning of this text: 'The devil sinneth from the beginning'

AND as for that which John says of the devil: 'The devil sinneth from the beginning,' if they make it natural to him, it can be no sin. But how then will they answer the prophets, as Isaiah, who, prefiguring the prince of Babylon, says: 'How art thou fallen from heaven, O Lucifer, son of the morning!' [3] and Ezekiel: 'Thou hast been in Eden in God's garden, every precious stone was in thy raiment'? This proves him once sinless: and so does that which follows more plainly: 'Thou wast perfect in thy ways from the day thou wast created.' [4] Which passages, if they have none other fitter meaning, do prove that he was in the truth, but abode not therein: and that passage of John, 'He abode not in the truth,' proves him once in the truth, but not persevering. And that also, 'He sinneth from the beginning,' means the beginning of sin, arising from his pride, but not from his creation. Neither must the passage of Job concerning the devil, 'He is the beginning of God's works, made to be derided by the angels,' [5] or that of the psalm, 'The dragon whom Thou hast made to scorn him,' [6] be taken as if God had made the devil at first fit for the angels to deride, but that it was ordained for his punishment after his sin. 'He is the beginning of God's works,' for there is no nature in the smallest beast which God made

[1] John viii. 44.   [2] Ps. xvii. 6.   [3] Isa. xiv. 12.
[4] Ezek. xxviii. 13, 15.   [5] Job xl. 14 (LXX).   [6] Ps. civ. 26.

not; from Him is all form, subsistence, and order: wherefore much more must the creature that is angelical, by the dignity of its nature have the pre-eminence over all God's other works.

CHAPTER XVI

Of the different degrees of creatures, wherein profitable use and reason's order do differ

FOR in all things that God made, and that are not of His essence, the living is before the dead, the productive before those that lack generation; and in the living, the sensitive before the senseless, as beasts, etc., before trees; and in things sensitive, the reasonable before the unreasonable, as man before beasts; and in things reasonable, immortals before mortals, as angels before men. But this is by nature's order. Now the esteem of these is as peculiar and different, as are their divers uses: whereby some senseless things are preferred before some sensitive, so far, that if we had power, we would root the latter out of nature, or (whether we know or know not what place therein they have) subordinate them to our profit. For who had not rather have his pantry full of meat than mice, or possess pence than fleas? No marvel: for man's valuation (whose nature is so worthy) will give more oftentimes for a horse than for a servant, for a ring than a maid. So that in choice the judgment of him that respects the worth is different from that of him that respects his own need or pleasure: the former estimating all things by their place in nature, the latter by the degree to which they satisfy his needs; the one valuing them by the light of the mind, the other by the pleasure or use of the sense. And indeed a certain will and love has gotten such predominance in reasonable natures, that although generally all angels excel men in nature's order, yet by the law of righteousness good men have gotten place of preferment before the evil angels.

CHAPTER XVII

That the vice of malice is not natural, but against nature, following the will, not the creation, in sin

WHEREFORE in respect of the devil's nature, not his will, we do understand this text aright: 'He was the beginning of God's works.' For where the vice of malice came in, the nature was not corrupted before: vice being so contrary to nature that it cannot but hurt it. Therefore were it no vice for that nature that leaves God to do so, unless it were more natural to it to desire adherence with God. The evil will then is a great proof that the nature was good. But as God is the best creator of good natures, so is He the just disposer of evil wills: that when they use good natures ill, He may use the evil wills well. Thereupon He caused that the devil's good nature, and evil will, should be cast down, and derided by His angels, that is, that his temptations might confirm His saints, whom the other sought to injure. And because God, in the creating of him, foresaw both his evil will, and what good God meant to effect thereby; therefore the psalmist says: 'This dragon whom Thou hast made for a scorn': that, in that very creation though it were good by God's goodness, yet had God foreknowledge how to make use of it in the bad state.

CHAPTER XVIII

Of the beauty of this universe, augmented by God's ordinance, out of contraries

FOR God would never have foreknown vice in any work of His, angel or man, but that He knew in like manner what good use to put it unto, so making the world's course, like a fair poem, more gracious by antithetic figures. *Antitheta,* called in Latin opposites, are the most elegant figures of all elocution: some, more expressly, call them contra-posites. But we have no use of this word, though the Latin, and all the tongues of the world, make use of the figure of speech. St. Paul uses it with rare charm in that passage to the Corinthians where he says: 'By the armour of righteousness on the right hand and the left; by honour and dishonour; by evil report and good; as deceivers and yet true; as unknown and yet known; as dying, and behold, we live; as chastened and yet not killed; as sorrowing and yet ever glad; as poor and yet making many rich; as having nothing yet possessing all things.'[1] Thus as these contraries opposed do give the saying an excellent grace, so is the world's beauty composed of contrarieties, not in figure but in nature. This is plain in Ecclesiasticus, in this verse: 'Against evil is good, and against death is life; so is the godly against the sinner: so look for in all the works of the highest, two and two, one against one.'[2]

[1] 2 Cor. vi. 7–10.　　　　　　[2] Ecclus. xxxiii. 14, 15.

CHAPTER XIX

The meaning of that text: 'God separated the light from darkness'

WHEREFORE though the obscurity of the scriptures be of good use
in producing many truths to the light of knowledge, one taking it
thus and another thus (yet so as that which is obscure in one place
be explained by some other plainer, or by manifest proofs: whether
it be that in their multitude of opinions, one lights on the author's
meaning, or that it be too obscure to be attained, and yet other
truths, upon this occasion, be admitted): yet verily I think it no
absurdity in God's works to believe that the creation of the angels
and the separation of the clean ones from the unclean took place
then, when the first light (*lux*) was made.   Upon this ground:
'And God separated the light from the darkness: and God called
the light day, and the darkness he called night.'[1]   For He only
was able to distinguish them, who could foreknow their fall ere they
fell, their deprivation of light, and their eternal bondage in darkness
of pride.   As for the days that we see, viz. this our natural light
and darkness, He made the two known lights, the sun and the moon,
to separate them.   'Let there be lights,' says He, 'in the firmament
of the heaven, to separate the day from the night.'   And by and
by: 'Then God made two great lights, the greater light to rule the
day, and the lesser to rule the night': He made both them and the
stars: and God set them in the firmament of heaven to shine upon
the earth, and to rule in the day and night, and to separate the
light from darkness.   But between that light which is the holy
society of angels, shining in the lustre of intelligible truth, and their
opposite darkness, the wicked angels, perversely fallen from that
light of justice, He only could make separation, who foreknows,
and cannot but foreknow, all the future evils of their wills not their
natures.

CHAPTER XX

*Of that verse of scripture spoken after the separation of the light
and darkness: 'And God saw the light that it was good'*

NOR may we overlook the fact that these words of God, 'Let there
be light, and there was light,' were immediately followed by these:
'And God saw the light that it was good.'   They are not recorded
after He had separated the light and darkness, and named them

[1] Gen. i. 4, 5.

day and night, lest He should have seemed to have shown His
liking of the darkness as well as the light.   For whereas the darkness which the conspicuous lights of heaven divide from the light
is blameless, therefore it was said after the division, and not before:
'And God saw that it was good.'   'And God,' says he, 'set them
in the firmament of heaven to shine upon the earth, and to rule in
the day and night, and to separate the light from the darkness; and
God saw that it was good.'   Both those He liked, for both were
sinless; but having said: 'Let there be light, and there was light,' he
adjoins immediately: 'And God saw the light that it was good.'
And then follows: 'God separated the light from the darkness, and
God called the light day, and the darkness night'; but here he
adds not: 'And God saw that it was good': lest he should seem to
allow well of both, the one being not naturally but voluntarily evil.
Therefore the light only pleased the Creator: the angelical dark-
nesses, though they were to be ordained, were not to be approved.

CHAPTER XXI

*Of God's eternal unchanging will and knowledge wherein He pleased
to create all things in form as they were created*

WHAT means that saying that goes through all: 'And God saw that
it was good,' but the approbation of the work made according to
the workman's art, God's wisdom?   God does not see it is good,
being made, as if He saw it not so ere it was made: but in seeing
that it is good being made, which could not have been made so but
that He foresaw it, He teaches, but learns not, that it is good.
Plato durst go further, and say that God had great joy in the beauty
of the universe.[1]   He was so foolish as to think the newness
of the work increased God's joy; but he showed that that pleased
Him, being effected, which had pleased His wisdom to foreknow
should be so effected; not that God's knowledge varies, or apprehends diversely of things past, present, and future.   He does not
foresee things to come as we do, nor behold things present nor
remember things past as we do: but in a manner far different from
our imagination.   He sees them not by change in thought, but
immutably, be they past or not past, to come or not to come.   All
these has He eternally present, not thus in His eye and thus in His
mind (He consists not of body and soul), nor thus now, and otherwise hereafter or heretofore.   His knowledge is not as ours is,
admitting alteration by circumstance of time, but exempted from

[1] *Tim.*, p. 37c.

all change, and all variation of moments: for His intention runs
not from thought to thought; all things He knows are present at
the same time in His spiritual vision.   He has no temporal notions
of the time, nor moved He the time by any temporal motions in
Himself.   Therefore He saw that what He had made was good,
because He foresaw that He should make it good.   Nor doubted
He His knowledge in seeing it made, or augmented it, as if it had
been less ere He made it; He could not do His works in such
absolute perfection, but out of His most perfect knowledge.
Wherefore if one urges us with: 'Who made this light?' it suffices
to answer, God.   If we be asked by what means, suffices this:
'God said, Let there be light, and there was light,' God making it
by His very word.   But because there are three necessary questions of every creature: Who made it, How He made it, and
Wherefore He made it, God says, quoth Moses: 'Let there be
light, and there was light, and God saw the light that it was good.'
Who made it?   God.   How?   God said but 'Let it be,' and 'it
was.'   Wherefore?   It was good.   No better author can there
be than God, no better art than His word, no better cause why,
than that a good God should make a good creature.   And this
Plato praised as the justest cause of the world's creation: whether
he had read it, or heard it, or got it by observation of the creatures,
or learned it of those that had this observation.

CHAPTER XXII

*Concerning those that disliked some of the good Creator's creatures,
and thought some things naturally evil*

YET this good cause of the creation, God's goodness, this just, fit
cause, which being well considered would give end to all further
investigation in this kind, some heretics could not discern, because
many things, by not agreeing with this poor frail mortal flesh
(being now our just punishment), do offend and hurt it, as fire,
cold, wild beasts, etc.   These do not observe what place in nature
these things occupy, nor how much they grace the universe (like a
fair state) with their contributions, nor what commodity redounds
to us from them, if we can know how to use them: insomuch that
poison (a thing in one way pernicious) being suitably administered,
procures health: and contrariwise, our meat, drink, nay, the very
light, immoderately used, is hurtful.   Hence does God's providence
advise us not to dispraise anything rashly, but to seek out the use
of it warily, and where our wit and weakness fails, there to believe

the rest that is hidden, as we do in other things past our reach: for the obscurity of the use either exercises the humility, or beats down the pride, nothing at all in nature being evil (evil being but a privation of good), but everything from earth to heaven ascending in a scale of goodness, and so from the visible unto the invisible, unto which all are unequal. And in the greatest is God the great workman, yet no less is He in the less: which little things are not to be measured by their own greatness, being near to nothing, but by their Maker's wisdom: as in a man's shape, shave his eyebrow, a very nothing to the body, yet how much does it deform him, his beauty consisting more of proportion and correspondence of parts than magnitude. Nor is it a wonder that those that hold part of nature bad, and produced from a bad beginning, do not receive God's goodness as the cause of the creation, but rather think that He was compelled by this rebellious evil of mere necessity to the task of creating and mixing His own good nature with evil for the sake of suppressing and reforming it, by which this good nature was so foiled, and so toiled, that He had much ado to recreate and cleanse it: nor can He yet cleanse it all, but that which He could not cleanse serves as the future prison of the captured enemy. This was not the Manichees' foolishness, but their madness: which they should abandon, would they like Christians believe that God's nature is unchangeable, incorruptible, impassible; and that the soul (which may be changed by the will unto worse, and by the corruption of sin be deprived of that unchangeable light) is no part of God nor God's nature, but by Him created of a far inferior mould.

CHAPTER XXIII

Of the error that Origen incurs

BUT the greater wonder is that some hold one beginning of all things with us, and that God created all things that are not of His essence, otherwise they could never have had being: and yet will not hold that plain and good belief of the world's simple and good course of creation, that the good God made all things good. They hold that all that is not God is inferior to Him, and yet that all is not good which none but God could make. But the souls, they say (not parts, but creatures of God), sinned in falling from the Maker: and being cast according to their deserts into divers degrees down from heaven, got certain bodies for their prisons. And thereupon the world was made (say they) not for increase of good, but restraint of bad; and this is the world. Herein is Origen justly culpable, for in his περὶ ἀρχῶν, or book of beginnings, he affirms this. Wherein I have much marvel, that a man so read in divine scriptures should not observe first how contrary this was to the testimony of scripture, that confirms all God's works with this: 'And God saw that it was good': and at the conclusion: 'God saw all that He had made, and lo, it was very good': averring no cause for this creation, but only that the good God should produce good things: where if no man had sinned, the world should have been adorned and filled only with good natures. But sin being committed, it did not follow that all should be filled with badness, the far greater part in heaven remaining still good, keeping the course of their nature. Nor could the evil willers, in breaking the laws of nature, avoid the just laws of the all-disposing God. For as a picture shows well though it have black colours in divers places, so the universe is most fair, for all these stains of sins, which notwithstanding being weighed by themselves do disgrace the lustre of it. Besides, Origen should have seen (and all wise men with him) that if the world were made only for a penal prison for the transgressing powers to be embodied in, each one according to the guilt, the less offenders the higher and lighter, and the greater ones the baser and heavier: that then the devils (the worst prevaricators) should rather have been thrust into the basest, that is, earthly bodies, than the worst men. But that we might know that the spirits' merits are not repaid by the bodies' qualities, the worst devil has an airy body, and man, though he be bad, yet of far less malice and guilt, has an earthly body, yea, and had ere his fall. And what can be more stupid than to think that the sun was rather made for a soul to be punished in as a prison, than by the providence of God to be the single source of the world's light and beauty, and of comfort to the creatures? Otherwise, two, ten, or a hundred souls sinning all alike, the world should have so many suns. To avoid which we must rather believe that there was but one soul sinned in that kind, deserving such a body, rather than that the Maker's miraculous providence did so dispose of the sun for the light and comfort of things created. It is not the souls whereof they speak they know not what, but it is their own souls that are so far from truth that they must needs be restrained. Therefore to these three which I commended before as fit questions of every creature, viz.: 'Who made it, how, and why?' the answer is: 'God by His word, because He is good.' Whether the Holy Trinity, the Father, the Son, and the Holy Ghost do intimate this unto us from their mystical height, or there be some place of scripture that prohibits us to answer thus, is a great question, and not fit to be dealt with in one volume.

CHAPTER XXIV

Of the divine Trinity, notifying itself (in some part) in all the works thereof

WE believe, hold, and faithfully affirm, that God the Father begot the Word, His wisdom by which all was made, His only Son, one of one, co-eternal, most good, and most equal; and that the Holy Spirit is both of the Father and the Son, consubstantial and co-eternal with them both. And this is both a Trinity in respect of the persons, and but one God in the inseparable divinity and one omnipotence in the inseparable power, yet so as every one of the three be held to be God omnipotent: and yet altogether are not three Gods omnipotent but one God omnipotent, such is the inseparable unity of three persons, and so must it be taught. But whether the Spirit, being the good Father's, and the good Son's, may be said to be both their goodnesses, here I dare not rashly determine: I durst rather call it the sanctity of them both, not as their quality, but their substance and the third person in Trinity. For to that this probability leads me, that the Father is holy, and the Son holy, and yet the Spirit is properly called holy, as being the substantial and consubstantial holiness of them both. But if the divine goodness be nothing else but holiness, then is it but diligent reason and no bold presumption to think (for exercise of our speculation) that in these three questions of each work of God, who made it, how, and why, the Holy Trinity is secretly intimated unto us: for it was the Father of the world that said: 'Let it be made'; and that which was made when He spake, doubtless was made by the Word: and in that, where it is said: 'And God saw that it was good,' it is plain that neither necessity nor use, but only His mere will moved God to make what was made, that is, 'because it was good': which was said after it was done, to show the correspondence of the good creature to the Creator, by reason of whose goodness it was made. If this goodness be now the Holy Spirit, then is all the whole Trinity intimated to us in every creature: and hence is the origin, form, and perfection of that holy city whereof the angels are inhabitants. Ask whence it is. God made it. How has it wisdom? God enlightened it. How is it happy? God whom it enjoys has framed the existence, and illustrated the contemplation, and sweetened the inherence thereof in Himself, that is, it sees, loves, rejoices in God's eternity, shines in His truth, and joys in His goodness.

CHAPTER XXV

Of the tripartite division of all philosophical discipline

HENCE was it (as far as we conceive) that philosophy got three parts: or rather that the philosophers observed the three parts. They did not invent them, but they observed the natural, rational, and moral, from hence. These are the Latin names, ordinarily used as we showed in our eighth book. Not that it follows that herein they had any idea of the Trinity: though Plato were the first that is said to find out and record this division; and unto him none but God seemed the author of all nature, or the giver of reason, or the inspirer of honesty. But whereas in these points of nature, inquisition of truth, and the final good, there are many diverse opinions, yet all their controversy lies in those three great and general questions. Every one makes a discrepant opinion from another in all three, and yet all do hold that nature has some cause, knowledge some form, and life some direction and sum. For three things are sought out in every artist—nature, skill, and practice; his nature to be judged of by wit,[1] his skill by knowledge, and his practice by the use. I know well that fruit belongs to fruition properly, and use to the user (and that they seem to be differently used, fruition of a thing which, being desired for itself only, delights us; and use of that which we seek for another purpose: in which sense we must rather use than enjoy temporalities, to deserve the fruition of eternity: not as the wicked enjoy money, and use God, not spending money for Him, but honouring Him for money), yet in common phrase of speech we both use fruition, and enjoy use. For fruits properly are the fields' increase, whereupon we live: so then thus I take use in three observations of an artist—his nature, skill, and use. From which the philosophers invented the several disciplines, tending all to beatitude: the natural for nature, the rational for doctrine, the moral for use. So that if our nature were of itself, we should know our own wisdom, and never go about to know it by learning, *ab externo*, and if our love had its origin in itself, and returned upon itself, it would suffice us unto beatitude, exempting us from need of any other good. But seeing our nature has its being from God our author, doubtless we must both have Him to teach us true wisdom, and to inspire us with the means to be truly blessed, by His high sweetness.

[1] *Ingenium.*

in them.   But whether the love that we love them with is to be
loved, that is to be declared.   It is to be loved.   We prove it,
because it is loved in all things that are justly loved.   For he is
not worthily called a good man that knows good, but he that loves
it.   Why, then, may we not love that love in ourselves, whereby
we love that which is to be loved?   For there is love whereby we
love that which ought not to be loved; and this love he hateth in
himself, who loveth that which ought to be loved.   They may
both be in one man; and it is good for a man that, his goodness
increasing, his evil should decrease, even to the perfection of his
cure, and full change into goodness.   For if we were beasts, we
should love a carnal sensual life: and this good would suffice our
nature without any further trouble; if we were trees, we should
not indeed love anything by motion of sense, yet should we seem
to desire fruitfulness and growth; if we were stones, water, wind,
fire, or so, we should lack sense and life, yet should we have a
natural appetite unto our due places; for the motions of weights
are like their bodies' loves, go they upward or downwards: for
weight is to the body as love is to the soul.   But because we are
men, made after our Creator's image, whose eternity is true,
and whose truth eternal, whose charity is true and eternal, and
who is the true eternal and loving Trinity, neither confounded
nor severed, we run through all things under us (which could not
be created, formed, nor ordered without the hand of the most
essential, wise, and good God), and so through all the works of the
creation; gathering from one more plain, and from another less
apparent marks of His essence; and beholding His image in ourselves, like the prodigal child we recall our thoughts home, and
return to Him from whom we fell.   There our being shall have no
end, our knowledge no error, our love no offence.   But as now,
though we see these three purely, trusting not to others, but observing them ourselves with our certain interior sight, yet because of
ourselves we cannot know how long they shall last, when they shall
end, whither they shall go, doing well or evil, therefore here we
take other witnesses, of the infallibility of whose credit we will
not dispute here, but hereafter.   In this book of the City of God,
that was never pilgrim but always immortal in heaven, being com-
pounded of the angels eternally coherent with God, and never
ceasing this coherence, between whom and their darkness (namely
those that forsook Him) a separation was made as we said at first
by God, now will we, by His grace, proceed in our discourse
already begun.

CHAPTER XXIX

Of the angels' knowledge of the Trinity in the Deity, and consequently of the causes of things in the Archetype, ere they come to be effected in works

THESE holy angels learn not of God by sounds, but by being present with that unchangeable truth, His only begotten Word, Himself, and His Holy Spirit, that undivided Trinity, of substantial persons: yet hold they not three Gods, but one, and this they know plainer than we know ourselves. The creatures also do they know better in the wisdom of God, the workman's draught, than in the things produced, and consequently themselves in that, better than in themselves, though having their knowledge in both: for they were made, and are not of His substance that made them. Therefore in Him their knowledge is day, in themselves, as we said, twilight. But the knowledge of a thing by the means it is made, and of the thing itself made, are far different. The understanding of a line or a figure does produce a more perfect knowledge of it than the draught of it in dust: and justice is one in the changeless truth, and another in the just man's soul. And so of the rest, as the firmament between the waters above and below, called heaven; the gathering of the waters, the appearance of land, the making of the sun, moon, and stars, growth of plants, creation of fowls and fishes of the water, and four-footed beasts of the earth, and last of man, the most excellent creature of all. All these the angels discerned in the Word of God, where they had the causes of their production immovable and fixed, otherwise than in themselves: clearer in Him, but cloudier in themselves: yet referring all those works to the Creator's praise, it shines like morning in the minds of these contemplators.

CHAPTER XXX

The perfection of the number six, the first that is complete in all the parts

AND these were performed in six days because of the perfection of the number of six, one being six times repeated: not that God was tied unto time, and could not have created all at once, and afterwards have bound the motions to time's congruence, but because that number signified the perfection of the work. For six is the first number that is filled by conjunction of the parts, the sixth, the third, and the half: which is one, two, and three; all which conjoined are six. Parts in numbers are those that may be described by how many they are, as a half, a third, a fourth, and so forth. But four being in nine, yet is no just part of it: one is the ninth part, and three the third part. But these two parts, one and three, are far from making nine the whole. So four is a part of ten, but no just part: one is the tenth part, two the fifth, and five the second: yet these three parts one, two, and five, make not up full ten, but eight only. As for the number of twelve, the parts exceed it. For there is one the twelfth part, six the second, four the third, three the fourth, and two the sixth. But one, two, three, four and six, make above twelve, namely sixteen. This by the way now to prove the perfection of the number of six, the first (as I said) that is made of the conjunction of the parts: and in this did God make perfect all His works. Wherefore this number is not to be despised, but has the esteem apparently confirmed by many places of scripture. Nor was it said in vain of God's works: 'Thou madest all things in number, weight and measure.'[1]

CHAPTER XXXI

Of the seventh day, the day of rest and complete perfection

BUT in the seventh day, that is, the seventh repetition of the first day (which number has perfection also in another kind), God rested, and gave the first rule of sanctification therein. The day that had no even, God would not sanctify in His works but in rest. For this is none of His works, such as being considered first in God, and then in itself, will produce a day's knowledge and an even's. Of the perfection of seven, I could say much, but this volume grows big, and I fear I shall be held rather to take occasion to show my small skill, than to respect others' edification. Therefore we must have a care of gravity and moderation, lest running all upon number, we be thought neglecters of weight and measure. Let this be a sufficient admonition, that three is the first number wholly odd, and four wholly even, and these two make seven, which is therefore oftentimes put for all: as here: 'The just shall fall seven times a day, and arise again,' that is, 'How oft soever he fall, he shall rise again.'[2] (This is not meant of iniquity, but of tribulation, drawing him to humility.) Again: 'Seven times a day will I praise thee':[3] the same he had said before: 'His praise shall be always in my mouth.'[4] Many such places as these the scripture has, to prove the number of seven to be often used for all,

[1] Wisd. of Sol. xi. 20.   [2] Prov. xxiv. 16.   [3] Ps. cxix. 164.   [4] Ps. xxxiv. 1.

universally. Therefore is the Holy Spirit called oftentimes by this number, of whom Christ said: 'He shall teach us all truth.' [1] There is God's rest, wherein we rest in God. In this whole, in this perfection is rest, in the part of it was labour. Therefore we labour, because we know as yet but in part, but when perfection is come, that which is in part shall be abolished. This makes us search the scriptures so laboriously. But the holy angels (unto whose glorious congregation our toilsome pilgrimage casts a long look), as they have eternal permanence, so have they easy knowledge, and happy rest in God, helping us without trouble, because their spiritual, pure, and free motions are without labour.

CHAPTER XXXII

Of their opinion that held angels to be created before the world

BUT if some oppose, and say that that verse: 'Let there be light and there was light,' was not meant of the angels' creation, but of some other corporal light, and teach that the angels were made not only before the firmament dividing the waters, and called heaven, but even before these words were spoken: 'In the beginning God made heaven and earth': taking not this verse as if nothing had been made before, but because God made all by His wisdom and word, whom the scripture also calls a 'beginning,' as He answered to the Jews when they inquired who He was: I will not contend, because I delight so in the intimation of the Trinity in the first chapter of Genesis. For having said: 'In the beginning God made heaven and earth': that is, the Father created it in the Son, as the psalm says: 'O Lord, how manifold are thy works! In Thy wisdom madest Thou them all': [2] presently after, he mentions the Holy Spirit. For having showed the fashion of earth, and what a huge mass of the future creation God called heaven and earth: 'The earth was without form and void, and darkness was upon the deep': to perfect his mention of the Trinity he added, 'and the Spirit of the Lord moved upon the waters.' Let each one take it as he likes: it is so profound that learning may produce divers opinions herein, all faithful and true ones: so that none doubt that the angels are placed in the high heavens, not as co-eternals with God, but as sure of eternal felicity: to whose society Christ did not only teach that His little ones belonged, saying: 'They shall be equal with the angels of God': [3] but he shows further the very contemplation of the angels, saying: 'See that you despise not one

[1] John xvi. 13.   [2] Ps. civ. 24.   [3] Matt. xxii. 30.

of these little ones, for I say unto you, that in heaven, their angels always behold the face of My Father which is in heaven.' [1]

CHAPTER XXXIII

Of the two different societies of angels, not unfitly termed light and darkness

THAT some angels offended, and therefore were thrust into prisons in the world's lowest parts until the day of their last judicial damnation, St. Peter testifies plainly, saying: 'For God spared not the angels that had sinned, but cast them down into hell and delivered them into chains of darkness to be kept unto damnation.' [2]   Now whether God's prescience separated these from the others, who doubts?   That He called the others light, worthily, who denies? Are not we here on earth, by faith, and hope of equality with them, already ere we have it, called light by the apostle?   'Ye were once darkness,' says he, 'but are now light in the Lord.' [3]   And well do they perceive the other apostate powers are called darkness, who consider them rightly, or believe them to be worse than the worst unbeliever.   Wherefore though that light, which God said should be, and it was, and the darkness from which God separated the light, be taken literally, yet we understand by these also two societies; the one enjoying God, the other swelling in pride; the one to whom it was said: 'Praise God all ye His angels,' [4] the other whose prince said: 'All these will I give Thee if Thou wilt fall down and worship me'; [5] the one inflamed with God's love, the other blown big with self-love (whereas it is said: 'God resisteth the proud and giveth grace to the lowly' [6]); the one in the highest heavens, the other in the obscurest air; the one piously quiet, the other madly turbulent; the one punishing or relieving according to God's justice and mercy, the other raging with the over unreasonable desire to hurt and subdue; the one allowed to be God's ministers to all good, the other restrained by God from doing the desired hurt; the one scorning the other for doing good against their wills by temptations, the other envying the gathering in of the faithful pilgrims.   We understand, I say, that these two so contrary societies (the one good in nature and will, the other good in nature also, but bad by will), since it is so explained by other places of scripture, are spoken of in this place in Genesis, the light and darkness being applied as denominative unto them both. Even though the author had no such intent, yet has not the matter

[1] Matt. xviii. 10.   [2] 2 Pet. ii. 4.   [3] Eph. v. 8.
[4] Ps. cxlviii. 2.   [5] Matt. iv. 9.   [6] Jas. iv. 6; 1 Pet. v. 5.

been unprofitably handled; because though we could not know the
author's will, yet we kept the rule of faith, which many other places
make manifest.   For though God's corporal works be here recited,
yet have they some similitude with the spiritual, as the apostle
says: 'You are all the children of the light, and the children of the
day: we are no sons of the night or darkness.' [1]   But if this were
the author's mind, the other disputation hath attained perfection:
that so wise a man of God, nay, the spirit of God in him, in reciting
the works of God, all perfected in six days, might by no means be
held to leave out the angels, either in the beginning, that is, because
He had made them first, or (as we may better understand 'In the
beginning') because He made them in His only begotten Word, in
which beginning God made heaven and earth: which two names
either include all the creation, spiritual and temporal, which is
more credible: or the two great parts only as containers of the
lesser, being first proposed in the whole, and then the parts performed in order according to the mystery of the six days.

CHAPTER XXXIV

*Of the opinion that some held, that the angels were meant by the
several waters, and of others that held the waters uncreated*

YET some there were that thought that the company of angels were
meant by the waters: and that these words: 'Let there be a firmament in the midst of the waters, and let it separate the waters from
the waters,' meant by the upper waters the angels, and by the
lower, either the nations, or the devils.   But if this be so, there is
no mention of the angels' creation, but only of their separation.
Some, however, most vainly and impiously deny that God made the
waters, because He never said: 'Let there be waters.'   So they
may say of earth: for He never said: 'Let there be earth.'   Aye,
but, say they: It is written God 'created both heaven and earth.'
Did He so?   Then is water included therein also, for one name
serves both: for the psalm says: 'The sea is His, and He made it,
and His hands prepared the dry land': [2] but the elementary weights
do move these men not to take the waters above for the angels,
because such an element cannot remain above the heavens.   No
more would these men, if they could make a man after their
principles, put phlegm, being instead of water in man's body, in
the head: but there is the seat of phlegm, most fitly appointed by
God, but as absurdly, as these men conceive, that if we knew not

(though this book told us plain) that God had placed this fluid, cold, and consequently heavy humour in the uppermost part of man's body, these world-weighers would never believe it. And if they were subject to the scripture's authority, they would still get some other meaning out of it. But seeing that the consideration of all things that the Book of God contains concerning the creation would draw us far from our resolved purpose, let us now (together with the conclusion of this book) make an end of this disputation of the two contrary societies of angels, wherein are also some grounds of the two societies of mankind, unto whom we intend now to proceed, in a fitting discourse.

THE TWELFTH BOOK OF
THE CITY OF GOD

CHAPTER I

Of the nature of good and evil angels

BEFORE I speak of the creation of man, wherein (in respect of mortal reasonable creatures) the two cities had their origin, as we showed in the last book of the angels, it seems requisite to speak of the congruity and suitability of the society of men with angels and to show that there are not four, but rather two societies of men and angels similar in quality, and combined together, the one consisting of both good angels and good men, and the other of evil. That the contrariety of desires between the good and evil angels arose from their diverse natures and beginnings, we may on no account believe, God having been alike good in both their creations, and in all things beside them. But this diversity arises from their wills, some of them persisting in God their common good, and in His truth, love, and eternity; while others, delighting more in their own power, as though it were from themselves, fell from that common all-blessing good to dote upon their own, and taking pride for eternity, vain deceit for firm truth, and factious envy for perfect love, became proud, deceitful, and envious. The cause of their beatitude was their adherence unto God; so must their misery's cause be the direct contrary, namely, their not adhering unto God. Wherefore if when we are asked why they are blessed, and we answer well: 'Because they stuck fast unto God,' and being asked why these are wretched, we answer well: 'Because they stuck not unto God': then is there no beatitude for any reasonable or understanding creature to attain but in God. So then though all creatures cannot be blessed (for beasts, trees, stones, etc., are incapable hereof), yet those that are, are not so of themselves, being created of nothing, but have their blessedness from the Creator. Attaining Him they are happy, losing Him unhappy. But He Himself is good only of Himself, and therefore cannot lose His good, because He cannot lose Himself. Therefore the one true blessed God we say is the only immutable good; and those things He made are good also because they are from Him, but they are mutable because they were made of nothing. Wherefore though they be not the chief goods, God being above them, yet are they great, in being able to adhere unto the

chief good and so be happy, without which adherence they cannot
but be wretched.   Nor are other parts of the creation better in that
they cannot be wretched: for we cannot say our other members are
better than our eyes in that they cannot be blind.   But even as
sensitive nature in the worst plight is better than the insensible
stone, so is the reasonable (albeit miserable) above the brutish, that
cannot therefore be miserable.   This being so, then this nature
(created in such excellence, that though it be mutable, yet by inherence with God, that unchangeable good, it may become blessed;
which cannot satisfy its own need without blessedness, nor has any
means to attain this blessedness but God) truly commits a great
error and enormity in not adhering unto Him.   And all sin is
against nature and hurtful thereunto.   Wherefore that creature
which adheres not unto God differs not in nature from that which
adheres unto God, but in vice; and yet in that vice is the nature itself
laudable still.   For the vice being justly blamed commends the
nature; the true dispraise of vice being that it disgraceth an honest
nature.   And therefore as, when we call blindness a fault of the
eyes, we show that sight belongs to the eye, and in calling the fault
of the ears deafness, that hearing belongs to the ear; so likewise,
when we say it was the angels' fault not to adhere unto God, we
show that that adherence belonged to their natures.   And how
great a praise it is to continue in this adherence, enjoying and living
in so great a good without death, error, or trouble, who can sufficiently declare or imagine?   Wherefore since it was the evil angels'
fault not to adhere unto God (all vice being against nature), it is
manifest that God created their nature good, since it is hurt only
by their departure from Him.

CHAPTER II

*That no essence is contrary to God, though all the world's frailty seem
to be opposite to His immutable eternity*

THIS I have said lest some should think that the apostate angels
whereof we speak had a different nature from the rest, as having
another beginning, and not God as their author.   Which one
shall the sooner avoid by considering what God said unto Moses
by His angel, when He sent him to the children of Israel: 'I am
that I am.'[1]   For God being the highest essence, that is, eternal
and unchangeable, gave essence to His creatures, but not such as
His own; to some more, and to some less; ordering nature's existence by degrees; for as 'wisdom'[2] is derived from 'to be wise,'

[1] Exod. iii. 14.   [2] *Sapientia*, from *sapere*.

so is essence [1] from 'to be.'   The word is new, not used by the old
Latinists, but taken of late into the tongue to serve to explain the
Greek οὐσία, which it translates exactly.   Wherefore unto that
especial high essence, that created all the rest, there is no nature
contrary, but that which has no essence: for that which has being
is not contrary unto that which also has being.   Therefore no
essence at all is contrary to God, the chief essence and cause of
essence in all.

CHAPTER III

*Of God's enemies not by nature, but will, which hurting them, hurts
their good nature: because there is no vice but hurts nature*

THE scripture calls them God's enemies, because they oppose His
sovereignty not by nature but will, having no power to hurt Him,
but themselves.   Their will to resist, not their power to hurt, makes
them His foes, for He is unchangeable and wholly incorruptible:
wherefore the vice that makes them oppose God is their own hurt,
and in no way God's; solely because it corrupts their good nature.
It is not their nature but their vice that is contrary to God; evil
only being contrary to good.   And who denies that God is the
best good?   So then vice is contrary unto God, as evil is unto
good.   The nature also which it corrupts is good, and therefore
opposed by it: but while it stands against God only as evil against
good, against this nature it stands as evil and hurt also; for evil
cannot hurt God, but corruptible natures only, which are good by
the testimony of the hurt that evil does them, for if they were not
good, vice could not hurt them: for what does it in hurting them
but abolish their integrity, lustre, virtue, safety, and whatever vice
can diminish or root out of a good nature?   And if this good be
not therein, vice takes it not away, and therefore hurts not: for it
cannot be both a vice, and hurtless; whence we gather that though
vice cannot hurt that unchangeable good, yet it can hurt nothing
but good; because it only exists where it hurts.   And so we may
say that vice cannot be in the highest good, nor can it be but in
some good.   Good therefore may exist alone, but so cannot evil:
because the natures that an evil will has corrupted, though in so far
as they be polluted they are evil, yet in so far as they are natures
they are good.   And when this vicious nature is punished, there
is this good besides the goodness of its nature, that it is not unpunished.   For this is just, and what is just is beyond question
good, and no man is punished for the faults of his nature, but of his

---

[1] *Essentia*, from *esse*.

will; for that vice that has grown from a custom into a habit and seems natural, had its origin from corruption of will. For now we are speaking of the vices of that nature, wherein is a soul capable of the intellectual light, whereby we discern between just and unjust.

CHAPTER IV

Of lifeless and reasonless natures, whose order differs not from the decorum of the whole universe

BUT it were ridiculous to think that the faults of beasts, trees, and other unreasonable, senseless, or lifeless creatures, whereby their corruptible nature is destroyed, are damnable: for the Creator's will has disposed of those thus, to perfect the inferior beauty of this universe, the beauty of the seasons, by this successive alteration of them. For earthly things are not comparable to heavenly: yet might not the world be without them, because the others are more glorious. Wherefore in the succession of those things one to another in their due places, and in the change of the meaner into qualities of the better, the order of things transitory consists. Which order's glory we delight not in, because we are involved in it as parts of mortality. We cannot discern the whole universe, though we observe how conveniently those parts we see are combined: wherefore in things out of our contemplation's reach, we must believe the providence of the Creator, rather than be so rash as to condemn any part of the world's fabric as imperfect. And yet if we mark well, by the same reason, those involuntary and unpunishable faults in those creatures commend their natures unto us, none of whom has any other maker but God, because we ourselves dislike that that nature of theirs which we like should be defaced by that fault: unless men will dislike the natures of things that hurt them, not considering their natures but their own profit, as in the case of those creatures that plagued the pride of Egypt. But so they might blame the sun because some offenders, or unjust detainers of others' right, are by the judges condemned to be set in the hot sun. Wherefore it is not the consideration of nature in respect of our profit, but as it is in itself, that glorifies the Creator. The nature of the eternal fire is assuredly laudable, though the wicked shall be therein everlastingly tormented. For what is more fair than the bright, pure, and flaming fire? What more useful to heat, cure, or boil withal, though nothing is so hurtful as fire burning? Thus that being penally applied is pernicious, which being orderly used is convenient: for who can explain the

thousand uses of it in the world? Hear them not that praise the
fire's light and dispraise the heat, respecting not the nature of it
but their own profit and disprofit. They would see, but they
would not burn. But they consider not that this light they like so,
being immoderately used, hurts a tender eye: and that in this heat
which they dislike so, many creatures do very conveniently keep
and live.

CHAPTER V

That the Creator has deserved praise in every form and kind of nature

WHEREFORE all natures are good, because they have their form,
kind, and a certain harmony withal in themselves. And when
they are in their true posture of nature, they preserve their essence
in the full manner as they received it. And that, whose essence is
not eternal, follows the laws of the Creator that sways it, and
changes into better, or worse, tending (by God's disposition) still
to that end which the order of the universe requires, so that that
corruption which brings all mortal natures into dissolution can
only dissolve that which was, that it may become afterwards that
which it was before, or that which it should be. Which being so,
then God, the highest being, who made all things that are not
Himself (no creature being fit for equality with Him, being made
of nothing, and consequently not being able to have been but by
Him), is not to be found fault with because offence is taken at the
creatures' faults, but to be honoured upon the due consideration
of the perfection of all natures.

CHAPTER VI

The cause of the good angels' bliss, and the evil ones' misery

THE true cause therefore of the good angels' bliss is their adherence
to that most high essence, and the just cause of the bad angels'
misery is their departure from that high essence, to turn back upon
themselves, that were not such. Which vice, what is it else but
pride? 'For pride is the root of all sin.' [1] These would not
therefore stick unto Him their strength, and having power to be
more perfect by adherence to this highest good, they preferred

[1] Ecclus. x. 13.

themselves that were His inferiors before Him. This was the first fall, misery, and vice of their nature, which though it were not created to have the highest being, yet might it have beatitude by fruition of the highest being; but which falling from Him becomes not indeed nothing, but yet less than it was, and consequently miserable. Seek the cause of this evil will, and you shall find just none. For what can cause the will's evil, the will being sole cause of all evil? The evil will therefore causes evil works, but nothing causes the evil will. If there be such a cause, then either it has a will or none. If it have, it is either a good one or a bad; if good, what fool will say that a good will is cause of an evil will? It should be if it caused sin; but this were extreme absurdity to affirm. But if it have an evil will, then I ask what caused this evil will in it. And to limit my questions, I ask the cause of the first evil will. For that which another evil will has caused is not the first evil will, but that which none has caused: for still that which causes is before the thing caused. If I be answered, that nothing caused it, but it was from the beginning, I ask then whether it were in any nature. If it were in none, it had no being; if it were in any, it corrupted it, hurt it, and deprived it of all good; and therefore this vice could not be in an evil nature, but in a good, where it might do hurt: for if it could not hurt, it was no vice, and therefore no bad will; and if it did hurt, it was by privation of good, or diminishing of it. Therefore a bad will could not be from eternity in that wherein a good nature had been before, which the evil will destroyed by hurt. Well, if it were not eternal, who made it? It must be answered, something that had no evil will. What was this — inferior, superior, or equal unto it? If it were the superior, it was better. Why then had it not a will, nay, a better will?

This may also be said if it were equal: for two good wills never make one another bad. It remains, then, that some inferior thing that had no will was cause of that vicious will in the angels. Aye, but all things below them, even to the lowest earth, being natural, are also good, and have the goodness of form and kind in all order. How then can a good thing produce an evil will? How can good be cause of evil? For the will turning from the superior to the inferior, becomes bad, not because the thing whereunto it turns is bad, but because the turning is bad and perverse. No inferior thing then depraves the will, but the will depraves itself by following inferior things inordinately. For if two men like in body and mind should behold one beauteous personage, and the one of them be stirred with a lustful desire towards it, and the other's thoughts stand chaste, what shall we think was cause of the evil will in the one and not in the other? Not the seen beauty, for it transformed not the will in both, and yet both saw it alike. Not the flesh of the beholder's face. For if so, why not the flesh of the other? Nor the mind, for we presupposed them both alike in body and mind. Shall we say the devil secretly suggested it unto one of them, as though he consented not to it in his own proper will?

This consent, therefore—the cause of this assent of the will to vicious desire—is what we seek. For, to take away one difficulty from the question, if both were tempted, and the one yielded, and the other did not, why was this, but because the one would continue chaste, and the other would not? Whence then was this secret fall but from the individual will, where there was such parity in body and mind, a like sight and a like temptation? So then he that desires to know the cause of the vicious will in the one of them, if he mark it well, shall find nothing. For if we say that he caused it, what was he ere his will became vicious but a creature of a good nature, the work of God, that unchangeable good? Wherefore he that says that he that consented to this lustful desire which the other withstood (both being before alike in body and soul, and beholding the beautiful object alike) was cause of his own evil will, whereas he was good before this vice of will; let him ask why he caused this—whether from his nature, or because his will was made of nothing; and he shall find that his evil will arose not from his nature, but from nothing: for if we shall make his nature the effecter of his vicious will, what shall we do but affirm that good is the efficient cause of evil? But how can it be that nature (good though it be mutable), before it have a vicious will, should do viciously, namely in making the will vicious?

CHAPTER VII

That we ought not to seek out the cause of the vicious will

LET none therefore seek the efficient cause of an evil will; for it is not efficient but deficient, nor is there effect but defect, namely falling from that highest essence unto a lower, this is to have an evil will. The causes whereof (being not efficient but deficient) if one endeavour to seek, it is as if he should seek to see the darkness, or to hear silence. We know them both, this by the ear, and that by the eye, but not by any forms of theirs, but privation of forms. Let none then seek to know that of me which I know not myself, unless he will learn not to know what he must know that he cannot know: for the things that we know by privation and not by form, are rather (if you can follow me) known by not knowing, and in knowing them, are still unknown. For the body's eye coursing over bodily objects sees no darkness, save when it ceases to see. And so it belongs to the ear and to no other sense to know silence, which notwithstanding is not known save by not hearing. So our intellect contemplates the intelligible forms, but where they fail it learns by not learning. For 'who can understand his faults?'[1] This I know, that God's nature can never fail anywhere or in any way: but all things that are made of nothing may decay. And yet in so far as these things achieve good results they have efficient causes; but in that they fail, and fall off, and do evil, they have deficient causes. And what do they then but vanity?

CHAPTER VIII

Of the perverse love, whereby the soul goes from the unchangeable to the changeable good

I KNOW besides that wherein the vicious will is resident, therein is that done, which, if the will would not, should not be done: and therefore the punishment falls justly upon those acts which are wills and not necessities. It is not the thing to which we fall, but our fall that is evil: that is, we fall to no evil natures, but against nature's order, from the highest to the lower. Herein is evil. Covetousness is no vice in the gold, but in him that perversely leaves justice to love gold, whereas justice ought always to be preferred before riches. Nor is lust the fault of sweet beauteous bodies, but the soul's that runs perversely to bodily delights, neglecting temperance, which scorns all company with those, and prepares us unto far more excellent and spiritual pleasures. Vainglory is not a vice proper to human praise, but the soul's that perversely desires praise of men, not respecting the conscience's testimony. Nor is pride his vice that gives the power, but the soul's, perversely loving that power, contemning the justice of the Most Mighty. So then, he that perversely desires a good of nature, though he attain it, is evil himself in the enjoyment of this good, and wretched, being deprived of a better.

CHAPTER IX

Whether He that made the angels' nature made their wills good also, by the infusion of His love into them through His Holy Spirit

SEEING therefore there is no natural nor essential cause effecting the evil of will, but that evil of mutable spirits, which depraves the good of nature, arises from itself, being effected in no way but by

[1] Ps. xix. 12.

falling from God, which falling also has no cause; if we say also that good wills have no efficient cause, we must beware lest they be held uncreated and co-eternal with God. But seeing that the angels themselves were created, how can their wills but be so also? But being created, were their wills created with them, or without them first? If with them, then doubtless He that made one, made both: and as soon as they were created, they were joined to Him in that love wherein they were created. And therein were some angels severed from others, because they kept their good wills still, and the others were changed by falling in their evil will from that which was good, whence they need not have fallen unless they had wished. But if the good angels were at first without good wills, and made those wills in themselves without God's working, were they therefore made better of themselves than by His creation? God forbid. For what were they without good wills, but evil? Or, if they were not evil because they had no evil wills either, nor fell from that which they had not, yet even so they were not yet so good as when they had gotten good wills. But now if they could not make themselves better than God (the best workman of the world) had made them: then verily could they never have had good wills but by the operation of the Creator in them. And these good wills, effecting their turning not to themselves who were inferiors, but to the supreme God, to adhere unto Him and be blessed by fruition of Him, what do they else but show that the best will should have remained poor, in desire only, but that He who made a good nature out of nothing and yet able to enjoy Himself, made it better by perfecting it of Himself, first having made it more desirous of perfection? For this must be examined— whether the good angels created good will in themselves, by a good will or a bad, or none. If by none, then none they created. If by a bad, how can a bad will produce a good? If by a good, then had they good wills already.

And who gave them those, but He that created them by a good will, that is, in that chaste love of their adherence to Him, both forming their nature, and giving them grace? Believe therefore that the angels were never without good will, that is, God's love. But those that were created good, and yet became evil by their own will (which no good nature can do but in a voluntary defect from good, that, and not the good, being the cause of evil), either received less grace from the divine love than they that persisted therein, or if they had equal good at their creation, the former fell by their evil wills, and the latter having further help attained that bliss, from which they knew they would never fall, as we showed in our last book. Therefore, to God's due praise we must confess that the diffusion of God's love is bestowed as well upon the angels as the saints, by His Holy Spirit destowed upon them: and that that scripture: 'It is good for me to adhere unto God,'[1] was peculiar at first to the holy angels, before man was made. This good they all participate with Him to whom they adhere, and are a holy city, a living sacrifice, and a living temple unto that God. And how that part thereof, namely that which the angels shall gather and take up from this earthly pilgrimage unto that society, being now in the flesh upon earth, or dead, and resting in the secret receptacle of souls, had its first origin I must now explain, as I did before of the angels. For of God's work, the first man, came all mankind, as the scripture says, whose authority is justly admired throughout the earth, and by those natures who (amongst other things) it prophesied should believe it.

CHAPTER X

Of the falseness of that history that says the world has continued many thousand years

LET the conjectures therefore of those men that fable of man's and the world's origin they know not what, not detain us. For some think that men, as the world, have been always. So Apuleius writes of men: 'Severally mortal, but generally eternal.'[2] And when we say to them: 'If the world has always been, how can your histories speak true in relation of who invented this or that, who brought up arts and learning, and who first inhabited this or that region?' they answer us: 'The world has at certain times been so wasted by fires and deluges, that the men were brought to a very few, whose progeny multiplied again; and so seemed this man's first origin, whereas indeed it was but a separation of those whom the fires and floods had destroyed; but man cannot have production, but from man.' They speak now what they think, but not what they know: being deceived by a kind of most false writings, that say: 'The world has continued many thousand years,' whereas the holy scripture gives us not yet full six thousand years since man was made. To show the falseness of these writings briefly, and that their authority is not worth a straw herein, that epistle of Great Alexander to his mother, containing a narration of things by an Egyptian priest unto him, made out of their religious mysteries, contains also the monarchies, that the Greek histories record also. In this epistle the Assyrian monarchy lasts five thousand years and over. But in the Greek history, from Belus the first king, it continues but one thousand three hundred years. And with Belus does the Egyptian story begin also. The Persian monarchy (says

¹ Ps. lxxiii. 28.   ² *De Deo Socrat.* 4.

that epistle) until Alexander's conquest (to whom this priest spake thus) lasted above eight thousand years: whereas the Macedonians until Alexander's death lasted but four hundred fourscore and five years, and the Persians until his victory two hundred thirty and three years, by the Greek story. So far are these computations short of the Egyptians', being not equal with them though they were trebled. For the Egyptians are said formerly to have had their years but four months long: so that one full year of the Greeks or ours is just three of their old ones. But all this will not make the Greek and Egyptian computations meet; and therefore we must rather trust the Greek, as not exceeding our holy scriptures' account. But if this epistle of Alexander being so famous, differs so far from the most probable account, how much less faith then ought we to give to those their fabulous antiquities, fraught with fabrications, against our divine books, that foretold that the whole world should believe them, and the whole world has done so: and which prove that they wrote truth in things past, by the true occurrences of things to come, by them presaged.

CHAPTER XI

Of those that hold not the eternity of the world, but either a dissolution and generation of innumerable worlds, or of this one at the expiration of certain years

BUT others there are that do not think the world eternal, and yet imagine it either not to be one world but many, or one only, dissolved and formed anew at certain intervals of time. Now these must needs confess that there were first men of themselves, ere any men were begotten. For they cannot think that the whole world perishing, any man could remain, as they may do in those burnings and inundations which left some men to repair mankind. But as they hold the world to be re-edified out of its own ruins, so must they believe that mankind first was produced out of the elements, and from these first was man's following propagation, as other creatures by generation of their like.

CHAPTER XII

Of such as held man's creation too lately effected

WHEREFORE our answer to those that held the world to have been *ab aeterno*, against Plato's express confession, though some say he spake not as he thought, the same shall be our answer still to

those that think man's creation too lately effected, having let those
innumerable spaces of time pass, and by the scripture's authority
been made as recently as within this six thousand years. If the
brevity of the time be offensive, and the years since man was
made seem so few, let them consider that nothing that has a limit
is continual: and that all the definite spaces of the ages being compared to interminable eternity are as a very little, nay as just
nothing. And therefore though we should reckon five or six, or
sixty, or six hundred thousand years, and multiply them so often
till the number lacked a name, and say then God made man, yet
may we ask why He made him no sooner. For God's pause before
man's creation being from all eternity was so great, that compare
a definite number with it of ever so unspeakable a quantity, and
it is not so much as one half drop of water compared with the
whole ocean; for in these, though the one be so exceeding small,
and the other so incomparably great, yet both are definite. But
any time which has an origin, run it on to never so huge a quantity, being compared unto that which has no beginning, I know not
whether to call it small or nothing. For, withdraw but moments
from the end of the first, and be the number ever so great, it will
(as if one should diminish the number of a man's days from the
time he lives in to his birthday) decrease, until we come to the very
beginning. But from the latter abstract not moments, nor days,
nor months, nor years, but as much time as the other whole number
contained (beyond the compass of all computation) and that as
often as you please, and what will it avail when you can never
attain the beginning, it having none at all? Wherefore that which
we ask now after five thousand years and the overplus, our posterity
may as well ask after five hundred thousand years, if our mortality
should succeed and our infirmity endure so long. And our forefathers soon after the first man's time might have called this in
question. Nay, the first man himself, that very day that he was
made, or the next, might have asked why he was made no sooner.
But whensoever he had been made, this controversy of his origin
and the world's should have no better foundation than it has now.

CHAPTER XIII

*Of the revolution of times at whose expiration some philosophers held
that the universe should return to the state it was in at first*

Now these philosophers believed that this world had no other
dissolution, but a renewing of it continually at certain revolutions
of time, wherein the nature of things was repaired, and so passed

on a continual rotation of ages past and coming; whether this fell out in the continuance of one world, or the world arising and falling gave this succession and date of things by its own renovation. And from this ridiculous mocking they cannot free the immortal nor the wisest soul, but it must still be tossed unto false bliss, and beaten back into true misery.   For how is that bliss true, whose eternity is ever uncertain, the soul either being ignorant of the return unto misery, or fearing it in the midst of felicity?   But if it go from misery to happiness never to return, then is something begun in time which time shall never give end unto.   And why not then the world?   And why not man made therein?   So we avoid all the false lures that deceived wits have devised to distract men from the truth.   For some will have that passage of Ecclesiastes: 'What is it that hath been?   That which shall be.   What is it that hath been made?   That which shall be made.   And there is no new thing under the sun, nor any thing whereof one may say, Behold this is new: it hath been already in the time that was before us,' [1] to be understood of these reciprocal revolutions, whereas he meant either of the things he spoke of before, viz. the successive generations; the sun's motions; the torrents' falls; or else generally all transitory creatures; for there were men before us, there are with us, and there shall be after us; so it is of trees and beasts.   Nay, even monsters, though they be unusual and diverse, and some have arisen but once, yet as they are generally wonders and miracles, they are both past and to come: nor is it news to see a monster under the sun.   Some however will have the wise man to speak of God's predestination that fore-framed all, and therefore that now there is nothing new under the sun.   But far be our faith from believing that these words of Solomon should mean those revolutions that they do dispose the world's course and renovation by: as Plato the Athenian philosopher taught in the academy that in a certain unbounded space, yet definite, Plato himself, his scholars, the city and school, should after infinite ages meet all in that place again and be as they were when he taught this.   God forbid I say that we should believe this.   'For Christ once died for our sins, and rising again, dies no more, nor hath death any future dominion over Him': [2] 'and we (after our resurrection) shall be always with the Lord,' [3] to whom now we say with the psalm: 'Thou wilt keep us, O Lord, and preserve us from this generation for ever.' [4]   The next verse I think fits them best: 'The wicked walk in a circuit': not because their life (as they think) is to run circularly, but because their false doctrine runs round in a circular maze.

[1] i. 9, 10.   [2] Rom. vi. 9.   [3] 1 Thess. iv. 17.   [4] Ps. xii. 7, 8.

CHAPTER XIV

Of man's temporal estate, made by God, out of no newness or change of will

BUT what wonder if these men run in their circular error, and find no way forth, seeing they neither know mankind's origin nor his end, being not able to pierce into God's depths, who being eternal, and without beginning, yet gave time a beginning, and made man in time whom He had not made before, yet not now makes He him by any sudden motion, but as He had eternally decreed? Who can penetrate this inscrutable depth, wherein God gave man a temporal beginning that had none before, and this out of His eternal, unchangeable will, multiplying all mankind from one? For when the psalmist had said: 'Thou shalt keep us, O Lord, and preserve us from this generation for ever,' then he reprehends those whose foolish and false doctrine reserves no eternity for the soul's blessed freedom, in adjoining: 'The wicked walk in a circuit,' as who should say: 'What dost thou think or believe? Should we say that God suddenly determined to make man, whom He had not made in all eternity before, and yet that God is ever immutable, and cannot change His will?' Lest this should draw us into doubt, he answers God presently, saying: 'In Thy deep wisdom didst Thou multiply the sons of men.' Let men think, talk, or dispute as they will (says he) and argue as they think, 'In Thy deep wisdom,' which none can discover, 'didst Thou multiply mankind.' For it is most deep, that God should be from eternity, and yet decree that man should be made at this time, and not before, without alteration of will.

CHAPTER XV

Whether (to preserve God's eternal domination) we must suppose that He has always had creatures to rule over, and how that may be held always created, which is not co-eternal with God

BUT I, as I dare not deny God's dominion eternal from ever, so may I not doubt that man had a temporal beginning before which he was not. But when I think what God should be Lord over from eternity, here do I fear to affirm anything, because I look into myself, and know that it is said: 'Who can know the Lord's counsels, or who can think what God intendeth? Our cogitations are fearful, and our forecasts are uncertain. The corruptible body suppresses the soul, and the earthly mansion keeps down the mind that is much occupied.'[1] Therefore many thoughts do I revolve in this earthly mansion, because out of them all I cannot find amongst them or beyond their number that one which is true. If I say there have been creatures ever for God to be Lord of, who has been ever, and has ever been Lord, but that they were now those, and then others by succession of time—lest we should make some of them co-eternal with the Creator (which faith and reason reprove), we must avoid the absurdity of saying that a mortal creature has been successively from the beginning, but immortal creatures had a temporal origin—in which time the angels were created (whether they be meant by the name of 'light,' or 'heaven,' of whom it is said: 'In the beginning God created heaven and earth'). They were not from the beginning, until the time that they were created; for otherwise they should be co-eternal with God. If I say they were not created in time, but before it, that God might be their Lord, who has been a Lord for ever, then am I asked, whether they were before all time, or how could they that were created be from eternity. And here I might perhaps answer that that which has been for the space of all time may not be unfitly said to have been always, and they have been so far in all time, that they were before all time, if time began with heaven's motion, and they were before heaven. But if time began not so, but were before heaven, not in hours, days, months, or years (for sure it is that these dimensions, properly called times, began from the stars' courses, as God said when He made them: 'Let them be for signs, and seasons and days, and years'), but in some other wondrous motion, whose former part did pass by, and whose latter succeeded, it being impossible for them to go both together—if there were such a movement amongst the angels, that as soon as they were made, they began to move in time, even in this respect have they been from the beginning of all time: time and they having origin both at once. And who will not say that what has been for all time, has been always? But if I answer thus, some will say to me: Why are they not then co-eternal with the Creator if both He and they have been always? What shall I say to this? That they have been always, seeing that time and they had origin both together, and yet they were created? For we deny not that time was created, though it has been for all time's continuance; otherwise, there should have been a time that had been no time. But what fool will say so? We may say, there was a time when Rome was not, when Jerusalem was not, or Abraham, or man himself, or when they all were not. Nay, the world itself not being made at time's beginning but afterwards, we may

[1] Wisd. of Sol. ix. 13–15.

say: 'There was a time when the world was not.' But to say: 'There was a time when time was not,' is as improper as to say: 'There was a man when there was no man, or a world when the world was not.' If we are referring to individuals, we may say, this man was when that was not; and so this time was when that was not. True. But to say time was, when no time was, who is so foolish? So then as we say time was created, and yet has been always, because it has been whilst time has been, so it does not follow that the angels, that have been always, should yet be un-created, seeing they have been always, but only in the sense that they have been since time has been: and because time could not have been without them. For where no creature is, whose motion may bring forth time, there can be no time: and therefore, though they have been always, they are created, and not co-eternal with the Creator; for He has been unchangeable from all eternity, but they were created, and yet are said to have been always, because they have been all time, and time could not be without them. But time, being transitory and mutable, cannot be co-eternal with unchanging eternity. And therefore though angels have no bodily transmutation, nor is one part past in them and another to come, yet their motion, by which time is brought about, admits the differences of past and to come; and therefore they can never be co-eternal with their Creator, whose motion admits neither past, present, nor future. Wherefore God having been always a Lord, has always had a creature to be Lord over, not begotten by Him, but created out of nothing by Him, and not co-eternal with Him, for He was before it, though in no time before it: nor foregoing it in any space, but in perpetuity. But if I answer this to those that ask me how the Creator should be always Lord, and yet have no creature to be Lord over, or how has He a creature that is not co-eternal with Him, if it has been always, I fear to be thought rather to affirm what I know not, than teach what I know. And so I return to the Creator's revealed will. What He allows to wiser understandings in this life, or reserves for all unto the next, I pro-fess myself unable to attain to. But this I thought to handle without affirming, that my readers may see what questions to for-bear as dangerous, and not hold them fit for farther inquiry; rather following the apostle's wholesome counsel, saying: 'I say through the grace that is given me, unto every one amongst you, presume not to understand more than is meet to understand, but understand according to sobriety, as God hath dealt unto every man the measure of faith.' [1] For if an infant be nourished according to his strength, he will grow up, but if he be strained above his nature, he will rather fade than increase in growth and strength.

[1] Rom. xii. 3.

CHAPTER XVI

*How we must understand that God promised man life eternal
before all eternity*

WHAT ages passed ere man's creation, I confess I know not: but
sure I am, no creature is co-eternal with the Creator.   The apostle
speaks of eternal times, not to come, but (which is more wondrous)
past.   For thus he says: 'under the hope of eternal life, which God,
that cannot lie, hath promised before all eternity of time: but His
word He hath manifested in time.' [1]   Behold, he talks of time's
eternity past, yet makes it not co-eternal with God.   For He not
only existed Himself before all eternity, but promised eternal life
before it, which He manifested 'in His due time.'   What other is
this than 'His Word'?   For that is 'eternal life.'   But how did
He promise it unto men that were not before eternity, save that
in His eternity and His co-eternal Word He had predestinated
what was in time to be manifested?

CHAPTER XVII

*The defence of God's unchanging will against those that argue that
God's works are repeated from eternity, in circles, from state to
state*

NOR do I doubt that there was no man before the first man's creation: but I deny the (I cannot tell what) revolution of the same
man (I know not how often), or of others like him in nature; nor
can the philosophers drive me from this, by objecting (acutely they
think) that *nullum infinitum est scibile*, infinite things are beyond
reach of knowledge.   And therefore God, say they, has finite
conceptions in Himself of all the finite creatures that He made;
yet must not His goodness be ever held idle, nor His works temporal, as if He had had such an eternity of leisure before, and then
repented Him of it, and so fell to work: therefore, say they, is this
repetition necessary; the world (which, though it has been always,
yet was created) either remaining in change or else being dissolved,
and renewed in this circular course.   Otherwise by giving God's
works a temporal beginning we seem to make Him disallow and
condemn that leisure that He rested in from all eternity before as
slothful and useless.   But if He did create from eternity now this
and then that, and came to make man in time, that was not made

[1] Titus i. 2, 3.

before, then shall He seem not to have made him by knowledge (which they say contains nothing infinite) but at the present time, by chance as it came into His mind. But admit those revolutions, say they, either with the world's continuance in change, or circular revolution, and then we acquit God both of this so long and seemingly idle cessation, and from all operation in rashness and chance. For if the same things be not renewed, the infinite variation of things is too incomprehensible for His knowledge or prescience.

These batteries the ungodly do plant against our faith, to win us into their 'circle': but if reason will not refute them, faith must deride them. But by God's grace, reason will lay those revolving circles flat enough. For hence is these men's error. Running rather in a maze than stepping into the right way, they measure the divine, unchangeable power by their human, frail, and weak spirit, in mutability and apprehension. But as the apostle says: 'Comparing themselves to themselves, they know not themselves.' [1] For because their actions that are suddenly done proceed all from new intents, their minds being mutable, they do imagine, not God, for Him they cannot comprehend, but themselves for God, and compare not Him to Himself, but themselves (in His stead) unto themselves. But we may not think that God's rest affects Him one way, and His work another. He is never affected, nor does His nature admit anything that has not been ever in Him. That which is affected suffers, and that which suffers is mutable. For His vacation is not idle, slothful, or sluggish; nor is His work painful, busy, or industrious. He can rest working and work resting. He can apply an eternal will to a new work; and begins not to work now because He repents that He wrought not before. But if He rested first and wrought after (which I see not how man can conceive), this first and after were in things that first had no being, and afterwards had. But there was neither precedence nor subsequence in Him to alter or abolish His will, but all that ever He created was in His unchanged fixed will eternally one and the same: first willing that they should not be, and afterwards willing that they should be; and so they were not, during His pleasure, and began to be, at His pleasure. This wondrously shows to such as can conceive it that He needed none of these creatures, but created them of His pure goodness, having continued no less blessed without them, from all unbegun eternity.

[1] 2 Cor. x. 12.

CHAPTER XVIII

Against such as say that things infinite are above God's knowledge

BUT such as say that things infinite are past God's knowledge may just as well leap headlong into this pit of impiety, and say that God knows not all numbers. That numbers are infinite is true; for take what number you can, and think to end with it; let it be ever so great and immense, I will add unto it, not one, nor two, but by the law of number, multiply it unto ten times the sum it was. And so is every number composed, that one cannot be equal to another, but all are different, every particular being different, and all in general infinite. Does not God then know these numbers because they are infinite, and can His knowledge attain one sum of numbers, and not the rest? What madman would say so? Nay, they dare not exclude numbers from God's knowledge, Plato having so commended God for using them in the world's creation: and our scripture says of God: 'Thou hast ordered all things in measure, number, and weight'; [1] and the prophet says: 'He numbereth the world'; [2] and the gospel says: 'All the hairs of your heads are numbered.' [3]

God forbid then that we should think that He knows not number, whose wisdom and understanding is innumerably infinite, as David says; for the infiniteness of number, though it be beyond number, is not unknown to Him whose knowledge is infinite. Therefore if whatsoever be known be comprehended in the bound of that knowledge, then is all infiniteness bounded in the knowledge of God, because His knowledge is infinite, and because it is not incomprehensible unto His knowledge. Wherefore if number's infiniteness be not infinite unto God's knowledge, and cannot be, what are we mean wretches that dare presume to limit His knowledge, or say that if this revolution be not admitted in the world's renewing, God cannot either foreknow all things ere He made them, or know them when He made them? Whereas His wisdom being simply and uniformly manifold can comprehend all incomprehensibility by His incomprehensible comprehension, so that whatsoever thing that is new and unlike to all others He should please to make, it could not be new, nor strange unto Him, nor should He foresee it a little before, but contain it in His eternal prescience.

[1] Wisd. of Sol. xi. 20.   [2] Isa. xl. 26.   [3] Matt. x. 30.

CHAPTER XIX

Of the worlds without end, or ages of ages

WHETHER He does so, and whether there is a continual connection of those times which are called *saecula saeculorum*, ages of ages, or worlds without end, running on in a predestinate difference (only the souls that are freed from misery remaining eternally blessed), or whether these words, *saecula saeculorum*, do imply that the world's idea remains firm in God's wisdom and is the efficient cause of this transitory world, I dare not affirm.   The singular may be an explication of the plural, as if we should say, heaven of heaven, for the heavens of heavens.   For God calls the firmament above which the waters are, heaven in the singular number, and yet the psalm says: 'And you waters that be above the heavens, praise the name of the Lord.'[1]   Which of those two it be, or whether *saecula saeculorum* have another meaning, is a deep question.   We may let it pass, for it belongs not to our proposed theme: but whether we could define, or but observe more by the discourse, let us not adventure to affirm aught rashly in so obscure a controversy.   Now are we dealing with the 'circular' persons that turn all things round about till they become repeated.   But which of these opinions soever be true concerning these *saecula saeculorum*, it does not support these revolutions, because whether the worlds of worlds be not the same world revolved, but others successively depending on the former (the freed souls remaining still in their endless bliss), or whether the worlds of worlds be the ideas[2] of these transitory ages, ruling them as their subjects: yet the revolutions have no place here howsoever.   The saints' eternal life overthrows them utterly.

CHAPTER XX

Of that impious assertion that souls truly blessed shall have divers revolutions into misery again

FOR what godly ears can endure to hear, that after the passage of this life in such misery (if I may call it a life, being rather so offensive a death, and yet we love it rather than that death that frees us from it), after so many intolerable mischiefs, ended all at length by true zeal and piety, we should be admitted to the sight of God, and be placed in the fruition and participation of that incorporeal light and unchangeable immortal essence with love of

[1] Ps. cxlviii. 4.   [2] In the Platonic sense.—ED.

which we burn, all upon this condition—to leave it again at length, and be re-enfolded in mortal misery and infernal mortality, where God is lost, where truth is sought by hate, where blessedness is sought by uncleanness, and be cast from all enjoying of eternity, truth, or felicity; and this not once but often, being eternally revolved by the course of the times from the first to the latter: and all this, because by means of these revolutions, transforming us and our false beatitudes into true miseries (successively, but yet eternally), God might come to know His own works, for otherwise He should neither be able to rest from working, nor know aught that is infinite? Who can hear or endure this? Which were it true, there were not only more wit in concealing it, but also (to speak my mind as I can) more wisdom in not knowing it. For if we shall be blessed in not remembering these things there, why do we aggravate our misery in knowing them here? But if we must needs know them there, yet let us keep ourselves ignorant of them here, and so be happier in our present expectation than in any future bliss; here expecting blessed eternity, and there attaining bliss, with the assurance that it is but transitory. But if they say that no man can attain this bliss unless he know the transitory revolutions thereof ere he leave this life, how then do they confess that the more one loves God the easier shall he attain bliss, for they teach the way how to dull this love? For who will not but love him lightly whom he knows he must leave, and whose truth and wisdom he must forsake, and that when by the perfection of his bliss he has come to the full knowledge of him? One can never love a friend faithfully, if one knows that he shall become one's enemy. But God forbid that this threatening of theirs that our misery should never be ended, but only interrupted now and then by false happiness, should be true. For what is falser than that bliss, wherein we shall be either wholly ignorant even in such light of our future misery, or otherwise continually afraid of it, while living in the highest citadel of felicity? If we know not that we shall become wretched, our misery here is wiser than happiness there. But if we shall know it, then the wretched soul had better live in a miserable state and go from thence to eternity, than in a blessed state to fall from thence to misery. And so our hope of happiness is unhappy, and of misery happy: and consequently, we suffering miseries here, and expecting them there, are in truth rather wretched than blessed. But piety cries out, and truth convinces this to be false. The felicity promised us is true, eternal, and wholly uninterrupted by any revolution to worse.

Let us follow Christ, our right way, and leave this circular maze of the impious. For if Porphyry the Platonist rejected his master's opinion in this circumrotation of souls, being moved hereto either by the vanity of the thing, or by fear of the Christian dispensation;[1] and had rather affirm (as I said in the tenth book) that the soul was sent into the world to know evil, that being purged from it, it might return to the Father, and nevermore suffer any such pollution: how much more ought we to detest this falsehood, this enemy of true faith and Christianity! These circles now being broken, nothing urges us to think that man had no beginning, because I know not what revolutions have kept all things in such a continual course of up and down, that nothing can be new in the world. For if the soul be freed, and shall no more return to misery, it being never freed before, there is an act and that a great one newly begun, namely, the soul's possession of eternal bliss.

And if this fall out in an immortal nature without any circum-volution, why is it not as possible in mortal things? If they say that bliss is no new thing to the soul, because it returns but unto that which it enjoyed always before; yet is the freedom new, for it was never freed before, being never before miserable, and the misery is new unto it, that was never miserable before. Now if this newness happen, not in the order that God's providence allotted, but by chance, where are our revolutions that admit nothing new, but keep all in one course? But if this novelty be within the compass of God's providence, be the soul given from heaven or fallen from thence,[2] there may be new accidents that were not before, and yet in the order of nature. And if the soul by folly procure itself new misery (which the divine providence foresaw and included in the order of things, freeing it from thence also by this provident power), how dare flesh and blood then be so rash as to deny that the divinity may produce things new unto the world (though not to Himself) which though He foresaw, yet were never made before? If they say it is no news that the freed souls return no more to misery, because every day and all days some are being freed from thence, why then they confess that there are still new souls created, to be newly freed from new miseries. For if they say they are not new souls, but souls existing from eternity, which are daily put into new bodies, and living wisely are freed, never to return; then they make the souls of eternity infinite: for imagine a number of souls ever so large, they could not suffice for all the men of these infinite ages past, if each soul as soon as it was free, flew up, and returned no more. Nor can they show how there may be an infinite multitude of souls in the world, and yet debar God from knowing things infinite. Wherefore seeing their revolutions of bliss and misery are dismissed, what remains but to aver that God can, when His good pleasure is, create what new thing He will, and yet because of His eternal foreknowledge

---

[1] *Tempora Christiana.*—ED.

[2] i.e. consigned to a human body by God's will or as a retribution.—ED.

never change His will? And whether the number of those freed
and not returning souls may be increased, look they to that, who
dispute about the limit which must be set to the infinity of things.
We end our disputation with a dilemma. If it may be increased,
why deny they that that may be made now that had no being
before, if that number of freed souls that was before be not only
increased now, but shall be for ever? But if there be but a certain
number of souls to be freed and never to return, and that number
be not increased, then whatever this number shall be, it never
existed before, nor can it increase to its consummation, except
from a beginning; and this beginning never existed. And so that
there might be this beginning, that man was created, before whom
was no other.

CHAPTER XXI

Of the state of the first man, and mankind in him

THIS hard question of God's power to create new things without
change of will, because of His eternity, being (I hope) sufficiently
handled, we may plainly see that He did far better in producing
mankind from one man only, than if He had made many: for
whereas He created some creatures that love to be alone, and in
deserts, as eagles, kites, lions, wolves, and suchlike; and others,
that had rather live in flocks and companies, as doves, stars, stags,
hinds, and suchlike; yet neither of those sorts did He produce of
one alone, but of many together. But man, whose nature He
made as a mean between angels and beasts, that if he obeyed the
Lord his true Creator, and kept his behests, he might be transported
to the angels' society; but that if he became perverse in will, and
offended his Lord God by pride of heart, he might be cast unto
death like a beast, and living the slave of his lusts, after death be
destinate unto eternal pains—him did He create one alone, but
meant not to leave him alone without another human fellow.
Thereby He the more zealously commended true concord unto
us, men being not only of one kind in nature, but also of one
kindred in affection. Nor did He create the woman He meant to
join with man, as He did man, of earth, but of man; and man whom
He joined with her, not of her, but of Himself, that all mankind
might have their propagation from one.

CHAPTER XXII

That God foreknew that the first man should sin, and how many people He was to translate out of his kind into the angels' society

GOD was not ignorant that man would sin, and so incur mortality both for himself and his progeny: nor that mortals should run on in that height of iniquity, that brute beasts should live in more agreement and peace among themselves, whose origin was out of water and earth, than men whose kind came all out of one for the commending of concord: for lions never war among themselves, nor dragons, as men have done. But God foresaw withal that His grace should adopt the godly, justify them by the Holy Spirit, pardon their sins, and rank them in eternal peace with the angels, the last and most dangerous death being destroyed: and those should make use of God's producing all mankind from one, in learning how pleasing to God was unity in mankind.

CHAPTER XXIII

Of the nature of man's soul, being created according to the image of God

THEREFORE God made man according to His image and likeness, giving him a soul whereby in reason and understanding he excelled all the other creatures, that had no such soul. And when He had made man thus of earth, and either breathed the soul which he had made into him, or rather made that breath one which he breathed into him (for to breathe is but to make a breath), which breath is the soul, then out of his side did He take a bone, whereof He made him a wife, and a help, as He was God; for we are not to conceive this carnally, as we see an artificer work up anything into the shape of a man by art. God's hand is His power working visible things invisibly. Such as measure God's virtue and power, that can make seeds without seeds, by those daily and usual works, hold this rather for a fable than a truth: but they know not this creation, and therefore think sceptically thereof; as though the works of ordinary conception and production were not strange to those that know them not, though they assign them rather to natural causes than account them the Deity's works.

CHAPTER XXIV

Whether the angels may be called creators of any, even the least
creature

BUT here we have nothing to do with them that hold that the divine
essence meddles not with those things at all.   But those that follow
Plato in affirming that all mortal creatures, of which man is the
chief, were made by the lesser created gods, through the permission
or command of the Creator, and not by Himself that framed the
world, let them but abjure the superstition wherein they seek to
give those inferiors just honours and sacrifices, and they shall
quickly avoid the error of this opinion; for it is not lawful to hold
any creature, be it never so small, to have any other Creator than
God, even before it could be understood.   But the angels (whom
they had rather call gods), though at His command they work in
things of the world, yet we no more call creators of living things,
than we call husbandmen the creators of fruits and trees.

CHAPTER XXV

That no nature or form of anything living has any other Creator
but God

WHEREAS there is one form given externally to all corporal sub-
stances according to which potters, carpenters, and others shape
forms and figures of creatures; and another inward containing
the efficient cause hereof in the secret power of the uniting and
understanding nature, which makes not only the natural forms, but
even the living souls, when they are not extant—the first each
artificer has in his brain, but the latter belongs to none but God,
who formed the world and the angels without either world or angels.
For from that all-dividing and all-effective divine power, which
cannot be made but makes, and which in the beginning gave rotundity both to the heavens and sun—from the same had the eye,
the apple, and all other round figures that we see in nature their
rotundity, not from any external effective, but from the depth of
that Creator's power that said, 'I fill heaven and earth'; [1] and
'whose wisdom reaches from end to end, ordering all in a delicate
decorum.' [2]   Wherefore what use He made of the angels in the
creation, making all Himself, I know not.   I dare neither ascribe
to them more than their power, nor detract anything from that.

[1] Jer. xxiii. 24.   [2] Wisd. of Sol. viii. 1.

But with their leave, I attribute the estate of all things as they are natures unto God, of whom alone they thankfully acknowledge their being. We do not then call husbandmen the creators of trees or plants, or anything else: for we read: 'Neither is he that planteth anything, neither he that watereth, but God, that giveth the increase.' [1] No, nor the earth either, though it seems the fruitful mother of all things that grow: for we read also: 'God giveth bodies unto what He will, even to every seed his own body.' [2] Nor call we a woman the creatrix of her child, but Him that said to a servant of His: 'Before I formed thee in the womb I knew thee.' [3] And although the woman's soul, being thus or thus affected, may put some quality upon her burthen, as we read that Jacob coloured his sheep diversely by spotted sticks, yet she can no more make the nature that is produced, than she could make herself. What seminal causes then soever that angels or men do use in producing things living or dead, or that proceed from the copulation of male and female, or what feelings soever of the mother dispose thus or thus of the colour or feature of her conception, the natures thus or thus affected in each of their kinds are the works of none but God, whose secret power passes through all, giving all being to all whatsoever, in that it has being: because unless He made it, it should not be thus, nor thus, but have no being at all. Wherefore if in those forms imposed externally upon things corporal, we say that, not workmen, but king Romulus was the builder of Rome, and Alexander of Alexandria, because by their direction these cities were built; how much the rather ought we to call God the builder of nature, who neither makes anything of any substance but what He had made before, nor by any other ministers but those He had made before: and if He withdraw His efficient power from things, they shall have no more being than they had ere they were created — ere they were, I mean in eternity, not in time. For who created time but He that made them creatures, whose motions time follows?

CHAPTER XXVI

The Platonists' opinion that held the angels God's creatures, and man the angels'

AND Plato would have the lesser gods (made by the highest) to create all other things, by taking their immortal part from him, and framing the mortal themselves: herein making them not the

---

[1] 1 Cor. iii. 7.   [2] 1 Cor. xv. 38.   [3] Jer. i. 5.

creators of ourselves, but of our bodies only.   And therefore Porphyry, in holding that the body must be avoided ere the soul be
purged, and thinking with Plato, and his sect, that the souls of
bad livers were for punishment thrust into bodies (into beasts' also
says Plato, but into man's only says Porphyry) affirms directly that
these gods whom they will have us to worship as our parents and
creators, are but the forgers of our prisons, and not our formers, but
only our jailers, locking us in those dolorous grates and wretched
fetters.   Wherefore the Platonists must either give us no punishment in our bodies, or else make not those gods our creators, whose
work they exhort us by all means to avoid and to escape: though
both these positions be most false, for the souls are neither put
into bodies to be thereby punished, nor has anything in heaven or
earth any creator but the Maker of heaven and earth.   For if there
be no cause of our life in the body but our punishment, how is it
that Plato says the world could never have been made most beautiful, but that it was filled with all kind of creatures?   But if our
creation (albeit mortal) be the work of God; how is punishment then
to enter into God's benefits, that is, our bodies?   And if God (as
Plato says often) had all the creatures of the world in His prescience,
why then did not He make them all?   Would He not make some,
though in His unbounded knowledge He knew how to make all?
Wherefore our true religion rightly affirms Him the Maker both
of the world and all creatures therein, bodies, and souls, of which
man the chief piece in earth was alone made after His image, for
the reason showed before, if not for a greater.   Yet was he not
left alone, for there is nothing in the world so sociable by nature
and so jarring by vice as man is; nor can man's nature speak
better either to warding off discord whilst it is out, or expelling it
when it is entered, than in recording our first father, whom God
created single (from him to propagate all the rest), to give us a
true admonition to preserve a union over the greatest multitudes.
And the fact that the woman was made of his rib, was a plain intimation of the concord that should be between man and wife.
These were the strange works of God, for they were the first.   He
that believes them not must utterly deny all wonders: for if they
had followed the usual course of nature, they had been no wonders.
But what is there in all this whole work of the divine providence
that is not of use, though we know it not?   The holy psalm says:
'Come and behold the works of the Lord, what wonders He hath
wrought upon the earth.' [1]   Wherefore, why the woman was made
of man's rib, and what this first seeming wonder prefigured, if God
vouchsafe, I will show in another place.

[1] Ps. xlvi. 8.

CHAPTER XXVII

That the fullness of mankind was created in the first man, in whom God foresaw both who should be saved, and who should be damned

BUT now because we must end this book, let this be our position—that in the first man the foresaid two societies or cities had their origin; yet not evidently, but unto God's prescience; for from him were the rest of men to come, some to be made fellow citizens with the angels in joy, and some with the devils in torment, by the secret but just judgment of God.   For seeing that it is written: 'All the ways of the Lord be mercy and truth,' [1] His grace can neither be unjust, nor His justice cruel.

[1] Ps. xxv. 10.

END OF VOLUME ONE

EVERYMAN'S LIBRARY
A CLASSIFIED LIST OF THE 966 VOLUMES

In each of the thirteen classifications in this list (except BIOGRAPHY) the volumes are arranged alphabetically under the *authors' names*, but Anthologies and works by various hands are listed under titles. Where authors appear in more than one section, a cross-reference is given, viz.: (*See also* FICTION). The number at the end of each item is the number of the volume in the series.

All the volumes are obtainable in the standard Cloth binding; selected volumes obtainable in Leather are marked L.

BIOGRAPHY

Audubon the Naturalist, Life and Adventures of. By R. Buchanan. 601

Baxter (Richard), Autobiography of. Ed. by Rev. J. M. Lloyd Thomas. 868

Beaconsfield (Lord), Life of. By J. A. Froude. 666

Berlioz (Hector), Life of. Translated by Katherine F. Boult. 602

Blackwell (Dr Elizabeth): Pioneer Work for Women. With an Introduction by Mrs Fawcett. 667

Brontë (Charlotte), Life of. By Mrs Gaskell. Intro. by May Sinclair. 318
    (*See also* FICTION)

Browning (Robert), Life of. By E. Dowden. 701
    (*See also* POETRY AND DRAMA)

Burney (Fanny), Diary. A selection edited by Lewis Gibbs. 960

Burns (Robert), Life of. By J. G. Lockhart. Intro. by E. Rhys. 156
    (*See also* POETRY AND DRAMA)

Buxton (Sir Thomas Fowell), Memoirs of. Ed. by Charles Buxton. 773

L Byron's Letters. Introduction by André Maurois. 931
    (*See also* POETRY AND DRAMA)

Carey (William), Life of: Shoemaker and Missionary. By George Smith. 395

Carlyle's Letters and Speeches of Cromwell. 3 vols. 266–8

  ,, Reminiscences. 875 (*See also* ESSAYS *and* HISTORY)

Cellini's (Benvenuto) Autobiography. 51

Cibber's (Colley) An Apology for his Life. 668

Columbus, Life of. By Sir Arthur Helps. 332

Constable (John), Memoirs of. By C. R. Leslie, R.A. 563

Cowper (William), Selected Letters of. Intro. by W. Hadley, M.A. 774
    (*See also* POETRY AND DRAMA)

De Quincey's Reminiscences of the Lake Poets. Intro. by E. Rhys. 163
    (*See also* ESSAYS)

De Retz (Cardinal). Memoirs. By Himself. 2 vols. 735–6

Dickens (Charles), Life of. By John Forster. Introduction by G. K. Chesterton. 2 vols. 781–2 (*See also* FICTION)

Disraeli (Benjamin), Life of. By J. A. Froude. 666

Evelyn's Diary. 2 vols. Introduction by G. W. E. Russell. 220–1

Fox (George), Journal of. Text revised by Norman Penney. 754

Franklin's (Benjamin) Autobiography. 316

Gibbon (Edward), Autobiography of. 511 (*See also* HISTORY)

Gladstone, Life of. By G. W. E. Russell ('Onlooker'). 661

Goethe, Life of. By G. H. Lewes. Intro. by Havelock Ellis. 269

Hastings (Warren), Life of. By Capt. L. J. Trotter. 452

Hodson of Hodson's Horse. By Capt. L. J. Trotter. 401

Hudson (W. H.), Far Away and Long Ago. 956

Hutchinson (Col.), Memoirs of. Intro. Monograph by F. P. G. Guizot. 317

L Johnson (Dr Samuel), Life of. By James Boswell. 2 vols. 1–2

  ,,   ,, Lives of the Poets. 770–1 (*See also* TRAVEL)

Keats (John), Life and Letters of. By Lord Houghton. Introduction by R. Lynd. 801 (*See also* POETRY AND DRAMA)

Lamb (Charles), Letters of. 2 vols. 342–3
    (*See also* ESSAYS *and* FOR YOUNG PEOPLE)

Lincoln (Abraham), Life of. By Henry Bryan Binns. 783 (*See also* ORATORY)

Mahomet, Life of. By Washington Irving. Intro. Prof. E. V. Arnold. 513

I

ssued June 1941

BIOGRAPHY—*continued*

CLASSICAL

ESSAYS AND BELLES-LETTRES

ESSAYS AND BELLES-LETTRES—*continued*

4

FICTION

FICTION—*continued*

FICTION—*continued*

FICTION—*continued*

FICTION—*continued*

Stevenson's Treasure Island and Kidnapped. 763
    "   St. Ives. Introduction by Ernest Rhys. 904
        (*See also* ESSAYS, POETRY, *and* TRAVEL)
Surtees' Jorrocks' Jaunts and Jollities. 817
Swift's Gulliver's Travels. Unabridged Edition, with contemporary
    maps. Introduction by Harold Williams. 60
L Tales of Detection. Edited, with Introduction, by Dorothy L. Sayers. 928
Thackeray's Rose and the Ring and other stories. Intro. Walter Jerrold.
    "   Esmond. Introduction by Walter Jerrold. 73 [359
    "   Newcomes. Introduction by Walter Jerrold. 2 vols. 465–6
    "   Pendennis. Intro. by Walter Jerrold. 2 vols. 425–6
    "   Roundabout Papers. 687
L   "   Vanity Fair. Introduction by Hon. Whitelaw Reid. 298
    "   Virginians. Introduction by Walter Jerrold. 2 vols. 507–8
        (*See also* ESSAYS)
L Tolstoy's Anna Karenina. Trans. by Rochelle S. Townsend. 2 vols. 612–13
    "   Childhood, Boyhood, and Youth. Trans. by C. J. Hogarth. 591
    "   Master and Man, and other Parables and Tales. 469
    "   War and Peace. 3 vols. 525–7
Trollope's (Anthony) Barchester Towers. 30
    "   "   Dr. Thorne. 360
    "   "   Framley Parsonage. Intro. by Ernest Rhys. 181
    "   "   The Golden Lion of Granpère. Introduction by
        Sir Hugh Walpole. 761
    "   "   The Last Chronicles of Barset. 2 vols. 391–2
    "   "   Phineas Finn. Intro. by Sir Hugh Walpole. 2 vols.
    "   "   The Small House at Allington. 361   [832–3
    "   "   The Warden. Introduction by Ernest Rhys. 182
Turgenev's Fathers and Sons. Translated by C. J. Hogarth. 742
    "   Liza. Translated by W. R. S. Ralston. 677
    "   Virgin Soil. Translated by Rochelle S. Townsend. 528
Voltaire's Candide and Other Tales. 936
Walpole's (Hugh) Mr Perrin and Mr Traill. 918
L Well's (H. G.) The Time Machine and The Wheels of Chance. 915
Whyte-Melville's The Gladiators. Introduction by J. Mavrogordato. 523
Wood's (Mrs Henry) The Channings. 84
Woolf's (Virginia) To the Lighthouse. Intro. by D. M. Hoare. 949
Yonge's (Charlotte M.) The Dove in the Eagle's Nest. 329
    "   "   The Heir of Redclyffe. Intro. Mrs Meynell. 362
        (*See also* FOR YOUNG PEOPLE)
Zola's (Emile) Germinal. Translated by Havelock Ellis. 897

HISTORY

Anglo-Saxon Chronicle, The. Translated by James Ingram. 624
Bede's Ecclesiastical History, etc. Introduction by Vida D. Scudder. 479
Burnet's History of His Own Times. 85
L Carlyle's French Revolution. Introduction by H. Belloc. 2 vols. 31–2
    (*See also* BIOGRAPHY *and* ESSAYS)
Chesterton's History of the United States. Edited by Prof. D. W.
    Brogan, M.A. 965
Creasy's Decisive Battles of the World. Introduction by E. Rhys. 300
De Joinville (*See* Villehardouin)
Duruy's (Jean Victor) A History of France. 2 vols. 737–8
Finlay's Byzantine Empire. 33
    "   Greece under the Romans. 185
Froude's Henry VIII. Intro. by Llewellyn Williams, M.P. 3 vols. 372–4
    "   Edward VI. Intro. by Llewellyn Williams, M.P., B.C.L. 375
    "   Mary Tudor. Intro. by Llewellyn Williams, M.P., B.C.L. 477
    "   History of Queen Elizabeth's Reign. 5 vols. Completing
    Froude's 'History of England,' in 10 vols. 583–7
        (*See also* ESSAYS *and* BIOGRAPHY)
Gibbon's Decline and Fall of the Roman Empire. Edited, with Introduc-
    tion and Notes, by Oliphant Smeaton, M.A. 6 vols. 434–6, 474–6
        (*See also* BIOGRAPHY)

HISTORY—*continued*

Green's Short History of the English People. Edited and Revised by
L. Cecil Jane, with an Appendix by R. P. Farley, B.A. 2 vols. 727–8
Grote's History of Greece. Intro. by A. D. Lindsay. 12 vols. 186–97
Hallam's (Henry) Constitutional History of England. 3 vols. 621–3
Holinshed's Chronicle as used in Shakespeare's Plays. Introduction by
Professor Allardyce Nicoll. 800
Irving's (Washington) Conquest of Granada. 478
   (*See also* ESSAYS *and* BIOGRAPHY)
Josephus' Wars of the Jews. Introduction by Dr Jacob Hart. ·712
Lutzow's Bohemia: An Historical Sketch. Introduction by President
T. G. Masaryk. Revised edition. 432
Macaulay's History of England. 3 vols. 34–6
   (*See also* ESSAYS *and* ORATORY)
Maine's (Sir Henry) Ancient Law. 734
Merivale's History of Rome. (An Introductory vol. to Gibbon.) 433
Mignet's (F. A. M.) The French Revolution. 713
Milman's History of the Jews. 2 vols. 377–8
Mommsen's History of Rome. Translated by W. P. Dickson, LL.D.
With a review of the work by E. A. Freeman. 4 vols. 542–5
Motley's Dutch Republic. 3 vols. 86–8
Parkman's Conspiracy of Pontiac. 2 vols. 302–3
Paston Letters, The. Based on edition of Knight. Introduction by
Mrs Archer-Hind, M.A. 2 vols. 752–3
Pilgrim Fathers, The. Introduction by John Masefield. 480
 Pinnow's History of Germany. Translated by M. R. Brailsford. 929
Political Liberty, The Growth of. A Source-Book of English History.
Arranged by Ernest Rhys. 745   [M.A. 2 vols. 397–8
Prescott's Conquest of Mexico. With Introduction by Thomas Seccombe
  ,, Conquest of Peru. Intro. by Thomas Seccombe, M.A. 301
Sismondi's Italian Republics. 250
Stanley's Lectures on the Eastern Church. Intro. by A. J. Grieve. 251
Tacitus. Vol. I. Annals. Introduction by E. H. Blakeney. 273
  ,, Vol. II. Agricola and Germania. Intro. E. H. Blakeney. 274
Thierry's Norman Conquest. Intro. by J. A. Price, B.A. 2 vols. 198–9
Villehardouin and De Joinville's Chronicles of the Crusades. Translated,
with Introduction, by Sir F. Marzials, C.B. 333
Voltaire's Age of Louis XIV. Translated by Martyn P. Pollack. 780

ORATORY

Anthology of British Historical Speeches and Orations. Compiled by
Ernest Rhys. 714
Bright's (John) Speeches. Selected with Intro. by Joseph Sturge. 252
Burke's American Speeches and Letters. 340. (*See also* ESSAYS)
Demosthenes: Select Orations. 546
Fox (Charles James): Speeches (French Revolutionary War Period).
Edited with Introduction by Irene Cooper Willis, M.A. 759
Lincoln's Speeches, etc. Intro. by the Rt Hon. James Bryce. 206
   (*See also* BIOGRAPHY)
Macaulay's Speeches on Politics and Literature. 399
   (*See also* ESSAYS *and* HISTORY)
Pitt's Orations on the War with France. 145

PHILOSOPHY AND THEOLOGY

 A Kempis' Imitation of Christ. 484
Ancient Hebrew Literature. Being the Old Testament and Apocrypha.
Arranged by the Rev. R. B. Taylor. 4 vols. 253–6
Aquinas, Thomas: Selected Writings. Edited by Rev. Fr D'Arcy. 953
Aristotle, The Nicomachean Ethics of. Translated by D. P. Chase.
Introduction by Professor J. A. Smith. 547
   (*See also* CLASSICAL)
Bacon's The Advancement of Learning. 719 (*See also* ESSAYS)
Berkeley's (Bishop) Principles of Human Knowledge, New Theory of
Vision. With Introduction by A. D. Lindsay. 483

PHILOSOPHY AND THEOLOGY—*continued*

Boehme's (Jacob) The Signature of All Things, with Other Writings. Introduction by Clifford Bax. 569

Browne's Religio Medici, etc. Intro. by Professor C. H. Herford. 92

Bunyan's Grace Abounding and Mr Badman. Introduction by G. B. Harrison. 815 (*See also* ROMANCE)

Burton's (Robert) Anatomy of Melancholy. Introduction by Holbrook Jackson. 3 vols. 886–8

Butler's Analogy of Religion. Introduction by Rev. Ronald Bayne. 90

Descartes' (René) A Discourse on Method. Translated by Professor John Veitch. Introduction by A. D. Lindsay. 570

Ellis' (Havelock) Selected Essays. Introduction by J. S. Collis. 930

Gore's (Charles) The Philosophy of the Good Life. 924

Hindu Scriptures. Edited by Dr Nicol Macnicol. Introduction by Rabindranath Tagore. 944

Hobbes' Leviathan. Edited, with Intro. by A. D. Lindsay, M.A. 691

Hooker's Ecclesiastical Polity. Intro. by Rev. H. Bayne. 2 vols. 201–2

Hume's Treatise of Human Nature, and other Philosophical Works. Introduction by A. D. Lindsay, M.A. 2 vols. 548–9

James (William): Selected Papers on Philosophy. 739

Kant's Critique of Pure Reason. Translated by J. M. D. Meiklejohn. Introduction by A. D. Lindsay, M.A. 909

Keble's The Christian Year. Introduction by J. C. Shairp. 690

King Edward VI. First and Second Prayer Books. Introduction by the Right Rev. Bishop of Gloucester. 448

L Koran, The. Rodwell's Translation. 380

Latimer's Sermons. Introduction by Canon Beeching. 40

Law's Serious Call to a Devout and Holy Life. 91

Leibniz's Philosophical Writings. Selected and trans. by Mary Morris. Introduction by C. R. Morris, M.A. 905

Locke's Two Treatises of Civil Government. Introduction by Professor William S. Carpenter. 751

Malthus on the Principles of Population. 2 vols. 692–3

Mill's (John Stuart) Utilitarianism, Liberty, Representative Government. With Introduction by A. D. Lindsay, M.A. 482

,, Subjection of Women. (*See* Wollstonecraft, Mary, *under* SCIENCE)

More's Utopia. Introduction by Judge O'Hagan. 461

New Testament. Arranged in the order in which the books came to the Christians of the First Century. 93

Newman's Apologia pro Vita Sua. Intro. by Dr Charles Sarolea. 636 (*See also* ESSAYS)

Nietzsche's Thus Spake Zarathustra. Trans. by A. Tille and M. M. Bozman.

Paine's Rights of Man. Introduction by G. J. Holyoake. 718 [892

Pascal's Pensées. Translated by W. F. Trotter. Introduction by T. S. Eliot. 874 [C.I.E. 403

Ramayana and the Mahabharata, The. Translated by Romesh Dutt.

Renan's Life of Jesus. Introduction by Right Rev. Chas. Gore, D.D. 805

Robertson's (F. W.) Sermons on Christian Doctrine, and Bible Subjects. Each Volume with Introduction by Canon Burnett. 3 vols. 37–9 (*Note: No. 37 is out of print.*)

Robinson's (Wade) The Philosophy of Atonement and Other Sermons. Introduction by Rev. F. B. Meyer. 637

Rousseau's (J. J.) The Social Contract, etc. 660. (*See also* ESSAYS)

St Augustine's Confessions. Dr Pusey's Translation. 200

L St Francis: The Little Flowers, and The Life of St. Francis. 485

Seeley's Ecce Homo. Introduction by Sir Oliver Lodge. 305

Selection from St Thomas Aquinas. Edited by The Rev. Father M. C. D'Arcy. 953

Spinoza's Ethics, etc. Translated by Andrew J. Boyle. With Introduction by Professor Santayana. 481

Swedenborg's (Emmanuel) Heaven and Hell. 379
,, ,, The Divine Love and Wisdom. 635
,, ,, The Divine Providence. 658
L ,, ,, The True Christian Religion. 893

POETRY AND DRAMA

POETRY AND DRAMA—*continued*

L Milton's Poems. Introduction by W. H. D. Rouse. 384
  (*See also* ESSAYS)
  Minor Elizabethan Drama. Vol. I. Tragedy. Selected, with Introduction,
    by Professor Thorndike. Vol. II. Comedy. 491–2
L Minor Poets of the 18th Century. Edited by H. I'Anson Fausset. 844
  Minor Poets of the 17th Century. Edited by R. G. Howarth. 873
L Modern Plays. 942
  Molière's Comedies. Introduction by Prof. F. C. Green. 2 vols. 830–1
  New Golden Treasury, The. An Anthology of Songs and Lyrics. 695
  Old Yellow Book, The. Introduction by Charles E. Hodell. 503
  Omar Khayyám (The Rubáiyát of). Trans. by Edward FitzGerald. 819
L Palgrave's Golden Treasury. Introduction by Edward Hutton. 96
  Percy's Reliques of Ancient English Poetry. 2 vols. 148–9
  Poe's (Edgar Allan) Poems and Essays. Intro. by Andrew Lang. 791
    (*See also* FICTION)
  Pope (Alexander): Collected Poems. Introduction by Ernest Rhys. 760
  Proctor's (Adelaide A.) Legends and Lyrics. 150
  Restoration Plays, A Volume of. Introduction by Edmund Gosse. 604
  Rossetti's Poems and Translations. Introduction by E. G. Gardner. 627
  Scott's Poems and Plays. Intro. by Andrew Lang. 2 vols. 550–1
    (*See also* BIOGRAPHY *and* FICTION)
L Shakespeare's Comedies. 153
L   ,,   Historical Plays, Poems, and Sonnets. 154
L   ,,   Tragedies. 155
  Shelley's Poetical Works. Introduction by A. H. Koszul. 2 vols. 257–8
L Sheridan's Plays. 95
  Spenser's Faerie Queene. Intro. by Prof. J. W. Hales. 2 vols. 443–4
    ,,   Shepherd's Calendar and Other Poems. Edited by Philip
      Henderson. 879
  Stevenson's Poems—A Child's Garden of Verses, Underwoods, Songs of
    Travel, Ballads. 768 (*See also* ESSAYS, FICTION, *and* TRAVEL)
  Swinburne's Poems and Prose. 961
L Tchekhov. Plays and Stories. 941
  Tennyson's Poems. Vol. I. 1830–56. Introduction by Ernest Rhys. 44
    ,,   ,,   Vol. II. 1857–70. 626
  Twenty One-Act Plays. Selected by John Hampden. 947
  Webster and Ford. Plays. Selected, with Introduction, by Dr G. B.
    Harrison. 899
  Whitman's (Walt) Leaves of Grass (I), Democratic Vistas, etc. 573
  Wilde (Oscar), Plays, Prose Writings, and Poems. 858
  Wordsworth's Shorter Poems. Introduction by Ernest Rhys. 203
    ,,   Longer Poems. Note by Editor. 311

REFERENCE

Atlas of Ancient and Classical Geography. Many coloured and line
  Maps; Historical Gazetteer, Index, etc. 451
Biographical Dictionary of English Literature. 449
Biographical Dictionary of Foreign Literature. 900
Dates, Dictionary of. 554
Dictionary of Quotations and Proverbs. 2 vols. 809–10
Everyman's English Dictionary. 776
Literary and Historical Atlas. I. Europe. Many coloured and line Maps;
                    full Index and Gazetteer. 496
  ,,   ,,   ,,   II. America. Do. 553
  ,,   ,,   ,,   III. Asia. Do. 663
  ,,   ,,   ,,   IV. Africa and Australia. Do. 662
Non-Classical Mythology, Dictionary of. 632
Reader's Guide to Everyman's Library. Revised edition, covering the
  first 950 vols. 889
Roget's Thesaurus of English Words and Phrases. 2 vols. 630–1
Smith's Smaller Classical Dictionary. Revised and Edited by E. H.
Wright's An Encyclopaedia of Gardening. 555 [Blakeney, M.A. 495

ROMANCE

Aucassin and Nicolette, with other Medieval Romances. 497
Boccaccio's Decameron. (Unabridged.) Translated by J. M. Rigg. Introduction by Edward Hutton. 2 vols. 845-6
Bunyan's Pilgrim's Progress. Introduction by Rev. H. E. Lewis. 204
Burnt Njal, The Story of. Translated by Sir George Dasent. 558
Cervantes' Don Quixote. Motteux's Translation. Lockhart's Introduction. 2 vols. 385-6
Chrétien de Troyes: Eric and Enid. Translated, with Introduction and Notes, by William Wistar Comfort. 698
French Medieval Romances. Translated by Eugene Mason. 557
Geoffrey of Monmouth's Histories of the Kings of Britain. 577
Grettir Saga, The. Newly Translated by G. Ainslie Hight. 699
Gudrun. Done into English by Margaret Armour. 880
Guest's (Lady) Mabinogion. Introduction by Rev. R. Williams. 97
Heimskringla: The Olaf Sagas. Translated by Samuel Laing. Introduction and Notes by John Beveridge. 717
    "   Sagas of the Norse Kings. Translated by Samuel Laing. Introduction and Notes by John Beveridge. 847
Holy Graal, The High History of the, 445
Kalevala. Introduction by W. F. Kirby, F.L.S., F.E.S. 2 vols. 259-60
Le Sage's The Adventures of Gil Blas. Intro. by Anatole Le Bras. 2 vols.
MacDonald's (George) Phantastes: A Faerie Romance. 732 [1437-8
    (*See also* FICTION)
Malory's Le Morte d'Arthur. Intro. by Professor Rhys. 2 vols. 45-6
Morris (William): Early Romances. Introduction by Alfred Noyes. 261
    "   "   The Life and Death of Jason. 575
Morte d'Arthur Romances, Two. Introduction by Lucy A. Paton. 634
Nibelungs, The Fall of the. Translated by Margaret Armour. 312
Rabelais' The Heroic Deeds of Gargantua and Pantagruel. Introduction by D. B. Wyndham Lewis. 2 vols. 826-7
Wace's Arthurian Romance. Translated by Eugene Mason. Layamon's Brut. Introduction by Lucy A. Paton. 518

SCIENCE

Boyle's The Sceptical Chymist. 559
Darwin's The Origin of Species. Introduction by Sir Arthur Keith. 811
    (*See also* TRAVEL)   [E. F. Bozman. 922
Eddington's (Sir Arthur) The Nature of the Physical World. Intro. by
Euclid: the Elements of. Todhunter's Edition. Introduction by Sir Thomas Heath, K.C.B. 891
Faraday's (Michael) Experimental Researches in Electricity. 576
Galton's Inquiries into Human Faculty. Revised by Author. 263
George's (Henry) Progress and Poverty. 560
Hahnemann's (Samuel) The Organon of the Rational Art of Healing. Introduction by C. E. Wheeler. 663
Harvey's Circulation of the Blood. Introduction by Ernest Parkyn. 262
Howard's State of the Prisons. Introduction by Kenneth Ruck. 835
Huxley's Essays. Introduction by Sir Oliver Lodge. 47
    "   Select Lectures and Lay Sermons. Intro. Sir Oliver Lodge. 498
Lyell's Antiquity of Man. With an introduction by R. H. Rastall. 700
Marx's (Karl) Capital. Translated by Eden and Cedar Paul. Introduction by G. D. H. Cole. 2 vols. 848-9
Miller's Old Red Sandstone. 103
Owen's (Robert) A New View of Society, etc. Intro. by G. D. H. Cole. 799
Pearson's (Karl) The Grammar of Science. 939
Ricardo's Principles of Political Economy and Taxation. 590
Smith's (Adam) The Wealth of Nations. 2 vols. 412-13
Tyndall's Glaciers of the Alps and Mountaineering in 1861. 98
White's Selborne. Introduction by Principal Windle. 48
Wollstonecraft (Mary), The Rights of Woman, with John Stuart Mill's The Subjection of Women. 825

TRAVEL AND TOPOGRAPHY

A Book of the 'Bounty.' Edited by George Mackaness. 950
Anson's Voyages. Introduction by John Masefield. 510
Bates' Naturalist on the Amazon. With Illustrations. 446
Belt's The Naturalist in Nicaragua. Intro. by Anthony Belt, F.L.S. 561
Borrow's (George) The Gypsies in Spain. Intro. by Edward Thomas. 697
  ,, ,,   The Bible in Spain. Intro. by Edward Thomas. 151
  ,, ,,   Wild Wales. Intro. by Theodore Watts-Dunton. 49
  (See also FICTION)
Boswell's Tour in the Hebrides with Dr Johnson. 387
  (See also BIOGRAPHY)
Burton's (Sir Richard) First Footsteps in East Africa. 500
Cobbett's Rural Rides. Introduction by Edward Thomas. 2 vols. 638-9
Cook's Voyages of Discovery. 99
Crèvecoeur's (H. St John) Letters from an American Farmer. 640
Darwin's Voyage of the Beagle. 104
  (See also SCIENCE)
Defoe's Tour through England and Wales. Introduction by G. D. H.
  (See also FICTION)   [Cole. 820-1
Dennis' Cities and Cemeteries of Etruria. 2 vols. 183-4
Dufferin's (Lord) Letters from High Latitudes. 499
Ford's Gatherings from Spain. Introduction by Thomas Okey. 152
Franklin's Journey to the Polar Sea. Intro. by Capt. R. F. Scott. 447
Giraldus Cambrensis: Itinerary and Description of Wales. 272
Hakluyt's Voyages. 8 vols. 264, 265, 313, 314, 338, 339, 388, 389
Kinglake's Eothen. Introduction by Harold Spender, M.A. 337
Lane's Modern Egyptians. With many Illustrations. 315
Mandeville's (Sir John) Travels. Introduction by Jules Bramont. 812
Park (Mungo): Travels. Introduction by Ernest Rhys. 205
Peaks, Passes, and Glaciers. Selected by E. H. Blakeney, M.A. 778
L Polo's (Marco) Travels. Introduction by John Masefield. 306
Roberts' The Western Avernus. Intro. by Cunninghame Grahame. 762
Speke's Discovery of the Source of the Nile. 50
L Stevenson's An Inland Voyage, Travels with a Donkey, and Silverado
  Squatters. 766
  (See also ESSAYS, FICTION, and POETRY)
Stow's Survey of London. Introduction by H. B. Wheatley. 589
Wakefield's Letter from Sydney and Other Writings on Colonization. 828
Waterton's Wanderings in South America. Intro. by E. Selous. 772
Young's Travels in France and Italy. Intro. by Thomas Okey. 720

FOR YOUNG PEOPLE

Aesop's and Other Fables: An Anthology from all sources. 657
Alcott's Little Men. Introduction by Grace Rhys. 512
L ,,   Little Women and Good Wives. Intro. by Grace Rhys. 248
Andersen's Fairy Tales. Illustrated by the Brothers Robinson. 4
  ,, More Fairy Tales. Illustrated by Mary Shillabeer. 822
Annals of Fairyland. The Reign of King Oberon. 365
  ,, ,,   The Reign of King Cole. 366
Asgard and the Norse Heroes. Translated by Mrs Boult. 689
Baker's Cast up by the Sea. 539
Ballantyne's Coral Island. 245
  ,, Martin Rattler. 246
  ,, Ungava. Introduction by Ernest Rhys. 276
Browne's (Frances) Granny's Wonderful Chair. Intro. by Dollie Radford.
Bulfinch's (Thomas) The Age of Fable. 472   [112
  ,, Legends of Charlemagne. Intro. by Ernest Rhys. 556
Canton's A Child's Book of Saints. Illustrated by T. H. Robinson. 61
  (See also ESSAYS)
L Carroll's Alice in Wonderland, Through the Looking-Glass, etc. Illus-
  trated by the Author. Introduction by Ernest Rhys. 836
Clarke's Tales from Chaucer. 537

FOR YOUNG PEOPLE—*continued*

Made in Great Britain at The Temple Press, Letchworth, Herts (Pj 589)

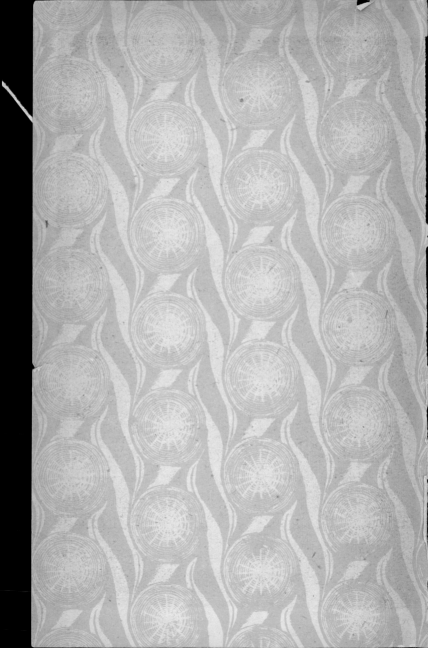